D0256007

POWER
CORRUPTION
and PIES Volume Two

First published in 2006 by WSC Books Ltd
17a Perseverance Works, 38 Kingsland Road, London E2 8DD
www.wsc.co.uk
info@wsc.co.uk

ISBN 13: 978 0 9540134 8 6
ISBN 10: 0 9540134 8 4

Printed and bound by Biddles Ltd, Kings Lynn, UK

Compiled & edited by Andy Lyons, Mike Ticher, Richard Guy and Ed Upright

Cover design by Doug Cheeseman
Cover illustrations by Dave Robinson, Tim Bradford, Jake Rickwood, Mick Marston
Cover Photos – Empics (2)

Chapter illustrations by Dave Robinson

Contents

3

2005

Editorials are by Andy Lyons, Mike Ticher & Philip Cornwall

Foreword

WHEN CHANNEL 4 LAUNCHED more than 20 years ago, one of its executives said they wouldn't be broadcasting much about sport or the monarchy because, in her view, it was impossible to broadcast intelligently about either. On the monarchy, I kind of took her point, and there's certainly an awful lot of brainless drivel written about football too; I should know, as I've been responsible for some of it. But no one could point the same finger at *When Saturday Comes*.

Quality writing about football used to be rare. The few examples of it shone as brightly as the FA Cup on first-round day when it makes an appearance at some poorly-floodlit non-League ground. Brian Glanville, Hunter Davies, Eamon Dunphy: we salute you.

Now, of course, it's different. There's so much good stuff to read that you don't know where to start. The received wisdom is that this state of affairs was made possible by the publication of Nick Hornby's *Fever Pitch* but, marvellous though that book was, I'm more inclined to give the credit to *WSC*. I remember reading it, wide-eyed with wonder, as a student in the late Eighties. It inspired me to think and talk about football in a different way, and it continues to do so.

Then, as now, the dedication of the editorial staff to the cause was exemplary. A friend of mine at university, Bryn Law, who now works for Sky Sports, did some work experience on the magazine. I well remember how he described it: "It was great," he said.

"What were the people like?" "They were exactly what my mother dreads I might become," he said approvingly. "Totally devoted to football with no women in their lives at all." I'm happy to say that it didn't work like that for Bryn's mum, and neither, now I've spent time in the offices myself, does it seem an accurate description of the editorial staff anyway.

I've found this collection as entertaining as ever. Many of the pieces fair throb with anger. There's a great one from a Bristol City fan still crying bitter tears about what Roy Hodgson once did to his club. The sight of Hodgson receiving plaudits at Blackburn Rovers is more than the writer can bear. As I now write City are riding high in what we must now call League One and Roy Hodgson is, well, I'm not quite sure where he is actually. For better or worse it all comes round, eventually. Strangely reassuring.

Less happily, there's a heartbreaking piece taking issue with the stuff we say every May about half the world's population (or whatever it is) tuning into watch the FA Cup final. Apparently, they don't; not least because you can't get it in most countries. Truly, this is an awful allegation and one I just won't accept. I'll continue to believe, no matter how compelling the evidence to the contrary is. I will suspend my disbelief – a vital skill to have as a football fan, no matter who you support.

Adrian Chiles
November 2006

Introduction

THE FIRST EDITION of *Power, Corruption and Pies* was illustrated with a reference to the football bandwagon that had gathered pace and hangers-on alike in the 1990s. In the decade since that appeared in 1997, the bandwagon has become more of a juggernaut, apparently with no one at the wheel. Back then, quaint customs and institutions that might baffle younger readers were still littering the landscape or fresh in the memory: a Conservative government; terraces; Ceefax; Wembley; fanzines; Wimbledon in the Premiership. This collection takes up where *Pies 1* left off, covering a decade in which fans largely learnt to do without such things but had to get used to lots of new ways of supporting their team – or, as it increasingly came to be known, consuming the product of football.

It was a decade when the Alfs and the Stans died out, and even the Jimmys, Jacks and Bobbys had to reflect more on their past achievements than any active role in the game. In their place came the occasional Wayne but, above all, foreigners. As more of them played for, owned and coached the top teams in the country (and England), the globalisation of football seemed unstoppable. A good thing if it means a less insular football culture; not so good when clubs become the latest must-have accessory for those with more yachts than they know what to do with.

In the Premiership, the Champions League regulars and wannabes became so inflated with self-importance they were in danger of floating away altogether. But despite the best efforts of ITV Digital, professional football survived at a more sane level in the lower divisions, no matter what name they like to masquerade under. Clubs that seemed doomed have rebounded, even after years of being run by Michael Knighton. Why? Mostly because fans were stubborn and bloody-minded enough to keep them alive, even when it meant starting again from the bottom.

So if there is something worth celebrating from a decade of excess, it is that football persists and even prospers away from the circus fuelled by the tabloids. It may be local, non-corporate and faintly illogical, but enough people care to sustain it. And the same goes for *WSC*.

Andy Lyons & Mike Ticher

1997

Message Understood

A howl of pain from 1997, when Sky's advertisements for their football coverage were based on a patronising and offensive depiction of the typical fan

WSC No 128, October 1997 ~ Editorial

THERE WAS NO ESCAPING football this summer. If you live anywhere near a major town you will have seen the huge billboards featuring text taken from the new Sky advertisement for its coverage of the 1997-98 season. "Football is our life," says one, above a picture of two fans, one celebrating, the other with head in hands. "Football is our religion," says another, over a picture of fans sitting on a fence overlooking a ground. The TV commercial from which the posters are derived only lasts a minute or so but it's one of the most disturbing things ever seen on satellite television, weirder even than the 24 hour shopping channel or episodes of *Scooby Doo* dubbed into German.

Monochrome close-ups of Premier League stars staring moodily into the lens are intercut with Sean Bean, star of the worst football film yet made (you may know the title), striding about, declaiming lines intended to strike a great big booming chord in the heart of football fans. Football, you see, is "ecstasy, anguish, joy and despair. It should be predictable but never is. It's a feeling that can't be explained".

The clincher comes at the end. "We know how you feel... we feel the same way." If only they did – then Sky would have to close down its entire operation and publicly apologise for having been the driving force behind football's grotesque kowtowing to television over the past five years. Instead it was left to a grafitti artist to add a ring of truth to one of the posters by adding the words "...about money".

Where to begin to describe the awfulness of this advertisement? Firstly, there's the patronising message – Sky, involved with football for all of five years, would have us believe that it understands the essence of football fan culture; something built up over a hundred years can be reduced down to stock images of men in replica shirts shouting and kids with painted faces.

Worse than that is the image of the fan as someone who has abandoned reason. This is a thread that has run consistently through the media depiction of football fans in the past few years. Innumerable advertising campaigns depict that new stock comedy character, the football nutter – sleeping in his scarf, painting his house in club colours, wearing his shirt 24 hours a day, naming a kid after a promotion-winning team. Every advertising agency now seems to want to catch on to football obsessiveness just as completely as they abandoned football altogether a decade ago in favour of the then fashionable American variety.

Obsessiveness has become a defining image of the fan, a badge of authenticity to be seized upon by any celebrity or politician keen to show that they've got the common touch, who will happily gabble on about how they would pack in their careers tomorrow for a chance to play centre-forward for their favourite club. Of course some fans are only too aware that football plays an unhealthily large role in their lives but to have this ailment appropriated, glorified and advertised back to them with such blatant insincerity feels like manipulation of the highest order.

For years, of course, the media seemed happy to suggest that if you were a football fan, you were abnormal. Now the opposite is true: the new stereotype suggests that you're not a real football fan unless you're incapable of conversing on any other subject.

This has understandably produced a reaction amongst those who happen not to like the game, in some cases, turning otherwise tolerant people against football fans, in the belief that all such people subscribe to the views in the Sky ad. In others it has reawakened an image of us as grunting knuckle-draggers which might have been understandable, however inaccurate, in the wake of Heysel.

As well as this reaction, the propagation of football as a commercial substitute for religion will create a hype monster that is sure to burst. Already there are stories of ten-year-olds who support Man Utd or Liverpool in order to stay in playground conversations but don't actually bother to watch the matches on TV.

Meanwhile Sky subscriptions have gone up again, and they have started to charge for Sky Sports 2, which was previously "free" to those who bought the other two channels. They make sure that their audience will pay for it, of course, by moving England's key World Cup games there from Sky Sports 1, the home of the Premiership. They will then, doubtless, spend the money on more degrading commercials, adding insult to extortion.

While the game undoubtedly needs money, English football is now as unbalanced as the fans in the adverts, with all control in the hands of people who hadn't managed to stay awake for a whole match before Italia 90, and will turn their backs if there are no more profits to be made.

Sky seem to believe that the whole of British football history has been one glorious progression leading to their arrival, that their involvement represents the pinnacle of football's achievement. What luck that our little game, struggling along as the most popular sport in the world, should have attracted the attention of the benevolent Mr Murdoch. ○

Focus Pocus

Saturday lunchtimes on BBC1 changed irrevocably when *Football Focus* was given a makeover. Cameron Carter surveyed the wreckage of a once-proud institution

WSC No 129, November 1997

I USED TO LOOK FORWARD to *Football Focus*. Probably because it used to be good. Ten years ago, during its golden Arthurian period, you got crumply old Bob Wilson with a pen in his jacket pocket (which sometimes crept into his hand during those traumatic live link-ups with experienced managers), lots of football clips and a special focus on Crewe Alexandra at the end. Now, you get last weekend's goals you've already seen on *Match of the Day* with a satiny Britpop underlay. It's not right, and deep down everyone knows it.

The rot set in when Bob left to work for ITV, presumably to provide a better standard of living for his family. A troop of people related to football, let us say, only by marriage – Ray Stubbs, Steve Ryder and the like – duly attempted to fill the gap, but were clearly only filling in while the BBC looked for a replacement with Bob Wilson's classic combination of authority and inoffensiveness. Finally they gave up and decided that what the kids wanted was a football DJ playing only the very latest stuff and so Gary Lineker has appeared on our screens ever since, squeaking away like a rusty fieldmouse.

It was quickly apparent what *Grandstand* had let us all in for. After a feature on the Liverpool team making a charity record in his first season in charge, Lineker undid a button on his pox-doctor's clerk's jacket and quipped: "I don't think Blur and Oasis have got anything to worry about." He probably thought this got him in with the kids. Well it didn't; we young people don't respect that kind of blatant currying of favour from people with stinking great streaks of grey in their hair, as a matter of fact, much preferring our football authority figures to remain conservative, remote and, therefore, dignified.

And anyway, there were people over 30 watching who rather like Mantovani and who fail to appreciate such lightning forays into the borderlands of youth-oriented humour. Chief among Bob Wilson's most alluring qualities, and I'm sure his wife would agree with me, was his obvious and profound ignorance of young people, their music and their lifestyle. A phrase like the one the man-child Lineker used that Saturday would be about as likely to pass Bob's lips as "Come on, let's trash the place", because he was and is a simple man who perhaps naively believed that football talk is what the viewers specifically want to hear when they tune in to a football magazine.

Now that we have Lineker with his Italian waiter cruise-ship charm, the material is extremely thin, like cheap toilet-roll your finger goes through, making you vow to buy the second-cheapest next time. A large percentage of each programme over the last two seasons has been taken up by a strenuous, in-depth Lineker interview with a current player in their beautifully appointed house in the suburbs. The footballing action was as limited as the questions: "Tell me, Jürgen/Bryan/Dennis, how does the English game differ from the one back home?"

"Was this a very difficult time for you?"

"Looking back now, do you regret your involvement in organised crime?"

After this patience-exploring period, Gary might pipe a slight joke if he was feeling confident, and then on we went to last Saturday's goals with guitar. As if this was not enough to convince the viewer that everything was better in the old days, there would generally then take place a folding of the hands for a serious chat with Mark Bloody Lawrenson about a player in the headlines, during which Gary would say "that's the nature of the man" as if he had hit on something final.

One hankers for Bob and the old days. You didn't have to look at Bob's jackets like you do Lineker's. They weren't meant to be looked at. They just Were. There was no gloss, no service-industry hokum, everything was purely functional. If the producers of *Grandstand* had ever approached Bob with the idea of managers' heads appearing in the middle of revolving footballs you can be sure that he would have told them gently but firmly to go back to lunch and he'd see them tomorrow.

The footballing public in Bob's day were given what they wanted – lots of clips. The top games of the day were lovingly previewed with action from the corresponding fixture the previous season, or maybe a few seasons before. There was a bit of context for you, a thread of care and preparation ran through the show. "The last time these two clubs met..." When did you ever hear Lineker introduce a piece of football action with those words? I'll tell you. You never did. Bob was always doing it, and that is why we loved him in a no-touching, share-a-bottle-of-whisky-with-him-when-we're-older kind of way.

Also, just as he came to the end of his enticing introduction to the clip, Bob would crinkle his eyes into some kind of smile and leave you with completely good karma until the excerpt was over. It is true that Lineker has begun to try this himself recently, but as this makes him resemble a wine bar Lothario coming on to the girls near closing-time one cannot take it as sincere.

Another extra you got with the old *Football Focus* was the "Focus On The Unfashionable Northern Club" bit. There'd be a dragging overhead shot of some disused dock or railyard accompanied by a Gubba figure droning an introduction they had written up in the library after a brief visit to the Geography section: "For nigh on four centuries the port of Hull has been famous for its shipbuilding, but today with the shipyards standing idle as they have done for the past 20 years, it is football that is providing the main talking-point in the pubs and offices of this historic northern city..."

Then there would be a very old guy on a leather sofa remembering things extremely slowly, interspersed with a few grainy old football clips of the club's past glories. Solid info-tainment for all the family, and they never seemed to run out of "Unfashionable Northern Clubs", either. The new boys can't be bothered with all that. Oh I know they can't use Nationwide League action nowadays, but they hardly ever use old material anymore in any context, not even when they were covering the FA Cup. It is almost as if the production team sacked two archivists to pay for the salary of one new set designer. Glitz and polish, you see, the modern disease. Never mind the quality – feel the service. As for Lineker, he won't shake your hand until you've been in make-up.

One last thing. In a recent edition, Garth Crooks' earnest little report was dressed up as an episode of *The Holiday Programme* by the boys in Titles & Effects. I was watching with a chap who had been living abroad for five years and I caught him staring in disbelief at the gyrating television screen in rather the same way people used to stare in disbelief at a man with no abdomen in a Victorian travelling circus. What could I say to him? That this post-modern grotesque was what his fondly remembered *Football Focus* had become? With its execrable, irrelevant theme tune and dreary live interviews with managers where the studio guest gets to ask a question and make a joke? In the end I didn't say anything, silence seemed the most appropriate response. Until now.

The way it's going at the moment, *Football Focus* will be presented a couple of seasons from now by Darren Day from inside a mocked-up ref's whistle to a background of heavy drum 'n' bass, with maybe the odd clip from last Saturday's big game included somewhere for nostalgia lovers among the deconstructional topical debate. This is a sad state of affairs because missing *Football Focus* (or *Top of the Pops*, incidentally) used to mean the whole week was a failure. Those days are gone. One recent Saturday I missed *Football Focus* because I was out in the kitchen testing myself on the exact ingredients of Alpen. ○

The Vauxhall Bridge

A new breed of wealthy club chairman was trying to
buy success – but in the Vauxhall Conference, not the
Premiership. Simon Bell explained

WSC No 129, November 1997

ONE OF THE MOST irritating things about the Vauxhall Conference is
the way it wants to be – really wants to be – the Football League. It's
a bit embarrassing. The Football League bars a club from entering
because its facilities aren't up-to-scratch (Kidderminster); bless my soul
if the Conference doesn't follow suit abjectly (St Albans and their now
infamous trees). The Football League applies a raft of strict financial
criteria for would-be entrants, ignoring the fact that most of its members
are perennially skint. As does the Conference, consigning Enfield and
Boston Utd to the never-never for a few more years.

The result is a league in limbo, a small pool containing a few potentially
league-sized fish and a rather larger shoal of tiddlers living beyond their
means in the fond belief that they will one day grow legs and scramble
out of the swamp – and to hell with the cost. So it is with the money
men, by and large. The League has Jack Hayward, self-styled Golden Tit
and increasingly grumpy employer of Mark McGhee. The Conference
has Max Griggs, proprietor of the Doc Martens empire and owner of
Rushden and Diamonds. Not short of a few bob, Max has built Nene
Park, Diamonds' home, from scratch, made sure that most of its 10,000
capacity is seated, and incorporated a venue for such extra-curricular
activities as snooker, and, er, more snooker. There's even a doorman to
show you into the bar, fer Chrissakes.

Max is not alone. Step forward Victor Green, chairman of Stevenage
Borough, described in the *Guardian* as "a feisty little rich guy". Thanks to
him, there's little chance of Stevenage being once again refused admission
to the League were they to win the Conference. League standard ground,
computerised turnstiles, Football in the Community scheme, you name
it. Unfortunately, the team doesn't look so hot this time out. Stevenage
have a £25,000 suspended fine hanging over their heads as a result of
conduct unbecoming an aspiring League club: they approached Torquay
United for money to "ensure" that they didn't sell leading scorer Barry

Hayles. Torquay would have been relegated if Stevenage had finished behind a club with a League standard ground in 1996.

This is a measure of the desperation some Conference chairmen feel for the Holy Grail of League football, a desperation which can sometimes seem to overstep the bounds of reason. Macclesfield, who at the time of writing are second in the Third Division, were bankrolled for their last few years in non-League football by Arthur Wood, a local businessman. For whatever reasons (and they are undoubtedly complex) Mr Wood shot himself in the summer of 1996. His company, Crosland Metals, is now in liquidation, and the receiver has been on the phone to Macclesfield Town FC regarding the whereabouts of some of Crosland's assets. Everyone in non-League football knows what happened to Maidstone, and what nearly happened to Barnet. The dream, of course, is to "do a Wimbledon", but one wonders what Conference chairmen see to attract them in the current superstar lifestyles of more recent recruits such as Scarborough, especially since the ladder to the serious money has been very firmly pulled up.

There's a good case for arguing that Wimbledon were the last side able to make the full trip. This sort of ambition sends freak shockwaves through football at all levels where players are paid. Non-League football is littered with examples of clubs who had a few good years on someone or other's money, only to plummet from view when forced once again to rely on their usually tiny hardcore of fans for material support. Colne Dynamos were bankrolled from the North West Counties League to the Conference before their backer pulled the plug, and they folded.

Likewise, Sittingbourne's future seemed so secure when they made a killing on the sale of their ground, but they hit hard times when the money evaporated within a couple of years. And there'll be more. The trouble is usually the same: a cash injection from the local rich geezer can buy you a defence and a couple of new bits of terracing, but it won't sustain you forever, and even megabucks from a ground sale can't guarantee the success that will keep punters coming through the turnstiles. Eventually, a club's aspirations will overcome its ability to organize itself competently, either on the field or off, and then the slide may not be long away. Hayes, currently living high on the hog on the ten per cent sell-on clause from Les Ferdinand's move to Newcastle, may soon find this out; £250,000 from the sale of Jason Roberts to Wolves will help, but sooner or later they have to address the issue of sub-1,000 gates if they are not to stagnate like most of the rest of the Conference.

It's a problem several of the middling Conference clubs face: just about too good to go down, but never quite well enough set up or supported to make the leap upwards. "Division Five", wherein 22 thrusting and ambitious clubs would joust for the right to play Hartlepool, has never quite become a reality. Macclesfield may make it. Although what "it" might be is a bit doubtful. Realistically, Division Two is probably the upper limit. And I wonder if Plymouth on a wet Tuesday will seem quite as enticing as it did when they were a Conference club?

Whatever, it won't stop the latest crop of lottery winners, scrap metal merchants and second-hand car dealers from acting out their fantasies of tea and Jaffa cakes in the boardroom at Chester by offering 20 grand a year to some knuckle-dragger who's just got the push from Shrewsbury reserves. And frankly, if they're that bloody sad, aren't you glad they're spending it on something relatively harmless? ○

The Trial of Roy

Roy Hodgson had just made a good start as Blackburn manager after building a reputation abroad. But Matt Nation had fraught memories of Hodgson's previous managerial stint in England, at Bristol City in 1982

WSC No 130, December 1997

ON TURNING TO THE front bit of your Sunday tabloid, you often find pages five to eight plastered with a "seedy past" exposé. The host of a sofa-based chat-show, for example, is revealed to have once visited a topless bar, dropped a couple of tabs and then thrown a cloakroom attendant through a plate-glass window. The nation smirks behind its collective hand for a couple of days, then loses interest, comes over all moral and decides to let bygones be bygones.

While he has never shared a settee and banalities with June Whitfield, Roy Hodgson is currently enjoying levels of attention which could, potentially, catapult him further towards the front of the paper. Already itinerant, tactically astute and a folk-hero in Switzerland, Roy could now also be credited with having pulled off a minor miracle in making Blackburn a great deal less unpopular than they were three or four years ago. In fact, it's difficult to imagine anybody less deserving of having muck and detritus from the past smeared all over them.

But it is precisely the nice guys, Roy, who get it in the neck, particularly when there are some people out there who just cannot let bygones be bygones. Like my father, who, on seeing your craggy-dressed-up-as-cosmopolitan features staring out from newspaper and television alike, went all of a doodah until his son helped him to place his head between his knees and draped warm towels over the back of his neck. Like my sister's first boyfriend, whose father-in-law-in-waiting threw him out of the house the very first time he came round because his first name was the same as yours, Roy.

I wonder whether you know just how much it hurt back then. When you and Bob Houghton managed to do what nobody else had ever managed to do, namely drag the City down into the Fourth Division at the beginning of the 1980s. I know the descent through the divisions had already started before you arrived, Roy; I know that the club was in a desperate financial position, that the backbone of the team was forced to tear up their contacts and accept voluntary redundancy; I know that you were only the assistant, Roy, and that it was Houghton who had the final word. Nevertheless, Roy, you were part of the big picture, that great big, farraginous Jackson-Pollock of an eyesore which, at that time, passed for Bristol City.

And you even became the boss for three months in early 1982, Roy, those unedifying three months when your charges won three games in 20. What on earth did you say during the pre-match team talks that made them go out onto the pitch with the verve of a long-term inmate of Death Row? "Go out there and get it over with"? "One day we'll all look back at this and laugh our heads off"?

Can you remember the players you imposed on us, Roy? Terry Boyle, the man who ran like Stan Laurel going the wrong way on a Travelator; Alan Nicholls, spindle-shanks centre-half with the bifurcate clearances, who would have been dragged out of position much more often but for the fact that he was never where he was supposed to be to start with; and what about Errington Kelly, Roy, possibly the only free transfer that even Bristol Rovers didn't want? You might be multi-lingual, but you didn't know that Errington is a name fit only for a big band leader or a North Sea seaside resort; it's not a footballer's name, Roy, not in any language.

You may not have signed all these players yourself, Roy, you may have inherited some, blooded some, or simply had no others available. But they are all inextricably linked with your time at the City; you filled in the team sheets, you let them stay when you could have banned them from the training ground.

These names mean nothing to most people and they probably mean even less to you, Roy. You will have consigned them to the murky twilight zone which you inhabited before you went away and got reinvented. In fact, if we ever manage to catch a glimpse of your CV, we'll probably find the years 1980-82 accounted for by some euphemism such as "travelling" or "managerial research in England". They've probably got a word in the Army for people like you.

What has become of the damage cases whom you left behind? My father is now retired and currently awaiting delivery of a defibrillator to counteract the effect of seeing you on *Football Focus*. My sister is happily married and appears to have suppressed the events surrounding the ignominious exit of her first love, save for the fact that she hasn't spoken since. Even the Roy the Boyfriend, who was so shaken by the whole affair that he has never married, seems to have come to terms with bachelorhood and the resultant evenings spent playing with electric train sets. They're settled, they're making do.

Maybe you should get settled too, Roy. You seem to have forgotten where you came from, and other people are doing their best to forget it as well. And should wanderlust or a Bristol City chairman asking you to name your price ever cause you to remember, then fight the urge to do anything about it. Make sure you never return to Bristol, unless you want to be sent packing back up the M5 with the toe of my father's slipper wedged up your backside. Leave my family alone, Roy, they've suffered enough. ○

Goalkeepers Are Different

From a series about great football literature, Ian Plenderleith
extolled Brian Glanville's story of a young keeper. The book
was republished after this review

WSC No 130, December 1997

HAS ANYONE EVER made football into fiction without incurring the
laughter of all those who know that it's three points for a win and that
you only play extra time in cup ties? It's a mysterious phenomenon that
so many have tried to turn sporting reality into art and, either on pulp or
celluloid, have consistently made such a mess of it.

Some even believe that the Great Football Novel is still to be written,
and no doubt publishers and agents across the country are gasping for
the appropriate manuscript to land on their desks so that they can cash
in on the current mania for printing unlimited crap with a round-ball
connection.

They can give up waiting because such a book has already been written,
published and, one suspects, largely forgotten over quarter of a century
ago. It's true that Brian Glanville's *Goalkeepers Are Different* does not,
strictly speaking, qualify as "adult" literature, but then neither do most
football books, and if you like a straight football story as much as the
next fan then you'll find yourself at the book's end in no more than two
or three sittings.

When I was 11 I must have been the only boy in the country playing
centre-forward for my school and secretly wishing that I was the
goalkeeper. It was all because of this book, which turned my head from
the trite, monotonous dross I was forcing myself to read in *Shoot!* every
week. I read it seven times (wearing out two copies), which is six more
times than any other book I've read in my life. Yet I've never met another
soul who has even heard of it.

What makes the book so convincing as a portrayal of life in the professional game is its disingenuous title. Narrator Ronnie Blake – the aspiring
keeper who makes his way up to become top stopper at first division
Borough United – proclaims in his opening sentence that goalies are
"not crazy, they're just different". Yet you couldn't meet a more normal
bloke than Ronnie.

He wants to be a pro, like all boys. When as a schoolboy he starts to get spotted by scouts he worries about his future, whether he'll make it, should he continue his education, and so on. There are setbacks, which he overcomes. He likes a couple of beers, but that's it. He observes that on the tube or in Mallorca there are "some nice birds". He's a dead regular geezer who just happens to play in goal. So instead of focusing the book on the alcoholic maverick or the gifted but temperamental serial-shagger, we meet a bloke who is pretty much like 90 per cent of all players – a bloke, whose overwhelming concern in life is doing well in the game of football. Simple, and it works perfectly.

Glanville applies his technical knowledge so realistically that you feel that at some point in his life he actually stood on a goal-line and felt the bulk of Jackie Charlton before him. You sense that you should know who Borough's temperamental Scottish manager Charlie Macintosh is meant to be, but you can't quite pin him down to a real-life figure. And reading accounts of fictitious games against real-life players made me look up in my *Rothmans* whether there really was a team called Borough United and that, somehow, I had overlooked them for the previous few hundred Saturdays.

This perfectly paced story is now apparently out of print, which is nothing short of a scandal in the present publishing climate. But according to the spirit of the times I'll lend you my copy for a hundred quid. ○

1998

Case for the Defence

Cris Freddi looked back at the career of the legendary Helenio Herrera, who had just died, and suggested a little reappraisal might be in order

WSC No 131, January 1998

ACCORDING TO CHANNEL 4, some of the Italian press have been calling him "the first real football coach", which is bollocks but shows the right respect. If you're an Inter fan, and aren't we all, HH was the only coach.

Not the best loved, I grant you. His nickname, Il Mago, means wizard or magician, but with undertones of sorcery, the black arts. This had to do with his emphasis on dark defence but also a certain exoticism: born in Buenos Aires, brought up in Casablanca, naturalised French, a new wife in every country he coached in. Some of the facts, naturally enough, don't match the legend.

For a start, he didn't start out as the high priest of *catenaccio*. His Barcelona side which won the 1959 Spanish League had a strong enough defence but above all a forward line made up of the great and the good: Kocsis, Czibor, Suárez, Kubala, Evaristo, not necessarily in that order. When Czibor and Kubala criticised his bonus system, he dropped them both before a European Cup semi-final. Barcelona lost each leg 3-1 to the hated Real Madrid, and Herrera was on his way within a month.

It was Barça's loss. While they had to wait until 1992 before winning the European Cup, HH was soon doing it twice in a row with Internazionale. Again, he didn't go with the intention of playing umpteen at the back, but once he realised attacking football wasn't going to succeed in Italy, he set out to defend better than any of them. And to carry on showing who was boss. Unlike Barcelona, Inter allowed him to sell the darling of the fans (Antonio Angelillo) and after that his flair for team selection wasn't in doubt. Allowed to use only two foreigners in the league, he bought exactly the right ones, persuading Barcelona to sell Suárez, before buying then selling the hard working England centre-forward Gerry Hitchens in exchange for the flying Jair. With a strong homegrown defence, Corso supporting Suárez on the left, and the great Mazzola up front, it was "today Serie A, tomorrow the world". When Inter won the 1964 European Cup at the first attempt, they were the first club to do it without losing a match.

Along the line, fact and myth became lost in the mists. The slogans pasted to changing room walls; Hitchens having to walk six miles back to the training camp because he and Corso were 20 seconds late for the team bus; Omar Sivori deliberately kicking the ball at Herrera on the bench; Liverpool cheated out of the 1965 semi-final by the referee; Celtic's Lions of Lisbon finally slaying the defensive dragon.

All the Celtic bullshit (and its 30th anniversary this year) overlooks the simple fact that Inter were without Suárez and Jair, so there was no springboard out of defence. Sarti and Co held out wonderfully well until they were beaten by an offside goal (see the BBC freeze-frame for proof). Meanwhile the Liverpool Affair concerns two allegedly illegal goals, Peiró kicking the ball out of the keeper's hands, Corso scoring direct from an indirect free-kick. Total cobblers. The ball was on the ground when Peiró nicked it away (Ian St John: "You must blame Tommy for dreaming") and the photo showing the referee with his arm raised for the free-kick is a still frame from the film: he was simply waving Corso to hurry up and take it. Anyway, where are the Scouse protests about the third goal, the one that sent Inter through? Picchi to Mazzola to Peiró, some cool passing through the middle, with no angles to play with, for Facchetti to thrash the ball low past Lawrence. David Coleman: "Oh, it's like a volcano!" A giant left-back appearing at centre-forward to score with his right foot. The term Total Football mean anything to you?

And that, though nobody ever said so, was Herrera's main legacy. Vilified for the consecration and spread of total defence, he was as misunderstood as Ramsey: hardly his fault if other coaches followed his methods but without the right players. At Inter he had the greatest playmaker of the decade, the sharpest striker, the fastest winger, and world class defenders who could step out from the back. His real heirs weren't Arsenal or any of the Argentinian choppers, but Cruyff's great Ajax, who ironically beat a declining Inter in the 1972 final, by which time he was long gone. People forget how few goals Ajax conceded (or scored), how content they were to quieten away crowds and win European Cup semi-finals 1-0 on aggregate. If that's the bastard child of Herrera's arcane practices, we can all live with it, and I suspect so could he. ◯

Financial Times

David Conn offered a preview of his book, *The Football Business*, which suggested that English football has been reshaped to suit the personal interests of club owners

WSC No 131, January 1998

BENEATH THE HIGH-PITCHED HYPE, English football presents some stark realities. Sir John Hall, former tireless warrior of the "Geordie nation", made £100 million for himself and his family out of Newcastle United when it floated on the Stock Market in April. He is now living mostly in Spain. Martin Edwards, chief executive of Manchester United plc, bought into United for £600,000 in 1978. He has recently made £33m cash from selling some of his shares, and retains a 15 per cent stake in United, worth around £60m.

Supporters are described in the City as "a captive market", and exploited by rising ticket prices, contrary to the recommendations of the Taylor Report. Many fans can no longer afford to watch their teams. Football League clubs struggle against increasingly difficult odds, in direct competition with Premiership and European matches on television nearly every night. Semi-professional clubs are going bust. School and youth teams are dependent on overworked volunteers. Sunday football is declining. And it is a sign of the depressing times that the commonest response to these facts is this: "So What?" The lack of opposition, protest and media debate is more than apathy, worse than ignorance. Jargonised excuses for greed such as "supply and demand" and "brand loyalty" hold Britain in thrall.

Of course football was never owned by the people; it was the property of a motley collection of self-made businessmen, often pursuing their own interests at the expense of the sport. Hillsborough was the catastrophe waiting to happen at the grounds they neglected. But this does not justify what has happened since. Hillsborough, as Lord Justice Taylor himself argued in his report, should have brought wholesale reform, "the fullest reassessment of policy for the game". Instead, football was taken over by those looking to get rich out of it. Make no mistake: the personal fortunes made recently by opportunist chairmen are the first ever made in football.

However incompetent or mean-spirited many old style chairmen were, they could not make big profits out of owning football club shares. Some may have been on the fiddle but the Football Association imposed rules early in the century to preserve football clubs as purely clubs, and not as exploitable companies. The rules are still in the FA handbook, as Rule 34. They restrict the payment of dividends and the earnings that can be made by directors and, importantly, provide that a football club cannot be wound up and its ground sold off.

Introduced around 1912, these rules protected clubs against speculation: a businessman could not get cash out via dividends or salary, nor could he profit from winding up the club. Directors described themselves as "custodians of the club for the town". However hypocritical this was in many cases, at least there was some protection. In the lower levels of the game people still talk of football like this, as a thing to be preserved. But the FA Carling Premiership has tossed aside any sense of football's value, beyond what coin it can turn.

In the Football League, television money was always redistributed throughout the four divisions. As the money got bigger, the Big Five grew less inclined to share, and muttered about breaking away. To its shame, the FA betrayed its responsibilities as guardians of the game, and puts its name to the tawdry venture to win a dismal turf war with the Football League. They knew the 1992 TV deal would be massive, and it was: £305m in 1992 over five years, now £670m over the next four. This, plus taxpayers' money via Football Trust grants, to only 22 (now 20) clubs, made Premiership football very attractive to businessmen.

As one accountant told me: "Clubs are no longer rich men's hobbies, but 'investment vehicles'." When a football club floats now, it specifically tells the City it is bypassing Rule 34. Holding companies are formed, to which the grounds are transferred. The football clubs become mere subsidiaries, officially paying rent to the floated plc.

Directors can pay themselves a fortune, even for part-time status, and for the first time ever football clubs can now be wound up and the grounds flogged off. The time of the greatest ever wealth in football, after a century of struggle, is the time when the game's money is least fairly distributed. The argument about this goes beyond mere mechanics, the surface arguments about whether the England team is better, whether there are too many foreign players or too many kit changes. In the age of market forces the FA has forgotten that money should be made to serve the game not the other way around. The governing body has failed to govern and is now a major part of the problem.

Football is supported by the government, in the World Cup bid and the £200m handed to the top clubs by the Football Trust, now being funded by the National Lottery. If the FA will not regulate as it used to, the government must impose regulation. A good case can be made for a windfall tax on the latest Sky deal, the proceeds to be spent on repairing football's threadbare fabric. Ticket prices should be kept affordable, as Lord Taylor urged. Football's hopelessly fractured administration should be unified into a single federation. If this doesn't happen, if the vaunted Task Force proves to be just a platform for the dismal David Mellor, football will be lost. ○

Standing to Lose

Ashley Shaw explained why matchdays at Old Trafford were being accompanied by confrontations between security staff and supporters who wanted to stand

WSC No 133, March 1998

WHEN EYE-WITNESS ACCOUNTS talk of scuffling in the stand between stewards and supporters, it is a clear sign that all is not well at Old Trafford. Some trouble had flared late last season when United fans in the East Stand Lower – the right-hand side of the ground for armchair viewers – made a stand at what they regarded as over-sensitive security. The trouble continued this season when, at the first home game of the season, the supporters behind the goal refused to sit down and United's in-house security ejected fans from the ground and confiscated season ticket books.

The backlash from other supporters culminated over Christmas during the games against Aston Villa and Everton. A typical incident affected season ticket holder Darrell Kinsey: "At the Villa game I was cheering the team on as were plenty of other fans around me. The atmosphere was better than normal when suddenly this security team turned up, they told me to sit down, but because everyone around me was standing and singing it would have meant that I wouldn't be able to see anything. Then they got a bit shirty telling me that standing up was illegal at Old Trafford and that they'd throw me out. Eventually I realised that they weren't going to go away – they were determined to make a scapegoat out of me, so they dragged me out and pinned me against a wall, gave me a caution and insisted that I hand over my season ticket.

"When I refused they started searching me and got a bit rougher. But they didn't really know what to do, I don't think anyone had questioned their right to do it before so they were a bit dumbfounded. I refused to tell them my name or my season ticket number, they warned me again and kicked me out of the ground. I know why they did it to me and not the others who were standing near me. They needed a scapegoat so they picked on the weediest looking guy thinking I would just cave in to them. I don't think they counted on my refusing to sit down, resisting arrest or my refusal to hand over the season ticket.

"By the next game against Everton on Boxing Day I turned up at the ground expecting some hassle but hoping that the club had seen sense. But when I reached my seat it was sealed off with green netting, then the security came over and made me leave. I've only just found out that they are giving me my season ticket back."

The return of Darrell's season ticket came along with an effusive apology from the club about a month after the incident, but the security gang in question still roams Old Trafford, although they have been removed from the vociferous East Stand Lower.

Special Projects Security, the force in charge of matches at Old Trafford, are headed by the shadowy Ned Kelly. He is supposed to have been one of the SAS men who stormed the Iranian embassy in 1980, while even stranger rumours say the SPS organisation has business links to a certain United board member. Ned Kelly's men are paid, unlike the voluntary ground stewards at exits. Their tactics appear more akin to club bouncers than the orange suited old-timers who patrol the stands. They represent the new face of football security, an extended arm of the control freaks higher up the Manchester United ladder.

It's true that United's Red Army was once at the vanguard of intimidatory techniques and proud of their record of inciting violence inside the ground. But the United fans involved in these incidents are far removed from the hooligan element of the 1970s. They are ordinary season ticket holding United fans trying to recreate the kind of atmosphere witnessed at the Barcelona Cup Winners-Cup game in 1984, the night that the United crowd produced the old European atmosphere as the team overturned a two-goal first leg deficit.

In recent games only the win against Juventus has come close to matching that night for vociferous support and nail-chewing tension. Indeed the current team are now so good that 50,000 Trappist monks would provide more than enough atmosphere for the average match, and perhaps that is the problem.

Supporters want to think that they can influence results. Superstitions and bawling at the telly are one thing but when you are in a stadium, either standing or sitting, supporters want to make their presence felt. For United's protesting season ticket holders the problem is how to do that with your backside tied to your seat. Many had hoped that Martin Edwards' early season call for a return to limited terracing would improve things, but the United board have quietly dropped plans to provide an alternative to the current bucket seat monopoly.

The official MUFC plc line remains that standing in games for prolonged periods contravenes Old Trafford's ground safety certificate and that United are only following the law of the land by forcing members of the crowd to sit down. They maintain that they are reluctantly forced to confiscate the season tickets of persistent offenders.

Alex Ferguson contributed to the debacle when he claimed in his programme notes that standing inside the ground was illegal, a claim later proved to be false – it is not illegal to stand at all-seater stadiums. Indeed the Premier League have no regulation covering standing for prolonged periods. The local council, by administrating the Ground Safety Certificates, make a judgement as to the safety of the fans and in this case it appears that Trafford Borough Council have decided that the ground is unsafe while fans continue to stand.

It will also explain why Chelsea allowed both home and away fans to stand through the whole 90 minutes of their third round FA Cup tie with United, an irony not lost on IMUSA's Andy Walsh: "We were allowed to stand for most of that game but when it comes to Old Trafford there seems to be no leeway. We have made progress though and it seems that the board are taking the terracing issue seriously, it is an issue we will be raising with Mellor at the FA Taskforce meeting."

A return to terracing however remains some way off. Tony Banks has been tacit in his refusal to even think about the issue. Meanwhile terracing continues to dominate the agenda of the Task Force roadshow, despite this issue being outside their official remit – a stance somewhat at odds with an article written by Tony Blair while in opposition which supported the return of safe standing.

But it is not hard to see why the authorities view a return to terracing with dismay – it will make supporters less identifiable and less controllable, enabling fans to protest in virtual anonymity causing more embarrassment for the club in the eyes of its shareholders.

However while a return to mass terracing is neither desirable nor possible, the technology surely exists for an improvement in the atmosphere at some of the Premier League's more corporatised grounds without inviting another Hillsborough. O

A First Time for Everything

Jeffrey Prest recalled his first experience of watching an evening kick-off, with spectators indulging in a range of behaviour he'd never seen on a Saturday afternoon

WSC No 133, March 1998

IT WASN'T THE NORMAL ROUTE to night-time football. There were no alluring floodlights visible above the rooftops; no hordes funnelling expectantly past my window. No, it was down to the Airey brothers, excused the last ten minutes of our Scout meeting every Wednesday so they wouldn't miss Spennymoor Utd's kick-off. I grew to envy them. The idea that the heroes I occasionally watched on Saturday afternoons were reconvening in the midst of a working week had the exotic flavour of stolen pleasure. The Aireys had sold me.

Spennymoor Utd by moonlight came at the perfect time in my life. Puberty was driving its wedge into my peer-group, dividing us into geeks or good-timers. To those of us for whom the Love Train had been delayed by points failure, sport was our only alternative means of embracing imminent manhood. If I had neither the nerve nor charisma to prop up a bar with some sixth-form siren, quaffing tequila slammers till dawn, then I would prove myself by watching Northern League football on windswept nights even King Lear might have turned his back on. Spennymoor Utd became my foreign legion – I went there to forget.

Less than an hour after I passed through the turnstiles that first evening, to see emerald turf against a jet sky, I knew that far more had changed than just the brightness control. Night-time heightens the senses as much as it deadens the toes. Every stimulus that distracts you from the awareness that your clothing is horribly mismatched with the ambient temperature is pounced upon. The pies smelt better, the Bovril like nectar and even the Capstan Full Strength vapours coming from the bloke behind took on a soothing quality.

People, too, had changed. Same faces but different mood. Shorn of the Saturday afternoon commitments that tied them to reality, personalities were being unleashed all around me. They hadn't got the kids with them, they hadn't got the in-laws coming round for Saturday tea, they hadn't got shopping to help out with afterwards. The night was theirs, all theirs. As half-time and the witching hour approached, I was conscious of the swearing becoming more sumptuous and experimental than anything I'd heard at weekends, while observation and anecdote took on a bawdiness that fleshed out the bones of the biology O-level syllabus at a furious rate.

That vague memories of the game itself recall a second-half clogging match would hardly be untypical of midweek fare. The free spirits emboldened by darkness weren't confined to the crowd. Sometimes it was as though the floodlights had trespassed upon some nocturnal spirit, the way football's gremlins emerged in night games. Bust-ups, cock-ups, burst balls, ripped shorts – they all came out at night.

Our only brush with the law, indeed, arose beneath a full moon, in a Northern League Cup replay. If the night had a thousand eyes, it wasn't sharing any of them with the referee, and Spennymoor passions became so aroused a policeman and policewoman were summoned from nearby Durham Road. Touched by this tribute to a menace we never knew we possessed, we gave them an ovation all the way down the touchline and then proffered ample advice as to how their evening together might progress once the shift ended.

About a year after my first sortie into this twilight zone, I followed the Aireys' example and left Scouting for good. We could pinpoint a non-League ground by night in a town of 30,000 people. We could endure sub-zero temperatures for up to two hours, during which time we would heavily interact with our community. We could sing, our sign language was crystal-clear and even in the great outdoors we knew how to rustle up pies and Bovril. We honestly felt there was nothing more Baden-Powell could teach us. ○

Sniffing Out the Truth

Richard Darn explained how Allan Clarke's departure as Barnsley manager led to an anxious few days in his life

WSC No 134, April 1998

WHEN THE PHONE RINGS it could – at least in a theory – be anybody. But you definitely don't expect it to be the wife of the manager of the local football club, thanking you for standing by her man. The background to this was the sacking of Allan Clarke by Barnsley in 1989. "Sniffer" had arrived back in town for a second spell four years earlier when – according to the local paper – the club was on the brink of going bust following the miners' strike and a slump in playing fortunes. The lingering death of Norman Hunter's regime and the stop-gap efforts of Bobby Collins left most fans suicidal after the sparkle of the early Eighties.

In his first incarnation at the club and against a similar background, Clarke became a revered figure. The dark days under his predecessor Jim Iley (the highlight being sixth in Division Four, before Iley was spirited away to Blackburn) were referred to as BC (Before Clarke). When the Blessed One arrived, his purpose was clear – to lead the "Ileyites" out of the wilderness. Which he did. So the greatness of Clarke for many fans, including me, was cast in stone. Short of pickling cats, pulling legs off spiders or sending his children to public school, he could do no wrong. We were no more than unlucky when the player-manager's team sank 7-0 to Reading in his final ever League appearance.

Until 1989 that was. Just 12 games into the new season, and after missing out on the play-offs by goal difference, he was sacked. By Clarke's own admission we were perhaps not ready "at the minute" for the top league (in fact he had 2,207,000 million minutes to solve that problem) but we were attractive to watch and solvent. So off went my first missive to the *Barnsley Chronicle*, and there was my letter on Friday morning stretched across the top of the page. It was all very cathartic. I'd done my bit. I'd told the truth.

Next the phone rang. "Hello, this is Allan Clarke's wife – Allan can't talk to you at the moment, but we'd just like to thank you for the letter, it's great to see the fans understand what's happened." Was this for real? Did this always happen when you write to the press?

I recovered my composure. "Er... thanks very much. All the best for the future and everything. Sorry it's come to this." After a nice chat, I put the phone down and decided not to write to Saddam Hussein about Iraq's human rights record just in case this was par for the course.

Within a couple of minutes, the phone rang again. This time it was the departing club chairman, who resigned when the rest of the board ganged up on him to have Clarke thrown out.

"I'd just like to thank you etc, etc, etc." This must have been one hell of a letter, I thought, as the dialogue continued. "But I'm sure a true supporter like you will stick with the team and be down there on Saturday cheering them on." Despite the bonhomie, I gave an honest response to this question and replied: "No, I'm boycotting the club."

But this wasn't the end. The next call was altogether more ominous. My mum rushed through the hallway, looking worried. "It's the club, the general secretary, asking for you by name."

"We'd like you to pop down, to see if we can iron out a few problems." This was getting quite sinister. From having a completely inflated sense of my own importance, my emotions switched to paranoia. What does the club do with dissenters? Are transformers involved, or just a cocktail of drugs, designed to make you placid?

The "suite" of offices at Oakwell at the time was a notch below the comfort offered by a night-watchman's hut. The shag pile had run out of pile and the single bar electric fire did its best to imitate a major health risk. The club shop, a two foot square hole in the wall, was blocked off by a plywood board when executive meetings were in progress.

The discussion was to "put me in the picture" and to explain the club's "reasoning". The picture that emerged was that everyone was pig-sick of Clarke. I'd walked into a major series of personality clashes that weren't in the slightest influenced by what went on out there on the pitch. Being a zealot, I thought we all loved the manager. But we clearly didn't.

Clarke had decided he hated the local paper's sports editor – who also wrote the Oakwell matchday programme – and matters came to a head when the manager's programme notes for a Port Vale home game, which went under the heading of "Having Said That", appeared as a blank page.

"He also refused to spend any money," protested the club secretary. "We had to drive him to Scotch Corner just to sign a player." What's more he wouldn't move from Scunthorpe when he took the job, as promised. Not moving from Scunthorpe to virtually anywhere else in the world is probably a major error of judgement, but it's hardly a hanging offence, I replied. Then in popped what looked like the refuse man asking where the "wheelie bin" had gone. I ignored him and his attempts to join in the conversation, until the club secretary referred to this character as "Mr Chairman".

By this stage I wanted to go home. I was more than prepared to accept that Clarke had become a bastard in his attempts to become Brian Clough Mark II and that's why they sacked him. I suddenly realised that I was in no position to give a character reference for a bloke I didn't know.

The November night drew in, the second cup of tea went cold in its glass mug, and I bade them farewell, promising to copy them in on any future correspondence, and wishing them well in their search for Jim Iley's remains.

This experience taught me a valuable lesson. The reality behind the façade of football clubs holds absolutely no interest for me. As simple vehicles for loyalty, hatred, passion and love they are perfect. But peer too closely and the magic goes and you end up looking like the idiot so many club chairman believe their ordinary supporters to be.

While I continue to quietly support Barnsley FC, Allan Clarke is now a salesman for an industrial ventilation firm in Scunthorpe. He remains a complete hero, but even I have to admit, he does seem to have a problem leaving Scunny. ○

Losing their Stripes

Ian Cusack reflected on the public disgracing of Newcastle directors Douglas Hall and Freddie Shepherd who had made unwise comments about the club's fans to a tabloid reporter

WSC No 135, May 1998

ISN'T IT GREAT to read about a team from the North East, playing in black-and-white stripes, with the whole community behind them, who have reached Wembley and are blessed with a decent and honourable chairman? Best wishes to Tow Law, population 2,208, for their trip to the FA Vase final. Now what about Newcastle United?

It took nine days from the publication of the first set of lurid allegations about Freddie Shepherd and Douglas Hall's private lives by the *News of the World*, via one adamant refusal to step down on the dubious grounds that they were both victims of a newspaper sting, to the announcement of their resignations from the board of Newcastle United plc. Significantly, none of the allegations about astonishingly vibrant sex lives and extremely heavy drinking has been denied. Perhaps they are pleased to be thought of in this way?

The announcement of their departure was made by non-executive director and ex-Rolls Royce boss Sir Terence Harrison and not by Hall and Shepherd themselves, who were believed to be donning hair shirts on a yacht in Portugal and a beach in Barbados respectively. It seems as if Harrison and two other obscure non-executive directors, thinking no doubt of their own good names and not of their investment portfolios, had issued an ultimatum to the disgraced two.

The spectre of Gerald Ratner has been invoked many times: slagging off the product, the customers, the customers' wives and high ranking employees, in one case for refusing to enter an Amsterdam brothel, is not taught as a model of good practice on the Harvard MBA.

However, there is a silver lining: cometh the hour, cometh the man. Emerging in their stead, from one hundred days in retirement, brandishing an unrivalled selection of contradictory and immoderate quotes, is the unelected President of the Geordie Nation, Sir John Hall.

Meanwhile, the plc announces half yearly profits of almost 12 million quid and, an FA Cup semi-final apart, the team continue to perform like a North Eastern equivalent of Man City. Dalglish's post-match interviews are somewhat reminiscent of John Major in his last days as prime minister, attempting to fob off the latest sleaze and sexual impropriety revelations, or in Kenny's case another pitiful home performance, with a shrug and a beatific smile. Season ticket holders and the wider population of Tyneside, having allegedly been demonised as drunken yobs and spendthrift simpletons by the clientele of a lap-dancing bar in Puerto Banus, are now supposed to go back to being subservient to the authority of the club and fanatical in their support of the team.

This may be difficult when the fact remains that Cameron Hall Developments, with 57 per cent of the shares, and Shepherd Offshore, with eight per cent, own a controlling interest in the club. Douglas and Freddie are off the board, but emphatically still on the payroll.

During the whole sordid saga Newcastle was awash with journos on a scale not seen since Keegan's resignation some 14 months previously. If the story is that rich businessmen are flying around the world on jollies, getting drunk, behaving obnoxiously towards women young enough to be their daughters and possibly dabbling in the staple crop of Faustino Asprilla's homeland, then there isn't really a story.

Arrogance and vanity amongst *nouveau riche* middle-aged men is again nothing new. Shepherd is a self-made man with a considerable personal fortune and Douglas Hall has been kept in his father's shadow until he was almost 40. Bearing in mind the world they move in, it is little wonder they are prepared to squander their money in such a demob fashion, boasting about supposed orgies to a man they've never met before. It has been a long time since the Old Etonian spirit of justice, fair play and discretion, as exemplified by the Hill-Woods at Arsenal and the Cobbold dynasty at Ipswich, has had a place in football club boardrooms. Indeed, one wonders just what Bob Lord could have got up to in the fleshpots of Burnley, if he'd been given access to the personal fortunes amassed by chairmen these days.

Barcelona in the Champions League excepted, the football Newcastle United have churned out this season has been so dismal that the national media has ignored the team, except during the public relations suicide pact with Stevenage chairman Victor Green. Indeed, one fanzine editor has gone so far as boycotting home games to voice his displeasure at the club. The local papers, sick of home defeats by Wimbledon and West Ham, have been their usual selves, wheeling out a so-called Newcastle fan, Coronation Street star Denise Welch, to comment on the allegation that Tyneside women are all dogs, or former chairman Gordon McKeag and his solicitor brother Clive, to make solemn and shallow pronouncements about how this sort of thing never went on when they were in charge and that it's the fans they feel sorry for. All of this despite the fact that Gordon described ownership of Newcastle United as "the family silver" not ten years ago.

However local coverage reached its nadir with speculation of a putative takeover by the Sultan of Brunei (an unfortunate name since the Geordie homonym "Broon Eye" means sphincter) who would of course bring back Keegan as manager. Whoopee, as most Fulham fans would say.

It does seem likely, from the noises Sir Terence Harrison made when announcing Sir John Hall's Lazarus act, that the Prince of Wynyard's comeback will be a short term measure, possibly heralding a share sale in the summer. For the sakes of their pockets alone, the board of Newcastle United plc will be keeping their fingers tightly crossed that Dalglish manages to rouse his team sufficiently to maintain a place in the Premiership. Personally, if someone could guarantee a Cup win at Wembley and three points at both Gigg Lane and Edgeley Park next season, I'd take it. I mean Boro seem to have enjoyed themselves this year. ○

Chaos Theory

A new report predicted that the European Super League would soon be upon us. Simon Evans explained why any such venture was likely to backfire on the participants
WSC No 135, May 1998

"THERE WILL BE a league formed outside of UEFA with a team from each country, sponsored by that country's biggest company... a super professional football league like American football, which will attract millions of viewers" – Silvio Berlusconi, president of AC Milan, 1998

Berlusconi is one of the most vocal supporters of the European Super League, but he is by no means the only one. According to a recent report by the financial consulting group KPMG, 69 per cent of a sample of "opinion leaders drawn from football clubs, the media and financial institutions" believe a European Super League is certain or likely. Most expect the new league to be up and running within five years.

The reasons cited for the inevitable emergence of the new pan-European championship are mostly financial. The Champions League has demonstrated that there is a market for European football – sponsors and television companies have paid more and more each season for the rights to the competition. Those clubs who qualify are receiving bigger and bigger rewards. A Super League appears to be a logical step forward, another way of maximising club revenues and dazzling us with stars.

The consensus emerging among Europe's top clubs is that the new league should run alongside domestic competitions and clubs that qualify (or are appointed) to the Euroleague should continue to play in their domestic competitions. The KPMG report indicates that opinion is in favour of weekend domestic leagues with Wednesday night Euroleague. To help make the fixtures manageable, domestic Premier leagues would be reduced to 14 or 16 clubs. With a similar sized Euroleague that would mean around 50 to 60 games a season for the top clubs, who would probably drop out of domestic cup competitions.

UEFA is against the idea. After all, they set up the Champions League as a means of stalling Super League plans and placating the big clubs. But it has merely had the effect of strengthening the hand of the elite clubs – the likes of Juventus, Manchester United, Bayern Munich and Barcelona, who with their Champions League cash can spend freely on maintaining their position at the top of their domestic championship and keep themselves inside the lucrative cash loop, are getting more and more powerful within the game as a result. They are now in a position to do their own TV deals and organise their own league, with or without the bureaucrats from UEFA.

While against the Super League plans, UEFA recognises that the current Champions League format needs change. Indeed there are strong signals that all three European club competitions are being reviewed with a view to a radical overhaul. The main problem with the Champions League is that it has created a large number of meaningless games. Whereas in the old knockout European Cup, every match was crucial, we now have fixtures like this season's Kosice v Feyenoord, where neither side can qualify and where only 3,000 people bother to turn up. Of course, domestic leagues are full of games where neither promotion or relegation are at stake, it is inevitable in any league, but European football has always been about games that matter.

But the Super League would not tackle this fundamental flaw in the current set-up, indeed it would by its very nature create more meaningless European games. Whatever moral, romantic or emotional arguments can be made against the creation of an elite continental championship (and there are many) the strongest argument against the Euroleague is a business one.

There appears to be an assumption that European football is a cash cow. TV companies will continue to pay higher and higher fees for rights, sponsors will fork out more and more to be associated with the games and fans will pay increased ticket prices. But TV, sponsors and fans are only interested in European football when it is an event. And European football is only an event when the result matters. In the Premiership, Liverpool v Manchester United is an event, regardless of the league position of the two clubs at any given time, because of a traditional and regional rivalry. A Euroleague game between eighth-placed Manchester United and ninth-placed Bayer Leverkeusen has neither tradition, rivalry or reason.

The situation could be further exaggerated by the changes that the super-clubs would have to make to their squad structures. Given the number of games they would have to play it is likely that Manchester United would expand their squad size even further. Presumably a weaker side would play on Saturday in the Premiership, while the full-strength squad would play in the Euroleague (a situation that has emerged at many top clubs during the Champions League era). But if in March, United were lying in mid-table, out of contention in the Euroleague, yet were in second position in the Premiership, the club's priorities would surely shift – a weaker team would play in Europe. Would Sky be happy to pay top rates for United reserves v Dortmund reserves? Would the fans pay to watch it?

The clubs should know better. Their success has created a national (even international in the case of United, Juve and Bayern) support and consumer base. But inevitably in the Euroleague, most of the almost-always winners will become also-rans. In the old European Cup, a defeat at the hands of another European giant was a brief disappointment, swiftly cured by a domestic league win. In the Euroleague, however, the likes of Ajax, Real Madrid and Glasgow Rangers could conceivably lose half of their games over the course of a whole season, with defeat after defeat severely denting their brand image.

Although concrete plans have yet to emerge, the recent meeting of the major leagues in Athens, comments from club officials and data from the KPMG report suggest that the proposed Euroleague would have heavy representation from those countries with strong leagues and the highest TV audiences. England, Germany, France, Italy and Spain would get two or three teams, with Holland, Turkey, Belgium, Scotland, Portugal and Sweden battling for a spot each. Eastern Europe would be locked out (sorry Dinamo Kiev, Spartak Moscow, Red Star Belgrade, Steaua Bucharest) and the occasional successful side from Scandinavia, Switzerland or Austria would have little or no chance to ever make a mark, consigned to the Euro equivalent of the Nationwide League.

The European Super League would have the major drawbacks of the English Premiership – an increasing gap between the big clubs and smaller competitors, oversized squads, spiralling transfer fees and inflated wages – but without the advantages. The danger is European football would be devalued as a competition, as a spectacle, or, in the terms of our age, as a product. ○

Favour of the Month

Richard Mason reported on a refereeing controversy in Italy – eight years before the "Moggigate" investigation that led to Juventus being relegated

WSC No 136, June 1998

THERE IS A CRISIS in Italian football. An unprecedented series of refereeing errors (or "favours", as many would prefer to believe) nearly all of which have benefited Juventus, has led to a degree of soul searching rare even in a country so frantically passionate about football as Italy.

The most recent occurred in the "match of the season", Juve v Inter of April 26, when Ronaldo was denied the clearest of penalties by referee Piero Ceccarini who then, within seconds, awarded a penalty at the other end. Admittedly, Del Piero missed it, but the damage had already been done. Inter President Massimo Moratti left the stadium 20 minutes from the end, commenting that referees were conditioned to favour Juve, and that he did not wish to be made a fool of any longer. Ronaldo called the decision "a disgrace". To add insult to injury, Inter's Ze Elias, sent off for a foul less heinous than one for which Juve's Davids was let off, was suspended for three matches and Ronaldo and Zamorano for two.

Had all of this been an isolated case of a referee having a bad game it would probably have blown over, even allowing for the importance of the occasion. But it wasn't. Throughout the season Juve have benefited from a series of decisions which can be euphemistically described as "strange". Back in the autumn, Ferrara cleared a shot from Udinese's Bierhoff when it was clearly over the line. The score at the time was 1-1, and the game was in the second half. The final result was 4-1, but it is reasonable to think that had Udinese been awarded the goal, a draw was probably the maximum that Juve would have achieved.

Then, in February, Roma were denied a clear penalty by international referee Messina for a foul by Deschamps with the score at 2-1 late in a game Juve won 3-1. Against Lazio in Rome, Italy's "top" referee, Collina, first sent off Nedved for protesting, then judged as involuntary a case of hands by a Juve defender as he jumped with a Lazio forward at a corner. It was the last minute and Juve won 1-0. On April 19 at Empoli, with 15 minutes to go and Juve winning 1-0, Bianconi's header was clearly over the line before Peruzzi scooped it out, but referee Rodomonti said no. Comically, television showed him mouthing "I saw it all, I saw it all".

As I write, Juve lead Inter by four points, but it could be argued that these five decisions presented them with ten points that they had not earned, and they are not counterbalanced by any points "lost" for mistakes against Juve. Also, the events I have described are only the most glaring – there have been many others of a more minor nature. There is also the fact that after 27 games Juventus have committed 625 fouls (only Atalanta have committed more) and had two players sent off, while Sampdoria, with 496 fouls one of the cleaner sides, have seen no fewer than 11 red cards.

The commonest theory, to which I subscribe, is that referees are "conditioned" to favour Juventus, and to a lesser extent the other big city clubs. Juventus are an institution as much as a football club, and possibly a third to a half of Italy's fans, whatever team they watch on Sundays, are Juve supporters at heart. Juve are also very strongly identified with the corridors of power because of their umbilical links with the Agnelli family, owners of Fiat. This can result, among other things, in staggering arrogance. After the Inter game, the nominal president, Vittorio Chiusano, denied the evidence of his own eyes in claiming that there was no penalty and that the referee had not helped Juve. The general manager Luciano Moggi contented himself with lecturing Ronaldo for "having learnt Italian too quickly". If we add the increasing commercialisation of the game, with the consequent "need" to be successful not occasionally but always, we can understand why a referee designated to control a Juventus match may not always be ecstatically happy. Especially if you consider that it has emerged that Rodomonti, the villain of the piece at Empoli, went more than three years without refereeing Juve after he was "guilty" of awarding Genoa a goal that wasn't in December 1994. This fact suggested to many that even if they don't actually pay referees, Juve can dictate who does or does not referee their games.

Now people are rushing to suggest all sorts of radical changes. They range from electronic equipment to determine whether the ball has crossed the line through two referees and even to the use of replays during matches. The first of these might be acceptable, though eventually one of these machines would be bound to give a false reading and then we would be back to where we started. As for the rest, forget it (I hope). If the thesis that referees are conditioned by the importance of certain teams is correct, it doesn't matter what technology you introduce, ways will still be found to favour those teams, and the game in the meantime will have been irreparably impoverished as a spectacle for no advantage.

I think there are simpler solutions. First, an end to the system whereby referees for Sunday's matches are announced on Wednesday and the newspapers regale us with details of their previous games – how many home wins, draws, away wins, penalties, red cards etc. Let people find out as they arrive in the stadium, as they do in England. Second, a bit more honesty and humility – when your team has clearly been the recipient of a piece of good luck, say so. Just a word in that direction from the Juventus backroom staff and perhaps some sympathy for Inter and the average fan in the street would have been satisfied. Third, remind referees that the old dictum, the best referee is the one nobody notices, happens to be true. Lastly, and most important of all, referees who are patently unable to apply the laws in the same way for all teams should be suspended indefinitely.

Of course, it is now quite possible that the pendulum will swing back against Juve for a time, as referees bend over backwards to be "impartial". In the meantime, Juve's last game is away to Atalanta. It is just possible that both teams will need the points for opposing reasons. If this is the case, any volunteers to referee? God himself, who is quite popular in this country, would have his work cut out to come of that one unscathed. ○

Waging Wars

Patrick Harverson examined the furore over a report detailing huge rises in footballers' wages in the previous year

WSC No 136, June 1998

ARE FOOTBALLERS PAID TOO MUCH? It is a simple enough question, but one that evades a simple answer. It can be, and often is, argued that footballers are paid too much in relation to the amount of money their clubs earn, or in relation to the performance they deliver on the pitch, or – as several tabloid newspapers suggested recently – in relation to the amount of money a nurse earns.

The latter earns on average about £15,000 a year, or more than 13 times less than the average Premiership player makes over the same period. Is this fair? Probably not. Low pay for nurses is a scandal, but that doesn't necessarily make high pay for footballers a scandal too. What we can be certain about is that today's top footballers in Britain operate in a global labour market in which their rare skills (don't laugh) are in great demand from employers willing to pay large amounts of money to secure their services. The same, obviously, cannot be said of nurses.

In this context, can players be blamed for accepting the riches on offer? Clearly not. But then try telling that to George Best. The great Irishman believes today's stars are overpaid, and said recently: "There is too much money in the game and we have seen it go out of control." Best's remarks were prompted by last month's report on the finances of the Premiership by accountants Deloitte & Touche. Their finding that the wage bills of the 20 Premier League clubs jumped by 35 per cent to £135 million last year – and are likely to rise by as much again this year – provoked a predictable round of media scare stories, plus the inevitable fatuous comparison with nurses' pay. A couple of points need to be made about the subject of footballers' pay before going any further. Firstly, when the media covers the issue of players' pay in football, accuracy is rarely at a premium. The huge sums bandied around on the back pages are often entirely speculative and must be taken with large doses of salt.

This situation persists because it is in the interests of the players, their agents, sometimes the clubs and certainly excitable newspaper sports editors to inflate the value of salaries. Only a handful of players in the top flight earn more than £1m a year, a point amply illustrated by the fact that the average annual pay in the Premiership is less than £200,000. That means a lot of players must earn less than £100,000. That is still a hell of a lot of money, but it is worth remembering when someone bangs on about all footballers being millionaires. Very few are.

Secondly, even if some players are paid as much as the papers say, so what? They deserve every penny. The oft-repeated arguments used by the players' union about short-lived careers, the risk of injuries and the lack of post-football opportunities are entirely valid ones. Also, if clubs are willing to offer footballers sackloads of money to play, why on earth should the players turn the offers down? Sir Tom Finney, who earned £20 a week in the late 1950s, showed a better grasp of football economics than George Best when he recently commented: "I've always said that an employer pays you what he thinks you're worth. Who can blame players if they are offered £15,000 or £20,000 per week?"

Obviously, when a player fails to deliver on the pitch, he deserves criticism for not giving his employers – and more importantly the fans – value for money. A greater element of performance-related pay in footballers' packages might be step forward in this respect, although it is unlikely the players or their agents would stand for it. The issue of pay has attracted so much attention in the past year not just because a few top stars are extremely well remunerated, but also because the speed at which wage rates at the top of football are increasing has become alarming. It is estimated that between 1992 and 1996 Premiership wages rose by an average of 25 per cent a year, with that rate rising to 35 per cent in 1997. The reasons for this remarkable surge are relatively easy to explain. Wages have shot up because the elite clubs have had much more money to spend, and because the players have been in a much stronger position to demand more money thanks to the changes in the transfer system prompted by the Bosman ruling.

If the huge rise in club revenues provided the fuel for the fire underneath football's wage structure, Bosman was the spark that lit the fire and fanned the flames higher. Since the ruling in the European court that out-of-contract players within the European Union could move to other clubs on free transfers, money that previously would have been spent on transfer fees has been diverted into players' wage packets.

The out-of-contract players from overseas had more bargaining power than those still in contract, and as their wages climbed sharply, so there was a knock-on effect elsewhere in England, with top players able to negotiate higher wages to match those of the incoming stars. That clubs have been able to meet the demands of players for hefty pay packets is thanks to the big increases in their revenues over the past few years, most notably from the sale of television rights. The latest broadcasting deal between the Premier League and Sky Television is worth £185m a year over four years to the top clubs, or 13 times as much as the 1988 deal was worth to the then First Division.

Much of that money, plus the extra income clubs are earning from gate receipts, merchandising and other commercial activities, has been spent on player wages and transfers. Alan Sugar may complain about the "prune-juice" economics of handing over much of the new money coming into clubs straight over to the players, but isn't that what the business of football should be all about – earning money to invest in the playing squad to improve the performance of the team? Yet he does have a point, in that what worried Sugar and many others from the business side of the game is that clubs are spending too much of their income on players' wages, and creating a worsening financial situation that could eventually lead some clubs into bankruptcy.

Last season wages and salaries (which admittedly include clubs' management staff) represented seven per cent of clubs' turnover in the Premiership. That is not a particularly worrying figure, but within it are some troubling instances of clubs spending as much as two-thirds, or in the case of Blackburn Rovers all, of its income in wages. Clearly, no business can survive if every penny that comes in the door goes straight out on payroll costs. The clubs that do spend a large portion of their income on wages defend the policy by saying it is a short-term phenomenon – they are investing heavily in the playing squad to improve performance and generate long-term benefits for the club. This is all well and good, but the strategy only works if the team is subsequently successful enough to bring in the extra revenues that eventually return the club to a more sustainable balance of income and expenditure. That, as anyone in football knows, is a very big if. Just ask Manchester City.

Ultimately, perhaps, the more immediate problem of rising player wages is that they give clubs a perfect reason/excuse for raising ticket prices. Chelsea offer a king's ransom to Brian Laudrup, then turn around and ask the fans to foot the bill. This might work while football is booming, but what happens when some of those newer fans of the game, who have jumped on the football bandwagon in the racy Nineties, get tired of the high prices and the hype and jump off again? At that point, the spendthrift clubs could find themselves earning less from ticket sales, merchandising and possibly television income, while still saddled with hugely expensive player contracts negotiated during earlier, more prosperous times. The sums would simply not add up, leaving the clubs facing serious financial problems. It is a sobering prospect. ○

Moving Targets

Phil Ball explained how the Grimsby winger Scott McGarvey, once a starlet with Man Utd, fell out with the home supporters at Blundell Park

WSC No 136, June 1998

CANTONA KUNG-FU PRECEDENTS? There are none that I know of, but there have certainly been some little *contretemps* in the past between actors and audience that suggested that Eric's leap of faith was going to happen sooner or later.

The 1987-88 season was a miserable one for Grimsby. Relegated the previous season from the old Second Division under the hapless Mick Lyons, the club was speeding down a creek without a paddle, with a hole in the boat for good measure. I seem to recall that the game was against Walsall, and that they were much the better side. It was a bitter afternoon, Grimsby were a goal to the bad, and in the old Findus Stand the wags of yesteryear were beginning to scowl.

Grimsby boasted a strike force of one Steve Saunders, lost in the fogs of obscurity, and Scott McGarvey, a somewhat more famous figure in the annals of Grimsby's substantial list of dysfunctional big-club refugees. Saunders, as was his wont, had just stumbled over the ball and kindly returned possession to Walsall when from across the frozen silence someone shouted: "Saunders – you're crap!" Something in the player's reaction, dropping his head slightly to contemplate the mud, told you that he'd heard it and that he'd recognised at least a grain of truth in the assessment.

McGarvey, loitering close by, walked deliberately over to where the shout had come from and stared long and hard into the stand, in a threatening gesture of solidarity with his team-mate. He was only a few feet from me when a Grimsby defender, having regained possession, tried to knock a long ball back upfield in McGarvey's direction, a fact that Scotty registered too late. The ball bounced from his foot as he attempted to control it, and dribbled out into touch.

None of this would have mattered too much if McGarvey had been even half humble. But he fitted the bill perfectly for a Blundell Park hate campaign. Though possessed of some skill, he clearly felt that his spell with Man Utd entitled him to some sort of special attention, and he strutted around like some fallen blond angel, amazed that he was having to make a living among such mundane company. He was never going to survive the wise men of Grimsby.

As the ball came to rest on the old wooden fence, an old guy to my left decided to come clean: "McGarvey, you're fucking crap," he intoned, and his group of mates joined in with the slanging. McGarvey's reaction was extraordinary. His face turned aubergine: "Fuck you!" he began, and turned his back on the game, for a Walsall defender had taken the throw-in. He pointed threateningly to his accuser, but the old man was already warming to the fight. "Fuck you an' all!" he countered, laughing through his false teeth. At this, McGarvey lost the plot completely and ran up to the fence, causing some supporters to flinch. All his pent-up feeling spewed out in a torrent: "Come on down an' try you fuckers!" he screamed, tugging his shirt from his shorts with the implication that his accusers could not play football themselves – hardly the point of course.

But he wasn't finished. In a slightly calmer voice he continued, as if lecturing his audience: "It's all right for you lot standing there every week, you bastards," and then he lost it again – I remember the whole exchange as if it were yesterday – and he began to stamp on the floor like a child denied some sweets, going silent for a moment and then exploding with a string of meaningless oaths aimed at no one in particular: "Fuckingbastardsfuckers-fuckoffshitbagsarrrr!", all the time dancing on one leg as the game carried on behind him.

I once saw Nicol Williamson play Macbeth at Stratford. During the floating dagger scene, when all was hushed in anticipation of the soliloquy, someone belched. Though the audience controlled itself, Williamson didn't. Sitting down on a stool, he began to lecture the audience about how he was there to teach us Shakespeare, and how he was not going to be distracted from delivering one of the greatest speeches in English drama. It was a bizarre moment, because he'd broken the spell, making you want to pinch yourself, to check that it was really happening.

And what McGarvey did was the same, because footballers, like actors, are not supposed to step over the line that separates them from the mortal world of mere spectators, whatever the problem might be. And when they do, albeit very rarely, the magic is somehow gone – as was Scott McGarvey, a few months later. ○

Double Jeopardy

Arsenal had just done the Double and become genuinely popular in the process. It was a painful transition for some, as Spurs fan Martin Cloake explained

WSC No 137, July 1998

COLUMNS OF BLACK SMOKE billowed into the night sky from the wasted shells of burning cars, helicopters clattered overhead and the sound of sirens pierced the air. Arsenal had just completed the Double, and some of their fans were trashing their own manor. A strange way to celebrate, but it was a strange season.

Arsenal used to be the team everyone loved to hate, but that's all changed. Sure, they've got an intelligent and likeable manager, have a creative midfield, the best defensive unit in the country, some great attacking players and play some flowing and exciting football – but come on folks, what have the Arsenal ever done for us?

Many people cite breaking the grip of Manchester United as reason enough to drop their traditional, and entirely natural, dislike of Arsenal. But enduring a few months of crowing from the "lifelong Gooners" who are already pouring out of the woodwork should soon restore some balance – these people make United fans look positively self-effacing.

Yet despite their many unattractive qualities, I feel sorry for Arsenal fans. Rather like the Labour Party, they've had to jettison everything they hold dear in order to achieve success. Remember "Lucky Arsenal", "1-0 to the Arsenal"? The chants of the glory days are but distant memories now. "Skilful, entertaining Arsenal with more than a hint of continental flair" doesn't quite trip off the tongue in the same way; "4-0 to the Arsenal" doesn't have the essential twist of irony that made "Boring, Boring Arsenal" such a hit.

Beneath all the bluster, they can't cope with all this adulation. They're so traumatised they turn their anger and confusion in on themselves – hence the destruction wreaked around Highbury on the evening of the Cup final. Worst of all must have been the antics of Tottenham Hotspur, the side they pretend not to see as rivals any more. At Highbury early in the season, a full- strength Arsenal failed to defeat an unadventurous Tottenham side reduced to ten men. Despite the airy disregard New Gooners affect when talking of Tottenham, they badly wanted to beat them that day, especially as an Ian Wright goal would have broken the club's scoring record. And so, as the teams trudged off the pitch, the Highbury faithful used, for the first time, the word "boring" as a term of abuse rather than pride. Boring Boring Tottenham? Where was the mad scientist who had swapped the personalities of the two clubs?

Spurs dogged them all season. Alan Sugar did his bit for social partnership when he brought one of the Double-winning side's most vital players, Emmanuel Petit, to England, then paid his cab fare to Highbury. This gift came on top of the already generous decision to give Arsenal a free run at Dennis Bergkamp, everyone's player of the year and a lifelong Spurs fan, because he would have been "a waste of money". Those who admire Sugar's business expertise know he wouldn't have been stupid enough to turn down such a quality player and – modest as ever – Sugar has refused to claim the credit.

Still Tottenham had a few tricks left up their sleeves. By adopting the clever tactic of being complete rubbish for long periods, they started to make Arsenal fans believe the treble was on – the League, the FA Cup, and Tottenham relegated. Spurs played it perfectly. When Arsenal beat Everton to clinch the title, that win also ensured Tottenham's continued presence in the top flight. This, as Rory McGrath – one supporter at least who has held on to the art of being boring – said in the papers, was extremely irritating.

It's almost possible to feel sorry for a set of fans who, tortured by success, can't enjoy a fine footballing side. Credit must go to Newcastle for being so inept that Arsenal didn't really have to try to beat them in the Cup final – completing the double in style would have been simply too much for them to bear. ○

Wembley Ways

Harry Pearson reflected on an unhappy trip to Wembley for a club from the North East

WSC No 137, July 1998

MIDWAY THROUGH THE SEASON my neighbour had a dream. He dreamed that four North East teams would get to Wembley but only one would return victorious. At the time this seemed rather unlikely, but as the months passed things gradually began to fall into place. First Middlesbrough obliged, losing with a clunking inevitability that has become the natural herald of spring in the areas where cuckoos never call. Next up came Tow Law Town of County Durham in the final of the FA Vase. "I can't say I don't want Tow Law to win," my neighbour said, "But with this dream and everything..." Newcastle United were playing the Cup final the following Saturday.

My neighbour was perhaps the only person in the North East who didn't give the Lawyers his unconditional support. Tow Law, 1,000 feet up on the edge of the north Pennines, has an almost unique ability to bring the region together. Walking up Wembley Way on the Saturday of the Vase final were men in Sunderland shirts with their faces painted in Tow Law's black and white stripes – the North East equivalent of seeing Ian Paisley in Celtic hoops.

Tow Law is the smallest town ever to send a team to a Wembley final. The north Pennine metropolis has a population of just 2,200. What this means in social terms can perhaps best be judged by one incident. A couple of weeks before the football team and its fans embarked on a trip to London local police advised club officials to take the area's most infamous burglar with them as a guest. That way, they said, the citizens of Tow Law would be able to enjoy their day out without worrying that their electrical goods would be missing when they got back. In a place the size of Tow Law creating a crime wave is a one-person job.

Tow Law is also arguably the coldest place ever to send a team to Wembley. When the Lawyers trounced Mansfield 5-0 in the FA Cup back in the Sixties the Stags' manager remarked that playing in Tow Law was "like playing at the North Pole". Mansfield's boss was neither the first nor last to make such comments about the "Siberian temperatures" at

Ironworks Road. Over the years so many teams have used Tow Law's singular playing conditions as an excuse for defeat it is tempting to say that, if Cowdenbeath are the Blue Brazil, then Tow Law Town are the Black and White Bolivia.

In the concourse beneath England's national stadium the 3,000 or so Tow Law supporters who have made the trip south mill around trying to come to terms with the price of Wembley beer. A middle-aged woman, perhaps suffering from the effects of low altitude, staggers about singing Tow Law Town's FA Carlsberg Vase final song, "All our dreams are coming true..." Judging by the look on the faces of her teenage kids this is not altogether the case for them.

Tow Law owe their place at Wembley to hard fought wins over the likes of wealthy Taunton and Sudbury Wanderers, but also to a change of attitude among the men who run the Northern League. For many years Northern League first division teams such as Tow Law entered the FA Trophy. This was a throwback to the days when the NL had been the dominant force in the amateur game. Up against the well supported and semi-professional outfits of the south-east and north-west, Northern League teams (many of whom, you suspect, are now more amateur than they were back in the glory years) had as much chance of winning the FA Trophy as they had of wining the FA Cup. Pride, however, kept Northern League first division clubs in the Trophy for over 20 years. When certain teams, such as Dunston, tried to drop down a level to the Vase, they were prevented from doing so by a Northern League administration which, when it came to the subject of falling playing standards, were in denial.

Realism eventually intervened in 1995. "A brilliant decision," Tow Law chairman John Flynn says, and it's easy to see why he thinks so. The results were almost immediate. Whitby Town won the Vase last year. They were the first Northern League team to lift a major trophy since North Shields won the Amateur Cup in 1969.

Tow Law failed to repeat the feat. For a team that play most of their games in a town where the Prince lament "Sometimes It Snows In April" makes even less sense than it does to the rest of the British population, the weather at Wembley on May 9 could hardly have been more favourable. The sun beat down, the breeze hardly stirred the corner flags. Conditions clearly favoured Devonian opponents Tiverton, but the Lawyers played attractive, passing football, had the most skilful player on the pitch in Jarrod Suddick and only conceded the decisive goal in the last ten minutes. For most of the fans that and a day out was enough.

A week after Tow Law's defeat Newcastle lost to Arsenal. After the game my neighbour came out into the front garden shaking his head. "It's all coming to pass," he said in amazement. "Three down and one left." He is a Sunderland fan. So much for the power of dreams. ○

French Lessons

The hype surrounding England's World Cup efforts only served to emphasise the undignified behaviour of the country's representatives, both on and off the pitch

WSC No 138, August 1998 ~ Editorial

AT THE RISK OF PROMPTING a wave of cancelled subscriptions, your old pals at *WSC* have to admit that in some respects we enjoy the World Cup more when England aren't in it.

This has something to do with being able to remember a time when football wasn't ubiquitous, when it existed for the benefit of those who were interested in it, but didn't intrude into the lives of everyone else. Nothing could support the weight of expectation heaped upon France 98 months before it started, and if England had not been there we might at least have been spared some of the crowing boorishness that surrounded the tournament.

It was apparent even during the ad breaks. A nasty, xenophobic stench hung around the commercials for one of the official sponsors, Vauxhall, in which foreign fans, players and managers were dubbed with voices and "dialogue" that would have been rejected as too crude in *'Allo 'Allo.* Worse still was the extraordinary beer commercial in which a group of supporters walk into a pub intending to watch a World Cup game but discover Vinnie Jones sitting by himself in front of the TV. He snarls at the group who back off immediately. The message was stark: respect the hard man, otherwise he may lose control – and it will be your fault if he does.

Many England fans, not the majority but still more than just the hooligan fringe, took this confrontational attitude with them to France. Determined not to adapt in any way to wherever they happen to be, they welcome the "provocation" that gives them the chance to demonstrate their toughness. And they keep receiving what could easily be construed as messages of support. Alongside the usual blather about the "shame" supposedly heaped on the nation by the fighting, the *Sun* produced a highly ambiguous front page on June 16 headlined **Two-Nil**, below which were pictures of Alan Shearer and one of the fat boneheads arrested in Marseille, two Englishmen making an impact at the World Cup given equal prominence.

In other papers, some of the fans who were subsequently arrested were shown wearing *Sun* bowler hats that had been distributed outside the bars in Marseille before the trouble started. Yet Des Lynam and sports minister Tony Banks were photographed wearing the same hats in the paper's build-up to subsequent England games. Banks will have had official approval for his stunt, given that the government is only too keen to cuddle up to Rupert Murdoch, but why should the BBC have allowed their main presenter to be aligned with a paper that was bound to take the most chauvinistic approach to reporting the World Cup?

Another reason for feeling ambivalent about England is the team itself, characterised during Glenn Hoddle's reign by petulance, immaturity and a refusal to acknowledge any fault – much the same tendencies displayed by the followers of the hooligans. The instinctive response of many fans in Marseille to blame someone else for provoking an English reaction was to be mirrored by the David Beckham incident which undermined England on the pitch. Beckham's dismissal was the low point of a bad night for the quartet of England players, Ince, Batty and Shearer being the others, who most frequently cross the line between legitimate aggression and intimidation and are also among the most reluctant to accept criticism.

Shearer, above all, seems to have cultivated a narky persona which refuses to engage with reasonable criticism or even normal standards of social interaction, as demonstrated by his leaden interviews in the build-up to England games. It fell to Shearer to explain the game where each player had to work a song title into his interview, which he did with obvious relish. True, the questions asked are almost invariably banal, but the open refusal to take them at all seriously showed a contempt for the viewer as well as the interviewer.

Shearer's sullen demeanour is matched by the man who made him captain. Glenn Hoddle plainly does not rate communication as one of the jobs of an international manager. His habit of giving out deliberately misleading information about injuries and his fatuous insistence that every selection he made was preplanned left him open to attack from those who might otherwise have given him the benefit of the doubt. Equally, his spiky, humourless manner left him with no reserves of affection when things went wrong on the pitch, dulled the enthusiasm generated by elements of the team's performance and did nothing to counter the poisonous legacy left by a faction of England fans wherever they went.

England's inability to admit defeat gracefully and depart with a semblance of dignity was familiar and wearisome enough. But the air of malice around England's campaign now seems set to continue into the domestic season in a new form – the ritual hounding of David Beckham. It might be tempting to respond that those who live by the hype also run the risk of dying by it, but not when some people seem to think that's what he literally deserves. Neither football nor England should matter that much. ○

Slow Coaches

At the World Cup, Matthew Roche found only one national team manager with interesting insights to offer. No surprise that it wasn't Glenn Hoddle

WSC No 138, August 1998

IT WAS ENOUGH TO MAKE any self-respecting journalist scream. Glenn Hoddle had just been asked at a press conference whether he thought the heat might be a problem during the game with Romania. "I don't know about that, but it's certainly hot enough in this room," he said with a witless smile, prompting a member of the accompanying media circus to put away his notebook. "It's at times like this that I want England to lose so I can go off and cover someone more interesting," he admitted. Wanted: Manager for national side. Must be able to provoke thought.

Although Hoddle might claim he was trying to bore the tabloid rat pack into submission, he did little to challenge the view that a crisp packet could have shown more originality in front of the media. The World Cup generated so many meaningless millions of words a day that we needed someone to stop playing mind games and cut through the bullshit.

Forget the players' drinking habits, forget the "How's the broken toenail today, Dennis?" and the "This player-interview has been specially arranged for our favoured television station, so everyone else get lost". Where was a story we could chew over? What about the managers, the men whose tactical choices made or broke the teams? Who could deepen our knowledge of the game by explaining how they made their decisions? Give us substance or give us a ticket home, we cried.

Step forward Claude Le Roy. Had the sides been given points for intelligent comments by the top man, Cameroon would have been in the final. The portly Frenchman was perhaps the only coach happy to sit down for an hour and discuss football, tactics and players without once repeating himself or descending into banalities. "This whole idea of compensatory play is absolute bollocks," he said one day after someone had criticised him for pushing too many men into attack. "If a defender goes forwards with the ball" – he moved his mobile phone up the table – "you have to send someone up to support him, not pull a player back to make up the numbers in defence." A bunch of car keys went forward to support the mobile phone. "There's no point dawdling near the goalkeeper when the guy with the ball is at the other end of the field."

Some managers would look for journalists from the team's next opponents before speaking but Le Roy made little attempt to hide his tactics. "We tell our players that once they've decided to do something, go for it and don't allow yourself to be distracted. All of football lies in those last 40 yards of the pitch where you can take risks," he said at a news conference. No one from Austria seemed to be listening, since the team looked mightily surprised the next night when defender Pierre Njanka scored a wonderful goal after running 60 yards with the ball .

Le Roy, the only manager who actually seemed to be enjoying himself, had little time for the closed training sessions so beloved by many. "If you want to protect your players, it's either because you're afraid or not confident enough in the quality of your work. It's a great game, eh? The pressure is such that some coaches would love it if there were no matches," he said.

Although some might say Le Roy's experience as a television commentator helped him formulate good soundbites, he showed an originality of thought matched by few of the dozen or so other managers I met. Some seemed to think that even mentioning the words "4-4-2" was tantamount to betraying state secrets.

Yugoslavia's Slobodan Santrac, for example, is rumoured to enjoy an exciting personal life, but behind a microphone he's about as lively as a bag of dust. Asked several times about his tactics for one match, he responded with a short mantra: "Yugoslavia will try to score one more goal than the opposition." That's all, folks. Wacky Bora Milutinovic, fleetingly in charge of Nigeria, spoke about six languages and made little sense in any of them. After rattling on in English he would translate his own quotes into French, then Spanish, then Italian and so forth, each time slightly changing the sense of his comments so that by the end of the monologue there were groups of journalists with somewhat different understandings of what had been said.

Everywhere you looked there was a manager trying to avoid interesting questions. Denmark's Bo Johansson looked affable enough, but he had a squadron of wasps hiding in his underwear. One hack had his head torn off for asking whether the team's greatest problem against South Africa might be over-confidence, while another was given a condescending lecture after daring to mistake the minute in which a player had been substituted.

While at least one correspondent cheered when the Danes were knocked out, a whole army of jubilant scribes hit the streets after the departure of Romania, whose team spokesman once announced he'd turned his mobile phone off because he didn't like being bothered by journalists. Perhaps Iordanescu and Co were too busy polishing those dreaded post-match untruths, which reached the status of an art form in the hands of Croatia's Miroslav Blazevic after an embarrassing defeat against Argentina. "It was a very pleasant game," he smiled. "I am very happy with our team. They can leave with their heads high."

Or perhaps they were studying endless match videos, although no one ever told us whether these sessions were any use. Le Roy had little time for them. "As a player I found it unbearable when the coach made us watch a long match video and then explained to us what we'd seen. It's like making an orchestra listen to a recording they've just made," he said, admitting he had other things on his mind.

"I want to change the psychology of my side. When someone is substituted the players need to think of it as fresh blood being injected into the team rather than an individual being punished. Once they've grasped that we'll have made a great stride forward," he said.

But this achievement is useless if there's no one left to be substituted, which sometimes looked likely after Cameroon's axemen had played the first half. It was frustrating to see a team with so much talent – they easily outplayed Italy and Chile for long spells with ten men – let down by rank indiscipline. Le Roy blamed youthful exuberance and biased referees rather than inherent malevolence. "The players know that if things go wrong I'll take responsibility. I will never blame them for not following my orders, which is an excuse I regard as a massive obscenity. If the players weren't following orders it's the coach's fault for choosing the wrong side," he said.

Now he's off to coach Strasbourg, leaving us to hope he'll be back in 2002. *"C'est une jouissance permanente, le foot,"* he said one day. Football is a permanent orgasm. For some. O

Sepp Mire

FIFA's new boss was distinctly similar to the old one. John Sugden and Alan Tomlinson put their view of the transition from Havelange to Blatter

WSC No 138, August 1998

AT FIFA'S 51ST CONGRESS in Paris, on the eve of the World Cup finals, Sepp Blatter – the man most responsible for outlawing the tackle from behind – felled Lennart Johansson with a late challenge that Tommy Smith would have been proud of. After a secret ballot, Blatter swept to the FIFA presidency by 111 votes to 80. The result stunned Johansson's supporters. Only days before they had been confidently predicting a comfortable victory for the man who for the past four years had been tirelessly promoting a campaign to reform FIFA based on principles of democracy and transparency.

Unfortunately for Johansson, democracy and accountability are alien principles to most of the 191 delegates entitled to vote. When, flanked by jogging, dark-suited bodyguards, the armour-plated limousine of Saudi Arabia's Prince Faisal bin Fahad nosed its way through the gates of the Equinox convention centre, one wondered how he would get his head around the principle of one person, one vote. In FIFA, all eligible national associations have one vote and each is equally valued – Germany and Brazil have no more weight than FIFA's newest members such as Palestine and American Samoa. It is through the manipulation of this system and the husbandry of the third world vote that the South American confederation (Conmebol), with only ten members, has been able to control FIFA for the past quarter of a century

During the count, João Havelange, the outgoing president of 24 years, gazed down approvingly from the tribune as the piles of ballot papers accumulated in favour of his protégé and former employee, the Swiss general secretary of FIFA, Sepp Blatter. On the surface this may have looked like Europe regaining its ascendancy. In fact, Blatter had been hand-picked to work his way up FIFA's totem pole by the late Horst Dassler, the key architect of the Adidas empire and the man who established ISL (Information, Sport and Leisure), the marketing agency which has virtually monopolised the media and sponsorship deals of FIFA and the International Olympic Committee for the past two decades.

Dassler spotted Blatter when he was an executive of Sports Timing in Switzerland. Dassler took Blatter to Landersheim, Adidas's secretive executive training school, before placing his recruit in FIFA where he married the daughter of the general secretary, Helmut Kaser, then took over his father-in-law's job. Blatter was soon divorced and bedded in as Havelange's chief of staff.

Blatter formally entered the race for the presidency earlier this year, only a week before the April 7 deadline. He was openly criticised by many FIFA executive committee members for using his position as general secretary as a campaigning base for an undeclared bid for his master's throne. Then, as Blatter's campaign gained momentum, the same voices called foul over the manner in which both Blatter and Havelange travelled the world in executive jets provided by allies in the Arabian Gulf and backed with resources from Swiss-based business partners.

The suspicion was that they were promising rewards and favours for votes. This tactic had worked for Havelange in 1974 when he ousted England's Sir Stanley Rous, and it was set to work again as some of those who had pledged their support to Johansson wavered. Significantly, Blatter and Havelange campaigned longest and hardest in the impoverished quarters of south-east Asia, eastern Europe and, most notably, Africa. This was viewed as a blatant attempt to undermine the alliance between Johansson's UEFA and Issa Hayatou's African confederation (CAF), which held the balance of power with more than 50 votes.

England's highly public last-minute defection to the Blatter camp was a further blow to Johansson's rocking campaign. Clearly, this was directly related to the English FA's hopes of staging the World Cup finals in 2006. Along with 49 other members of FIFA, England had signed a letter promising support for the Swede. Once the cradle of football tore up their covenant, it was easier for other nations to abandon their pledges to Johansson. Shamefully, and not for the first time, in the FA's calculations getting the World Cup was worth more than keeping promises and being a good European player.

Even with the game running away from him, the night before the elections Johansson believed he had enough votes to win. However, as he prepared for bed in Paris's Le Bristol, the favoured hotel of the FIFA executive and its guests, he was disturbed by his aides who told him that across the Seine, at the Montparnasse Meridien, where all the national associations were accommodated, Blatter supporters from the Gulf were working the corridors. Johansson's supporters sped across Paris to try to prevent a haemorrhaging of their vote but, as one insider put it, "it was too late, it had become a tidal wave".

Perhaps Blatter, with his smooth politician's manner and his multilingual stage skills, won because he is the best man for the job, but we doubt it. It is equally likely that the continuity candidate prevailed because Johansson's collectivist ideals simply proved to be less appealing than patronage and personal gain.

At his post-election press conference, when asked about rumours of vote buying, Blatter responded smugly by saying "the match is over". Indeed, inside the FIFA club, solidarity and silence soon replaced outspoken outrage among the losers. However, outside the gates, there may still be enough people who, in the words of the FIFA motto, "care about football" enough to carry forward the investigation. This game may be longer than Blatter thinks. ○

Brought to Book

Harry Pearson was appalled by the sheer awfulness of Glenn Hoddle's Diary, which presented the England manager's views on the World Cup

WSC No 140, October 1998

THE HODDLE BOOK. A betrayal of trust; a gross error of judgement; an action in which personal gain has been put ahead of the public interest. Yes, there's no doubt about it, by charging £17.99 for 236 pages of this mind-numbing rubbish Andre Deutsch really have brought the English publishing game into disrepute.

Where to begin? The tedious golf games with Ray Clemence, perhaps, or the endless repetition of the words "positive" and "focused" or maybe the positive, focusing sound of M People's *Search for the Hero* as it echoes around the team coach. Oh, no, let's start with the tortured prose style, shall we?

As a player Glenn Hoddle was hardly noted for bruising physicality, but when it comes to tackling the English language it's a different matter. After a few paragraphs in his company our native tongue is carried off on a stretcher groaning and begging for mercy.

Hoddle is a football manager. No one expects him to be able to write like Flaubert or even Harry Harris. That is the point of having a ghost writer. The England boss's spectral scribe is the FA's Director of Public Affairs, David Davies, though reading sentences such as " We were ready for just about everything, even the slightly changed role from what we'd expected of Gianfranco Zola" it is hard to avoid concluding that the prolific Seventies playwright Ernest Wise was also involved.

Interviewed on Radio Five Live Hoddle outlined the reasons he had written *My 1998 World Cup Story*: "My main concern was to get a quality book out in the sense of what was running more from my mind and my reactions of situations through a World Cup and putting things down on record to a certain degree and having that memory and giving people a bit of an insight." The best thing that can be said for David Davies is that he has captured the authentic voice of the England football manager.

Amidst the linguistic carnage it's often hard to pick out meaning or significance. The book appears to have been written contemporaneously with events, but on odd occasions suddenly lurches into the past tense. Is this just another cock-up? Or does it mean that bits were inserted later with the benefit of hindsight to point up the England manager's vision? It's impossible to tell, but certainly there are moments in *My 1998 World Cup Story* in which there appears to be a sly method in the syntactical madness.

Here, for example, is Glenn Hoddle on the sending off of David Beckham: "We'd warned him at Le Tournoi a year ago about not getting involved with silly antics, but he obviously hadn't learned... If he hadn't got sent off we'd have had 11 men on the pitch and would have won the game – I was convinced of that. I also told him that I'd done my best to avoid putting a greater burden on his shoulders by naming scapegoats." Except in a book, obviously.

Jack Charlton once summarised his doubts about Hoddle the player with the words "The lad lacks passion". Maybe so. He certainly doesn't lack self-belief, however. Doubts creep into *My 1998 World Cup Story* even less often than good music (Hoddle opts to tell the players he is dropping from the squad the bad news to the accompaniment of Kenny G. No wonder Gazza went berserk). The England manager justifies every decision with the forthrightness of someone who has been totally vindicated by events; his only regret that he did not take faith-healer Eileen Drewery to France with the squad. Sadly, there is more conviction in his arguments than logic. For example, Hoddle talks about the "lack of focus" he had detected in David Beckham before the tournament began. He then uses the Man Utd player's sending off in the Argentina match to justify his decision not to start with him against Tunisia or Romania. All of which leaves you wondering which dimwit it was who picked this walking liability to play in St Etienne.

Much of the "I told you so" element of the book (and it forms a considerable portion) is directed at "the media". Hoddle finds many football writers' grasp of the game laughable. And who is to say he is not correct in his judgement? There are, however, odd holes in his own knowledge.

Middlesbrough fans will doubtless be interested to learn, for instance, that Emerson's many absences were partly explained by the fact that he was often away on international duty with Brazil.

Nor would Hoddle have made any money, as he seems to believe, by betting on Paraguay to beat Spain. Yet, though Hoddle resents media criticism of his methods, he feels no compunction about outlining the mistakes made by referees with whose decisions he disagrees. This is a prevailing vice among football managers, many of whom will happily expend thousands of words outlining the errors of match officials only to explode with rage if anyone has the temerity to question the wisdom of their team selection.

Hoddle is touchy about his beliefs, too. He feels people leap to judgement without considering the evidence. Whatever. There is a dividing line between faith and superstition and the England manager crosses it regularly. Hoddle believes in astrology, faith-healing, negative and positive vibrations, intuitive feelings and, apparently, that dreams may predict the future. He believes that Jesus "was a normal run-of-the-mill sort of guy who had a genuine gift, just as Eileen [Drewery] has got". (I am no theologian but my understanding was that Christ was the son of God. Hardly normal, you would think, even in Essex.)

He also believes that if we had beaten Argentina we would have gone on to win the World Cup, doubtless brushing Holland, Brazil and France aside like the football weaklings they are. In the end, though, what he believes in this context is worthless. In spiritual matters faith may take precedence over facts, but when it comes to World Cups results alone matter. England played four games and lost two of them (Hoddle thinks we would have beaten Romania but for a couple of defensive errors. Ah, those defensive errors, if it wasn't for them and the fact our opponents keep scoring more goals than us England have won every World Cup we've ever entered). Our record in the tournament was comparable with that of Paraguay or Chile, worse than that of Denmark. That is the truth. And no amount of Hoddle's believing will alter it. ○

Wash and Go

A driveway in Yorkshire would always mean something special to Dave Cohen and his chamois leather

WSC No 140, October 1998

WHENEVER I COME TO LEEDS on the train, I still experience a shudder of recognition as we chug past Elland Road, even though the ground now resembles the hundreds of superstore complexes already passed on the way up from London, where I now live. But the most significant footballing address I remember is number 41, The Drive, Leeds 17 – the modest suburban semi that for a few years was the home of Peter "Hot Shot" Lorimer, and a mere ten minutes walk from my teenager abode.

Growing up in north Leeds in the early 1970s, celebrities were thin on the ground. I did bunk off school once to go to the Radio One Road Show, but Dave Lee Travis was hosting and even then, at the height of his success, that was not a name you could drop in double chemistry unless you wanted to be bullied. The only other time I ever got to see anyone famous was once a fortnight at Elland Road.

One way I discovered of paying for my football habit was to go car washing on Sunday mornings. Today, if you entrust your motor to a 14-year-old, you may expect it to be returned as a burnt-out wreck after an all-night session of drag racing and handbrake turns. But car washing was big business back then, when a Fairs Cup ticket could be purchased with the profits from half a dozen sparkling Hillman Imps.

It was during one such motor-soaking Sunday morning that I first discovered my celebrity address. Looking up from a car I was cleaning in the road, I saw in the bay window of 41 The Drive none other than Hot Shot himself, gazing at the begonias on his front lawn, probably while reminiscing over a 40-yard scorcher that nearly tore the goal netting off. It was him all right.

I froze with indecision. Should I wait for him to spot me, staring rudely into his front room, or should I march towards his rather dinky looking sports car and mime a cleaning ritual with my bucket and sponge?

Actually, I felt so humble at the thought of being mere feet away from one of United's finest, that I finished the job I was doing and ran away as fast as I could.

I thought long and hard about how I could use this new-found knowledge to my advantage. Knowing where someone famous lived could buy me a lot of street cred. In my fantasy I became a great big Somebody – The Boy Who Would Be Peter Lorimer's Car Washer. I dreamed of saying to the anti-Semites giving me a hard time at school: "I dare you all to call me names in front of Peter Lorimer. He's Scottish, he understands what it's like to be a member of a white minority. He's my mate. I wash his car."

But it was not to be. As the weeks passed, I concentrated all my car-washing efforts around The Drive, never once plucking up the courage to ring on the doorbell of number 41. The time was never quite right. Maybe I would be too nervous. Maybe United lost the day before and

I wouldn't want to see him brooding over the missed opportunities. Maybe, deep down, I realised that I would have to deal with my racist classmates without his help.

After weeks of obsessive prevarication, I walked out one Sunday morning determined to cross the rubicon, to leap over the threshold from my dull reality into the glamorous world where Peter's Triumph resided and anything might be possible. I imagined turning on the cold water tap in his kitchen while chatting breezily about the previous day's game. I arrived at his house and started to walk towards his front door. Within seconds the man I had adored from afar – Hot Shot Lorimer, Superman, freedom fighter, racist basher and all-round hero – had waved me away as dismissively as Ray Tinkler during a Leeds v West Brom match.

All my illusions were shattered in that moment when, for the first time in my eyes, he became an ordinary human. But the next Saturday he ran out on the pitch in his all-white shirt and became a God again. I realised that was how I wanted my footballers to be – untouchable heroes whose cars were washed by angels in another galaxy.

The racist kids got bored and moved on to something else, there were plenty of other cars to wash and I never did find out the great man's views on the multicultural society. Although, bizarrely, he ended up becoming a football manager in Israel for a short while, making him a dead cool anti-racist or a rampant Zionist, depending on your point of view. O

As Good as Gould

His team sank to defeat after defeat yet Bobby Gould soldiered on as Wales manager. Nigel Harris paid tribute to a remarkable talent

WSC No 141, November 1998

FIVE YEARS AGO, Wales, beating the likes of Germany and Brazil, were ranked 27th in the world and heading towards USA 94. Then Paul Bodin missed that penalty. Welsh football has never recovered. Today, Wales are ranked 107th, behind Malawi, Vietnam and Myanmar.

The right appointment was vital following the acrimonious departure of Terry Yorath, a one-match debacle with John Toshack and further disaster under Mike Smith. Enter Bobby Gould, previously employed as the host of the Sky Sports phone-in. Fans choked at this appointment. Some were also concerned about that one continuous eyebrow across his forehead. Choose any criteria and he fails.

Results? Prior to this month's games versus Denmark and Belarus, how does six defeats and a draw in seven Euro/World Cup qualifying games sound? There are no easy games in international football, apart from Wales against Holland (who scored seven), Turkey (they got six though Wales scored four), Tunisia (four) or Leyton Orient, who won a friendly. Tactics? Gould admits wrong formations, tactics and line-ups in past matches. He hasn't learned. Against Italy last month, Mark Hughes was in midfield, Ryan Giggs played as a striker and Dean Saunders was dropped because, in Gould-speak, Giggs cannot play behind a front two. Morale? When the Euro 2000 draw was made, Gould said Wales will not qualify. Thanks, Bobby.

Then, of course, there are continual clashes with respected Welsh internationals and former managers. The hit list runs into double figures and includes Terry Yorath, John Toshack, Mark Hughes, Ian Rush, Nathan Blake, Gary Speed and now Robbie Savage. More speak to the press anonymously, in fear of retribution. Vinnie says players "can't wait to go back to clubs", which is possibly affirmed by the regular withdrawals of established internationals before friendlies, not always through injury.

Vinnie is not international class, but would you drop him for a League of Wales player who, despite trials, was not signed by any League club? Hartson's club goals and performances are ignored while Gould asserts he is overweight and unfit. Nathan Blake refused to play, calling him a racist. This fracas was the consequence of continual jibes and references to Blake's colour. At best, they were grossly naive and hinted at a man out of touch with modern times. Peace is restored, for now. One Welsh fan that complained was invited by Gould to sound out the views of black players who had worked under him. Gould's list included the late Laurie Cunningham.

The barrel was firmly scraped before the Italy international last month, when Gould instructed Savage to leave the camp for being disrespectful after he'd playfully he tossed away a Paolo Maldini shirt (Savage also jokingly called Welsh defenders "Third Division" – Italy's opening goal suggests this was lavish praise). After the manager met with senior players, Savage was reinstated but relegated to substitute. In defeat, Wales' performance was credible but Bobby had an encore. Reading

teletext in bed later that night, he seethed at a headline, Lacklustre
Wales Lose. He woke Ceefax's editor at home in the early hours to get the
headline changed. It was. The following day witnessed one of the most
skin-tingling examples of football man man-agement imaginable as
Gould again rounded on Savage at a specially arranged press conference.
A hardened media watched in stunned silence.

Gould himself put a green Welsh shirt in a dustbin during a new kit
launch last June but denied hypocrisy. "Some of us are superstitious," he
said, adding that Wales were "unlucky in green". It is no surprise that the
new reserve strip worn in Tunisia a few days later was green.

Demands for his censure or dismissal are overwhelming. The press
comment that he has "lost the plot", fan letters fill Welsh newspapers,
the Football Association of Wales (FAW) email server strangely stopped
working shortly after being bombarded by irate supporters and Manic
Street Preachers sang "Bobby Gould Must Go" instead of "Everything
Must Go" at recent gigs. Gould deserves some credit however:
membership of the Welsh FSA doubled in a week.

The FAW remain silent when asked to explain why Gould seemingly
has the safest job in world football. In fact, his power is extended. He now
oversees younger age groups and designs Welsh shirts. Keith Haynes,
author of *Come On Cymru*, a review of Welsh football, also criticises the
FAW for being "haphazard in their thinking and methods, failing to
achieve any sort of stability" and allowing "dire management".

The ordeal and agonies look set to continue. Will Bobby Gould be
recalled as one of the most bonkers international managers in football
history? Sadly, I'm certain there is more to come. ○

Support for All?

Towards the end of a decade of great change for the average supporter, Ian Plenderleith reflected on the evolving nature of fanhood itself

WSC No 142, December 1998

I USED TO LIVE with an Arsenal fan. He knew sod all about football and had only started going to watch them in the mid-1980s because that's what all the people he met at college did on Saturday afternoon. When Arsenal won the Cup-Winners Cup in 1994 he told everyone that Arsenal had won "the European Cup". And asked to name his current England XI he put down Niall Quinn. On the left wing.

Laughs all round at his expense, then, but the thing was he didn't care. It wasn't that important to him that he could not name any players from the 1970s or that he couldn't keep up with a conversation in the pub where the rest of the circle were comparing knee scars from falls on jagged terracing at the age of six. But for those with a more fundamentalist view on the role of football, genuine-fan credentials seem to have become – to borrow a phrase employed by commentators to describe every game broadcast live on TV – absolutely essential in the age of Skyperbole. For it would seem that a despicable new breed, seduced by the appeal of having a satellite dish on the side of their house and, perish the thought, buying a replica shirt, is now ruining the game for everybody.

For many fans the identikit lounge-layabout seems to have become the epitome of evil and a tool by which they now measure their own credibility. So those wry, nostalgic conversations of ten years ago about sideburns, flares and flick-knives (which went on to constitute 50 per cent of fifth-rate, sub-*Loaded* glossy football magazine journalism in the Nineties) have been replaced by chest-out proclamations starting with those ominous words: "In the 25 years that I've been watching football..."

Those of us who have been watching football longest, you see, believe that we own the game. The further back your initiation, the greater your moral entitlement to pontificate on the latecomers who spent their youths unaware of the world-shaking importance of events taking place within Blundell Park and Plainmoor. Worse still, somewhere along the way we lost our sense of humour and became like the indie-pop clan, those gloomy guardians of hip who berate the vacuity of the pop charts, but who then huff and puff when their favourite band gets famous: "It's not fair, I liked James years ago when they were on Factory and no one had ever heard of them." What did they want – compensation or cultural copyright?

Of course it is a wonderful thing that fans have found their voices over the past few years, that supporters' associations have gained respect in the media and are consulted and quoted by the great and powerful, and that Brigg Town boasts eight independent fans' magazines. The question is, however, do football fans really have much more worth saying now they seem to spend so much time harping on about the remote control addicts, supposedly killing football in their living rooms? (Real football fans, as well as having supported their local side from the womb, have never ever watched a game on Sky.) A reflection of this trend is the fact there are now only three jokes left in football: all Man Utd fans live down south; all Scottish goalies are rubbish; the Arsenal back four likes to step up with its collective arm in the air.

These have all been repeated so often that no one has noticed they are not even slightly funny any more, illustrating once more that the game as a whole has become too important to too many people. Have you read a fanzine lately? Was it funny or did it call your striker a leg iron and your local rivals scum? What about a witty terrace chant (of course not, it's been scientifically proven that sitting down paralyses the vocal chords)? Have you talked to a fellow fan lately? What did you moan about first, the chairman's failure to spend 20 million quid on new players or the imminent death of the game?

Watching your football team should mean one and a half hours of oscillation between tension, dread, despair and ecstasy. It doesn't matter if you watched your first game last week or last century, if you watched it on your arse at home or off your head on the terrace – if you go through these emotions then you're involved. Only, once that game is over, it would be nice to go back to the days when we didn't take it all quite so seriously and supporting a football team wasn't a crutch for the socially challenged. ○

A Passing Trade

As part of a series commemorating important historical
sites, Al Needham paid tribute to a long-departed
programme shop in Nottingham

WSC No 142, December 1998

To SAY THAT RELICS of the glory years of Nottingham Forest are thin on
the ground is a bit like saying it was rather hard to get your hands on a
Cabbage Patch Kid on December 24, 1984. In fact, I can only think of
one. Programme World. It did exactly what it said on the tin, and then
some. In times like these, when you can't even nick a ruler from WH
Smiths without being trapped in an avalanche of football magazines, it
seems odd that one could make a living from selling programmes, but
when I first came across it in 1980 it was positively thriving.

The owner of the shop was Terry, a Jason Kingalike who owned another
place up the road called Soccer City, a haven of silk scarves and daring
abstract interpretations of club badges – Forest's tricky tree, for example,
looked like Jimmy Greaves's liver with an octopus's tentacle snaking out
of the bottom.

He was a County man, but went all round Europe with Forest gobbling
up programmes left and right. Once, after my best mate Gormy Dawny
and I had been on a daring raid and ripped up handfuls of grass from
the Trent End goalmouth, Terry conned us into buying cheap wooden
display cases to mount our booty in. Then he told us to piss off, because
he was about to merge the two shops together in a big refurbishment
job and he couldn't hang about talking to a couple of mongs in scabby
Harringtons. I asked him if he needed a hand, and before I knew it I had
my first ever job.

God, I loved that shop. Every single square inch of Programme World
told a tale of matches long ago and far away, from the four-page County
v Forest reserves programme that marked the debut of Trevor Francis
to the ultra-glossy Forest v Hamburg European Cup final programme.
There were thousands and thousands of the things (he also had a shop
in Mabelthorpe), and I must have leafed through all of them, drinking
in the heritage of Bovril adverts, "Pen Pix", and the glorious publication
of the late Sixties that was the *Football League Review*. My duties were

simple – every Saturday and Wednesday during the season, I'd roll up early, sweep up, mind the till. At about one o'clock, I'd nip outside with an armful of that day's programmes and bellow "CAAAAM 'n' GIT yer PROGRAAAAMMMES" in a strangely Cockney accent. Then at 2.50 I'd peg it to the Trent End, leaving with ten minutes to go for the post-match rush or riot, if the away supporters could break free of their police escort. As we shut up at 7pm, I would wave to the Forest players as they drove past in their cars, all from a Ford dealership with their names on them. Martin O'Neill was the only one who never waved back. I got two quid, a ticket to the game and a big wodge of programmes. It was bliss.

Naturally, like all good things, it was never going to last. Terry had a goldmine on his hands, with Forest at the peak of their success, but one by one the body blows rained down. Forest opened a club shop in the middle of town and, to our horror, they were selling away programmes miles cheaper than us. A new role was added to my job – I had to go up the club shop and buy 40 programmes at a time, armed with the alibi that I had a lot of pen friends. Then attendances slumped, and one evening during a League Cup second round tie Terry took me to one side and gently broke the news that I was surplus to requirements. I never returned to the shop.

Until the other day, on a rare excursion to my home town. Mooching around the train station waiting to go back to London, I came across it. It was like seeing the girl you were in love with at school pushing a pram with bleached hair, bad make-up and a tatty Giorgio sweatshirt from the market. The shop window was full of 1980s slasher videos, and Terry was fiddling with a battalion of second hand fridges with dodgy lights. All the old paraphernalia was on the walls – faded photos of Munich and Madrid, pennants from Sofia and Zurich and Athens. It was frozen in time.

Things started to go wrong when the fanzine boom kicked in, said Terry, as he made me a cup of coffee. Then Forest started to take charge of their branding, and cut off his supply of matchday programmes. He owns the cafe next door, and I think he's doing all right. I hope so, anyway. In times like these, where Chelsea can sell scooters with the club badge on and still keep a straight face, it's a tragedy that shops like Programme World have declined. If you're ever travelling by train to a Forest game, keep the flame alive – go and buy a fridge off him. ○

1999

All Bar One

**Matthew Hall saluted the only World Cup captain
to frequent a bar in Wollongong**

WSC No 143, January 1999

THE BARMAN AT KEMBLA HEIGHTS BOWLING CLUB, a breezy two-hour drive
south from Sydney, probably would not be able to enlighten you too much
about the local football scene. But the chances are he's pulled a few beers
for Peter Wilson, Australia's most enigmatic and mysterious sporting
legend. And that makes this place a classy joint.

"Big Willie" pitched up in Wollongong in 1968, aged 21, having spent
four unproductive years at Middlesbrough. Built like a Viking, he cut an
imposing figure at South Coast United and it wasn't just his silk shirts
and flared trousers that got him noticed. He played as a sweeper, was
calm in times of trouble and, despite being a quiet bloke off the pitch,
was a deft organiser on it.

He soon came to the attention of Rale Rasic, then national coach.
Rasic was never orthodox in his manner or views. Prior to a 1973 World
Cup qualifier in Tehran he told the Iranian media that Australia would
triumph over the home team simply because they were "the superior

race" (T Venables take note). Rasic's choice of Wilson to lead the team was surprising, but inspired. Wilson introduced the music of Tim Buckley and Van Morrison to the dressing room (touché, so-called "Crazy Gang"), wasn't much of a drinker (but once quaffed 16 pints to find out what the fuss was about) and led Australia to the 1974 World Cup finals.

Compared with the sophisticated European and South American professionals the Socceroos were a virtual novelty act in West Germany. It wasn't just the curious multicultural melange of European migrants and home-grown talent, which included Harry Williams, the one and only Aboriginal Australian to grace a World Cup. Bona fide part-timers, the majority of the squad took holidays from work to make the tournament. Their plastic flip-flops, dangerously tight shorts and marsupial mascots also endeared them to the German public, yet the Socceroos were far from disgraced on the pitch.

They frustrated eventual champions West Germany enough for the home crowd to boo their own team and start chanting for Australia. At the final whistle, despite having won 3-0, Franz Beckenbauer stormed off the pitch, refusing to swap shirts with the Australian skipper. Peter Wilson claimed the moral victory as one of his greatest games.

Wilson and the Socceroos should have returned home to gilt and glitter but the game's administrators once more failed to seize a moment to push soccer into the forefront of a hungry public. It wasn't until last year's infamous Melbourne showdown with Iran that the 1974 team was publicly honoured. It was even left to a former player to organise the first-ever squad reunion just two months before that.

By 1982, Wilson had forgone his Viking image, replacing it with a voluminous moustache, and resembled a giant walrus. It was also the year he played his last-ever competitive game, a Cup final in front of just 5,000 people at Melbourne's Olympic Park. Then player-manager of Sydney's APIA-Leichhardt, blood poured from a cut above his right eye as he led APIA to a 2-1 win over Melbourne's Heidelberg. When the final whistle blew Wilson walked right out of the stadium and never spoke of football again.

Willie returned to Wollongong and his job as a coalminer. He skipped through the loop that circles former players, the media and the hangers-on. He grew his hair to his hips, added a beard to match, became a vegetarian and switched his interests to vintage Harley-Davidson motorbikes. Planet football? Wilson fell right off it.

Over the years, journalists have occasionally tried to obtain a quote, a story, even an explanation. None succeeded. All requests were, and still are, met with awkward silence. An Australian fan from Hanover in Germany is the only person known to have had any success. A brief exchange of letters ensued before Wilson sent a gift. It was the torn-off national crest from one of Wilson's spare Socceroo shirts – the one he wore against West Germany in 1974. "I hope you can find some use for it," Wilson wrote. In exchange, he requested some European motorbike magazines.

So, the only chance to brush shoulders with a true colossus of the Australian game is at Willie's local watering hole – the Kembla Heights Bowling Club. With its views over the Pacific and its slow, sunny pace it's the perfect place to idle away an afternoon and shoot the breeze with the locals. Just don't ask the tall bloke in the corner with the beard around his ankles to spin another one of those World Cup yarns. Not that he'd answer, anyway. ○

Score to Settle?

Hans Segers explained his role in the betting scandal that also involved John Fashanu and Bruce Grobbelaar. Matthew Roche, present in court, was unimpressed

WSC No 144, February 1999

FOR HANS SEGERS to put his name to a book on the two 1997 Winchester match-rigging trials is a little like Torquay's chief air raid warden penning a personal history of the Second World War. Segers was a bit-player in the affair and this is reflected in a thin and disappointing book which reveals little about "soccer's trial of the century".

Segers, John Fashanu, Bruce Grobbelaar and Malaysian businessman Richard Lim were accused of rigging matches to benefit Far Eastern betting syndicates but walked free after the second jury believed the stars had merely provided match forecasts which Lim passed on to the gamblers.

The trials asked some serious questions about modern football and we could do with a probing account of the affair, but despite the efforts of ghost writer Alan Thatcher this book is extremely flat. Segers does not come across as a particularly deep man and it is debatable whether the humdrum memoirs of a middling Dutch goalkeeper would have been printed had it not been for the trials. Even so, the book is shamelessly padded out and you can imagine a frantic editor pleading: "You haven't written enough. Is there nothing else you can add? What was your favourite colour as a child? Which foods don't you like?"

It can be no coincidence that well over half the book was written by Segers's solicitor Mel Goldberg and even he is reduced to spinning out his material by including the full charge sheet, adding plenty of tedious courtroom "humour" and then reprinting word for word the lengthy closing defence speech for Segers which he didn't even make. The last chapter, entitled "My Greatest Save", tells how Segers discovered Christianity. All very admirable, but not the kind of thing you expect in the final chapter of a book about match-rigging trials.

But for all its faults the work is not without interest. It was clear to those of us who sat in the press box that the case against the four was flawed. The prosecutors relied on vast logs of mobile phone calls made between the defendants and video tapes recorded by Chris Vincent, a former business partner of Grobbelaar's, in which the keeper appeared to admit he had thrown games. Crucially, there were no recordings of the mobile calls themselves and many of the Vincent tapes were of appalling quality.

Segers notes the charges against him were changed early on and then again after the first trial, where he had been accused of throwing matches. "In the second trial that accusation switched to trying to influence results. All the time their case was getting weaker and they changed their tactics to suit themselves," he writes.

Goldberg dismissed the prosecution's case as "nonsense. It is surely difficult, if not impossible, to influence the outcome of a match... unless all 22 individuals, plus the referee and linesmen, are in collusion." Most attempts to influence games seem to involve putting pressure on the referee, not the players.

How do you prove a player has thrown a match? It is very hard to draw any conclusions from slow-motion frames of goals, however many times you see them. Unless a keeper boots the ball into his own net and then throws himself into the arms of the opposing strikers, how can you prove he was acting deliberately? And what about retrospective action? Chelsea fans remember the two atrocious goals Dave Beasant conceded a few years ago against Norwich – will there now be a probe into whether he was bribed? Are we going to see shareholders take legal action against a goalkeeper for making a mistake which results in relegation or a striker whose miss robs the team of a cup victory?

Segers naturally portrays the defendants as heroes and the account therefore lacks any sense of how tawdry the proceedings were, of the evidence which could only help kill the romance of football by showing our sporting heroes to be as base as the rest of us. Did we really want to know Grobbelaar smokes, that he kept £25,000 in his sock drawer and is in love with one particular obscenity when drunk?

Listening to tabloid reporters phoning in excerpts from the court transcripts of the Grobbelaar tapes had a certain surreal quality to it. "Just you know, see what f***ing person I am and if I'm f***ing genuine. I like to f***ing win. I don't like to f***ing lose." "So what happens if I say, right fine, f***ing Man United are playing f***ing next day at Man United and I say, right, Man United are going to f***ing win. And it's not my f***ing team. And I'm just taking the f***ing...right?" "This is how f***ing dangerous it is. When you're playing with f***ing dangerous men, it's f***ing dangerous."

In the book Segers rhapsodises about his love for wife and family but it emerged at the trial that he had been having affairs. And we learned that John Fashanu, core of the Crazy Gang, simply switched off at the final whistle. "He had a relatively limited knowledge of the specifics of football, the anorak side," said his agent. Oh yes, those anoraks who regularly shell out to watch the team and buy the excremental new strip every few months, the ones who help keep the club in business.

Goldberg unwittingly identifies the book's main problem by relating what he suspected after Segers had performed badly under cross-examination by the chief prosecutor, who was clearly using the Dutchman for target practice. "Is he warming up for Bruce?" the solicitor wondered.

And that's the point. The definitive book about these trials should surely be written by Grobbelaar, who was both the central figure and the most interesting of the defendants, a former soldier who saw his friends killed in Rhodesian war and someone who seriously considered giving up football after Hillsborough. So come on, Bruce. Sit down, turn on your word processor and hit those asterisk keys. ○

Fouls of the Century

Cris Freddi's series about the worst football feats of the
century included an assessment of its most heinous fouls

WSC No 145, March 1999

NO SHORTAGE OF MATERIAL in this category. We've all got our nominations
and it becomes a question of which to leave out. One that gets in without
much argument was perpetrated in Manchester United's Champions
League match against Feyenoord in 1997, when Paul Bosvelt crashed
his studs into Denis Irwin's calf, a really dangerous foul. Sándor Puhl,
who didn't even show a yellow card, was dropped from the rest of the
competition as well as France 98, missing the chance of becoming the
first referee to take charge of two World Cup finals.

Other horrifying one-offs include Torino's Fabrizio Poletti breaking
Bobby Collins's thigh in 1965, which takes some doing, and Walter
Skocik's tackle from behind which crippled Jim Baxter the previous year,
after which he was never quite the same again (Slim Jim turning into
Whisky Jim). Terry Yorath's early attack on Björn Andersson in the 1975
European Cup final was described by Uli Hoeness as "the most brutal
foul I think I have ever seen. His leg was a mess, and it was eight or nine
months before he could play again."

The worst damage of all was inflicted on Dixie Dean, no less, who was
only 17 when Rochdale's centre-half kicked him so hard that he lost a
testicle, apparently the origin of the "don't rub 'em, count 'em" story.

Kevin Keegan was lucky to escape a similar fate when he elbowed the
fearsome Romeo Benetti in the face at Wembley in 1976, "knocking out
a couple of teeth", which was like sticking one on a rottweiler. Benetti's
threat ("I get you Keegan, before finish") was carried out when our Kev
made Brooking's first goal for England. As the pass leaves his foot,
Benetti's own arrives at the top of the screen, the Italian knowing the
referee will be following the ball. Even at this range, the memory still
makes your shins shudder – as does one of Johan Neeskens's fouls in the
1978 World Cup, when Renato Zaccarelli's shout of pain was picked up
by the TV microphones at the other side of the pitch.

The 1966 tournament threw up its share of classics. Not so much João
Morais's famous double assault (Pelé had missed the previous match

after being softened up by the Bulgarians) as Rafael Albrecht getting himself sent off for kneeing Wolfgang Weber in the groin, which must have been a formidable part of his anatomy: Albrecht was limping as he walked off. But perhaps the leading representative of Argentinian football in those days was Carlos Pachamé of Estudiantes, who cut Bobby Charlton's shin to the bone and broke Joop van Daele's glasses when he scored Feyenoord's winning goal in the 1971 World Club Championship. Alf was right about the animals.

Pachamé and Neeskens are also leading candidates for the lifetime achievement award, which goes not to serial early bathers like Mark Dennis or Vinnie Jones but to one of the more skilful breed, who either didn't have the timing to make clean tackles or did have the timing to make unclean ones. The likes of Peter Osgood, Mike Summerbee, Allan Clarke ("he would leave his boot in just a bit longer than he should have done," said Jack Charlton), Souness and Asprilla, and the undisputed No 1: Michael John Giles of Leeds. Or, as George Best put it, "most especially Johnny Giles".

Giles once had his own leg broken "and I'm going to make sure nobody ever does it again". I see, said Charlton, "so every bugger in the league is going to get punished because you once got your leg broke". But according to Big Jack, "it wasn't just them, it was us he was putting at risk. John caused us a lot of hassle at Elland Road over the years."

He caused George Best a fair bit too. "Because we were playing Leeds, I was wearing shinguards," which saved him from a broken leg. Giles's studs ripped through his sock, split his shinpad and cut his shin open, "almost ending my career". Giles was one of the leading playmakers of his day, but it's impossible to remember him with any affection.

But even he doesn't win the portfolio award for a single match, which goes to the astounding Mihai Mocanu of Romania, unheard of before England's opening match in the 1970 World Cup but now a legend. First he kicked Keith Newton's knee so badly he had to go off, then he took Franny Lee's legs, then went after Newton's replacement Tommy Wright ("I thought my leg had snapped, my eyes watered like they've never done before"). Lee felt "he must have created a new tackle, leaving identical bootprints on each knee". Any one of those fouls would have earned a red card today, but Mocanu wasn't even booked. And people are still nostalgic about the Seventies.

Of the challenges that ended a player's career, the worst is a toss-up between John Fashanu's elbow on John O'Neill (who settled out of court) and Dean Saunders on Paul Elliott (who didn't). A personal opinion? Saunders was lucky. As for Fashanu's elbows, no strangers to court-rooms, they also broke Gary Mabbutt's cheekbone and earned the Bash a booking on his international debut for catching Chile's Fernando Astengo in the face.

Other famous elbows were wielded by Leonardo Nascimento of Brazil and Jan Wouters of Holland. In the 1994 World Cup, Leonardo caught the USA's Tab Ramos in the temple, fracturing his skull, almost killing him, and even moving Brian Moore to reprimand Kevin Keegan for trying to excuse it. England didn't reach the finals, partly because Paul Gascoigne had to be substituted after Wouters caught him in the face at Wembley, forcing him to wear that grotesque face mask. Hard to believe the Dutch would have come back to force a draw if Gazza had stayed on. Mind you, his famous hack at Gary Charles in the 1991 FA Cup final was as bad as anything he suffered himself. Referee Roger Milford admitted he could have sent him off for an earlier foul ("I couldn't bring myself to do it") and the self-inflicted damage to Gazza's knee effectively killed off his status as a world-class player, though it's taken a long time to die.

The golden fist award ought to go to Leonel Sánchez of Chile, whose father was a boxer of some repute. In the infamous World Cup match against Italy in 1962, Sánchez reacted to a series of kicks by jumping up and flattening Mario David with a left hook. English referee Ken Aston took no action but did send David off for taking belated revenge with a flying kick to the neck. An Italian publication also pointed the finger at Sánchez when Humberto Maschio had his nose broken in the same game. If Sánchez wasn't responsible for that, the award goes to Paul Davis of Arsenal, banned for nine games after breaking Glenn Cockerill's jaw in 1988.

The most influential foul was committed by West Germany's centre-half Werner Liebrich in the 1954 World Cup finals. Brought in against Hungary, he changed places with Jupp Posipal during the match and kicked the great Ferenc Puskás on the back of the ankle. A clear foul (he was booked), it kept Puskás out of the next two matches and reduced his input in the final, which the Germans won. The Liebrichs getting winners' medals instead of the Puskáses was a central theme of the first five World Cups.

In the next, Vavá of Brazil made two important contributions to Brazil's win in the 1958 semi-final, volleying the opening goal then smashing the shin of his immediate opponent, France's classy centre-half Bob

Jonquet, who spent the rest of the game limping on the wing. The 5-2 scoreline was a mockery: before Vavá's foul it was 1-1.

The next time they reached the semi-final, in 1982, the French suffered a similar blow, my choice as the foul of the century, with no apologies for lack of originality. At first glance, Harald Schumacher's full-frontal on Patrick Battiston looked like a follow-through he couldn't avoid (no free-kick, let alone a red card). Then you watch the replay and see the pause, the leap, the turned shoulder. Battiston, who was stretchered off and given oxygen, had several teeth broken – Schumacher rather crassly offered to pay to have them capped. When people wonder if Michael Schumacher was a relative, this is what they mean. It affected the result, too: France were forced to use their second substitute, so there was no one to chase Karl-Heinz Rummenigge's fresh legs when they came on and pulled a goal back on the way to that penalty shoot-out.

Amazingly, Battiston not only forgave the German, he made him best man at his wedding. But Schumacher still deserves his infamy, alongside other villains like Souness, Gentile, Benetti, Stielike and Tommy Smith. Some of the worst moustaches of the century. ○

This Town ain't Big Enough

Ken Gall explained why fans were fuming at the press response to the proposed merger of the two Dundee clubs

WSC No 146, April 1999

WHEN PETER MARR – nightclub owner and chairman of Dundee FC – raised the possibility of his club merging with neighbours Dundee United, there was, unsurprisingly, uproar among the fans of both clubs. Slightly more surprisingly, there was also a flurry of favourable comment in the Scottish press.

To most fans in the city of Dundee, the reason for Marr's proposal seemed clear enough. Dundee, facing relegation if they fail to comply with the Scottish Premier League's rules on stadiums and possible financial calamity if they did, had eyed up their comparatively asset-rich neighbours 150 yards down the road and come to the seemingly all-too-logical conclusion that one team in the city would be better than two.

However, the attitude of the Scottish footballing press to this barely thought-through proposal – based, apparently, on a 57 per cent approval rating in a highly dubious phone poll conducted by a local newspaper on what was obviously a slow news day – was staggering in its complacency and all too indicative of the undercooked thinking and reporting that typifies the Old Firm-obsessed Scottish media.

Even allowing for the nosebleeds and double vision that must have accompanied the efforts of the hacks to write about football in Dundee, most of the articles bore all the hallmarks of resulting from a few leisurely half-hour typing sessions to fill substantial spaces in the various papers. "Merge or submerge" suggested Darryl Broadfoot in the *Herald* – and that was very much the theme played out by all the other papers.

The *Scotsman* seemed to imply that the deal was a *fait accompli*, and that all that remained was the waving of tear-stained hankies as we said goodbye to nearly a century of rivalry. To its credit, the *Scotsman* did include an anti-merger piece by Mike Watson, the former Labour MP and author of Dundee United's official history, whose views surely must have matched the vast majority of supporters' of both clubs.

The *Scotsman* also took the opportunity to name a "Joint Dundee" starting XI, made up of current players from both sides; a side which, it was suggested, would provide the serious challenge to the Old Firm that was currently missing from the city of Dundee. The presence in that XI of Dundee's Willie Falconer, however, seemed to blow that theory clean out of the water.

Even the old warhorse, Doug Baillie of the *Sunday Post* – a paper owned by the Dundee-based DC Thomson Ltd and the last true defender of all things tartan and traditional in Scotland – suggested that "merge or die" was the only sensible course for the clubs.

However, the most risible piece of them all came from the lugubrious James Traynor, once a respected broadsheet writer for the *Herald* and now a shock-horror merchant at the *Daily Record*. "It stands to reason," wrote Traynor, "that the new body should be stronger." What? Why should the combination of the playing staffs of two mediocre football clubs provide anything other than a larger mediocre football club?

Traynor's main point of contention seemed to be that in this era of multi-million-pound expenditure by the Old Firm, true competition in Scottish football could be reproduced only by the sort of super-club proposed by Marr. The question of whether the notion of competition and sporting achievement in Scottish football has been anything other than destroyed by David Murray's annual spending of £20-30 million to win the Scottish championship remains unasked and unanswered by the hacks, who know on which side their bread is buttered and to whom they owe the shirts on their backs.

Like most fans of both clubs, I want to see my club do well. If Dundee United are successful, I will be delighted. If they are relegated and spend years in the wilderness, so be it. I am not so much in need of the "success" or "progress" referred to by Traynor and others as to want to sacrifice something that has been a big part of my family for 40 years. Traynor may deem such sentiment to be an example of the "traditional feelings and loyalties" of fans which "sometimes can be a drawback" as he spelt out in his article. I would suggest that without the "loyalties" of fans in Dundee, there would not be two clubs in the city to merge.

And then we come to Traynor's most absurd comment of all – that "petty prejudices and maybe even old grudges must be discarded". This, in a newspaper whose entire football coverage is geared towards pandering to fans of the Old Firm, a large constituency of whom exhibit palpably the worst examples of "petty prejudices" and "old grudges" in Scottish life. I fear that Traynor and his colleagues should, in future, return to commenting on matters where their footing is more sure – namely the interminable contractual wrangles of Celtic's Mark Viduka and the alleged affiliations and "petty prejudices" of Andy Goram, one of the least appealing characters to have emerged in Scottish football in my lifetime.

In the 25 years that I have been watching Dundee United, I have seen the club win all the Scottish domestic trophies, as well as reaching the UEFA Cup final and a European Cup semi-final. My father's generation grew up with a Dundee side boasting the likes of Alan Gilzean and Charlie Cooke, which was undoubtedly one of the best sides in the early 1960s. Nostalgia can be limiting, but the histories of each club are important to those who care for football in Dundee. Those people want both clubs to have a future, and they deserve more from the Scottish footballing press than a handful of half-hearted efforts at journalism from people who really ought to know better. ○

Leaning Towers

Jeff Hill paid tribute to Wembley Stadium, which was about to be demolished

WSC No 146, April 1999

THE WEMBLEY THAT WE ALL LOVE OR HATE – the dog track with a football ground in the middle – will soon be no more. Next year it will be pulled down, and by 2002 or thereabouts only the famous twin towers are likely to remain of the present structure. Barring last minute hitches, the rest is to be transformed into a multi-sports National Stadium. So England will have a site to equal the Stade de France and all those other sporting venues which are supposed to symbolise "the nation".

But in a country where four nations inhabit one state this has always been a problematic concept. England (or Britain) is not France, and English national identity is a far more elusive thing than its French counterpart. Where Paris serves as a focus for the idea of France, London often does the opposite; the metropolis is seen as a symbol of English or southern dominance and provokes a sense of local identity.

This has been one of the glories of Wembley; a place rich in ambiguity of meaning, where the sporting rivalries of British people have been acted out and a site of memory through which we have continued to identify ourselves by our past achievements. Since many of these are not to do with Englishness, Wembley represents the diversity as well as the unity of Britain. Some of the greatest sporting victories of the "fringe" nations have taken place there. In fact, until the 1950s most of England's international fixtures, with the exception of the biennial Scotland match, were not held at Wembley. It took 1966 and all that for the spectator passion usually associated with the visitors to be generated for England.

For many, then, coming to Wembley has been the occasion for proud assertions of "otherness". Northern Ireland's victory over England in 1957, for example, was a glorious celebration of the quality of pre-Best Irish football, of what Danny Blanchflower, Jimmy McIlroy, Peter McParland and Harry Gregg brought to the English League. The Wembley Wizards of 1928 similarly confirmed what Scottish folk had been saying ever since the modern game was invented: that their football, based on passing and dribbling skills, was superior to England's "kick and rush".

And how many supporters of now ill-considered clubs in the lower divisions think of Wembley to remind themselves that they once possessed a great team which had its moments in the Cup and, in some cases, actually won it? These memories are still important to supporters in Preston, Burnley, Huddersfield, Brighton and many other places. They help to keep them on the football map.

It is not just football which provides such sentiments. Rugby League, synonymous with the north, has played its Challenge Cup final at Wembley since 1929, when Wigan met Dewsbury, a team whose members all came from within six miles of the town. Wembley has played a similarly iconic role for countries such as Hungary and Denmark, whose victories over England in 1953 and 1983 were key moments in their football history. To compress all these associations – local, regional, national and international – into the idea of a "national" stadium seems churlish. Wembley is all things to all people, and that is perhaps why it commands such affection.

There is another side to the place, of course. Wembley has always had an air of pomposity about it, a whiff of the football establishment. Why is it still so difficult to get a Cup final ticket? We all know the reasons, and the complaints about the restrictions go back years. The FA first took control of the allocation after that disastrous first final of 1923, when admission was possible at the turnstiles (and via many other routes as well). When the all-ticket system was introduced the following year, it also ushered in the entry of the "blazerati" – the FA officials and their guests who kept out the real fans.

JPW Mallalieu, writer, Labour MP and (as he saw himself) a real fan, went to the 1947 final and railed against all those who came for the social occasion. The people who had followed their teams all season were left outside, he claimed, while many inside were "people who don't care which team wins, who don't know the rules, and who chatter". Simultaneous with the rise of the chattering classes was the ritualisation of the final: marching bands, community singing and royalty were not normal features at English football grounds. Fans value their independence, and don't like to be directed. There has often been a rather desultory response to the attempts to engage Wembley crowds in singing, though in the inter-war years particularly, Abide With Me usually went down well.

This increasing stage-management prompted some old-timers to look back with nostalgia to the carnival atmosphere of the Crystal

Palace finals before the First World War. "There was ample room," said William Pickford of the FA, "for crowds to move about the charming grounds, watch the entertainment under the famous glass roof, listen to the great organ and lunch in comfort... I can see the branches of the tall trees opposite the pavilion black with eager climbers." Where the Crystal Palace had been an anarchic celebration of fandom, Wembley became more of a state occasion, its crowd structured into price-related status groups, watched over by the controlling gaze of the monarch in the royal box.

Of course, the stadium had always been intended as a serious statement. It was built as the centrepiece of the Empire Exhibition of 1924-25, which symbolised the supposed "one soul and mind" of the empire. During these two summer seasons the stadium held pageants depicting the rise and unity of the empire and its peoples. Lofty aims demanded an august style. If anyone thinks that only stately homes and town halls have "architecture", look at Wembley. Where do those squat twin towers and rounded arches originate? If they look familiar it's because Wembley is the Colosseum of Rome transported to the North Circular Road, the style of a Mediterranean empire borrowed for a British one of global proportions.

There are still today, alongside the Wembley Arena (another name from Rome to conjure with), a few neo-classical facades of old Exhibition pavilions. A reminder of the imperial splendour in which the stadium was originally set, they now look like remnants from the backlot of a Hollywood epic.

So, Wembley has its special place. No other ground was lucky enough to stage its opening match in such desperate circumstances and get away with it. It could all have ended in tragedy. Instead, a national legend was born. The crowds were marshalled by the policeman on his white horse and the final went ahead. Thus was created an instant myth of orderly, decent English people, who refuse to get carried away in minor crises. For two generations the myth of the white horse fuelled the idea that bad behaviour at football grounds was something that foreigners got up to.

Wembley has meant all this in its 76-year history. The new stadium will have a rich and varied inheritance. It too will arouse feelings of love and hate. If it can somehow revive some of the traditions of the old Crystal Palace and avoid some of Wembley's pretensions, we are likely to warm to it. ○

Ten Short Years

On the tenth anniversary of the deaths of 96 Liverpool fans at Hillsborough, John Williams assessed the issues arising from the day of the disaster

WSC No 147, May 1999

IS IT REALLY TEN YEARS? I have to say it seems like fewer to me though, God knows, it must seem like a life sentence to people still struggling to find out what happened to their lost loved ones after they were waved off, catastrophically as it turned out, simply to see a football match in Sheffield on the morning of April 15, 1989. For those who have followed the case – and in Liverpool, even now, Hillsborough is seldom ever really off the public agenda – certain key phrases about the inquiry hearings have now taken on an almost totemic resonance: "the 3.15 pm cut-off point"; "accidental death"; "defective camera 5"; "missing video tapes" and so on.

TV coverage has also put some of these in the national domain; it is incredible just how many people seemed to know so little of the important detail of the incidents in Sheffield until the recent drama-doc hit home. That is why, of course, Jimmy McGovern's campaigning film was so important. None of this has been put to bed, either, by the blame allocated to, and now apparently accepted by, the South Yorkshire police, or by Jack Straw's recent judicial scrutiny of the evidence which was chaired by another High Court Judge (aren't they just the guys to get to the bottom of this?) Lord Justice Stuart-Smith. The latter could find no reason to open a new inquiry, much to the obvious disgust of the Hillsborough Family Support Group.

With no individuals yet held accountable and no police officers prosecuted or disciplined, we now move on to the private prosecutions of key police officers by the families. Much as one would like to say differently, there seems likely to be no satisfactory end to this, one of the reasons why Straw is also examining the verdicts available to inquests, the rules on early retirement through "sickness" of accused police officers, and the relationship between public inquiries and inquests into disasters of this type and scale. None of this will cut any ice at all with the Liverpool group and their determined and unending search for "justice".

I was at the game in 1989, initially at least, as a fan. I remember being told about the alleged "broken gate C" at the Leppings Lane end and later examining it with officials as distraught supporters who had been in the area – I was in the North Stand – told us that the police themselves had opened it. No shame there it seemed at the time; after all, fans had been pleading with police for a release from dangerous overcrowding outside which itself had threatened serious injury or worse. Why was no one properly organising the crowds outside? Having no plans to distribute the supporter flood into the ground away from the already crowded and inescapable central pens was what eventually proved fatal, of course. Would a more experienced chief officer have done things differently?

Frozen inaction in the face of CCTV pictures and one's own eyes that said that fans were clearly in trouble in the central areas compounded the initial crucial error. Not that the design of the stadium offered much scope for remedial action at that late stage. Given this awful, but hardly unimaginable, catalogue of police mistakes, Hillsborough was like many other football grounds then – a potential death trap. The general chaos, horror and lack of preparedness for something on this scale at football meant that the seriously injured, who might now be saved in similar circumstances, then had little chance.

If the disaster itself was avoidable and tragic, the treatment of the families later by the police was little short of inhumane and repellent. Personal and professional damage limitation – the attempted cover up – soon swung into action. What was truly shameful here were the police attempts to continue to fly the drunken fans/broken gate stories, later aided disgracefully by the *Sun*, and to treat the bereaved like little more than contemptible rubbish.

After all, these were just football supporter families (many people on Merseyside would add "from Liverpool" here), people with no obvious power to organise or to question the police case or their own despicable treatment at the hands of the South Yorkshire force. "They can be rubbished" must have been the thinking of these so-called public "servants". How little the police knew.

Ironically, many of those supporters who died would have been among the very first in the ground, arriving early to get a good vantage point. They would, in fact, have been among the very last supporters to have been "on the ale" on the day. Many Liverpool and Forest fans at Hillsborough had been drinking, of course. There is no shame in this.

This was English FA Cup semi-final day, after all, traditionally a major day for a football "bevvy", as many fans still know.

Police questioning on this aspect implied that having a drink somehow made innocent fans culpable for their own deaths. But McGovern's Hillsborough TV drama documentary takes obvious but important liberties on this and other points, presumably for dramatic and possibly "political" effect. Apparently, no fan goes ticketless to Sheffield, or even for a single pint before the match, as the police later pummel away grotesquely with questions to bemused and broken parents about football and drink. Drinking, in fact, is strategically expunged by McGovern from the culture.

Nor do we get any sense from the TV version of quite how damaged relations had generally become between some young supporters and the police at this time (though we do get it from the real doctor and ordinary police constable statements which emerged much later). This, sadly, was just one of the reasons why police responses were completely inappropriate on the day.

In fact, until quite disastrous policing decisions intervene, McGovern's ultimately tragic football day looks, oddly, much more like the spruced up "new" football experience of the late 1990s than it does an account of the then sometimes deeply troubled sport and the macho posturings "across the barricades" more characteristic of policing and fan cultures at football in the 1980s. One learns nothing here, for example, about how or why these ugly, sunken pens – real death traps – had come almost to be accepted by many fans then, and in one of our most "modern" football grounds. The centrality in the TV account of the terrible case of the deaths of the two daughters of the almost impossibly brave and artic- ulate and resourceful Hicks family also rather accentuates these other "absences". Some other context is probably also important here in order to understand exactly how the police – but also ourselves – could get it so badly wrong at football those ten short years ago.

Looking now at the Hillsborough ground as it was in 1989 – and comparing it to grounds today – it seems almost unimaginable that we would have thought this one of our most up-to-date football venues. We did; it was. Today, of course, the killing fences have gone and so, at the big clubs, have the terraces. When Tony Banks commented in October 1997 that he might look again at the terrace question he was taken immedi- ately to task by the Hillsborough families who spoke of the important progress on safety and on hooliganism at football since 1989.

The symbolic shift to seats is probably also important here; a sign of the sport finally moving on from an often desperate period in the 1980s. Ironically, in Liverpool, where the families' cause is otherwise assiduously supported, they are opposed by some on the seats issue. A local fanzine commented recently that this was "too important" an issue to allow the families' views to hold sway. Banks, shrewdly, withdrew. Seats, surely, are here to stay, though the campaigns will probably go on, even in some parts of Merseyside.

Clubs, not the police, are now made to take responsibility for the safety and management of supporters at football. This is a major change. In the 1980s it was "Get 'em in, get 'em out" and worry about the niceties later. Not now. But "safety" is also becoming an increasingly contentious issue at football. When do proper concerns about supporter safety become, for example, thinly veiled attempts to cleanse and market the sport to a nice, middle-class family "audience"?

All things are under assault here from those who query the new "safety culture" at football, including the anti-racist Kick It Out campaign, down to daft club responses to supporters who want to bring flags and the "carnival" back into the game. This issue will also run for some time yet; it raises important questions about the quality and range of experiences supporters expect from football and also what we expect from ourselves, all of which are now closely scrutinised, inevitably, in the shadow of Hillsborough.

Generally, football supporters are dealt with rather differently now. Like it or not, we are a little more cared about these days. We probably also care about each other at the match a little more now, too, than we sometimes did in the 1980s. But new abuses have emerged. If there was a Thatcherite contempt for the public and for public services and spaces a decade ago, now, in times of relative plenty for the sport, there is a new contempt, this time for the much trumpeted football customer. Clubs have followed the letter, but hardly the spirit, of Lord Justice Taylor's recommendations on seats and new facilities. He envisaged access for all at reasonable prices, which is certainly possible. The reality, as we all know, has been very different.

In a couple of weeks' time Liverpool, appropriately, visit Nottingham Forest, our horror-struck partners on that Sheffield afternoon a decade ago. Incredibly, the last time I went to the City Ground we were taunted about Hillsborough by some local "fan". That was nothing, however, to the bile and abuse heaped that day by the rest of the home crowd on the hapless Collymore. This time all Liverpool supporters will be asked to pay £25 to attend a clash between the relegated and the simply inept.

Profiteering is an ugly term, especially at this time, but it probably fits here. There is no protest about this from my own club as, apparently, we all live now in the age of the market. Clearly, I can't rely on them to defend my interests. Not everything, it seems, changes. ○

Predictions of the Century

Cris Freddi continued his trawl through some of the less celebrated football moments of the 20th century with an examination of the least accurate predictions

WSC No 147, May 1999

COLIN WOOD, the *Daily Mail*'s football correspondent in Liverpool, once wrote: "This team will dominate the Seventies... nothing can stop it becoming one of the greatest club teams of all time." Given that Liverpool won four European trophies in that decade, plus the League title four times and the FA Cup in 1974, these look like prophetic words. "Er, not exactly," said Wood. "I wrote them about Everton."

I like that one. It's got a certain style, and it couldn't have been more wrong, especially if you're from Liverpool. If you're from Portsmouth, this one's better. Peter Harris was a speedy winger who holds the club record of 194 League goals and helped them win the title in 1949 and 1950, which led one reporter to think: "Round about 1952 the name of Peter Harris will appear in England teams with the same joyful frequency as Stanley Matthews. That's a safe prediction." Harris won a grand total of two caps, against the Republic of Ireland in 1949 and Hungary in 1954. The first match was England's first home defeat by a country from outside the Home Championship, the second was England's biggest defeat by anybody.

Before the latter, Stanley Rous was asked for a prediction. "We will win," quoth he. Even allowing for the need to rally the troops after the 6-3 home defeat by the same country, this was stretching it a bit. Something along the lines of "We know Puskás and Co aren't bad, but we're going there to compete" might have been smarter – but maybe

Rous was only taking his lead from Yugoslavia's famous half-back Zlatko Cajkovski, who insisted "the England defence was strong enough to stop the Hungarians from scoring". It wasn't quite. Hungary won 7-1.

Four years later, when Sweden reached the World Cup final at home, their English coach George Raynor hoped for an early goal against Brazil, who would then "panic all over the show" like all "darkies" who don't like it up them. Sweden scored after only four minutes but lost 5-2.

People were still underestimating these foreigners years later. Try this from Franny Lee's ghostwriter after England lost in Rio in 1969: "This game showed us one thing, that Brazil would not be a problem to us, and my immediate reaction was that I wished I could stand all the bets laid on Brazil to win the World Cup… with their suspect temperament they were not a team that deserved to carry a ha'penny of anybody's money in the World Cup." Alan Ball had much the same opinion in Mexico, though he was less long-winded about it: "We'll beat these." We didn't, of course. We lost the match and Brazil won the Cup.

When Austria won at Wembley in 1965, Jimmy Hill stuck his neck out by saying England had no chance of winning the next World Cup. "But don't blame Alf. No one could win it with players like these." Mind you, Ramsey himself was a tad worrying at times: "I like the look of Graham Taylor as England manager. In many ways he reminds me of me." Eek, surely not.

In the light of what has been happening to the German national team recently, let's hear it from Kaiser Franz. With the 1990 World Cup just won and reunification round the corner, Beckenbauer told us: "The choice will become even bigger and nobody will be able to beat us for years. I'm sorry for the rest of the world, but that's the truth."

Andy Roxburgh's "We have nothing to fear from Costa Rica" is a well worn classic, but the greatest World Cup prediction was probably made by Geoff Hurst: "That hat-trick gave me a great start in life, but it is not – it is not – going to be the one thing I'm remembered for." One of Peter Knowles's quotes belongs in the same league. Cyril Knowles's brother, a skilful ball player who played for England Youth and Under-23s, he gave it all up to become a Jehovah's Witness in 1969 – probably because he thought he was short of time: "We believe the world will end in 1975. If you study the Bible, it'll tell you." Wouldn't mind a percentage of every Bible sold since 75.

After Man City had won the 1967-68 League title by strutting their attacking stuff (Lee, Bell, Summerbee) you could forgive Malcolm

Allison for proclaiming they were setting out to "frighten the cowards of Europe". The continent didn't have time to tremble at the knees: City went out in the first round to a Fenerbahçe team Big Mal didn't bother to have watched. Five years later, taking over at newly relegated Crystal Palace, he declared "We will walk this division", which they did, but not in the direction he meant: Palace went down again in his first season.

The most vivid European Cup prediction looks so daft it has to be tongue-in-cheek but was apparently perfectly serious. After a 5-1 defeat by Ajax in 1966, only Bill Shankly could have thought Liverpool would win the return 6-0 ("and I said so"). They drew 2-2 at Anfield, leaving Shanks with nothing but irrelevancies: "We should have won the second game... they were lucky to get a draw near the end."

Frederick Wall, the fossilised old walrus who was FA secretary for 39 years, was chiefly responsible for the great Charlie Roberts winning only three caps because of his Players Union activities. In 1935 Wall admitted he "cannot easily predict an era when the sorcerers of science may easily turn night into day as they now talk to a man on the other side of the world". Translated: clubs will never install floodlights.

You couldn't keep club chairmen out of an article like this. When Derek Pavis appointed Howard Kendall as manager of Notts County in 1995, he went on TV to declare that no County supporter could find fault with the appointment: "I might just have done it this time." He had, too. Kendall lasted ten weeks before being fired "because of the way the club was being run" (euphemism for naughty goings-on at the ground, allegedly). They finished bottom and were relegated to the Second Division. "I think our fans know how to behave. I don't believe there will be any problems. Those days are behind us now." So said Millwall chairman Reg Burr, just before the riot at a play-off with Derby County in 1984.

But let's leave the last words to the press. Ian Stirrup, for instance, in the *Daily Star* before the 1995-96 season: "If Manchester United finish above Liverpool, my backside will be on display in Trafalgar Square in June." Any anticipation was probably restricted to the pigeons.

The *Mirror*'s notorious **Achtung! Surrender!** headline not only made them look like a bunch of xenophobic panderers but wasn't much of a forecast: "For you, Fritz, ze Euro 96 is over." While Fritz went through to the final for the fifth time and won it for the third, poor Tommy still hasn't appeared in one.

A strong candidate for most offensive prediction of the century, but nobody'll mind if the big prize goes to the *Sun*, which exceeded even its own standards in Italia 90. It started after England's dismal draw with the Republic of Ireland: "The *Sun* speaks its mind. Bring them home." After the last-minute win over Belgium, the tone changed: "We never seriously doubted England's chances of clawing their way through the World Cup field." By the end of the tournament, the about-face was complete: "Around Gazza and his young gang we can build a team to rule the world. Four years on, remember you read it first in the *Sun*." Don't worry, we won't forget. That or Hillsborough. ○

Abroad Sweep

Ronald Reng explained why foreign players often had difficulty integrating at English clubs

WSC No 149, July 1999

IN THE CROWDED TOILET of a Barnsley nightspot called The Theatre I learned what it means to be a foreign football hero in England. As I walked in with Lars Leese, Barnsley's giant German goalkeeper, one of the men relieving themselves turned around and welcomed Lars with a hint of poetry: "Oh, Lars Leese/Tall as trees." Then the man gently stepped back to offer Lars his place at the urinal. During all this he kept on pissing, now on the floor.

Lars had offered to show me around Barnsley to prove that his accounts of life as a footballer in an English town were not exaggerated. They definitely were not. We were stopped in the street by two 14-year-old girls who desperately wanted to discuss the latest run of Barnsley reserves, we were press-ganged into becoming guests of honour at a birthday party, and offered approximately 233 drinks by total strangers. "When you lose a game in Germany," he said, "you lock yourself in, afraid of fans who would beat you up. In Barnsley, you face a different problem. You are drunk after 30 minutes because everybody wants to buy you a beer to console you."

By his own admission, Leese did not do much to earn such adoration. He made 24 appearances for Barnsley in two years, a few outstanding, but hardly the stuff to make you the small-town cult-figure he seems to be. Leese knows better: "The fact that I am 6ft 5in tall and from

Germany, home of the European champions, seems enough to assure them that I am a sensational keeper." He comes from far away, we paid a lot of money for him, so he must be great: this romantic perspective still exists in the English game and makes it the best place to be for a foreign journeyman footballer – if only such worship did not so easily turn into contempt at the slightest hint of disappointment.

After four years when foreigners were "seven-language-speaking, cappuccino-drinking, much-more-intelligent-than-our-lads" professionals one week and "big-mouthed, big-headed poofs" the next, I thought the 1998-99 season might be the first in English football when it was normal to be foreign. But then came the Van Hooijdonk saga, the Di Canio incident, Leboeuf's moaning. We also had, for example, the Robbie Fowler affair, but whereas Fowler's wrong-doings were simply explained by his personal character (or lack of it), the misbehaviour of Van Hooijdonk, Di Canio and Leboeuf were immediately generalised: Oh, these foreigners again.

Ruud Gullit keeps telling us that "a Frenchman is not a foreigner any more". But Gullit knows he still has to convince us of it, as in English football foreigners are still seen – and still see themselves – as a different species. Interestingly, the English game may be the first to amalgamate common national prejudices: It's not "the Italians who are cheating" any more, not "the Croatians who are arrogant", not "the Brazilians who are dancing Samba with the ball". They are all "the foreigners", and we are still debating how we can learn from "them" or whether "they" are ruining our game.

No other major European league has had to cope with such a large influx in such a short time. In Spain, Italy and Germany they have employed players and managers from abroad for decades, getting used to different tactics, football cultures and each other in a steady evolution. It was like a permanent drip from a tap. In England, the foreigners came in one big waterfall. Suddenly there were people in the dressing room asking questions like: Where can we get a massage? Why do you drink so much beer? And, do you call it a tactics session when the gaffer shouts: "Move your arse, you fucking dickhead"? Any country would have problems coming to terms with it.

At the Rams Arena, training ground of Derby County, Jim Smith is in a good mood when we come to talk to him about the foreign invasion. "Hello, what are all these women doing here?" he shouts, entering the players' canteen. In fact, there is one woman, a translator for Francesco

Baiano. "I'll see you in a minute," Smith tells the woman, then he goes into his office and forgets about her for the next hour. "I am quite modern, although I am getting old," he says. "I am prepared to look seriously at anything which will enhance our performance and, yes, a lot of new things came from the foreign players. For example we are now providing the food for the squad at lunchtime, Italian style. They are getting pasta, rice, salad. We've taken the chocolate away." He beams. "Now I get all the Kit-Kats, Snickers and Mars." The phone rings. It's Jan, a Danish agent, who watches the Scandinavian market for Smith. "Yes, Jan, say again, what's his name? Fuel? Ah, Flo, right." [Norwegian striker Håvard Flo, then at Werder Bremen.] "See, that's another thing with all the foreigners," Smith says. "You get millions of faxes from agents from all over the world saying 'I've got a player for you'. Then they send a video with his ten latest goals – or at least that's what they tell you. Later you find out he's only scored nine in his whole career."

It was inevitable that with so many foreign players arriving, they could not all be super-heroes and bargains, but also failures and braggarts. Though naturally that discovery has not helped ease the pain of integration. At Barnsley, for example, a lot of the local players, who signed their contracts two or three years ago, still earn three or four time less than the imports. "That was the biggest problem when the influx started three or four years ago," Smith claims. "Our own players were cross. But now it's just normal."

On the surface, perhaps. But below it you can hear both foreigners and locals expressing their discontent. "There is no question that the media critics do not apply the same standards in judging me as they do Alex Ferguson," Gianluca Vialli said at the beginning of the season, when Chelsea's multinational team suddenly went from one praised for enriching English football to being "the team of mercenary multi-millionaires". Of course, he was speaking to an Italian, not an English paper. It's a situation that replays itself endlessly. Someone complains back home about the English training sessions, the English weather or, in the case of Barnsley's Macedonian striker Georgi Hristov, about the ugliness of English woman. Irritated English players counter-attack, like Paul Gascoigne telling Emmanuel Petit in January: "I don't like the foreign lads coming in, moaning and saying the league is too long." And in the heat of the battle some critics fall into the trap of generalising, as the *Daily Telegraph* did when writing of "foreign parasites".

Nowhere is the difference in attitude between English players and foreigners so obvious as in their public demeanour off the pitch. English players are brought up to shun the media (in no small part thanks to a uniquely venomous tabloid press) and not to say anything controversial. Foreign players – and here I think it is fair to generalise – are taught the value of speaking out. Someone like Newcastle's Didi Hamann learned at Bayern Munich that: "You have to raise your voice from time to time, strongly and publicly, otherwise you do not survive." Guess who created a storm when he commented on Newcastle's turmoil in late December.

Hamann's compatriot Uwe Rösler, now back with Kaiserslautern, says most foreigners realise the kind of things they are expected to say at home are not welcomed in England. "But if you are frustrated by your own or the club's situation, you just fall into your old habit," Rösler says. In 1997 nothing was going right at Manchester City. Relegated to the First Division, they saw off four managers in five months and Rösler suddenly found himself chatting away to a German journalist. "I knew the rules, I knew the story would come back to haunt me, but still I could not stop myself complaining," he says.

The headlines of either the "whinging" or "much-more-intelligent-than-our-lads" foreigners will presumably go on as long as English clubs continue to advise their players not to speak their minds. In comparison to such professionals the foreign view will always sound articulate and often controversial. Steve Heighway, director of Liverpool's Youth Academy, said at the opening of his institution: "The definition of players is changing. We have to bring through boys who can communicate, represent our industry better." But communicating is also about saying what you really think. Even if English players are brought up with the slick PR-speak of "representing the industry", the differences between them and "the foreigners" will still seem huge. And it is the foreigners who will continue to be unreasonably praised and blamed in equal measure. O

My Kind of Town

Steven Askew offered some guidance to anyone with a spare afternoon in Scunthorpe

WSC No 149, July 1999

SCUNTHORPE UNITED'S TOP SCORER last season, Jamie Forrester, outraged locals by describing the town as "a shed" in a recent interview with top onanist's periodical Loaded. In the inevitable media storm that followed (well, one publicity seeking local politician blowing a fuse in the town's nightly excuse for a newspaper) Forrester neatly attempted to sidestep the issue with the same precision as he might finish off a move on the pitch. He claimed he had "never actually used the word 'shed'", as if this were crucially distinct from the words he actually uttered. Clever. "All I said was that there was nothing to do and nowhere worth going," he disclaimed.

The matter finally whimpered to a halt when United manager Brian Laws went on the local television news to firmly point out that "Jamie Forrester was not being derogative". The confusing intellectual mind-games he was employing seemed to appease the outraged councillor. Forrester's mildly defiant attitude ("you know what journalists are like") caused sales of *Loaded* in Scunthorpe to drop by, ooh, two or three copies a month.

But it is a really offensive indicator of the mercenary attitude of footballers in this day and age when you consider how little respect, and how little real interest, Forrester must have shown in the town when he first signed. Scunthorpe may well be less than a hotbed of activity, but the town does have its redeeming features. If he had bothered to ask, and then had the patience to look, Forrester would have discovered there are actually myriad modestly stunning locations in the borough, all connected to the history of his employers.

Following redevelopment and the club's trend-setting move to a purpose-built stadium on the edge of town, a national-chain supermarket now stands on the site of United's original home. The Old Showground was used by the club in tandem with local agricultural business to display their sale stock – some might say that somewhere along the line the two got mixed up. Those of us old enough to harbour real emotional ties to the gloriously ramshackle but innovative stadium (which boasted the first cantilever stand in Britain) still find ourselves keenly touched by the hand of history as we pick up our Shredded Wheat. Who could fail to be nudged closer to tears by the sight of a disco-ball on a super-market ceiling, suspended poignantly over aisle six's cereals – the very spot where a significant centre-circle had once been?

The PlayStation-less kids who gamely fulfil their societal roles as shoplifting urchins may well evade the security guards by hopping across the car park wall into King Edward Street. It was here, to his modest *Coronation Street*-style terraced lodgings, that teenage apprentice Kevin Keegan ran one morning after a bout of extra-curricular laddism during which he crashed and wrote off the club tractor. He didn't last much longer at United after that and the club offloaded him as soon as some mug came in with an offer.

Just round the corner is the house from which actor Donald Pleasance, in repertory theatre in the town during the late Sixties, would stride purposefully up to The Old Showground to stand on the terraces and shed the shackles of luvviness. A brick's throw from Don's old pad is the seemingly endless boulevard, Doncaster Road, once home to Tiffany's, a Seventies/Eighties nightclub of the utmost taste, which features promi-nently on our tour because it was from this very establishment that goalkeeper Joe Neenan and Ian Botham (yes) stepped, minutes before assaulting a local man who had the audacity to question Beefy's creden-tials as the libero grande of the team. Botham lasted about six or seven games in a United shirt, was made vice president and then wandered off into the long grass, never to return. He was finally sacked from his honorary position a couple of years back after club officials woke briefly from a perpetual stupor and noticed he'd not even bothered to come and watch a match, let alone invest a penny, since his playing days.

The pavement outside what is now an amusement arcade in the town's shopping centre was itself host to my own first social encounter with a Scunthorpe United player. In the mid-Seventies, when I was six or seven years old, midfielder Mike Czuczman (pronounced something like "Churchman") was my hero and, due to the complete unavailability of posters of the United team, I had pinned a picture of TV lawyer Petrocelli to my bedroom wall with the words "Mike Czuczman" carefully spelled out in felt-tip beneath. I was astonished to see Czuczman leaving the High Street dry-cleaners Zerny's one close season afternoon. Over his arm was a terrible black and grey pinstripe suit.

I raced over for an autograph and, as he signed, he dropped the hefty piece of gum he had been chewing on to the ground. The lump is there to this day, though it's a little greyer. I often pause and look at it, wondering where the years have gone, and what happened to Mike. My autographed copy of Tiger has long since vanished, though I do remember quite clearly that his signature read "Mike Czzzzzzzzzzmzzzzzzzzzn, skill". I may well have added "skill" myself.

The Gunness Straight is a very long road which leads away from Glanford Park, away from Scunthorpe and out into the wilds, beyond which lie Yorkshire and other foreign places. United's squad are often to be seen engaging in their training runs up The Straight, as it is imaginatively nicknamed. So it was one Monday morning recently as I was driving along it. Curiously, a transit van travelled alongside them for almost the entire length of the road. As I passed it I slowed down to a similar pace and wound down my window to shout some sort of encouragement to the team, only to hear the van-driver get there first.

Undeterred by the squad's decision to keep their heads down and jog on in ignorance, he was shouting all manner of constructive criticism, the kind which would make even Ian Botham blush, before finally he gave up and ended his gargantuan tirade with a cursory cry of "Faster, you absolute bastards". He gave a few wheel-spins for good measure, showering the team in mud and gravel, and then sped off. He had a Scunthorpe United scarf dangling from his rear-view mirror. It's that kind of town. They're that kind of team. ○

Break for the Border

Carlisle United were about to come under new ownership. Roger Lytollis explained why the club's supporters would be delighted to see it happen

WSC No 152, October 1999

WHEN JIMMY GLASS blasted his shot towards the Plymouth goal, Carlisle United's 71-year Football League life was one-and-a-half seconds from ending. As furious chants of "Fat, greedy bastard!" battered Brunton Park, Michael Knighton found himself the centre of attention, not for the first time. For seven years the story of Carlisle United has been the story of Michael Knighton. The chairman has used his majority shareholding to indulge his many and varied whims. He took over when the club was bottom of the league. He revived it. And then he almost killed it.

Back in 1992, Carlisle supporters soon learned that the new chairman's promises could not always be relied upon. An hour before his first match Knighton declared to a TV crew: "We will not lose. We cannot lose." We lost. Undeterred, he promised Premier League football within ten years. By the year 2000 Brunton Park would house 25,000 fans for every game. Utter bollocks, of course, but far better than the previous board's lack of ambition. In 1995 Carlisle won promotion. Instead of building on this success, however, Knighton tried to do it on the cheap. The team took their place in the Second Division without any new players and struggled from the outset. On transfer deadline day, in the midst of a relegation battle, Paul Murray and Tony Gallimore were sold for £1.2 million. Carlisle went straight back down.

Relegation was regarded by fans as a disappointing setback. Knighton had made mistakes but deserved another chance. The press were more concerned with the chairman's encounter with aliens – the ones who interrupted his journey along the M62 to tell him: "Michael, don't be afraid." In November 1996 Knighton resigned in protest at the media's portrayal of him as some sort of nutter, before reinstating himself three days later. Carlisle came straight back up and won the Auto Windscreens Shield under Mervyn Day's astute management. In July Knighton resigned again to write a book about his Old Trafford adventure. Six weeks later, back in the Second Division, he came out of retirement in spectacular style. He sacked Mervyn Day after just six matches and appointed himself head coach, as well as chairman, chief executive and director. Also drawing salaries were his wife (marketing director) and his son (publications co-ordinator).

It would be generous to describe Knighton's 15 months in charge of the team as farcical. Midway through the season he emigrated to the Isle of Man for tax purposes. He still managed to conduct a bizarre feud with the local paper, the *News and Star*. His programme notes included this reference to a *News and Star* journalist: "Tis he who must lead the crusade to see the Chairman slain. Slain according to the righteous moral high ground of the new Titan, wielding his titanic hammerhead God-like to smash the Anti-Christ into unconditional submission." Well, it made a change from "The lads are gutted".

After winning his first match as coach Knighton had gloated: "Who needs a manager?" Eight months later Carlisle were relegated, ten points adrift of safety. At least the chairman didn't give himself an unfair advantage over his predecessors, selling Matt Jansen and Rory Delap for £2.9m during the club's latest relegation battle. Back in the Third Division in 1998, the frenzy of selling continued. Nick Wright and Allan Smart were off-loaded to Watford for a bargain £250,000. The only new players were the usual assortment of free transfers, loan signings and trialists. Knighton's pre-season comments included: "Only a fool makes predictions, but we'll be in the top four at Christmas." By December Carlisle were 89th in the Football League.

Nigel Pearson was appointed head coach but could not stop the slide. As transfer deadline day loomed, Carlisle's rivals strengthened their squads. Michael Knighton adopted a different policy, one he had used in two previous relegation scraps. On deadline day he sold three first-teamers. One was goalkeeper Tony Caig, an ever-present for three years. He joined Blackpool for £50,000. He was the club's only fit keeper. The fans were in uproar. Conspiracy theories abounded. Clydebank wanted to merge with Carlisle and play in the Scottish League from Brunton Park. Knighton called the plan "interesting". One theory was that he saw money-making potential in Scotland and thought Carlisle fans' opposition would wilt if the alternative was Conference football.

Tony Caig was replaced for the most important match in the club's history by a loan signing – Richard Knight from Derby County – who had never played a league game. Knight was recalled after six matches. Enter Jimmy Glass. The day before Glass's great escape, the club announced record profits of £1.4m – more than Liverpool, Leeds and Tottenham. Knighton, who owns 93 per cent of Carlisle United, proclaimed the profits as proof of his business acumen. His critics accused him of asset-stripping. Since 1996 the club has spent £300,000 on players while generating £6.1m from sales.

A month after Glass's goal, someone called Keith Mincher was appointed head coach. He took one training session and walked out. The man seeking to eclipse the Mincher Minutes is Martin Wilkinson, previously chief scout. Knighton has resigned as chairman, again, while retaining his shareholding. He rejected a buy-out by a local millionaire and claimed that two consortiums were about to make offers. Three months on there is no sign of them. The new chairman Knighton said would be in place before the new season has not materialised.

Carlisle supporters were for a long time reluctant to criticise Michael Knighton. That has changed. Their concerns have repeatedly been ignored and the fans he once described as the best in the game are now "yelping idiots". An independent supporters' group is being formed with the aim of buying a seat on the board. This plan has already been dismissed by the club.

Cumbria lost Workington and Barrow from the Football League in the 1970s. Only an on-loan goalkeeper's injury-time goal preserved League football in England's second-largest county. When Michael Knighton promised Premier League football within ten years, no one realised he meant the Unibond Premier. ○

League Ladders

The North Atlantic League had been proposed as a competition for clubs who dominate their own league but flop in Europe. Ken Gall, however, was sceptical

WSC No 155, January 2000

IN HIS UNJUSTLY NEGLECTED 1911 classic *The Devil's Dictionary*, the great American satirist Ambrose Bierce accurately defined once as "enough". Sadly, however, Bierce's assertion that there can be too much of a good thing seems anathema to the individuals in charge of the big European clubs. The latest to demonstrate that undeniable truth are the chief executive of Celtic, Allan MacDonald, and his contemporaries at two of Europe's other sleeping giants – or fading has-beens, depending on one's point of view – Ajax and PSV Eindhoven.

These men, gazing upon the fixture-congested mass that is the Champions League, have decided that what is needed is another, similar competition. However, this pan-European, not-quite-Champions League would come with a twist – namely that Celtic, Ajax, PSV and others so minded would leave their domestic leagues to play in it exclusively. Other great names of yesteryear – such as Benfica and Anderlecht – as well as aspirational Scandinavians such as Rosenborg would be invited to jettison their domestic rivals in the feverish hunt for the dregs from the seemingly bottomless barrel of Euro TV money. Ajax chief executive Frank Kales was first out of the traps with his suggestion of a "North Atlantic League" – a vague and somewhat disturbing title which, for some reason, conjures up images of Oswald Mosley. Kales's "idea", such as it was, was backed by Harry van Raay, the chairman of PSV, apparently a long-term advocate of just such a competition involving the bigger clubs from the Netherlands, Belgium and Scandinavia.

However, it was MacDonald's performance at Celtic's October AGM that brought a hitherto unheard-of project to the front and back pages of the Scottish press. Celtic: We're Out Of Here was the typically subtle two-inch headline in the *Daily Record* on the day after the AGM. Breathlessly, the paper reported Kenny Dalglish's statement: "In five years, I'd like to see the club operating in a different league." Scottish fans, aghast at the prospect of losing one – or perhaps both – of the much-loved Old Firm were doubtless choking on their cornflakes at the news that Celtic were looking to "escape" the Scottish Premier League to join a "lucrative European super league". (It can be noted that just as indictments are always "damning" and increases always "dramatic", a European super league is always "lucrative".)

It was taken as a given, naturally, that were Celtic to leave the SPL, Rangers would quickly follow, leaving the Scottish Premier League as a wasteland. All television and sponsorship contracts would be ripped up, and football in Scotland would become as commercially viable as shinty or badger-baiting. MacDonald – who succeeded Fergus McCann, another man fond of the publicity-grabbing soundbite – gave a performance at the AGM to gladden the hearts of all who cherish romance in football. Shareholders were told that the "economic model" of Scottish football could not generate success; that, in their "strategic review", Celtic were "looking at the market" in which they operate; and, wonderfully, that Celtic were looking to "invest in our playing portfolio". One wonders whether Jock Stein, on seeing a less-than-exemplary performance from the Lisbon Lions, ever turned to the then Celtic chairman to say, "I think we need to invest in our playing portfolio."

The argument, which does not become less wearying by repetition, is that poor old Celtic, Rangers, Ajax, PSV and so on are being left with only a few bawbees to play with while the millionaire Eurotrash from Barcelona, Milan and London throw money around like sailors on shore leave. The reason for this, as MacDonald made clear, was simple: "It all comes down to TV audiences."

Across the North Sea, Ajax spokesman Erik van Leewan was singing from the same hymn-sheet, comparing the Scottish and Dutch situations and highlighting the fact that, in both countries, a handful of big clubs did not "earn the kind of rewards we are due". One can imagine him stamping his foot while saying this. Removing his gaze from the crystal ball, Van Leewan speculated airily that while Ajax v Celtic or Rangers would be of immense interest to the Dutch couch potato, Ajax v Hearts would have him reaching for the remote quicker than a guest appearance by Jim Davidson on Noel's House Party. Clearly, therefore, the Jam Tarts, Twente Enschede, Standard Liège and others similar would not be receiving the embossed invitations to this one. Because of their business backgrounds – MacDonald was previously a senior executive with British Aerospace, while Ajax's Kales worked for IBM – the men behind this half-cooked plan are credited with seer-like wisdom by the sporting media, which probably would treat with equal seriousness any footballing proposals by John DeLorean.

However, these supposed visionaries of the stock market and the financial pages seemed to lose their touch when faced with demands for more concrete proposals. How would the creation of such a competition leave each national league? What was the view of UEFA or FIFA? Would the winners of the competition go into the Champions League? "Everything is theoretical," said Van Leewan at Ajax. "Everything is hypothetical," added a PSV spokesman. MacDonald, however, was categoric: "I don't know what the outcome will be." These men have noted, astutely, the way in which European TV viewers have foamed at the mouth in anticipation of big-time Champions League encounters such as Sparta Prague v Willem II Tilburg. They have concluded, again astutely, that the 75,000 empty seats at the Bernabéu for Real Madrid's first Champions League encounter provide irrefutable evidence that what the European fan wants is more – much more – of this sort of thing. This is what is known as commercial acumen.

Sadly, the joyless administrative face of the SPL's chief executive Roger Mitchell and others quickly put a dampener on the party, with much talk of rule books, laws and injunctions against any club contemplating participation in any "super league". Rangers' chairman David Murray went further, committing his club to Scottish football and stating that all efforts should be focused on getting another place for Scotland in the

Champions League. That might appear to be that. But those clubs which seem to have outgrown their domestic competitions but do not have the means to compete consistently at a higher level may use similar threats to hold domestic football associations to ransom when future television contracts are negotiated. Was this the hidden agenda behind the whole business? Surely not!

Celtic, Ajax and PSV once dominated European football by the judicious marshalling of their own assets and playing abilities. Now, the only playing field on which they are interested in competing against the giants of Italy, Germany, Spain and England is the financial one. Sporting ambition and achievement – and other such archaic concepts – are simply beyond them. ○

Broken Record

Archie MacGregor surveyed the Scottish press's attitude towards the English in the wake of the two countries' Euro 2000 qualifying play-off

WSC No 155, January 2000

SO THAT WAS THE BATTLE OF BRITAIN. To paraphrase an apposite remark, surely never in the history of Scottish journalism has so much hype and mindless posturing been so relentlessly sustained by so few. In Scotland, the sight of the national team once again performing its party piece of glorious failure has been greeted with something approaching fatalistic acceptance. Yet mixed in with the anguish, ennui and glee (at the Wembley result) there is also a tangible sense of relief that the goddam war is over. All that remains in the run-up to the season of goodwill is a deep-seated wish that the tabloids abide by the terms of the ceasefire. Some hope.

The advent of devolution may signify Scotland's coming of age as a modern nation state, but while the rest of us have been growing up, some of our tabloid newspapers have apparently opted to stay in the kindergarten. From that fateful moment on October 13 in Aachen when "international football's oldest rivals" were paired together in the Euro 2000 play-off draw, the Scottish *Sun* and *Daily Record* in particular set about working through the A to Z of tabloid-induced hysteria with ferocious zeal. The symbolic existence of the Scottish parliament as a catalyst for an ongoing reappraisal of the relationship with our southern neighbour? Forget it.

By the following morning it was the familiar Neanderthal fare of the screaming headlines with stories continued inside on pages 2, 3, 4, 5... On its front page the *Record* concocted its now infamous "Boastbusters" theme, a spoof on the Ghostbusters logo featuring Kevin Keegan with a saltire plastered over his mouth, and considerately instructed its readers to "help Scotland shut Keegan up with our cut-out-and-keep poster". Uncannily, the *Sun* featured, yes, a close-up photo of Keegan with a saltire over his mouth. What a pity for them that, whatever his other shortcomings, Keegan was a model of diplomacy in his public relations and assiduously avoided raising Scottish hackles with presumptuous pronouncements on the likely outcome.

On the inside pages we had reheated tales of English bias in the London-based media, English thuggery on the terraces and mock outrage that Tony Blair had had the temerity to pronounce his support for England. Typical of the *Record*'s skewed perspective was its feature on players with unusual surnames who have been selected for England, including the unfortunate SR Bastard in 1880. The piece was given an unnecessarily acerbic twist by an over the top headline, **Here's The First English B********, and an attempt to suggest modern day equivalents – step forward Bobby Robson, Sir Alf Ramsey and Alan Shearer for their alleged hatred of the Scots. In subsequent days an increasingly defensive *Record* was to protest its innocence against charges of incitement by pointing out that its editorial on October 14 had asked its readers to Be Nice, Even To English (sic). Cynicism was the only appropriate response to the *Sun*'s attempts to play the Tartan card – especially when you know only too well that the English editions will be full of Jock-baiting trash.

Yet again football has been a casualty of the circulation wars. The Scottish tabloids are a dab hand at it – at least four times a season they get the opportunity to inflate a Celtic v Rangers match into the most important meeting in the history of the Old Firm. Then they wring their hands when it descends into the sort of disgraceful mayhem that enveloped the title decider at Celtic Park last May. What made the tone of the *Record*'s coverage both bemusing and reprehensible was that the paper's political stance is pro-New Labour and virulently anti-SNP, while its editor Martin Clarke is English and has a CV which includes a spell at the helm of the stridently right-wing Scottish *Daily Mail*. Scottish-based English folk will have been consoled to discover, however, that there are others in the *Record*'s cannon fodder caste system for whom it reserves even greater disdain – these being the SFA, BSkyB, the English FA, Glasgow council workers and, when the wheels came off on the field, Craig Brown.

The broadsheets mercifully provided an antidote to the rabble-rousing. The *Sunday Herald*'s editorial on October 17 contained a barely concealed dig at the *Record*'s antics: "It is only a game and those 90-minute patriots are not doing us any favours by invoking the sort of naked nationalism which has nothing to do with love of country but much to do with insti-gating hatred of our neighbours." There was healthy coverage given to the thoughts of England supporters living amid the tabloid siege while, in keeping with a trend that emerged during France 98, there were even a few writers brave enough to question the "support anybody that's playing England" knee-jerk.

So was it the red-tops or the broadsheets that provided the most accurate barometer of Scottish opinion? The level of opprobrium directed towards the *Record* for its opening salvos lends encouragement to the belief that it was the latter. For the more cynical, however, there was also the realisation that, despite all the emphasis on separate identities and distinctness of culture, Scotland and England really do have rather a lot in common – mediocre national teams, inept football authorities and a tabloid press that is an embarrassment to us all. ○

Greyer Shade of Blue

Trevor Francis – fabulous Seventies icon or dour Nineties time-server? John Tandy found Birmingham City fans unwilling to abandon faith in their then manager

WSC No 156, February 2000

IT'S THE EARLY EIGHTIES. Birmingham City are well into the downward spiral that will shortly see them drop into the Third Division. Trevor Francis is at Sampdoria. The song rings out: "My Trevor lies over the ocean, My Trevor lies over the sea... Oh bring back my Trevor to me..." Fast forward to 1996 and the dream comes true. With all the bunting and tickertape you would expect for a Homecoming Queen, Francis let himself be talked out of retirement (ie Sky TV) and into the manager's chair. It wasn't all unbridled joy. There were those who worried that anything less than walking on water would only serve to tarnish the memory of our Greatest Player Ever. There were those who pointed to his less-than-inspirational management career at QPR and Sheffield Wednesday. There were even those who (perish the thought) suggested his contributions to Monday Night Football demonstrated less than razor-sharp wit and tactical awareness.

Three years down the line and we find a tangle of contradictions that Anthony Clare would die for. It's hard to reconcile the style of the player with the tactics of a manager striving for that elusive 1-8-1 formation that will one day change the face of football. *Catenaccio*-esque, I guess you'd call it. On a good day. Francis is distant to the point of supercilious with staff, yet prizes team spirit above all (he ended Christopher Wreh's loan spell early for a lack of it at a time when he was the only fit striker at the club).

You have a man who demands unswerving loyalty while making it clear he doesn't need the job and has tried to walk out several times. You have a man who demands the flexibility of a squad system, yet whose own stubbornness would see him lose Ian Bennett, our finest goalkeeper since the Fifties, rather than back down in a squabble over a few quid. His team selections appear to owe more to favouritism than to strategy: if you're in, you're in for ever (Martin Grainger, Jon McCarthy, Paul "half-a-season" Furlong), if you're out, you're on your bike (Paul Devlin, Nicky

Forster and Paul Tait all sold for peanuts, while Eddie "massive-fee-from-Chelsea" Newton took a matter of days to earn himself a permanent place in the reserves). You have a man whose public persona is bland to the point of non-existence yet who somehow communicates a single-minded determination and commitment.

So where does this leave the average consumer? To find out I undertook an objective, verifiable, triangulated research project. I asked a load of Blues fans. The results weren't far short of unanimous. Trevor Francis apparently still is God. Walking on water is now taken as read and we are eagerly awaiting progression to the more challenging miracles: healing the lame, reaching the play-offs, that sort of thing. We have the strongest squad we have had for 20 years – your heart hardly ever sinks these days when they read out the team list. We are playing the best football many of the fans have ever seen (a sizeable chunk of the supporting demographic have never seen Francis play, he's just a piece of living history, like Neil Armstrong or Les Paul, so they don't have any of the "icon" hang-ups). We may be bland, but at least people don't laugh any more. There is the conviction that Francis has taken the club to heart ("you can see how much it hurts him when we lose" is a frequent comment). The stubbornness is seen as single-minded, the walkouts a challenge to an unsupportive board.

There is even the feeling that our place in the table (11th and sliding at the time of writing) is a credit to Francis, given an injury crisis that makes *Titus Andronicus* look like a Boyzone gig. Against West Ham in November we had our second-choice full-backs on either wing with a centre-back and an on-loan winger up front. Tackling has been banned in training and even then one player dislocated his thumb when it tangled in someone else's shirt, and another fell downstairs at home. Like *Titus Andronicus* it would be funny if there wasn't so much blood.

When we lost to Watford in the play-offs last season Francis spoke of the pain of losing with a passion we'd never heard before. In some ways that seems to have been a defining moment. It's hard to judge how long the feelgood factor will last, but it has certainly survived a lot of things that would normally have caused rumblings of discontent by now. Whether he gets us anywhere or not, one thing's for sure. Trevor Francis somehow manages to irritate the hell out of Villa fans, like a burst of eczema that's been festering since the Seventies. For that, if for nothing else, he will always be sure of a place in our hearts. O

Saint Matthews

Cris Freddi paid tribute to arguably England's greatest footballer, Sir Stanley Matthews, who died in March 2000

WSC No 158, April 2000

IT'S ALMOST AS IF HE just fancied seeing in the new millennium. Or maybe he thought 85 was quite a round number. We all assumed Stan would go on for ever. That's partly because he did. League football from 1932 to 1965, a 22-year international career, Footballer of the Year at 48 – tributes to the legendary fitness that explained why he always looked the same sort of age, ie old, the rather wizened appearance of the very slim and fit (Tom Finney and Lester Piggott had it).

His various obits have all been emphasising what a perfect gent he was: for example not a single booking in 700 League matches. There's no reason to doubt it, and it's good to hear, but I'm not particularly interested unless it was part of his armoury; maybe the fact he didn't react made him relatively untouchable in the way Bobby Charlton's supposed to have been. If not, it's irrelevant. I mean, if you take his only real challengers as Greatest Outside Right of the Century, Garrincha had kids all over the place, left his wife for a nightclub singer and died in poverty; and in between World Cups the amazing Helmut Rahn grew as round as a barrel of the lager he was so fond of. All I care about is how good Stan was as a player.

There were doubts at the time. He won only 54 caps compared with Finney's 76, he scored only 11 goals in those internationals, his concern with beating a man was criticised for slowing down the attack – and we all know he was a one-trick magician, some of his contemporaries are adamant about it. Shuffle up to his full-back, dummy inside, scoot past on the outside. He was so quick he got away with it time and again. But it's hard to believe he could have survived at the highest level for 30 years, even with only one man to beat, if he hadn't had other strings to his bow. The obit in the *Gazzetta dello Sport*, for instance, recalls him lying deep against Italy in Turin in 1948, drawing left-back Alberto Eliani upfield before punching long balls up the right wing for Stan Mortensen to use his speed, first to thrash in a freak goal, then to make the second for Tommy Lawton. Against a team based on the Grande Torino, England won 4-0. Eliani wasn't capped again. There's also the story of Stan pulling a comb out of his shorts before Eliani came in for a tackle, but that's just typical *Gazzetta*.

Then against Brazil in 1956, at the age of 41, Matthews destroyed Nílton Santos, the greatest left-back of all time. Although there's a famous picture of him with the ball at his feet and Nílton left lying on his side, again most of the damage came from passes pushed behind the defender. It's presumably the performance that made him the first European Footballer of the Year ahead of Di Stéfano and Kopa. He'd been the first English equivalent in 1948 and won it again for taking Stoke into the First Division in 1963.

All right, so he was a two-trick wizard. So put one of today's man-markers on him and goodnight. Except they'd have to cope with that much-filmed acceleration and the ability to run all day – and anyway there was even more to his game. His passing and perfect ball control stood him in good stead when he came inside. When England were reduced to nine fit men against the talented Czechoslovakians in 1937, he moved to inside-right and scored a hat-trick, including the late winner in a 5-4 win, all with his left foot, which isn't in the script you usually read.

And that's the main thing when you try and decide his place in the pantheon. Whereas Finney had two anonymous World Cups and a bad FA Cup final, Stan was always likely to do it on the big occasion. All right, he only made the winner in "his" Cup final because Bolton were down to ten men – but in the 1954 World Cup he was all over the pitch against Belgium ("England threw away all Matthews's brilliant work") and the best player against the holders Uruguay, even at the age of 39. The Swiss match programme knew what it was doing when it listed him as St Matthews.

As for how he'd get on today, you're having a laugh aren't you? The fact that England are having to use Beckham in the No 7 shirt says it all. There's only ever been one Stan the Man. O

No Riot Answers

Simon Evans looked at the causes and consequences of the worsening football violence in eastern Europe

WSC No 160, June 2000

WHILE POSSIBLE VIOLENCE at Euro 2000 occupies the minds and column inches of the west European media, the continent's other half, as usual, is dealing with much more real and pressing problems. The second weekend of April saw serious crowd violence in St Petersburg, Budapest, Lodz and Bucharest. These were not western-style scuffles or skirmishes. Hooliganism in eastern Europe is proper stuff: rubber batons and tear gas, head-splitting and hospitalising. The most serious clashes were in St Petersburg, where one fan died during the latest in a series of full-scale riots that have greeted the start of the Russian season.

In Poland, an elite anti-terrorist squad was called in to quell violence at the match between Widzew Lodz and Legia Warsaw. It is the second time this season that the unit, designed to deal with armed criminals and the mafia, has been called on to deal with the hooligans who are increasingly plaguing the Polish game. The Budapest derby between Ferencvaros and Ujpest has become a battleground in recent years, and this year's match saw 50 fans injured and 12 arrested after fighting outside Ferencvaros' Ulloi ut stadium. With 2,000 visiting Ujpest fans matched by an equal number of home supporters, the jaded phrase "mindless minority" hardly applies. At derby matches in the east the problem is rarely restricted to a minority.

Brutal, organised violence at football matches has been increasing ever since the collapse of communism, but while the governments and football authorities in the former eastern bloc have been crying out for help, little has come. The German and British police could offer some advice from their struggles against football violence. UEFA's officials could use some of the organisation's wealth to help improve stadium safety and security instead of just rolling their eyeballs when they turn up at grounds. Very little of this is happening. It is not seen as our problem, and in a sense it is not. There will never be a major tournament in the east while the current economic divide in Europe and European football remains. Even

Hungary's joint bid with well organised and reliable Austria to host Euro 2004 got little serious attention. Most of the region's teams get knocked out of European club competitions before Roy Keane and Rivaldo have returned from their summer holidays.

Nor is there anything for the organisers of Euro 2000 to worry about. Of the four venues for violence in April, only Bucharest have representatives at the championship and those Dinamo fans who wrecked the away stand at Rapid can't afford the train fare. A teenage fan was killed at the Belgrade derby this year, but the Yugoslav national team is unlikely to be tarnished by the behaviour of its fans this summer. At France 98, Yugoslav supporters consisted of émigrés and Belgrade businessmen. Poverty meant Partizan's notorious "gravediggers" group stayed at home. But violence in eastern Europe should be concerning UEFA and western football authorities. For a start, European football would be a damn sight more interesting if there were teams from the east who could once again challenge for honours in the way Red Star, Dinamo Kiev and Steaua Bucharest used to. More prosaically, if the west doesn't come to eastern clubs, their hooligans will eventually come to the west.

Lack of capital is the biggest problem facing clubs in the east, but with the yobs literally in charge of the terraces, the clubs find it hard enough to keep hold of their fan base, let alone attract new supporters. In Hungary, TV images of a pensioner being punched in the face by a young fan of his own Ferencvaros team did more than just shock viewers. In the 12 months since that incident, the club's attendances have halved. "I used to follow Fradi regularly," says Peter, a 26-year-old Budapest marketing executive. "Even when the football became basically crap I still went because it was where I had always gone with my dad on a Saturday afternoon. But when you hear and see what is going on at the games now, it is not something you want to deal with. It's not worth it."

Without the Peters of this world, east European clubs with huge potential, like Ferencvaros, are seeing their market shrink. Western advisors tell them to expand their merchandising and increase ticket prices, but there are fewer and fewer people who identify with the clubs. How many sponsors want to be associated with people who punch pensioners? The problem for the west is that while the clubs are struggling financially, some parts of the east are getting wealthier. Hungary, Poland and the Czech Republic will soon enter the EU. The small band of VIPs who currently follow eastern teams in Europe may soon be supplemented by the less refined supporters who will be able to afford travel and won't need a visa. Then the problem will land on UEFA's doorstep. The television companies won't be happy at spending millions on the rights to Champions League matches abandoned after anti-terrorist units are forced to intervene to stop skinheads attacking Ajax supporters.

UEFA won't accept that. They will fine and ban clubs with trouble-makers. The east European clubs will be out of sight again, with less money and less chance than ever of getting on level terms with the west. And European football will be even less diverse, less colourful and less interesting than it is now. ○

Eurovision

Rangers and Celtic declared that they wanted to leave the Scottish Premier League. Gary Oliver felt that it couldn't happen soon enough

WSC No 164, October 2000

THE NEW PREMIER LEAGUE SEASON had barely begun when BBC Scotland breathlessly announced that Rangers and Celtic intend to quit Scottish football, the pair ganging up with soul mates from abroad within two years. For viewers who had just switched over to Friday Sportscene from Channel 4, and who felt they had heard this one before, it was perhaps appropriate that the story was broken straight after Eurotrash.

Celtic's desire to forsake Scotland is well documented, and their recent announcement of a £6 million trading loss has concentrated minds still further. For much of last season, chief executive Allan MacDonald talked up the prospects of a renegade North Atlantic League, in which Celtic would band together with the most powerful clubs in Holland, Belgium, Portugal and Scandinavia.

The proposals then were vague and contradictory and the notion of an ersatz Champions League evidently did not impress UEFA. Now it is envisaged that much the same B-list teams will compete together instead of at home, the domestic competitions to feed the new monster. No one has yet explained how this set-up might interact with the Champions League, though rest assured the clubs involved are not contemplating life without wallowing in that trough too. With relatively few countries reported to be involved, it is a format that might seem to have a very limited shelf life. Nevertheless, Rangers, hitherto wary of compromising any Champions League involvement, have now performed a handbrake turn and come out in support of such an arrangement.

Yet it is only a few months since chairman David Murray, proclaiming his "sense of responsibility", denounced Celtic's posturing as "detrimental to Scottish football". But now, warning that "something dramatic must be done", he judges that "we are hindering Scottish football... it would be better for other clubs not to financially strain themselves trying to keep up with Rangers and Celtic". This is the man who in January claimed that without the Old Firm Scottish football would be "all over bar the shouting". One must therefore assume that Murray's summer *volte-face* was prompted not by altruism, but by the embarrassment of various foreign strikers declining to take his shilling.

The history of the Scottish Premier League is of clubs maximising and preserving their fixtures with Rangers and Celtic. It is perhaps surprising, then, that this latest Euro model has received general approval from other clubs within the SPL. The possibility of at least one other Scottish side becoming involved, plus the promise of compensation payments to the rump, has ensured that most club officials are on-message. "The league is a logical extension of how businesses are marketing themselves in Europe now," observed Hearts' Chris Robinson, possibly sensing an opportunity to recoup some of the £1.4m lost by his club in the past six months.

Lex Gold, the chairman of the SPL, has insisted that for SPL clubs of all levels the Euro proposal is "win, win, win". And most pundits are also quite relaxed at the prospect of a Scottish League shorn of the Old Firm. One dissenter on Radio Scotland, Keith Jackson of the *Daily Record*, opined that Scottish fans would miss the "razzamatazz" that surrounds Rangers and Celtic. Yes, much as the people of Northern Ireland would miss the "razzamatazz" of the Drumcree march. A few other pessimists have warned of the remnant sinking to the level of the League of Ireland; however, Aberdeen's UEFA Cup humbling by Bohemians indicates it is a little late to be worrying about that particular comparison.

With Rangers and Celtic now openly contemptuous of the domestic competition, many opposing fans will feel that the sooner they go the better. A league bereft of the duo should certainly produce what most Scots yearn for – a top division that is truly competitive. But whether the Scottish champions would then be allowed on board the gravy train, even temporarily, is anyone's guess. Any European league designed to cosset clubs already oligarchic at home is unlikely to be a genuine meritocracy.

Now all the talk is of how the larger television audience will enable clubs to inflate even further the wages they offer. Small wonder, then, that Stig Nilsson of Swedish league leaders Halmstad rejected the group's pecuniary priority, condemning the agitators as "people who let themselves be hypnotised by thoughts of money". But only if UEFA now reacts by further expanding its existing competitions are Rangers, Celtic and the others likely to snap out of it. ○

Passing the Port

Tim Springett explained why Portsmouth fans still thought of their club as regional top dogs, despite statistical evidence in Southampton's favour

WSC No 164, October 2000

THE RIVALRY BETWEEN Southampton and Portsmouth is arguably as intense as exists between any two clubs in the country. More than 20 miles separate the two, but in football terms they represent something of an outpost. For the clubs of Hampshire's main seaports, supremacy of the south coast and indeed the whole of the south of England is at stake.

Quite why the feeling between the two is so fierce is not easy to understand, though there are obvious starting points. The two cities have a great deal in common – their populations are of similar size and both are major seaports. Neither is the county town of Hampshire (that honour belongs to Winchester) so there is no "natural" pecking order between the two. One theory is that ill feeling was originally fostered by an occasion early in the 20th century when non-union labour from Southampton was brought in to break a dock strike in Portsmouth. One (probably far-fetched) interpretation of the term "scummer" which fans of each club apply to the other, is that it was an acronym for a particular collective of non-union dock workers.

To the chagrin of Portsmouth fans and the amusement of those of Southampton, it is now 40 seasons since Pompey were in a higher division than Saints. Yet it is a brave soul who suggests in the vicinity of Fratton Park that the Saints are the principal football power of the region. Whether caused by fond memories of past glories or simply a bloody-minded refusal to accept the evidence provided by form since the early Sixties, the idea held by Portsmouth folk that theirs is the important club in the area appears unshakeable. For much of the 20th century, Portsmouth were the more successful side. Southampton FC predates its neighbour by 13 years, won the Southern League in the 1890s and reached the FA Cup final in 1900 and 1902. But Pompey soon developed into a force themselves and both clubs were founder members of the Third Division South in 1920. Pompey reached the top flight by 1927 – 39 years before the Saints made it that far.

After the war, manager Bob Jackson steered Pompey to the First Division championship in 1949 and 1950. In the year of Jackson's departure, 1953, the Saints dropped back down to the Third Division South, further emphasising the supremacy of the Fratton Park club. But the balance would soon change. In 1959 Pompey slipped into the Second where Saints rose to meet them the following year. From that point on Saints were strongly in the ascendancy. In 1966 Ted Bates led them into the First Division and, aside from a four-year absence in the mid-1970s, they have remained in the top flight ever since. It was during the Saints' spell back in the Second Division that they brought the FA Cup back to the south coast, beating Manchester United 1-0 in the 1976 final. Particularly galling for Pompey fans was the fact that the scorer of the goal, Bobby Stokes, was born and bred in Portsmouth. Even more depressingly, Pompey dropped into the Third Division that year and two years later they found themselves relegated to the basement – just as Southampton were returning to the top flight.

Why did Pompey fall so far while the Saints were rising inexorably? The clubs' managerial roll-calls provide a clue. From the end of the Second World War to 1991, the Saints had six managers. In the same period Pompey had 15. Southampton, apart from the 1996 stock market flotation and the recent managerial muscial chairs, have been a stable, solvent club whereas Pompey have changed owners regularly and lurched from one financial crisis to another. And while Saints have been renowned for years for the quality of their youth system, Pompey scrapped all teams other than the first team in 1964 in order to cut costs. Future England captain (and Southampton stalwart) Mick Mills was a casualty of this falsest of economies before the youth system was reinstated.

Almost certainly the desire to prove Portsmouth's claim to be the region's top club was a significant factor behind the desperate financial imprudence that has afflicted the club for so long. Back in 1971-72 Pompey's accounts showed a loss of £92,000, but just two seasons later, with John Deacon installed as chairman, £400,000 was spent on new players. This was at a time when only one player in the whole country had ever been transferred for more than £250,000. But three seasons on, with Pompey in 22nd place in the Third Division, Deacon was forced to call a public meeting to launch SOS Pompey, which raised £35,000 to keep the club in business.

How painful it must have been for Pompey to watch the Saints' progress. The 1976 FA Cup win was followed two seasons later by promotion back to the top flight, then the arrival of Kevin Keegan, described at the time as the transfer coup of the century. Regular high league placings culminated in the runners-up spot in 1984. Even Keith Chegwin rubbed salt into the wounds. During a Radio 1 roadshow in Southsea he spoke on air to a youngster who said he liked football. Cheggers' corking response was: "That's not surprising with Southampton and Kevin Keegan just up the road!" In the 1980s Pompey, now sandwiched geographically between two top flight outfits with Brighton having joined Southampton among the elite, staged a recovery, finally returning to the First Division in 1987. But they lasted just one season and Deacon sold out to ex-QPR supremo Jim Gregory. Nevertheless, their fans did at least enjoy the satisfaction of a 2-0 victory in the last league derby at The Dell.

Local derbies are rare these days. Aside from that 1987-88 season the only meetings between the two sides since the mid-Seventies have been two FA Cup ties. The first was at Fratton Park in January 1984 – a game billed as the "match of the decade" in the local media and watched by a crowd of 36,000. As far as Saints fans were concerned the description was entirely apposite. Steve Moran scored the only goal of the game in injury time and Lawrie McMenemy famously made light of the coins and fruit hurled at Mark Dennis and Danny Wallace respectively during the game. "We've got a good result, £4.50 in small change and two pounds of bananas to take home," he beamed afterwards.

Twelve years later came the most recent encounter, in the third round at The Dell. Though they had been struggling to find any sort of league form, the home side strolled to a comfortable 3-0 win. Pompey's abject performance that Sunday morning should have shattered any illusion that they, rather than their Premiership neighbours, were the region's top team. But try telling that to anybody in the Fratton End. O

A Special Occasion?

As part of a regular series, Chris Fyfe exploded the myth that the FA Cup final is watched around the world

WSC No 164, October 2000

IF YOU TELL A LIE often enough it becomes the truth. In the days when *World of Sport* and *Grandstand* both covered the FA Cup final, Frank Bough and Dickie Davies told us that two billion people were watching the game live. We believed them.

Even those of us who watched the Scottish Cup final instead believed them, despite the evidence of our own eyes. For no sooner had the world been welcomed to Wembley than we would be transported to Archie MacPherson in the BBC *Sportscene* studio or to the slow motion world of Arthur Montford on STV. But Scotland is a small country and there could easily be another two billion around the world watching the English final. Frank Bough wouldn't lie.

May 1992, Guyana. Roll forward 15 years and I am a VSO volunteer in Georgetown. With a few other friends we embark on the hunt for someone with a telly who knows what channel will show the match. I ask my Guyanese colleagues which channel will have the Cup final. I get bemused looks. Responses vary from "Why would anyone want to watch football when we can't even get Test matches?" to "What sport is that?". We listened to the match on the World Service.

May 1993, Guyana, 10.30am (1.30pm BST). Roll forward one more year. A Brazilian diplomat surreptitiously helps us to open up his embassy, which has a six-foot gyroscopic satellite dish that fries any passing tropical birds. We have a dish, we have someone who knows how to work it, we're near the equator and there are 90 minutes to go through every channel in the world. We did go through every channel in the world. We saw the *Bold and the Beautiful* in English, we saw *Dallas* in French, we saw numerous Argentinean soap operas (including an episode about the secret drug habit of the world's best footballer), we saw lots of Brazilian motor sport. We got Canal Plus, we got Russian current affairs programmes, we got more American religious broadcasting than anyone could stomach.

Wembley, 2.45 pm. The crowds have moved from singing *We Are The*

Champions to *Abide With Me*. The Princess/Duchess of Wherever is in the royal box. Meanwhile, back in Georgetown, the thought dawns: we have been systematically lied to. No one else is interested in the FA Cup final; no one else thinks Wembley is the home of football. Few know that the match is even taking place and fewer care.

Three pm. *God Save The Queen* has been belted out in a manner ill-befitting a dirge. The captains have tossed up and shaken hands. The ref blows the whistle and supposedly the greatest football occasion on the planet commences. There is a power cut in the Brazilian embassy in Guyana; the lights flutter out and a debate is started on whether to put the generator on or just go to the national park and play football. One last chance. On we go, trying and trying, winding the dish across the heavens.

Three-fifteen pm. No idea what's happening at Wembley. We give up. Such was our belief in the power of Frank Bough that no one thought of bringing a radio to listen to the game. We trooped off to the park, despondent and defeated, where we were even more outclassed by the Brazilians than usual.

May 1995, Goma, Zaire. There is a large satellite dish attached to the house in which I am staying. I make discreet enquiries. The TV can, I am told, pick up a local channel, a few French ones and... Canal Plus. My heart sinks as I remember. I persuade people to wind the satellite around to try all the channels available. It doesn't take long. Sure enough, there is no coverage in Zaire, nor in nearby Rwanda or Burundi. It's like finding out that Santa Claus doesn't exist or Elvis is dead. You can't get the FA Cup final live in 200 countries. A childhood truth smashed. ○

Forward Move

The European Commission wanted to scrap football's transfer system. Pierre Lanfranchi and Matthew Taylor argued that such a move might bring the industry up to date
WSC No 165, November 2000

IMAGINE FOOTBALL without transfer fees. Journalists, financial analysts and sports lawyers – not to mention directors, managers and players – have apparently been doing little else since the European Commission's "shock" announcement that the present system of clubs profiting from the movement of players must come to an end. In Britain at least, predictions have tended towards the catastrophic: take away transfer fees and small clubs would die, top players would earn even more and all manner of chaos would ensue.

The Commission's intervention has been widely interpreted as a reaction to the spiralling fees in European football which culminated this summer in the deals involving Hernan Crespo and Luis Figo. More specifically, it was prompted by the action of Perugia in successfully objecting to the payment of a fee for the transfer of Massimo Lombardo from Grasshoppers Zürich. In truth, however, the EC's intervention is not really about Crespo, Figo or Lombardo. It is the latest – possibly the last – offensive in a long battle to force football to accept its status as an industry like any other.

Introduced in England in 1890, the transfer system was primarily intended to control the mobility of players. Where they had been free agents able to sell their labour to the highest bidder, footballers were now effectively the property of their employers. In order to prevent the poaching of players and ensure a stable workforce, the Football League created a system which deprived footballers of the basic right to freedom of movement. Clubs as well as players were often critical of the system but preferred to curb its excesses rather than abolish it. In 1908, the FA imposed a maximum limit of £350 on fees but this was evaded by the purchase of makeweight players and lasted only three months. Between the wars, Arsenal and Everton led a series of unsuccessful campaigns by the richer clubs to cap transfers in an attempt to reduce costs.

By the 1960s, there was a general feeling that the transfer market was out of control. Incensed by the vast sums changing hands for transfers in Britain and abroad – specifically the £250,000 which Roma paid Mantova for Angelo Sormani in 1963 – *World Soccer* called for urgent legislation, even putting forward its own suggestion of a surcharge on all transfer fees which would then be divided among clubs of the appropriate national league.

France alone rejected the need for a formal transfer system. In 1969, an agreement between the players' union and the national league abolished the "life contract" which had bound players to a club until the age of 35. New regulations stipulated that at the end of a contract "whose duration was agreed by both parties", the player was free to sign for whichever employer he chose. Unless it was the player's first move – in which case "development compensation" was paid – his former club was entitled neither to oppose the transaction nor ask for compensation. Transfer rules in other European countries became less rigid in the control of player movement, but the legitimacy of the system itself was rarely questioned.

One reason the transfer system has survived unchallenged for so long is the idea that it is fundamental to the survival of football as we know it. This rests on a number of related assumptions. The sale of players from smaller to larger clubs, it is argued, allows the former to stay afloat, while the redistribution of income ensures the economic viability of the competition as a whole. Transfer payments are also believed to act both as a reward for, and a stimulant to, the development of young talent, and the system is assumed to guarantee a certain amount of continuity in playing personnel. Without it, in the words of PFA boss Gordon Taylor, "Football clubs would become like Euston station, with different players arriving, staying for a short while and leaving again almost non-stop."

We tend to accept all this because the football authorities have been telling us as much for over 100 years. From the beginning, the transfer system was defended as a means of maintaining some degree of competitive balance between teams by preventing the wealthier clubs snapping up the best talent. As early as 1906, the England and West Bromwich Albion forward William Bassett, later to become a director at The Hawthorns, was convinced that without the sums received from selling players, clubs like his would be forced out of business. Such assertions have been repeated so often over the years that they have come to be regarded as established facts.

Yet there is surprisingly little evidence that the transfer system has ever done what its defenders say it has. Recent studies have called into question the "common sense" view that it has operated to the benefit of football as a whole. Transfer money has rarely simply trickled down from the top to the lower divisions. Most trade has always been confined to bigger clubs and even when funds have filtered down, they are often concentrated at a small number of selling clubs. Some smaller clubs may have used the transfer system as a means of survival, but many others have consistently shown a transfer deficit, spending more on players than they receive in return.

If the transfer system has been ineffective in redistributing wealth, then its abolition might actually be beneficial by convincing the authorities to consider more explicit means of subsidising the poor. It was less than 20 years ago that schemes existed for sharing revenue from gate receipts and television contracts. The greed of the top clubs and then the creation of the Premiership put an end to that, but if we are genuinely interested in the fate of the small fry there is no reason why something similar cannot be put in place.

It is much too easy to be suspicious of the EU and its alleged attempts to "interfere" with football. Such an attitude is in keeping with the arrogance of an industry which has chosen to ignore European law for decades. National federations have remained convinced that community law did not apply to sport, despite the fact that two cases which reached the European Court of Justice in the 1970s confirmed it was illegal to restrict movement on the basis of nationality.

The Bosman ruling should have put an end to all this. Yet we continue to hear about football's right to be seen as a special case. The sooner we realise that football is not a world within a world, the sooner we can search for a system which will guarantee the rights of players and secure the financial future of clubs. Or is that asking too much? O

2001

Always Afraid to Miss

Tony Cascarino's exceptional autobiography told some harsh truths about himself and about players' lives, said Dave Hill

WSC No 167, January 2001

OH BOY. HARK AT THIS: "It has often been said that the joy of scoring goals is greater than sex but personally I'd compare it more with masturbation. I've always found sex to be an absolute pleasure, but scoring goals has only ever brought relief." The search for relief – by foot rather than by hand – and the misery of not finding it, is the key theme and metaphor of this book: a book which, at its best, is almost unbearable.

"Fifty thousand Celtic fans jump to their feet... They see Tony Cascarino slipping his marker and breaking free. They see the winger cross the ball low to the striker's feet. They see a million pound player in front of an open Rangers goal with a glorious opportunity at his feet... They do not see the fear on my face at that moment. They do not believe their eyes when I swipe frantically and completely miss the target. They do not feel compassion when I fall to my knees and cover my face in shame."

There are lots of other voices in *Full Time*. There's the voice of Jack Charlton, for example, explaining to Cascarino why he had dropped him from the Ireland team after a poor showing in training: "You were fucking crap!" Ken Bates gets a word in: "I don't want another fucking disaster like Cascarino." And then there's Liam Brady, his manager at Celtic: "What the fuck is going on, Tony? You were a disaster! I've never seen you play so badly!" A Celtic fan, too, makes this fragrant contribution: "You're fucking shit, you. You're a useless big bastard."

But most vividly of all there is the little voice of doubt inside the striker's own head. Here it is January 1984, when Cascarino, playing for his first club Gillingham, bears down on Neville Southall in the last extra-time moments of an FA Cup replay, with no Everton defender for miles around, the score 0-0, and giant-killing glory within his grasp:

"Any striker worth his salt will put this ball in the net."

"Yeah but..."

"This is your big chance."

"It's not as easy as it looks, you know."

"You're shitting yourself, aren't you?"

"No, I..."

"You're going to miss."

He did. It was a miss he would relive a thousand times, a miss captured by television cameras and reshown over and over as one of the great misses, a miss that probably helped save Howard Kendall's job, as the then Everton manager reminds Cascarino every time they meet.

The news angle on this book has been its revelation that Cascarino was never actually qualified to play for Ireland: only later did he discover that his mother – maiden name O'Malley – had been mistaken in her belief that her parents had been born in the Republic thereby entitling her son to pull on the green shirt. But the real story here is that a professional footballer has given us a look at his own soul and with it the soul of the game he played until his hair was turning grey and his knees could take no more.

The publishers describe *Full Time* as "a football autobiography that reads like a novel" and they're not far wrong. The nearest thing to it that I have read previously is an unjustly forgotten pre-soccerati novel called *Striker* by Michael Irwin, a professor of English. Its fictional anti-hero, one Vin Gilpin, had much in common with Cascarino: chronic crises of confidence, failures of form and attitude he couldn't understand, a sporting life of drift and gloom as well as some rich rewards.

Full Time tells of good times: up front with Sheringham at Millwall, adventures with the Irish, his strange Indian summer in France with

Marseille and Nancy. The dominating mood, though, is of pathos and regret. Cascarino looks back ruefully at boozy indiscretions, the card schools, the lure of BMW catalogues, the two million quid in earnings he has somehow frittered away. But there is much, much more than just the hazy self-pity of a fading athlete afraid of facing up to the remainder of his life.

He reflects candidly on his sexual infidelities and the resulting distance between himself and his two sons. He looks back on his own childhood, his unhappy family, his love for his mother, the brutal beatings he endured from his father. And he provides telling insights into dressing room cultures where players inspire and police each other to remain in a state of permanent puerility, often stupid, sometimes poisonous, but so seductive nonetheless. What was there to do except join in?

Cascarino's openness is exceptional and welcome. So too is the way he appears to have worked with journalist Paul Kimmage, chief sportswriter with Ireland's *Sunday Independent*. Even the best "ghost job" football memoirs reflect master-servant relationships between the star and the hack, who is generally obliged to put PR before the truth. *Full Time*, by contrast, has the refreshing feel of a true collaboration; the player provides the anecdotes, the experiences, the emotions, the writer weaves them into a prose that does them proper justice. If only all books about football men were even half this good. ○

Gurgle No More

Lots of people said nice things about veteran commentator David Coleman when he retired from the BBC. Harry Pearson wasn't one of them

WSC No 168, February 2001

TRYING TO DECIDE who is the best football commentator of all time is clearly a pointless exercise, on a par with arguing over who is the better looking, Kevin Phillips or Phil Stamp. Nevertheless, the news that the BBC will not be renewing David Coleman's contract has provoked just such a debate and a recent convening of the Radio Five sports panel, among others, unanimously declared the septuagenarian gurgler from

Stockport the greatest ever. Friends who know about such things assure me this is complete rubbish and that Martin Tyler is much better. But that, of course, depends on what you see as the football commentator's prime role. It would be nice to think commentators were like referees – best when you didn't notice they were there. Unfortunately, this is not the case. My considered opinion based on 30 years' experience is that the TV companies do not choose individuals such as Alan Parry and Tony Gubba by mere fluke.

No, these men have been selected only after careful scrutiny by a panel of experts who have judged them solely on their ability to bore into the viewers' subconscious and then remorselessly hammer away until even the most mild-mannered citizen finds him or herself out of their chair yelling "What game are you watching, you moron?" at images of Roy Keane spitting. If their ability to irritate is the criterion by which commentators are to be measured (and all the evidence says it is) then there is little doubt that David Coleman is indeed unparalleled in history.

John Motson may get your goat with his bizarre belief in the significance of trivial facts or Barry Davies send you round the twist with his portentous phrasemaking. Possibly Brian Moore had you grating your teeth by adopting that Churchillian rasp whenever Tony Adams flattened a foreigner or maybe Clive Tyldesley's ability to sound as though he is shouting even when he is talking normally has you pinging off the walls. Compared to Coleman, however, these men are nothing. They are one trick ponies, he is the circus.

First there is the voice, a cross between a blocked drain and a rather pompous sea-lion, with that pubescent break that always cut in at moments of high excitement. (Coleman was rarely more than one stop away from high excitement – on Cup final day even the sight of the Duke of Kent coming out to greet the teams had him croaking and wheezing like an asthmatic bullfrog in the throes of sexual ecstasy.) Nobody, not even secret agents trained to resist North Korean brainwashing techniques, could listen to that for 90 minutes without at some point hitting their head repeatedly against an immovable object.

Then there were the words. Let's deal first with Coleman's beloved catchphrase, "Wwwwon-nil!". A true masterpiece, you might say, the very quintessence of the TV commentator's art, since it tells us absolutely nothing we cannot see for ourselves. Indeed, its sole function seems to be to afford the viewer the chance to shout "Thank you so much for sharing that insight with us" in a sarcastic voice.

When he got fancy things were even worse. Coleman apparently regarded himself as a hard-nosed journalist (whether, as rumoured, he really had to beat off the challenge of Woodward and Bernstein to host *A Question of Sport* is hotly debated in press rooms across the land) but much of his phrasemaking sounded more like Edward Lear than Ed Morrow. After Liverpool's opener against Newcastle in the 1974 Cup final, Coleman warbled: "Goals pay the rent and Keegan does his share." This, on first hearing, appears to make absolutely no sense, but on closer analysis it is revealed, in fact, to make absolutely no sense whatsoever.

Liverpool's third goal that day provoked an even stranger outburst: "And Newcastle were completely undressed." This bizarre utterance has lived with me ever since I first heard it as a 13-year-old. What other commentator could have conjured up the nightmarish vision of Tommy Smith and Emlyn Hughes with practised hands deftly removing Bobby Moncur's undergarments, and thrust it into a nation's sitting rooms on a sunny afternoon in May? No, indeed, there will never be another like him. Thank God. ○

G Forces

Who were the G-14 and what did they want? John Sugden investigated the gathering threat to UEFA's control of European club football

WSC No 168, February 2001

MANCHESTER UNITED, ARSENAL AND LEEDS are all through to the second group phase of the Champions League but, while that may induce a sense of wellbeing in England, we should not be blinded by the glitz and glamour to the reality that European club football is mired deep in crisis. Already reeling from the unfolding consequences of Bosman and the latest European Union attack on the transfer system, UEFA are faced with a new double challenge to their monopoly over the European game. As usual, the essence of the latest crisis boils down to money, or, to be more precise, who generates the cash and who gets their hands on the lion's share of it.

Leading the challenge to UEFA's authority are G-14, the self-styled elite of clubs who have established an exclusive lobbying cartel and set up offices in Brussels. The G7 group of the world's most powerful national economies inspired the name and G-14 comprises mainly the richest clubs from Italy, Spain, England, Germany, Holland, Portugal and France. Like the Cosa Nostra, the exact formula for membership is mysterious, but it clearly has to do with money, success and potential television audience. Not surprisingly, the richest club in the world, Manchester United, is in, but Chelsea and Arsenal, ranked fourth and tenth respectively in the world club rich list, are not. Liverpool, at No 11, are included, whereas Lazio, ranked No 8, are not.

G-14 portray themselves as nothing more than a group of like-minded football club owners and administrators, but the fact that they head-hunted UEFA's fixtures co-ordinator to head their Brussels operation suggests otherwise. There can be little doubt that G-14 is the thin end of a wedge that looks likely to pioneer the establishment of a breakaway European super league. What sets G-14 apart from previous failed breakaway attempts, such as the Murdoch-backed Media Partners initiative of 1998, is the fact that G-14 includes the clubs which are the leading producers of the European football industry. Without their co-operation, UEFA are out of business.

The motive behind the G-14 initiative is blindingly simple – greed. It is estimated that globally football generates in excess of $250 billion, of which more than 75 per cent comes from Europe. The G-14 clubs argue that it is they who provide the facilities, fans, and muscle and blood, without which none of this cash would flow, and therefore they should have more say in how the spectacle is produced and where the money ends up. Incidentally, this is the very argument that G-14 club presidents decry when it comes from players and agents, accusing them of being too greedy.

Under UEFA's current arrangements for the Champions League, G-14 feel they are getting a raw deal. In response to earlier threats of secession, UEFA relaxed the criteria for inclusion in the Champions League, allowing entry for up to three clubs from the strongest leagues and two from the weaker countries, in order to ensure that as many of the big clubs as possible qualify. This led to an expanded format within which the mega-clubs, somewhat ungraciously, now claim they are required to play too many meaningless games against lesser teams in an already over crowded domestic and international football calendar. As illustrated by Barcelona's untimely exit this season, no matter how hard UEFA try to rig it, there can be no guarantee that the big clubs will always get through to the lucrative final stages of the competition. With massive wage bills, impatient and success-hungry shareholders, sponsors and fans, "maybe next season" is no longer good enough for the business planning of Europe's top clubs. The G-14 also object to the way UEFA taxes the rich to feed the poor, taking a slice of Champions League revenue, ostensibly to prop up weaker European clubs and leagues, but also to bankroll its own operation in Switzerland. If G-14 set up on their own, they reason, payments such as these would be unnecessary.

UEFA's initial response to the establishment of G-14 was bellicose. With the backing of most national football associations, UEFA threatened to expel G-14 members from all European football, domestic or otherwise. It was a threat that didn't cut much ice with Karl-Heinz Rummenigge who, speaking on behalf of G-14, pointed out: "Twelve of these 14 clubs are Champions League clubs. The same day that they kick us out of UEFA they can close their Champions League shop."

To make matters worse, clubs on Europe's northern and western fringes, including a sprinkling of G-14 members, have also proposed the establishment of an Atlantic League, a transcontinental, weekend competition for clubs who have significant local and continental followings, but who play most of their football in relatively minor leagues. The odd derby match notwithstanding, clubs like Rangers and Celtic, Ajax, Benfica and Anderlecht cannot sustain big enough television audiences to attract the massive media-sponsor contracts that have inflated the football cash bubble elsewhere in Europe. Combining would give them a potential TV audience of 60 million. Of course, the Atlantic League would require participating clubs to withdraw from existing domestic leagues, virtually guaranteeing the collapse of professional football in some countries, particularly the smaller ones such as Scotland.

Faced with this second front, UEFA's hard man tactics look to be failing. General secretary Gerhard Aigner has conceded: "The Champions League in its current format has reached the end of its life. We must find a new formula in which there will be fewer matches, but the proposal to install a special league for a limited number of clubs is not the solution." We have heard this all before, of course. In fact, it was the same argument that led to the development of the Champions League in the first place and its subsequent expanded format. It usually results in a fudge, whereby the big clubs get most of what they want in new and increasingly elite competitive structures, but still nominally under UEFA control. In a belated attempt to limit the scope of such restructuring, UEFA have immodestly issued what they call their "ten command-ments" as a framework within which European club competitions can be discussed. This smacks of high-minded protectionist hypocrisy. The Champions League was always a business concept and never a football development. From day one it has been driven by a closeted network of media and commercial interests held together by TEAM, UEFA's media-marketing partner.

If between them, instead of looking after their own short-term financial and status interests, UEFA and FIFA had established and operated principles such as these 20 years ago, then perhaps football might have been saved from total surrender to the entertainment industry. Now it's probably too late. Rather than protecting the European game from the more pernicious effects of naked entrepreneurialism, UEFA have been serious collaborators in its total commodification. It is naive of UEFA to think that they, the instigators of the Champions League, can now hold back the commercial tide. ○

Johnny Foreigner

For a feature on the UK's football emigrants, Phil Ball profiled John Toshack, who was then the only British coach working at the top level in a major European league

WSC No 169, March 2001

"WHETHER IT'S WITH A BOTTLE OF CLARET, a good rioja, a glass of raki or a decent port, the attraction's still the same – come away after 90 minutes with the three points," said the peripatetic Welshman John Toshack, in an article penned just before Christmas from St Etienne for *El Diario Vasco*, the Basque newspaper with whom he had signed a contract at the beginning of the year to write a weekly column. His Bacchanalian refer-ences were, of course, a nod to all the countries in which he has managed a football team, although he seems to have had some problem recalling his Welsh spell, unless he was alluding in the opening clause to some new strain of Swansea claret. Toshack's current interests are clearly identi-fiable in his cultural shorthand, but one should beware of assuming that the only reason for his now impressive international credentials is that he is constantly in search of the good life. What Toshack seems unable to resist, to quote that old curriculum vitae cliche, is a challenge – and this fact, combined with his now famous tendency to ruffle feathers wherever he goes, has meant that he has moved around quite a bit since cutting his management teeth at the Vetch Field all those years ago.

Toshack has come a long way from his original Cardiff roots, and, Bobby Robson aside, has succeeded in becoming practically the only high-profile British footballer ever to manage such an array of top clubs in different countries. Real Madrid twice, Sporting Lisbon, Besiktas, Deportivo de La Coruña, St Etienne and his beloved Real Sociedad – to whom he has just returned for a third spell – plus Swansea and a brief flirtation with the Welsh national side. You might be forgiven for thinking he was older than his 51 years.

It's an impressive haul, and one in which he has rarely gone too long without some sort of success– be it the giddy romp through the divisions with Swansea, the league title with Madrid, the Spanish cup with Real Sociedad, the Turkish one with Besiktas, third place in the Spanish league with Deportivo in 1997 and two months with St Etienne in which he at least got them off the bottom of the league. Although Robson's own record cannot be sniffed at, as a footballer he belongs to a different generation. There remains a sneaking feeling about "the great procrastinator", as Brian Glanville once called him, that he has somehow stumbled amiably through Europe, inheriting great sides, never quite understanding the cultures he had landed in, ending up back at his roots pretty much the same old guy that he had been at the beginning.

Toshack, although his playing career belonged to the distant era of dodgy sideburns, is a postwar baby, "Euroman" incarnate; a working-class product who has succeeded in burying his roots to such an extent that the only place which now seems closed to him is England. Once upon a time his name would occasionally be linked with the job at Liverpool (even Newcastle after Kevin Keegan quit) and although he could undoubtedly contribute his experience to the Premiership you get the feeling, when you listen to him speak, that it just wouldn't be his scene any more. He doesn't spend much time in Britain now, except when he is between jobs and is hauled in for some Euro commentary analysis. He bought a house some years ago in Zarautz, a pretty coastal resort west of San Sebastián, and the Basque Country has always been his refuge, not Wales or Liverpool.

A couple of years ago Keegan, being interviewed on a late-night British chat-show, was linked up live to Toshack, in Madrid, on a large screen in the studio. Keegan came over as lap-doggish, almost naive, speaking to Toshack as if in awe of his sophistication. Toshack himself seemed to have left his old mate light years behind, tolerating his embarrassing reminiscences with a paternal smile and indulging him with a rather tired sort of matiness. The whole episode was vaguely discomforting, and it wasn't difficult to spot Toshack's boredom.

He has never suffered fools easily. He has been involved in some astonishingly bitter episodes over the past 15 years, but it has never put other directors off signing him. What you seem to get in the package now is a hard-bitten tactical nous, meticulous attention to detail and a "Don't mess with me" sort of stare that impresses a certain kind of president and player. In 1986, his first season with Real Sociedad, one of the players dared to laugh during the post-match hotel supper in Oviedo, where they had lost rather lamely 2-1 in a cup match. Standing up in the midst of the throng Toshack ordered the players to be on the bus at 4.30am for the trip back to San Sebastián. When they arrived home at about 9am he ordered them off the coach and on to the training ground – a legendary incident that they still talk about in the city.

In a sense, he only got away with it because something in his manner suggests he is both sympathetic and open to the cultures he often confronts. The Basques, not an easy people to win over, like him and treat him almost as one of their own, even forgiving his two spells in Madrid. Toshack likes the Basques too, and makes no secret of it. When he went to manage Deportivo over in Galicia in the mid-Nineties, he failed to win their confidence precisely because they suspected him of spending too much time playing golf in Zarautz and not dedicating enough to La Coruña. During a barren spell there, Toshack stood up and faced the crowd as they celebrated a rare goal, famously mouthing "¡Sí – auplaudid cabrones!" (Yeah – you're applauding now, you bastards), a sort of personal challenge to a whole community whose culture, he was implying, was not up to it as far as he was concerned. Toshack has not only managed in many countries but also in three very distinct cultures within Spain – Galicia, the Basque Country and Castile – and he has understood, if not necessarily liked – all of them.

At Besiktas, he became notorious for his lack of sympathy with the young goalkeeper Fevzi, which did not greatly enhance Toshack's standing when the player attempted to commit suicide (though there is no evidence to suggest one caused the other). He also fell foul of the press by suggesting military service was unimportant and should not interfere with a player's career. Despite all this, he only left because he could not resist the challenge of sorting out Real Madrid, and the Turks would apparently take him back tomorrow were he available. Back at Madrid, called in by the floundering president Lorenzo Sanz to sort out the ego problems in the changing-rooms, Toshack set about alienating just about everyone as if he no longer cared. In his first spell there in the late Eighties, he had refused to be cowed by the capital's notoriously bitchy press, and they had got him sacked in the end.

This time it was his endearing tendency to translate phrases from English directly into Spanish that finally moved Sanz to give him the push. Toshack declared to the football tabloid *Marca* that he would rather "see pigs fly over the Bernabéu" than take back what he had said the previous day about the higher echelons of the club. In Spanish, the phrase made it sound as if Toshack was referring to Sanz himself – a famous misunderstanding, but one that saw Toshack leave through the back door for the last time. At least he knows how to speak the language, idiosyncratically but fluently. Like Michael Robinson, another import turned native, he seems funnier and smarter in Spanish than in English, as if he has genuinely benefited from the alter ego that another language can provide. And now he's back at Real Sociedad, with his pals down the golf club and the Michelin forked restaurant next door to his house.

After the 4-1 win at Santander at the end of January, a mate of mine claimed to have seen him dining in a San Sebastián restaurant with Luis Arconada, the goalkeeper who failed to stop Gerry Armstrong's shot back in 1982. The Real Sociedad presidency is up for grabs in April and Arconada may stand. Toshack, a member of the club, was either weighing up his vote or, who knows, maybe eyeing the throne himself. He's certainly got the money. Watch this space. ○

Green Giant

None of Devon's three clubs can claim glorious, trophy-laden histories, yet, as Nick House showed, one seems to attract more than its fair share of attention

WSC No 169, March 2001

SOME YEARS AGO, Harry Pearson wrote a wonderful book about football in the north-east of England. By calling it *The Far Corner* he unwittingly paid a compliment to football west of Taunton Deane services by not labelling Devon as English football's outpost. Unfortunately, others continue to do so, portraying Devon football fans as wretched individuals who spend Saturdays travelling to Old Trafford courtesy of Taw and Torridge Coaches.

The Bideford Reds exist, as do the Hatherleigh Reds, the South Molton Reds and, sadly, the Torbay Reds. Yet an important geographical fact needs to be established –Devon is a big county. Barnstaple, for example, lies 40 miles from Exeter, 65 miles from both Torquay and Plymouth. The county's expanse has created two footballing Devons. North of Dartmoor is the land of Cities and Uniteds beyond the county boundary. Here, there is some interest in Plymouth, less in Exeter and very little in distant Torquay. The north boasts a Screwfix quartet but only Tiverton Town, further east, offer vibrancy. Twice winners of the FA Vase, now climbing into the Dr Martens, the county is sensing some kind of fourth force. In Devon, it is possible to become excited about having a half-decent non-League team.

The worry is that the other footballing Devon, the Exeter-Plymouth-Torquay triangle, may soon provide a non-League team of its own. The casual observer of this season's league tables is advised to read from the bottom up. Cup football has been worse: a solitary LDV victory against Bristol City reserves all season.

It's not a rich history. Certainly there have been promotions, a Sherpa Van final and seemingly numerous Wembley visits since Devonport Dockyard Apprentices played there in a 1970s youth club competition. Yet in terms of real national success there has been nothing more than Plymouth's 1984 FA Cup semi-final, two League Cup semi-finals and fourth places in the old second division when footballs were laced. The other two teams have never progressed beyond the present Second Division. Lack of success should not mask the intrigue of a football micro-culture. Rivalries are neither bitter nor vindictive, but they are keen and long established. Devon's football miracle is that Exeter have retained League status since 1920, Torquay since 1927. A shared local media, with just three clubs to cover (plus a bit of surfing and endless Cornish rugby), perpetuates the self-contained nature of the county's football. It is impossible to follow one team without being fully aware of the others.

Herein lies the grievance that fuels rivalries. Viewed from without, the absence of a big club suggests the local media might effortlessly divide its attention three ways. It does: 40-30-30 when even-handed, 50-25-25 when something exciting is happening at Home Park. Ever since Don "Argyle" Arnold fronted *Westward Sports Desk* in the 1960s (alongside youthful versions of Gary Newbon and David Vine) allegations of unseemly bias have been directed at Argyle Country TV, the *Western Morning Argyle*, the *Sunday Argyle* and BBC Radio Argyle. This, of course, is the staple of regional media and football supporters everywhere. The cries of anguish emanating from Exeter and Torquay will be no different than those coming from Swansea, Portsmouth, Middlesbrough, Bradford and Hull, but the imbalance is particularly transparent in an area with plenty of media and comparatively little sport to report. The dream team is only Plymouth Argyle after all. Not exactly a colossus to overshadow the rest.

But, if not huge, Plymouth is the most significant team in the county and, alone, enjoys support extending into Cornwall and other parts of the region. At times this is exaggerated to contrast Argyle with "parochial" Torquay and Exeter. This reached absurd proportions in 1996 when West Country TV reported Argyle's Third Division play-off victory as the greatest event in football history. Alas, the green-bedecked newscasters neither provided the context of this being the club's sixth promotion (the others being at a higher level) nor did they utter the unspoken truth that the region's most popular club is also the most unpopular.

Plymouth's local pre-eminence acts as a double-edged sword. When things go wrong at Home Park, as they frequently do, the regional media sinks its teeth into the club, whereas it could not be fussed to do so with Torquay or Exeter. Although this suggests the other two clubs matter less, it provides great entertainment for their supporters. Particular mirth arose when, as former manager Neil Warnock used the *Western Morning News* as his mouthpiece, the *Sunday Independent* provided a similar function for chairman Dan McCauley. As long as Desperate Dan remains at the helm there will be fun for all.

The fiercest rivalry, by far, is between Plymouth and Exeter, exacerbated by the rival city dimension. Exeter is the county town, Plymouth the largest centre. Exeter has legal and ecclesiastical pre-eminence, Plymouth commerce, industry and the media. Universities and rugby clubs compete. Torquay, by contrast, is somewhere to go for a nice time, a hard place to dislike. Torquay and Plymouth enjoyed a fiercer rivalry in the old Third Division together in the late 1960s. Middle-aged Torquay fans, mindful of the 6-0 defeat in 1969, may still see Plymouth as the team to beat, while younger fans, raised on games against Exeter, mostly see this as the main rivalry. Inevitably, on derby days, Torquay supporters are reminded of their irrelevance by opposition chants of "We only hate Argyle" and "We only hate City". It can be hard not being hated.

As Torquay and Exeter struggle at the bottom of the Third Division, it is apparent football in Devon will lose heavily if one is relegated. In wishing ill will upon their local rivals many may come to appreciate what will be lost by their departure. A partisan view is that, for all their failings, Exeter and Torquay remain the true heroes of Devon football and share an affinity of sorts. The cup semi-final appearances, the seasons in the old Second Division and the 33,000 fans at Wembley are all Argyle's. The better future is probably Argyle's. Yet Plymouth remain the great underachievers. Green-edged propaganda such as "if they were in the Premiership they'd get 35,000 down there every week" merely leads to knowing, wry smiles up the A38. ○

The Big Mismatch

Stan Collymore had retired after a career of unfulfilled promise. David Wangerin came to the conclusion that he simply ended up in the wrong job

WSC No 171, May 2001

SHOULD HAVE, WOULD HAVE, COULD HAVE. Dalian Atkinson springs to mind. All the tools you could want: strong, quick, good in the air, a nose for goal and always capable of the extraordinary. Should have been an England regular, could have guided Aston Villa to a championship or two, would have been one of the top strikers the club has ever seen. Drag out the video of his wonder-goal at Selhurst Park in 1992, the one where he runs through the entire Wimbledon team and plants the ball in the net with such graceful nonchalance. Even the strains of Clive Tyldesley's post facto commentary can't remove the lustre of such genius.

And what happened after that? You tell me. Dalian went on to miss a lot of first-team football at Villa, for reasons which remain unclear to many. He never figured in an England manager's plans, never played for a title contender, never came close to doing on the pitch all that he should have. Depending on who you listen to he was too lazy, too arrogant or hung out with the wrong crowd. The last I heard he was in Saudi Arabia, yet another member of the If Only Club.

To Villa fans, this is hardly uncommon. Indeed, they have seen it again very recently. Fast-forward a few years and there he is, Stan Collymore – Stan the Man, Big Stan, the Number Nine the Holte End had waited for ever since Peter Withe threw his last wrist-bands over the perimeter fence. Since then, many had come and gone – Aspinalls and Thompsons, McInallys and Cascarinos – but Cannock-born Stan, we were told, was the genuine article, Villa through and through. This was no Savo Milosevic, this was the guy Liverpool had whipped out eight-and-a-half million clams for. He was all but the missing ingredient in the club's bid for supremacy.

As you know, this never happened. It never happened in spades. In two seasons at Villa Park, Stan managed fewer goals than many players we've never heard of. Offloaded in ignominy, he became the biggest bust in a club history littered with busts. His career continued to sail a turbulent, troubled course, ending, it seems, in relative obscurity at Real Oviedo where he lasted slightly longer than an eye-blink.

Now, barely 30 years old, Stan has apparently decided to bring his footballing career to an end, for reasons best known only to himself. The writing had probably been on the wall. Few gave him much chance of getting his act together on the continent. By then Stan the Man had become Troubled Stan, Controversial Stan, Unsettled Stan. Talk of him spearheading the England attack had long since descended into talk of him turning up to play. Perhaps the story would have been different had fate been slightly kinder to him at Leicester. His partnership with Emile Heskey had the makings of one of the most lethal in the Premiership. But then Heskey was sold and Stan broke his leg and Martin O'Neill went to Celtic. Rotten luck, or all part of the game?

Did Stan deserve fate to be kinder to him? It is hard to think of anyone who has been given more second and third chances without taking advantage of any of them. His time at Villa Park was desperate, plagued as it was by a string of off-the-pitch incidents, mental difficulties and a singular inability to inspire the confidence of John Gregory. At Liverpool, he'd been fined for thoughtless remarks about team-mates and the manager. And we all still remember his lonely goalscoring celebrations at Forest. On and on it goes, right back to his YTS days at Walsall, where his contract wound up being cancelled. It's more irritating than depressing.

Despite the 55-goal partnership with Robbie Fowler at Anfield, or the 41 goals he scored in 65 games at the City Ground, it's unlikely that anyone ever coaxed the best out of Collymore, and certainly not the heights his transfer fees demanded. Each new employer was offered a promising debut and a sprinkling of impressive performances thereafter, but much misery and controversy along the way. And so, after ever-diminishing intervals, Stan would be put back on the market. Even the most facile review of Collymore's behaviour must have filled any suitor with second thoughts. The clubs that took him on must have done so as a challenge, either arrogant enough to think they could succeed where everyone else had failed or cold-blooded enough not to care about his conduct off the pitch. Or maybe they were all just blinded by those goals.

Even now, managers like Southend's David Webb try to tempt him back. Stan, though, claims his mind is made up. And with the increase in his free time, one hopes he will put some of it towards a little reflection. Does he consider the £17 million spent on fees in his name good value for the clubs concerned? Were the three England caps a fair representation of his international potential? If not, why not? Was any of it down to his attitude and behaviour, or were these blameless and simply misinterpreted by a hostile media? Would he admit to any errors in judgement, or would he still do it all the same way again?

To many – to most – Collymore probably represents the epitome of the modern dysfunctional footballer, a young man who accumulated too much money and met too few genuine friends along the way, someone who collapsed under the weight of his own ego and scarcely deserves our sympathy. To others, he is seen as an iconoclast, gifted but misunderstood, a guy who deserved to be cut a little more slack than the steady, unspectacular players alongside him. More sympathetic handling might have been all that separated him from a gleaming career: a stroke of the ego here and there, more ready forgiveness for the odd dose of youthful high spirits or anger. So what if he screwed up now and again? We accept that kind of behaviour in other fields of entertainment.

But maybe neither was the case. Maybe it's just this. Football is not a career for everyone – and the presence of talent does not necessarily alter that fact. Not everybody who signs for the big money is capable of putting the abundant free time and income to constructive use, particularly when – so the stereotype would have us believe – footballers are scarcely noted for their prudence. Equally, football is a team sport, and as such demands that players maintain a certain level of trust and respect for each other and their manager. Often, this can be more important than individual talent. Few would argue that Collymore had the physical traits to succeed in the game; perhaps it was these other things that were missing.

It would be nice to imagine that over the past few weeks Stan did give his position plenty of thought and, marooned in some Iberian hotel, reached the conclusion that football ultimately was not the life he was meant to lead. Granted, wishing to become a film star is no saner an option. But it may be naive to expect someone so accustomed to bright lights and fast living to be satisfied with, say, running a country pub.

Let's take that thought and go home with it. Classify Stan as a failure if you like, but for now restrict it to the game he played. Maybe, in terms of self-fulfilment, his best is yet to come. And if we never hear from the guy again, perhaps it will be best for all concerned. ○

Lax Deduction

The Football League's verdict on charges of financial irregularities against Chesterfield threw the Third Division into confusion. Hartlepool fan Ed Parkinson was among those left unimpressed

WSC No 172, June 2001

IN A CONFUSINGLY DISHONEST WORLD full of spin, deceit and greed it is usually possible to gain some respite by indulging an obsession with lower division football, a reasonably plain-speaking sporting backwater still dominated by traditionalists and mercifully free of prawn sandwiches. The recent events involving Chesterfield would suggest that this rare pool of comparative sanity is in danger.

In March the Football League found Chesterfield guilty of two serious charges of financial irregularities, at least one of which has had a direct impact on results this season. Having considered a huge volume of evidence the hearing decided that the club had submitted false gate receipts – hence avoiding payment of the three per cent levy charged by the League – this aspect of the case may be what triggered a surge of interest from the Inland Revenue.

Although this charge may prove hugely damaging to Chesterfield as a business, many might dismiss it as a harmless fiddle, a crime with no victim. This would be wrong. By disconnecting some turnstiles the club had no means of accurately counting entrants to some sections of their ageing Saltergate ground. It is worth remembering that the tragic events at Hillsborough happened because two sections of the Leppings Lane End were overfilled, while the number of people in the ground as a whole remained within a notionally safe capacity. It seems incredible, given the safety implications, that switching off turnstiles seems to be widely regarded as Chesterfield's lesser offence. From a Third Division fan's point of view, however, this is less immediately disturbing than the dishonesty surrounding the recruitment of Luke Beckett.

Beckett is one of the division's better front players and was a sought-after signing when his club Chester City lost their League status last year. Beckett chose to join Chesterfield and his goals and general play have been a key feature of their dominance of the Third Division this season. But he was signed dishonestly. He acquiesced in the production of a false contract in order to aid his new employers in reducing the fee payable to his previous, struggling club. The bogus contract halved his real wages and more than halved his signing-on fee: these false figures were part of the equation which a tribunal used to decide on a transfer value of £150,000. This seems low for a proven goalscorer of Beckett's age (24).

To make matters worse, the degree of proof required to find the club guilty on other charges seems bizarrely extreme. Jim Brown, Chesterfield's commercial manager, told the enquiry he believed players had been given cash in envelopes, the money being prepared by Sharon Wood, the club lottery manager. She told the inquiry: "I knew that the cash used for that bonus came out of the gate receipts for a home match against Exeter." Apparently this confession by two of the accused organisation's own officials did not constitute sufficient evidence and the charge of making illegal payments was unproven.

Now it might seem reasonable to expect a harsh punishment based on the proven irregularities alone. The League's decision to deduct nine points and fine the club £20,000 would in most circumstances have been a severe penalty. However, Chesterfield, despite their dilapidated ground and chaotic finances, have assembled a team which had built a big lead at the top of the division until overhauled by Brighton in the last weeks of the season. The deduction still left them five points clear of fourth-placed Hartlepool on the day it was announced. In other words, the proven cheats were still odds-on favourites for automatic promotion. The apparently harsh punishment was a paper tiger.

So have Chesterfield talked up their considerable blessings and apologised for their wrong doings? No. Luke "Two Contracts" Beckett said: "We can't believe the hearing has recommended a nine-point penalty." Some reports on their 1-0 defeat of Kidderminster suggested that "by rights" they should already have been promoted, as if the points deduction was an unjustified imposition. To add insult to injury for fans of other Third Division clubs, John Green, the club's chief executive, told reporters they would appeal. This was partly because they felt they had a case, but Green also joked that "someone in the car park said our barrister was that good we might win the appeal, get 12 points back and start next season with three points". Nicky Law, the manager who signed Beckett, claimed it would be "a catastrophe for the management, players and supporters had we been denied promotion". Not as big a catastrophe as it will be for Barnet or Torquay as they head for the Conference knowing that a few "irregularities" which might have worked in their favour would have gone unpunished even if they had been caught.

It is tempting to look for conspiracies to explain this decision but the simplest reason is often the most appropriate. I suspect the sentence was carefully calculated to avoid further wranglings with a good barrister offering a robust defence. If this is the case then the abject cowardice of the football authorities, who had clear precedent in the case of Swindon to work from, is to be condemned.

The real sickener was the gloating, barefaced denial of the successful cheats and it is nice to imagine that this provoked the next twist in the tale, with the Football League asking its disciplinary panel to reconvene. In the opinion of the League board, the punishment "did not sufficiently reflect the damage done to the integrity of the competition". Astonishingly, Sports Minister Kate Hoey went further and actually reflected the feelings of many fans: "The penalty, which would have still allowed the club to benefit from breaking the rules at the expense of other clubs, who have abided by the rules, is just not right."

Chesterfield's point of view was cleverly summed up by their assistant manager Ian Banks when he made a transparent bid to solicit sympathy, stating: "It's another kick in the goolies." The offending gonads were miraculously transformed into guts and teeth to spare the hypersensitive readers of the *Daily Mail* and Ceefax from alarm, but the basic message remained the same. The crooked Spireites were still playing the innocent victims.

This act should not impress anyone. Due to Chesterfield's actions, compounded by a disciplinary panel which appeared to lack the resolve to actually discipline, the rest of the Third Division is left with a chaotic closing programme. No one, least of all the completely blameless followers of Chesterfield, can be quite sure what results will mean in the end. It seems likely at the time of writing that the hearings and any consequent appeals will go on past the season's end and could also affect the play-offs. The final stages of the competition have been distorted by the spin, deceit and greed that many of us naively hope to leave behind us when we enter a football stadium. O

Riga Mortis

Gary Johnson had been sacked as Latvia coach after a draw with San Marino. Daunis Auers explained what he was doing there in the first place

WSC No 173, July 2001

GERIJS DZONSONS (or Gary Johnson as the English spelling would have it) bounced into Latvian football at the tail end of yet another doomed campaign for the national side, a respectable but ultimately unsuccessful attempt to qualify for Euro 2000. Johnson offered a colourful contrast to the grey, dour Soviet negativity of Revaz Dzodzashvilli, his Georgian predecessor, with his bubbly, upbeat, chirpy cockney (I could go on, but I think you know what I'm driving at) demeanour that had never been seen in Latvian football, or, come to that, anywhere in Latvia. However, Johnson left Latvia a forlorn, tragi-comic figure after the disgrace of drawing with San Marino on April 25 (on a comparative scale, we are talking Real Madrid drawing with an injury decimated Corby Town) and losing even a mathematical possibility of qualifying for the 2002 World Cup. So what went wrong?

During the 50 years of Soviet domination, Latvian football was absorbed into the hinterlands of Soviet lower league football while ice hockey and basketball stole the limelight. After independence in 1991 it seemed likely that football would go the way of these other, more popular, sports and see a rapid exodus of sporting stars to the West while financial crisis crippled the domestic league. However, this did not happen, for two reasons. First, there were no Latvian football stars. Second, a knight in suspiciously shiny armour emerged from the shady post-Soviet economy. This was Guntis Indriksons, ex-KGB agent turned managing director of the Skonto group of companies. He founded and bankrolled the obviously named Skonto FC (winners of the Latvian league for the past nine years – in fact, since its creation), based in the capital Riga and now proud owners of a brand new 10,000-seat capacity stadium smack in the centre of the city.

The club developed an extensive scouting and youth coaching system that is now beginning to pay dividends. Indriksons formalised his domination of Latvian football when he took over as president of the

Latvian FA in 1998. In many ways, club is country, as the overwhelming majority of the national team are either current or former Skonto players, the coaching staff are virtually identical and the national side now plays at Skonto's new stadium. Compared with other ex-communist countries, football in Latvia is as organised as the Arsenal back four in the George Graham era. It seems strange then that a journeyman English player and coach should have got in on the act.

By the late 1990s the Indriksons empire began running into financial difficulties. This made it increasingly difficult for money to be siphoned off to the football club, his great passion. However, a possible solution proposed itself in 1999 with the sale of star Skonto striker Marians Pahars to Southampton. Pahars' goals kept the club in the Premiership that year and scouts seeking cheap talented players began to look to the amber-laden shores of Latvia. But this trade still required some kind of contact man on the English end to prevent Skonto from being ripped off. Step forward the Bob Hoskins lookalike Gary Johnson, formerly a hard working but limited player and manager at Cambridge, and by now Watford's youth coach.

Dzodzashvilli had left for sunnier and wealthier climes in Saudi Arabian club football. Johnson met Indriksons (they had first been in contact on Skonto's pre-season tour of England the previous year) and apparently talked his way into the job with an incessantly perky view of the potential of Latvian football. Johnson initially charmed the press with his openness, his willingness to drone on about football for hours on end and his confidence in Latvia's ability to qualify for a tournament. Moreover, the press were slightly in awe of this man from the "home of football" (clearly none of them had ever seen Cambridge or Watford play) and his large selection of shellsuits. He wooed the fans by buying them a set of drums (come on, we're poor) and asking for more vocal support, as well as promising, and initially delivering, a more attacking style of play. Alas, in eight qualifying games, Johnson managed just one win – 1-0 in San Marino.

However, there was more success on the business side. Johnson performed a facilitating role in the sale of Vitalijs Astafjevs to Bristol Rovers, Imants Bleidelis to Southampton, Andrejs Rubins and Andrejs Kolinko to Crystal Palace, and Igors Stepanovs to Arsenal (where he has disappeared since "starring" in the 6-1 defeat at Old Trafford). The money has helped pay for further development of the stadium, although rumours have swept Riga that the transfer fees have also been used to help service the large debts of the Skonto empire. Johnson's English network appears the only valid explanation for the FA president's reluctance to sack him, even after the San Marino game. By this point both press and the fans had turned on Johnson. At the end of the game, the stadium echoed to the chant of "Dzonsons go home", to a rhythm set by the drums he himself had bought. Johnson managed to make things worse by physically attacking a football reporter after the game and then blaming press negativity for the result. The next day, headlines talked of The Blackest Day in Latvian Football and resignation was finally wrestled out of him.

Since that eventful evening, abuse from Latvian coaches as well as the press has been heaped on Johnson's head. The Skonto manager has taken over the national team, continuing the cosy relationship between club and country. Indriksons now says he wants to buy a club in England when he has paid off his debts (which he estimates at nearly £5 million from football alone). "I will begin at the bottom, and build a club up," he claims. Look out Cambridge. ○

Child's Play

The global trade in young footballers had reached disturbing new levels. Neil Wills detailed some of the cases that led to European clubs being accused of abuse and even slavery

WSC No 175, September 2001

IN JUNE, a 12-year-old, Marco Quotschalla, was sold by Bayer Leverkusen to Cologne for £60,000. Remarkably, it wasn't even his first transfer, since Cologne had sold him to Leverkusen just a year before. Marco's signing caused a stir in the German media principally because he is German and there's a sense that such a thing should not happen to a nice European child. Sadly, much less attention is paid to the thousands of youngsters who are being brought over to Europe from South America and Africa in increasing numbers with promises of big money and stardom.

There are two main methods for corralling up cheap local talent. The first involves an agent arriving somewhere suitably impoverished, holding a trial and selecting the best half dozen boys. These will typically be between ten and 14 years old, though there have been reports of boys as young as six being "spotted". The parents, hoping their son's ability will take the family out of poverty, sign a document releasing the child and are paid a token sum, sometimes as meagre as $20. The second approach is the setting up of football academies. According to Emmanuel Huesu of *African Soccer* magazine, "youth farms" have sprung up all over the African continent, either fully owned by European clubs or, in the case of Mali, by the former African Footballer of the Year Salif Keita. Where the "farms" are owned or sponsored by European clubs, the best players are sent to the mother club. If they don't work out, they can always seek to offload them to smaller clubs or simply dump them. It's a very inexpensive way of maintaining a youth policy. Among others, Feyenoord own a school in Ghana, Inter have one in Argentina and Lyon are said to be investigating the possibilities in Nigeria.

Some smaller European clubs have used the fact that they just happen to be football teams to make some money out of the trafficking of children. One such case concerns Arezzo, an Italian Serie C club. Six boys, all in their early teens, were brought over from Argentina in 1999 with promises of a possible future with the club. Their life became one of training, Italian lessons and more training, occasionally being pitched in with the pros for "friendlies" to enable scouts from bigger clubs to have a look at them. The six went back to Argentina for the holidays and quite understandably decided they didn't want to return. The money their families were promised for the time the boys stayed at the club never materialised.

In many ways, though, they can count themselves lucky. Saro Pettinato, a member of the Italian parliament and former president of Serie C side Atletica Catania, told the *Clarín* news website: "Someone rang me and said that his brother-in-law in Argentina could send me boys. Each one cost $5,000. He was not selling me the rights [to their football skills], he was selling me the boys themselves."

According to George Weah, many children get no further than a trial on European soil. When, inevitably, the vast majority don't perform to a sufficient standard, they are simply abandoned to survive in a country they don't know, with no contacts and often not a word of the local language. Unless they come from a developed nation, no one looks out for them. Even then, it can be dicey. Twelve Australian teenagers were taken to Turin in 1998 and 1999 and then "disappeared" – it was only when the Italian consul in Brisbane was alerted to the fact they hadn't returned that a search was set in motion.

However, every so often an Ariel Huguetti comes along. The Argentinian, at 14, was the subject of a scrap between Barcelona and Real Madrid, who reportedly offered $1 million for him this year. The prospect that there might be more like him out there has prompted companies such as Deloitte & Touche to invest in Argentina, Brazil and Uruguay. D&T director Eduardo de Bonis lays out the game plan: "We're not looking for a Maradona but ten or 20 decent players who, together, will be worth what Maradona was." Venture capitalists the Exxel Group have scraped together $40m in Europe and the US to buy child footballers in South America. They've promised their backers a 25 per cent return over four years.

But never fear, for swooping over the horizon comes FIFA, albeit a full ten years after Issa Hayatou, the current president of the African Football Confederation, first blew the whistle on the trade in child footballers. Principles set out by the world body governing the involvement of minors in football were accepted by the European Union in March this year and should come into effect on September 1. The new regulations state that, for those under the age of 18, international transfers or first registration of players are permitted if "the family of the player moves for reasons not related to football into the country of the new training club" or, within the European Economic Area (the EU plus Iceland, Norway and Liechtenstein), "suitable arrangements are guaranteed for their sporting, training and academic education by the new training club".

Spot those loopholes. No doubt European lawyers are already advising clubs on how to wriggle through them. For example, how do you prove that a family has not emigrated for reasons other than football? It may be pesky having to arrange some "job" for a parent, but if their offspring is good enough, it's a small price for the club to pay. Furthermore, the regulations won't put an end to the succession of boys coming to Europe for trials only to be abandoned.

The largest importers of child footballers are Italy, France and Belgium. However, before we become too self-righteous, we should remember that British clubs have no qualms about importing under-age stars (among others, Mikael Forssell and Carlos Marinelli were both 17 when joining Chelsea and Middlesbrough respectively) and would doubtless be as heavily involved in the Third World as our neighbours if it weren't for the fact that employment laws here make it almost impossible for non-EU teenagers to obtain work permits. When prices for home-grown flesh went through the roof, English clubs looked to cheap European imports. All European clubs are doing is following the same principle, only a little further down the age scale. It's sweat shop economics applied to the business of football. O

Working from Home

As part of a series on defunct competitions, Ken Gall argued that the demise of the home internationals left Scotland chasing irrelevant targets such as the World Cup

WSC No 175, September 2001

WITH BJÖRN BORG-STYLE skinny-fit tracksuits and Gola trainers in the shops, and *Planet of the Apes* set to be the summer's hit movie, surely all we need to complete a nostalgia-fest for jaded thirty-somethings is the return of the home internationals. For Scots fans of that age, the memories linger: Brian Moore in the commentary box with Sir Alf; male relatives drinking cans of beer in the afternoon around the television; the Hampden roar; the offensive chants about Jimmy Hill.

Even without the retro-chic appeal, a resurrected home internationals could inject a bit of passion back into a somewhat jaded Scottish national set-up. Some years ago, it was decided (on our behalf, naturally) that what we did not want was the insularity of trips to Cardiff and Belfast and the mind-bending importance of the England tie; what we really wanted was to qualify for the final stages of World Cups and European Championships. Throw in the increasingly dreadful behaviour of those attending the matches, and it became all too easy to pull the plug on the competition. But for all that we have gained from our modern outlook and our worldwide series of morale-sapping defeats, Scotland and its fans seem to have lost something fundamental. In the Fifties and Sixties, Scotland had some of the greatest players in the world, backed by the most passionate fans. However, we qualified for nowt. Now, we qualify all the time, but the nagging question remains: what is it all for?

For Scots, the home internationals meant, in essence, the England match. The games against Wales and Northern Ireland were largely treated as preliminaries to the main event, something that men such as John Toshack were often only too glad to exploit. But a win over the Auld Enemy and, really, who needed the World Cup anyway? Scotland's attitude to the World Cup until the mid-1970s was similar to Bill Clinton's public attitude to marijuana; tried it once, didn't like it, ain't gonna try it again.

The reputations of many of the Scottish game's greatest heroes were made by their achievements in the home competition – the Wembley Wizards, Jim Baxter, Denis Law, Kenny Dalglish, Ray Clemence. Other, less-familiar heroes are also held dear, including Mike Pejic, perpetrator of a humdinger of an air shot that allowed Peter Lorimer to score Scotland's second goal at Hampden in 1974. Of course there are also the Scottish footballing equivalent of the untouchables: Frank Haffey (9-3 in 1961), Fred Martin (7-2 in 1955), Stewart Kennedy (5-1 in 1975). Let us never speak of them again.

Jock Stein, a man who had taken on and defeated the footballing world, started the process of looking beyond the home internationals, feeling that Scotland's inordinate focus on the end-of-season tournament was a hindrance in terms of what he regarded as the real business, namely the World Cup. Craig Brown's exemplary record in terms of championship qualification shows that Stein may have had a point. This may also go some way towards explaining why Jim Baxter did not play in the final stages of a World Cup, but Gordon Durie did. Hungary, Holland, Denmark and now France have all benefited from golden generations of players that took previously less-heralded footballing nations to glory on the world stage. Scotland's finest seemed content with a point against the Irish and a narrow defeat at Ninian Park, just so long as they beat you-know-who. (For example, it has been conveniently forgotten that the 1967 Wembley heroes – the true "world champions", if you will – lost 1-0 to Northern Ireland in Belfast just a few months later.)

However, it is the bloodless attitude to the Scottish national side that makes one long for the return of the British championship. Rather than a Welsh booze-up as a precursor to the life-or-death Wembley or Hampden bash, Riga and Tallinn are now the Tartan Army's favoured destinations. The matches themselves seem almost to be a sideshow or afterthought, while the fans go about cementing their reputation as the "nation's kilted ambassadors". But the fire was put back in the national belly by the Euro 96 Wembley match against England and the play-offs for last year's competition. Fans who had grown weary of the interminable wait for a goal in any number of matches against San Marino and Latvia were enthused once again. Only, of course, to be disappointed once again.

Frankly, given the propensity of broadcasters and the game's authorities to squeeze blood out of the proverbial stone, it is staggering that the game's oldest international competition has not yet been resurrected for the Sky generation. And in a World Cup and European championship-free year such as this, the prospect of Wales v England at the Millennium Stadium (Giggs v Beckham!), or even – to avoid the dreaded Unionist tinge that the championship might otherwise have – the inclusion of the Republic of Ireland, should be enough to have your average TV executive foaming at the mouth.

Of course, the English FA, media and Sven 'n' Tord probably feel they are all a bit beyond this parochial nonsense now. But one wonders whether three highly competitive internationals with the home nations would not serve them better than their recent spate of extremely friendly friendlies. For instance, the game against Mexico in June was probably about as useful to England in terms of international football as a tie versus the current cast of *Big Brother*. (Here we see another idea that the television companies may wish to explore.)

Those who are worried about the "security considerations" which, in part, led to the ending of the tournament, should recall that the rigid application of such considerations would have prevented England from competing in any international competition over the past 25 years. But in these days of named tickets, CCTV and travel restrictions, any of the home internationals should be no more or less difficult to police than any other major match. It is merely a question of the will of the nations concerned.

Northern Ireland and Wales could certainly do with the money from a rejuvenated home international series, while England could probably do with the competitive edge. And Scotland? Well, we've seen Zaire, Iran, Costa Rica and Morocco; perhaps now would be a good time to return home. O

Early Warning

We asked Cameron Carter to sit down and watch as much of ITV's Premiership coverage as he could stomach. He emerged unscathed but unsympathetic

WSC No 176, October 2001

ITV HAVE GOT FOOTBALL. It's like the Childcatcher and, frankly, I'm scared. With the first edition of *The Premiership* going out at the *Blind Date* time of 7pm, ITV were always going to have one eye on the committed fan and the other on its family audience. I sat down to watch it with two packets of Frazzles and a heavy heart.

First, why *Beautiful Day* by U2? I bet Bono doesn't even like football. It's an old pop song probably about the singer's ex-girlfriend having a breakdown in Miami. Bad start. And the time. You cannot have a credible football programme on when it's still light outside. I kept thinking I was watching the highlights on the news. In fact, I was completely disorientated and wanted to go outside.

Still having trouble with the glare from the window, I then became unhinged by the speed at which the programme was passing. The transition from first half to second was marked by a freeze-frame on the last action of the first half, followed by a small blue sign in the bottom right-hand corner saying "second half". Otherwise, you were on your own – no establishing shot of fans having their half-time pork pie, no John Motson statistic. The main Middlesbrough v Arsenal match was rushed through as if it were the extra match at the end and the whole programme had the air of someone in a medical hurry.

The first match's highlights were nine minutes long, Liverpool v West Ham took eight minutes and Sunderland v Ipswich was still far too long at six. The programme's extra 15 minutes over the hour were almost entirely subsumed by three four-minute advertisement breaks. By the time the last game was being analysed, this runaway vehicle was going so fast there was no time to include the interviewer's question about Robbie Fowler, making Gérard Houllier's isolated comments appear needlessly enigmatic.

Of course there were going to be innovations. What's the point of having ideas people on the payroll otherwise? Of the two introduced,

Prozone seemed likely to be more successful than Andy Townsend in a trailer showing a moody defender his mistakes. Terry Venables' explanation of Michael Owen's first goal must have given Michael Carrick goose-bumps. (Though ITV clearly disagreed, cutting the slot after the press savaging of *The Premiership* in order to squeeze in a bit more action.) Taken as a whole, this hideously slender programme suggested that ITV believe the population's short attention span is decreasing daily, when in fact football fans are among the last few left in our society who can genuinely concentrate on one event for 90 minutes.

The second programme, at 11.15, was much better. Des started off properly with a joke ("We at ITV do it twice a night on Saturdays") and the extended highlights gave you time to relax in your chair. The team of Des, Venables and Ally McCoist is the best yet assembled by ITV and the painful yearning for Alan, Trevor and even Gary is already starting to heal. Of course, where ITV nearly always get it wrong is in the near-total absence of class, grace and dignity, but this seems to have been given some consideration by the production team. The half-expected Sky style of over-presentation didn't materialise. Occasionally a statistic popped shyly out of the team names in the top corner ("Score last season: Liverpool 3 v 0 West Ham"), but there was little other embellishment and the programme steered a sober course. Never mind that half the people watching it at this time were drunker than a pirate on shore leave.

The commentary team was able enough and, unlike Barry Davies with that salivatory desire to show off his reading, largely unobtrusive. Except for Jon Champion, who, rather than being "poached" from the BBC, seems to have been inherited, like a chipped gravy-boat. During the Sunderland v Ipswich game, when Titus Bramble had been penalised and Kevin Phillips was preparing to take the penalty, Champion said – he actually said – "Bramble ruminating, Phillips hoping to be fulminating". I ask you.

That aside, the late *Premiership* was a pleasant surprise. The problem is, if you've seen the first programme there's not much point staying up for this one, and if you deliberately miss the early edition – a choice I will be making with all my strength – a quarter-to-midnight is a mighty long time to wait. It's all very well Des looking at his watch at 7pm and murmuring "Better for us, better for you", but at this time of night he's up against a quiz show on the other side. Football was never meant to be up against a quiz show.

Monday at 11pm brought us the third evil triplet. The Premiership

Parliament with Gabby Yorath (now officially Logan) and Ally McCoist is a fine example of ITV spreading a successful ratings-puller very thinly. She began with "If it moves in the top flight, we've got it covered" and that pretty much set the tone for the night. It's lines like that one that demonstrate the BBC simply has better scriptwriters. Gary Lineker, although in isolation about as funny as a management techniques weekend, still came up with pearlers on a weekly basis. The gradual unravelling of Gabby's late night personality was quite disconcerting, like watching a respected primary school teacher on two pints of snakebite.

Then there was the sustained confusion over whose turn it was to speak, with some contributors not only barely audible but only visible when the camera finally swung over to them, just as they were trailing off. The fans' "parliament" was audible enough. In fact, its members' articulacy and objectivity seemed to disappoint the show's presenters. Obviously, at the planning stage this was going to be a live, stirring bear-pit of a programme. Its low-key sprawling shoddiness must have been a big disappointment to its makers as well as its audience. ○

2002

Rising from the Ashes

Though appearing to be a flawed idea from the start, the Phoenix League was a worryingly real possibility at the time

WSC No 179, January 2002 ~ Editorial

So, THE PHOENIX LEAGUE. If we are to believe what the *Daily Mail* says, and who wouldn't, "revolution" is afoot. Some time soon, possibly next season, more likely in 2004 when the current TV deal expires, 14 clubs will leave the Football League to form a second tier of the Premier League, where they will be joined by two clubs demoted from the top level, together with Celtic and Rangers.

Top secret talks have apparently been going on for a while. Simply deciding which mythical creature to use as a code word – unicorn? sasquatch? gorgon? – must have necessitated several clandestine meetings between the interested parties, of which there appear to be a lot. According to the *Mail*'s front page exclusive on Saturday November 24, six "rebel" clubs would serve notice of intention to quit the Football League on December 11. The same paper has since claimed that another eight First Division clubs are to join the "scramble to climb aboard".

There would, it seems, be one promotion place set aside each season for the champions of what will surely come to be known as The Rump (just think of the logo possibilities). Confusingly, however, it would appear that places may also be set aside for lower division clubs with nice big stadiums, such as Stoke and Huddersfield.

Rangers and Celtic are to be invited in primarily because their presence will tickle the fancy of television executives who believe, according to the *Mail*, that "audiences are already tiring of a diet of the same top teams on the screen". Similar concerns are voiced by Richard Scudamore, chief executive of the Premier League: "We might have to do something like the Phoenix idea to keep the game varied and interesting to broadcasters when the next negotiations take place." As opposed to keeping it "interesting" for, say, the people who pay to watch it every week.

This issue goes to press before the meeting of Nationwide League chairmen on November 29. However, it seems pretty clear what the principles are. Clubs that have recently been in the Premier League, or who have spent a fortune trying unsuccessfully to get there, want to narrow the gap between their income and that of those still clinging by their fingertips to the edge of the cliff that leads to the Promised Land. (Think of Rupert Lowe hanging on, mouth open to ingest an avalanche of gold coins, but with David Sheepshanks stamping on his fingers.)

Clubs of all different sizes who have embarked on foolish spending sprees funded by television are in a blind panic about the likelihood of revenues falling when the current contract expires. But those who see themselves as too good for the First Division but maybe not quite good enough to be sure of staying in the Premier are most at risk of suffering unpleasant financial downturns.

So they hope to create some new "product", spice it up with added ingredients (Rangers and Celtic) and cut away the ragged masses below them. Prepare the way by spreading the word that all of this is "inevitable" and it will surely happen. ("A Premier League Two is inevitable and Watford will be part of it," says the friendly Hertfordshire club's chief executive, Tim Shaw. "It's almost inevitable," agrees his counterpart at Nottingham Forest, Mark Arthur. Write those names down.)

The only problem is that it is far from obvious where the money is coming from to bail out clubs who in many cases have got themselves into an almighty mess. Not from the Premiership, presumably, whose whole premise is to keep themselves separate, both for marketing reasons and to create a more or less permanent financial advantage. Not from the lower divisions either. Incorporating their cut of the Nationwide TV deal, even the present over-valued one, is not going to pay for many John Hartsons. There is no logic similar to that of the original Premier League plans that suggests this scheme, however formulated, must work.

Maybe we've missed something blindingly obvious that the business brains of Geoffrey Richmond, Bryan Richardson et al have cottoned on to while their clubs plunge into debt. But it seems unlikely. O

Rights to the Wire

The players' union threatened to strike in a row over TV money. John Harding assessed the dispute and concluded that the PFA had retained important principles

WSC No 179, January 2002

ON THE SURFACE this year's PFA dispute seemed an eerie rerun of the TV cash row of a decade ago, when a similarly rock solid vote gave Gordon Taylor a mandate to secure a deal with the newly formed Premier League. However, this time around it's been a darker, murkier struggle. In 1991, Taylor was football's White Knight, who had never put a foot wrong, was the saviour of small clubs, a doughty opponent of Thatcher and so on. There were no "dirty tricks" and no club chairmen firing off vitriolic broadsides.

At that time the PFA felt marginalised by the FA and the Premier League and, like others working at the grassroots, had been worried about where the game was going and what the future held for lower division players. The 95 per cent mandate for action the Association received at that time was, according to Taylor, one of the highlights of his career. With such solid backing, he went on to re-establish the principle that the PFA was entitled to a percentage of TV cash.

In a sense, the current struggle has primarily been to secure that same agreement again, a determination by the PFA to "draw a line in the sand" against repeated attempts by the Premiership clubs to swap the percentage principle for "ballpark" figures that can change according to who's currently on the pitcher's mound. It's arguable whether the PFA can claim a clear cut victory or not. However, the two-month saga has certainly revealed just how wisely the Association has used its cash allocation since the early Nineties. And it's a measure of that success that so many chairmen appeared seized with the notion that it was time to curb the PFA's burgeoning influence.

The PFA has grown dramatically in the past decade. It now has offices in Manchester, Birmingham and London. It employs 50 full-time and 250 part-time staff working in coaching and education, financial management and Football in the Community. It runs its own website and has fingers in a variety of media pies (such as an International Hall of Fame). The PFA also boasts a collection of memorabilia and art, including the famous Lowry painting, that is unrivalled outside Preston's National Football Museum. It's certainly a union unlike many others, though whether that makes its external activities suspect, as the chairmen often implied, is another matter.

What's more, as the president of FifPro, the umbrella organisation for all Europe's players' unions, Taylor has moved on to the European stage with some skill. His outmanoeuvring of the Premiership and FA over the new European Contract of Employment came as a shock to many (particularly those presently engaged in attacking him personally).

Thus, from being virtually unrecognised, though never unregarded, Taylor is now a senior administrator in the British game. Not surprisingly, therefore, he became the prime target for abuse: his "inflated" pay, the "extravagant" Lowry, his mannerisms and even his girth were all subjected to unpleasant scrutiny. He responded angrily at times, but, significantly, was able to rebut the smears and misinformation via a carefully orchestrated publicity campaign spearheaded by the PFA's GiveMeFootball website.

This publicity arm has been crucial because, for the first time in such a dispute, not only Taylor himself but the very nature of the PFA has been questioned. Its apparently bulging assets, its role as a "commercial" operation rather than a "traditional" union, even its honesty have all been put under the spotlight. How much does it really spend on old pros and their hip-joints? The latter arguments were made against a back drop of "revelations" concerning top players' salaries, and underpinned by doomsday scenarios concerning the way broadcasters had overreached themselves in paying for screening rights. The clubs, in an ambiguous position since it is they who are funnelling the cash into players' pockets, wondered why their wealthy employees couldn't pay for their own replacement hips.

Top players' salaries are not the PFA's concern or responsibility, but ever since professionalism was allowed in football, the public have preferred to believe that all players were well paid, if not overpaid. Even when the maximum wage existed, fans failed to grasp that the majority of players didn't receive it. The "greedy" player has always, therefore, been a useful stick to beat the union with (to which we can now add the "greedy" union leader).

Unpleasant though it has been, the dispute has nevertheless been a good opportunity for the PFA to highlight its role in supporting players at the end of their career – whether that comes prematurely through injury or via retirement. This work has been greatly expanded, for example by funding research into players' long-term head injuries, but it has become increasingly expensive, as has insuring players against such fates. Much of Taylor's anxiety for the future stems from these rising premiums, and contrasts with the short-term, almost gauche approach of relative newcomers to the scene such as the Premier League chief executive Richard Scudamore, who pointed to monies spent in years past and drew irrelevant conclusions.

Despite last-minute claims (and David James) to the contrary, most commentators conceded that the PFA won the publicity battle hands down. This was one major strand of their campaign. The other was the determination of Taylor to establish critical "rules of engagement". The PFA's relationship with football's governing bodies and employers has been at the heart of most disputes ever since the old Players Union staggered into existence in 1909. To state the obvious, the PFA is not a client of the Premier League nor of the FA. It is a free-standing organisation that owes its existence and its status to its members alone.

The money it receives from the TV share-out is owed to it by right. When television first offered money for highlights, the players claimed, through their union, that their appearances before the cameras were worth a share of the revenues. In the Fifties and Sixties, players appearing in TV matches were paid individually, a practice long since voluntarily abandoned but still relevant to today's arguments. The players agreed to give their shares to the PFA. Thus, the much disputed percentage isn't a donation from the clubs or the Premier League. It's a payment from the players as a whole to the PFA.

If that principle were to be abrogated and the idea established that the Premiership was handing over a cut of "its" money, then club chairmen like Doug Ellis could feel free to poke their noses into PFA business whenever they liked, checking up on where "their" cash had gone.

(Ironically, it might do them some good, as they might learn something about what kind of animal the PFA really is.) It's this latent, stubborn paternalism towards players that affords men like Ellis and David Gold the leeway to moan about how much Taylor is paid or how much they think the PFA has in its coffers. None of this is their business. If the PFA is relatively rich, it's because it has known what to do with its cash, not to mention its shrewd marketing of the PFA "brand". If the Premier League finds itself with no assets (as Scudamore admitted may be the case), whose fault is that? Greedy players? Or greedy chairmen?

Football isn't an industry in the traditional sense for one crucial reason: the player is both worker and product. Thus, the PFA is and isn't a union. It is when it looks to the welfare of its members. That's what all unions do. But it isn't when it creates a massively influential department to deal with the education and training of all young professionals entering the game, in the new terminology, as "scholars". What other union devotes so much time and expertise towards helping lazy employers train their fledgling employees? It is a union when it offers financial and legal help to members where contracts are concerned, despite dark mutterings about conflicts of interest and union "agents". But it isn't when it implements sophisticated coaching schemes and programmes that raise the level of performance and expertise of those players TV companies are so anxious to feature.

The PFA has also worked long and hard to improve the quality of the game in the widest sense – witness its pioneering role with initiatives such as Football in the Community and anti-racism campaigns. Traditional unions leave such crucial salesmanship to the employers. Fortunately, the PFA didn't sit back and allow football to be promoted by clubs alone during the years when the game seemed to be dying on its feet. We should be thankful, too, that the present dispute resulted in a reassertion of the principle of PFA independence and financial security. Otherwise, the game's future might look much bleaker than it does. O

Stares from Tattooed Men

Two Leeds players, Lee Bowyer and Jonathan Woodgate, were accused, but acquitted, of assaulting a young Asian man. Soheb Panja, a West Ham fan who had lived in Leeds, compared attitudes towards race at the two clubs's stadiums
WSC No 180, February 2002

AT UPTON PARK the flimsy Let's Kick Racism Out Of Football sign is sandwiched by the pitch and the notorious Chicken Run, a small stretch at the corner of the East Lower Stand where it meets the Bobby Moore Stand. The most vitriolic abuse heard anywhere in the ground is aimed at petrified players wandering over to take corners (just ask David Beckham). From my comparatively placid vantage point in the West Stand, I always check who the unlucky left midfielder is on the opposing side. I think I can confidently say, however, that the abuse these days is always because of the colour of the player's shirt and not the colour of his skin. I always think it is too much of a coincidence that the campaign's sign should be placed where it is.

As the bananas are no longer raining on the pitch and the howls of monkey noises are rarely heard, racism in football is said to be on the wane. Recent publicity about racism at Millwall has been dismissed as "an exceptional case". But I have yet to see a football stand anywhere with even the remotest similarity to the one projected by Sky television's introduction to their live games: a carefree blonde girl sitting among a range of "non-white" people.

Having followed West Ham at home and away, and spent three years studying in Leeds, I feel I am in a position to make some first-hand judgments about the differences between the two. There is a bit of an edge that comes with West Ham's away games. I have now become used to semi-threatening stares from heavily tattooed men. But the little open racism I've heard induces embarrassment rather than fear. It is certainly an awkward feeling when a section of the fans near me are singing "I'd rather be a Paki than a scouser" while I can feel the looks of disdain as well as sympathy directed towards me.

While in Leeds, I often went to Elland Road. Nowhere, in my experience of Premiership grounds, is there a more malevolent atmosphere. Last season, many Leeds fans seemed to take the lack of censure for Bowyer and Woodgate as a sign (and a welcome one) that the club was somehow racist. That all the players shaved their heads during their Champions League run-in didn't help.

Leeds is a strange city demographically. Although other big cities have distinct "ethnic" areas, they are generally in close proximity to predominantly white areas. In Leeds, the working classes live in isolated settlements some distance from the city centre and the demarcation lines are very clear. One evening in Leeds a friend's car broke down in a particularly white area. One boy in a Leeds shirt wandered over on his bike as we called the AA awaiting a new battery. He casually said to me: "I bet the AA man's like you, a Paki." He didn't seem malicious but had just imbibed the culture and attitudes of his area.

On the few occasions when watching England play away I have felt conspicuously not English. At France 98 I was asked: "Why's a fucking Paki got an England shirt on?" The questioner had a tattoo on his forearm that read "LUFC". As the Bowyer/Woodgate trial dragged on I noticed the odd Asian face in the crowd at Elland Road. I can only imagine their sense of divided loyalty. I would hate to be in a situation where I feel alienated from West Ham because I'm Asian.

Ironically, Leeds and West Ham, two Premiership clubs with bad reputations for racism, are also the only two with Asians on their books. Both clubs recognise the need to tap into the local reservoir of support and talent. Community initiatives go some way to bridging the gulf between football culture and the reality of multicultural cities in Britain. However, there is still a huge disparity between the noises in the boardroom and the noises from the stands. ○

Axed Stanley

March 2002 marked the 40th anniversary of Accrington Stanley's controversial ejection from the Football League. Mike Gent explained what went wrong

WSC No 182, April 2002

"PROBABLY THE MOST FAMOUS football team in the land" is how a Lancashire County Council website describes Accrington Stanley. A contentious claim, but there is no doubt that the Stanley's continued notoriety stems not from the club's modest playing record but from a series of off-pitch calamities which culminated in their departure from the Football League in March 1962. Since then, the spectre of Accrington Stanley has been regularly invoked whenever football clubs sink towards bankruptcy.

History was not on their side. Stanley were not the first team from the town to drop out of the League because of financial difficulties. Accrington FC, one of the 12 founder members of the Football League in 1888, resigned because of crippling losses just five years later, before the start of the 1893-94 season. The remnants of th'Owd Reds, as the original club was known, merged with junior side Stanley Villa to become Accrington Stanley. In 1920-21, the Football League expanded with the formation of the Third Division South and the northern section was added the following season. Accrington Stanley were founder members. Fifth place in that first term was their best for many years, though Stanley like to remember that they were top of the division with three wins out of three when league football was suspended in September 1939.

The immediate postwar period showed little improvement, but Glaswegian Walter Galbraith transformed the club on being appointed manager in 1952. In an era when only the champions of the Third Divisions went up, Stanley finished second, third and third from 1955 to 1957, often playing with an all-Scottish team. The reorganisation of the League at the end of the 1957-58 season led to promotion, of a kind. Runners-up position in the final Third Division North table meant that they played in the new national Third Division in 1958-59. Their elevated status was short-lived, however. Stanley were relegated in 1959-60, nine points adrift at the bottom, having conceded 123 goals. Their demise after that point was painfully swift – 18th in 1960-61, then, instead of 24 clubs, the final Fourth Division table for 1961-62 shows only 23.

The club had been no strangers to penury – a bazaar held in the town saved the club from extinction during the Depression in 1932. It was in late 1961 that Stanley's latest financial difficulties became public and in December they were barred from making any transfer deals because they owed £3,000 to other clubs. A local Alderman launched a "Save Stanley" fund, hoping to raise £20,000, but the appeal only netted £450. Gates fell to 1,500, half the break-even point, a far cry from their first season in the League when season tickets for the unfinished Peel Park were over-subscribed.

In February 1962, with the club at the bottom of the Fourth Division, former Stanley chairman Sam Pilkington, together with Bob Lord of neighbouring Burnley, tried to put a rescue package together. However, a debt of £62,000 proved insurmountable. The only advice that Lord could ultimately offer was that Stanley should resign from the League, leaving disappointed supporters with a convenient scapegoat for their club's downfall. A 4-0 defeat at Crewe on March 2 turned out to the their last League game.

A letter of resignation was sent to the League's headquarters in Lytham on March 6. Two days later, the club's president Sir William Cocker sent a second letter withdrawing the resignation and claiming that a group of local businessmen had put up the money to save Stanley, with the approval of the creditors. The fate of the club hung in the balance for three days, awaiting a meeting of the League in London on March 11. The town's mayor sent a telegram in support of the club and the directors and club solicitor attended the meeting to argue their case. It was to no avail. The League's decision, read out by its secretary Alan Hardaker, relied on "well-established legal precedent" and claimed that the League had no alternative but to accept the first letter. Accrington Stanley were out of the League. The results of their matches were declared null and void and the records of the players for the season were expunged from the official statistics.

The club's fall from grace was shockingly sudden. Only a few years earlier they had been one of the first teams to use floodlights and had attracted big crowds to Peel Park for friendlies, usually against Scottish First Division teams. The ground record of 17,634 was set on November 15, 1954 for the visit of Blackburn Rovers for a floodlit friendly. Ambitious plans for a new two-tier stand at the Burnley Road side, including a suite of offices and a ballroom, were drawn up, then shelved. Instead, the club purchased a second-hand 4,000-seat stand from the Aldershot Military Tattoo. Not only did it end up costing the club ten times the purchase price of £2,000 when dismantling, transportation and re-erection costs were added, but it was impossible to see the pitch from certain parts of a stand not designed for watching football. The episode effectively crippled the club. For his part, Sir William Cocker was in no doubt where the fault lay – the Football League. Angered by its high-handed reliance on legal precedent, he claimed the League had actively tried to rid itself of smaller clubs like Stanley by reorganising the regional Third Divisions, arguing that the inevitable result was prohibitive expenses.

The club's place in the League was taken by Oxford United, but the name of Accrington Stanley refused to die – it is, after all, such a great name. The original club struggled on in the Second Division of the Lancashire Combination before folding in 1963. Peel Park fell into disrepair and became derelict before ending up as a school playing field. Accrington Stanley reformed in 1968 but didn't play a competitive game until two years later when the team rejoined the Lancashire Combination. Turning out for them that season was Terry Tighe, a wing-half who had played for the old club in the Football League. Since then, Stanley have risen to the Premier Division of the Unibond League.

Forty years on, the feeling lingers that Stanley could have been saved. The Accrington public and its business community appeared unaware of the seriousness of the club's plight until it was too late. The League's attitude is puzzling, falling back on legalities in spite of Cocker's salvation plan. Teenage inside-forward Mike Ferguson was sold to Blackburn Rovers in the same month as Stanley's resignation and then on to Aston Villa for £60,000 – just short of the club's total debt in 1962.

In the intervening years, only two other clubs have been forced to resign from the Football League for financial reasons. Almost exactly 30 years later, Aldershot did a Stanley, dropping out of the League mid-season in March 1992. Six months later, Maidstone United resigned just before the start of 1992-93, after only three seasons of League football. Despite the concentration of wealth in the Premiership and the regular choruses of doomsayers, League clubs continue to display remarkable survival instincts. Perhaps the best tribute to Accrington Stanley can be found in the successful efforts of other clubs to avoid following their example. O

Must Do Better

With FIFA president Sepp Blatter being accused of malpractice, Alan Tomlinson looked at how the organisation might reform itself

WSC No 183, May 2002

FIFA'S MOTTO IS: "For the good of the game." The slogan is often parroted by the insiders in the FIFA elite, as they gloat from their luxury rooms in the world's top hotels, or welcome you to their bunker-like FIFA House in the exclusive hillside suburb overlooking Lake Zürich, the Alpine summits across the water and the self-satisfied gloss of Zürich's Banhofstrasse, with its top designer stores and morally dodgy banks. The FIFA elite is comfortable here. The wives of FIFA's top brass like the lobbies and the stores. The FIFA men themselves like the loot and the secrecy.

It has been assumed for years that the elusive FIFA finances are rotten to the core, though it has never been easy to get to the heart of the multi-million dollar accounts. One well placed observer of global sports politics has commented, albeit a mite melodramatically, that any independent researcher or journalist who really got hold of the details of IOC or FIFA finances might not survive in the best state to see them published. With FIFA, you're welcomed so far and then it's very arms-length indeed. With Sepp Blatter fighting for his survival as president after the collapse of FIFA's marketing partner ISL and amid claims that he bribed FIFA delegates to get elected, the openness towards outsiders has hardly improved.

Even walking up to FIFA House feels like a criminal activity. I was the only pedestrian. There were no signposts pointing up the hill, only pointing from the top down. I made it to the exclusive Aurora Strasse, though – "FIFA House? There, on top of the mountain," my city contact had gestured. It was a steep climb, too, in Zürich's most sought-after neighbourhood – Tina Turner's house is just a door or two along the road. Aurora was the Roman goddess of the morning. What is FIFA doing here, amid the aura of classicist allusions and the glitziness of this superstar and bankers' hideout? FIFA House itself lacks style, but has serious substance. It is bunker-like, as Keith Cooper, FIFA's director of communications, put it to me. When the money rolled in on the back of the massive expansion of the World Cup's commercial potential from the 1980s onwards, the quaint old Swiss chalet-style house occupied by FIFA was razed, and a modern square-metered and measured monster erected in its place.

Sepp Blatter was general secretary from the early 1980s through to 1998. He nodded me a cautious welcome as I was given a tour of FIFA House by Cooper. Media files, sponsor files and a number of the other most interesting documents were immediately branded as "classified, confidential". Blatter's boss, his predecessor as president, was Dr João Havelange, who is still talked of in hushed tones – always as "the president". I was told of how, when the phone goes in FIFA House and it's Havelange on the line, the arched backs of the FIFA apparatchiks straighten and stiffen. The man is in South America; the FIFA secretariat is in central Europe. But when he's on the phone, it's like a royal visit. *"Oui, Monsieur le Président,"* was the reported general response to any such calls. No discussion, just the affirmative. FIFA House is like a court of the *Ancien Régime*. Running FIFA is a matter of mastering not the football rulebook, more Machiavelli's *The Prince*.

Havelange's achievement was to expand football across the globe by bringing the interests of world football closer than ever to business interests, fuelled by the ruthless ambitions of aspirant autocrats and international businessmen and politicians from newly independent countries of the developing world, and then from the heartlands of the developed economies, the US and Japan. Blatter has continued striking deals with such allies, particularly from small countries in Africa, Asia and the Pacific region. Everyone has had a bit more of the expanding action – in World Cup places, new tournaments for younger age categories, the women's World Cup, the Olympics, the club championship. In the classic style of the Havelange/Blatter era, FIFA has kept everyone happy with increased expense accounts for its inner circle, regular (unmonitored and unaccounted for) payouts of a million dollars to every one of its 204 or so member football federations, reconciliation for troublesome members of the FIFA family.

But perhaps Blatter has gone an incentive or few too far in persuading those delegates to vote him in as president in 1998 and, with the collapse of long-standing financial and marketing partner ISL in 2001, lost credibility within the power base of the core committees. If the Cameroonian Issa Hayatou – or anyone else, for that matter, in 2004 or 2006, if not

Seoul this June – were to topple the dynasty of Havelange and Blatter, there would be a great opportunity to put the unthinkable on the agenda – the reform of FIFA.

What would that reform look like? FIFA could seek to gain some credibility in the eyes of a sceptical public by opening its books, coming out from behind the veil of Swiss secrecy and banking laws that have protected world sports organisations, as well as hoarders of Nazi gold, for half a century and more. It could ask those national federations that have accepted huge and regular handouts to say precisely where the money has gone. It could look to use the profits from bonanzas such as World Cup finals to develop the game at the grassroots. It could make moral interventions in the richest pastures of the world game, the European leagues. It could review the membership and composition of key committees, so that henchmen of the president don't sell on media rights for FIFA events to their own cronies or even their own companies. It could give the executive committee proper and useful functions, such as setting the budget and advising and consulting on major contracts and genuine tenders. It could begin to act with integrity for the good of the game, rather than for the egos of the Fifacrats and the lifestyle of the hangers-on.

Led by the African, Asian and European members of the FIFA executive committee, some of the questions that could lead to such reform may well be put. But Blatter will have answers, and the audit committee appointed to look at FIFA's finances represents all the complex and warring interests of the factions within FIFA. It is hard to see how FIFA might radically reform itself from within. There is too much at stake – everyone is an insider, a beneficiary, a club member. As in any corrupt dynasty, the courtiers are likely to perish with the Prince – Blatter won't mind who goes down with him. He'll have always known that "it is much safer for a prince to be feared than loved". It is this 16th century manual for survival that Sepp Blatter is likely to cling to, rather than the FIFA statutes, as the governing body of world football lumbers towards its centenary year between the 2002 World Cup and Germany 2006. It's hardly likely that an organisation that tamely allowed Blatter to write himself a large cheque, for half as long again as his initial presidential tenure, would find the wherewithal to oust him.

There may be some whiter-than-white heir apparent around the corner, ready to take over when Blatter is willing to step down at the centenary party. Franz Beckenbauer, having won the World Cup as both player and coach, would make a popular figure in Germany, especially after his efforts to secure the 2006 tournament. But even Beckenbauer is not entirely an outsider. How did Germany get those last-minute votes to edge out South Africa for 2006? We may never know, but the answer may lie somewhere in the general direction of the Arabian Gulf.

Reforming FIFA might be an idealistic dream, a hopeless impracticality mired in the messy dynamics of global business and international politics. But football deserves better. The undoubted successes of the Havelange/Blatter era have been achieved at a high price, with deception, evasion and hypocrisy more normal than openness, honesty and transparency. For the good of the game, it is time for FIFA to stand up and be counted. ◯

Green Gauges

Many Irish fans seemed to think Mick McCarthy's squad did well to reach the knockout stage of the 2002 World Cup. Paul Doyle said they should have higher standards

WSC No 186, August 2002

THE JAPANESE WORLD CUP organising committee voted Ireland's fans the best of the tournament, and yes, the Green Army spread the word craic with great gusto. But were all Irish supporters a "credit to their nation"? What, for example, are we to make of the 100,000 who gathered with giddy delight in Dublin's Phoenix Park to greet Mick McCarthy's "heroes" on their return home? What were these strange folks saying about their country's ambitions? Perhaps it was something like: "Anything above naked humiliation will do for us."

Yes, little ol' Ireland battled to the last 16 in the world, emerging unbeaten from cataclysmic clashes with giants such as Holland, Portugal, Spain and even eventual finalists Germany. "And don't forget, we should have beaten the Germans!" But we didn't. We nearly beat silky Spain too. But we didn't. They were deprived of Raúl, were down to ten men in extra time, including the almost totally incapacitated Luis Enrique, and we were awarded two penalties, one after an opprobrious dive from Damien Duff. They were there for the taking! But we didn't take them. "Yeah, but we nearly did! We took them all the way to penos!"... and then took three of the most atrocious spotkicks in the history of Irish football.

We might also have avoided Spain, of course. But we didn't. If Ireland had topped Group E by earning actual victories, as opposed to the wildly celebrated "moral victories" against Cameroon and Germany, we would have had to beat Paraguay, the US and South Korea to claim a historic place in the World Cup final. Now that would have been something to shout about. That would have been the perfect excuse for the Football Association of Ireland to declare a free bar in their sumptuous hotel for hundreds of liggers until 6am, as they did after the draw with Germany.

But we didn't, and we may never get a better chance. Can we really be happy to say, "Ah well, we gave it our best shot"? Do we even care? Or, as Roy Keane famously lamented, are we really only along for the party? The fiasco in the Phoenix Park would actually have been quite fun if Keane had been there. We might well have seen him spontaneously combust right in front of our bleary eyes – surely our fearsome captain wouldn't have been able to contain his fury at the sight of so many of his compatriots basking so smugly in mediocrity. "Martin Luther Keane", as some supporters have dubbed him, was, of course, not there. In their eyes he was shot down for trying to uplift his people. It seems Keane's commitment to what he regarded as the highest professional standards unsettled the Irish camp, perhaps even puzzled some people who revel in the popular Irish self-image of lovable oddballs, full of fighting spirit and a will to, er, do quite well but not dominate (God no, that's for imperialists).

Any number of questions remain about the whole episode. Why did so few of the Irish players protest about conditions in the Saipan training camp as loudly as Keane did? Steve Finnan and Kenny Cunningham were unable to start against Cameroon because of "knocks" picked up on the parched Saipan surface – did either of them express their frustration to McCarthy? Who were the two players who Keane claims told him privately they agreed with everything he said, but didn't support him because they were afraid of being sent home too? It is hard to believe that McCarthy would have sent home three players, but then perhaps Keane was treated in an exceptional way because he has had a long-running, albeit mostly latent, war of attrition with the manager.

That war was intensified by McCarthy's failure to seek a workable resolution. Was it not negligent, for example, for the manager not to so much as telephone his captain and best player after he collapsed in Manchester United's Champions League clash with Deportivo La Coruña? We can't imagine Sven-Göran Eriksson refusing to speak to David Beckham, or Roger Lemerre playing hard to get with Zidane. Keane may be a difficult character to deal with, but McCarthy was inviting conflict by allowing their enmity to fester – indeed, he may even have fanned the flames with the cheap provocation of allowing his World Cup diary to be penned by the Irish journalist most critical of his captain. Some might ask why Keane, whose desire to prolong his career as long as possible led him to request playing in as few friendlies as possible, was the only one of the starting 11 not to be replaced at half-time in Ireland's pre-tournament friendly with Russia.

Do you have to be blindly loyal to the manager to enjoy playing for Ireland? Certainly, loyalty and length of service seem to have strangely prominent places in McCarthy's definition of a meritocracy. Steven Reid is a fine player, who made a powerful impact when he came on against Cameroon, but he was only in Japan because McCarthy's prize pupil, Mark Kennedy, a dunce in most observers' eyes, got injured. And why, as Ireland tried to finish off a reeling Spain, did McCarthy resort to David Connolly, who has simply never looked like an international player, instead of the comparatively swashbuckling Clinton Morrison?

Maybe McCarthy's diary will explain all. It's due out at the end of August, as is Keane's autobiography, which is to be ghost-written by a very visible phantom: Eamon Dunphy, the Irish journalist most critical of McCarthy. We wait to discover whether anything we read will dispel the bizarre mood of jubilation which currently prevails in Ireland, this perverse pride in saying: "We could have – but we didn't." ○

Horror Shows

The World Cup produced some truly awful TV. Barney
Ronay lamented the humiliation of Paul Gascoigne

WSC No 186, August 2002

I LOVE PAUL GASCOIGNE. After the 1990 World Cup, I travelled around
eastern Europe wearing a T-shirt with his face on it and the slogan
"Gizza Goal Gazza" across the front. Wherever I went, the eyes of men
with mullets and snow-washed jeans would light up. "Gazz-scoyne,"
they would say, excitedly. "Yes," I would reply, strangely relieved that this
was the entire extent of the vocabulary we shared. In those days, you see,
everyone loved Gazza.

But it turns out that even love has its limits. And Gazza's appearances
as an ITV pundit during the World Cup have been truly heartbreaking
stuff. Right from the start, from his first slump-shouldered outing on
the sofa, he looked terrified. Propped up between Terry's Sta-Prest and
Ally's Man at Gap single-cuff, he looked as though he was sitting in the
dock waiting to be sentenced. Remember those advertisements before
the World Cup, the ones with a picture of Gascoigne with his mouth taped
up? Hmm, nice idea, you started to think, as he kicked off his punditry
career with the now-infamous: "I've never even heard of Senegal."

But we could forgive Gazza his dodgy start. Maybe he was just keeping
his powder dry; maybe... oh God, he's trying to say Trezeguet. As Gazza
mumbled something about "Trees... are green... tirade", the most
distinctive aspect of his punditry style began to emerge. No one could
understand a word he was saying. We're not talking accents here. This
wasn't a Geordie thing. This was a slur-like-a-drunken-six-year-old thing.
When he wasn't stunned into a palm-sweating silence by the simplest of
questions, there were moments when Gascoigne appeared to be quietly
gurgling to himself while Des nodded patronisingly from his armchair.

That was when he wasn't beginning every sentence with the words
"Like I said before..." (presumably in conversation with the rest of the
lads in the Green Room); or waking up from a quick nap to interrupt a
lengthy discussion of Rivaldo's fine for play-acting against Turkey with
the show-stopper: "I'll tell you what – that ball never even hit him in the
face!" Er, thanks for that, Paul.

When he did manage a few sentences, they tended to include the kind of words that are guaranteed to get the Independent Television Commission hot under the collar. Attempts to complete the phrase "I've got a lot of admira... adrimation... adminiat..." culminated in a sweating Gazza blurting out: "You know what I f***ing mean" – the last two syllables of which were headed off by a remarkably on-the-ball Gabby. Of course, ITV must take the blame. I mean, what were they thinking? Gazza Meets the People... Gazza trots around outside the LWT studios collecting vox pops from tourists who have no idea who he is or what he's talking about. Is he trying to mug them? No, thank God. Now, quick, let's get out of here.

The most notable of Gazza's walkabouts ended up with him leaping around in Trafalgar Square after the England v Argentina game, at one point dunking his entire head into a fountain. "Thank Christ," you could almost hear him thinking, "thank Christ I'm out of that studio. If I can just stay in this fountain, Des can't ask me any more questions." Gazza, of course, is terrified of Des. Picture the scene. The time has come for Des to solicit the "reaction" of his assembled experts to the morning's action. First up is Ally McCoist: jovial, chirpy, reassuringly Scottish. Speaks with the confidence of a man who regularly makes Sue Barker piss herself laughing just by saying "I'll go for No 2, Sue". Next, cut to Robbie Earle: laid back, check-shirted. Not afraid to sit on the fence in a twinkly-eyed kind of way. Jokes lethargically with Des. Could, and probably does, do this in his sleep. And finally, cut to Gazza. A pair of hollow, red-rimmed eyes gaze into the camera. Sweat is already glistening on his forehead. He grimaces; he gasps. The back of Des's head looms ominously in the corner of the screen. Just as it seems the silence, all two seconds of it, just can't go on any longer, Gazza begins, with the air of a man about to climb a mountain: "Like I said before ..."

In Hollywood they say you should never die on screen. It's the first rule of a successful career. Just don't let it happen. During the World Cup Gazza died on our screens every day for two weeks. And there he was the next morning, miraculously risen and ready to go down in flames all over again. Gazza, I don't quite know how to tell you this. But at least we'll have the good times. We'll always have Germany in Turin, that goal against Scotland and, of course, "Fuck off Norway". Unfortunately – and this really is unfortunate – we'll also always have Des Lynam saying: "I think you'll find it's been part of Africa for some time now." ○

Sins of Commission

An arbitrarily appointed FA body sanctioned Wimbledon's move to Milton Keynes. Ian Pollock reported on the staggering logic of a hugely damaging ruling

WSC No 186, August 2002

JUST BEFORE THE WORLD CUP STARTED, a special three-man commission of the FA came to one of the most profound decisions any football authority in England has ever made by giving permission for Wimbledon to move 60 miles north to Milton Keynes. With most fans' attention firmly fixed on events in Japan and South Korea, it is not surprising that hardly any scrutiny has been given to the ruling handed down by the commission on May 28. After all, it only concerned Wimbledon, so who cares?

The three men on the commission were the Aston Villa director Steve Stride, Ryman League chairman Alan Turvey and FA legal adviser Raj Parker. Their arguments – agreed by a vote of two to one, with Turvey believed to be the dissenter – have destroyed two of the essential elements of the way British football has traditionally been organised: that clubs should be based in the area from which they draw their identity; and that progress through the leagues should be on merit.

The essence of the commission's 67-page report is that it is better to let Wimbledon move than to die. The club's owners made it clear that if a move was not sanctioned, it would go straight into liquidation and out of business. Yet the commission appears to have given this supposed "fact" no scrutiny at all. According to the report, the owners claim: "WFC's 2000-01 operating loss was greater, at £10.8 million, than all but two of the other 91 professional clubs in England." However, in a glossy brochure sent to Wimbledon fans just after the decision, the club adds a rider that puts a completely different complexion on the figures: "In the 2000-01 season, the club made a loss of £10.8 million (operating loss before player trading)."

What is glossed over by that phrase "before player trading" is the fact that during that season the club sold Carl Cort to Newcastle for £7m; Ben Thatcher to Tottenham for £5m; Hermann Hreidarsson to Ipswich for £4m; Marcus Gayle to Rangers for £1m; and John Hartson to Coventry for an undisclosed fee. These sums clearly should have eradicated the club's losses and left it with a healthy surplus (the money spent on players coming in was puny by comparison). In the season just ended, another £4m came in through the transfer of Jason Euell to Charlton. What has happened to this money? If it is in the accounts (which have yet to be filed at Companies House) they should show Wimbledon to be solvent.

The club stated that it could not afford to move to a redeveloped Plough Lane site, and therefore had to go to Milton Keynes. Yet on the evening after the decision, one of the club's owners appeared on Norwegian television stating that he would now be authorising the release of £40m to assist the club in its move, significantly more than was required to make Plough Lane a reality. So much for the club's owners, two of the richest men in Europe, having no money.

Quite independently, however, the FA commission managed to conjure up two arguments for the move that should astonish most football fans. Believe it or not, one of the most important reasons for the decision was that: "Milton Keynes provides a suitable and deserving opportunity in its own right where none exists in south London." Savour that concept: the suitable and deserving opportunity. In one glib, ignorant phrase the commission has swept aside more than 100 years of football clubs trying to advance themselves by actually beating their opponents and winning games. Just to rub it in, and to make it clear that league placings should have little to do with merit any more, the commission quoted approvingly the view of an earlier Football League arbitration panel which said: "It should be in the interests of football as a whole that major new stadia are encouraged where there is an untapped demand for major league football, such as in new towns. It is true that a route does exist through the pyramid structure to achieve this, but it is a somewhat tortuous one."

There we have it. You are a new town or maybe a big town. You have no club or maybe a very unsuccessful one. The answer is simple. Don't bother with the long-winded and tedious business of building up a local outfit into something bigger and better. Just get another one to move in! This is a policy familiar to people in the US and Canada. It is called franchising, where teams disappear overnight, only to reappear on the other side of the country in a more prosperous location, or one that has fewer competitors in the vicinity.

Intriguingly, the commission peppers its reports with assertions that it has not set a precedent; that franchising is bad; and that it won't happen anyway. It says much for the intellectual rigour of the commission that it could so blatantly deny the most obvious conclusion of its own decision. The plain fact is that any unscrupulous chairman could now sell his club's ground, move to a "temporary" location, claim poverty and then demand a move. How could the football authorities argue against it? What could they say if an existing club in a big town or city (like, say, Bristol, Swindon, Bradford or Coventry) went bust and another club came along and asked for permission to move in and take over the "franchise"? The incoming club would only have to point to the example of Wimbledon in order to succeed.

For their part, Wimbledon fans have set up a new club (which they will own and control through the Dons Trust) so that they can watch football this coming season and actually enjoy it. AFC Wimbledon narrowly failed to win election to the Ryman League, but were accepted by the Combined Counties League and the season kicks off on August 17 after a flurry of friendlies. With a target of 1,000 season ticket holders, and having established a groundsharing arrangement with Ryman Premier League Kingstonian, it will be by far the best supported club in that league and promotion to the Ryman First Division is the initial goal.

What about Milton Keynes though? Members of the Wimbledon Independent Supporters Association will continue to campaign vigorously against their old club's move. But most WISA members have given up on the football authorities doing anything to help. Both the Football League and the FA ducked their responsibilities. They asked three people who represented no one but themselves to make the decision instead.

The football authorities, bizarrely, now say the decision is one they don't like and which worries them. But will they do anything about it, such as repudiating the commission's findings, or refusing Wimbledon FC the move its owners desire? No chance. Pusillanimous hand-wringing is the order of the day when the authorities are faced with the demands of rich businessmen to make a profitable return on their misguided investment in football. ○

Brother World

Harry Pearson welcomed a biography of the Charlton brothers that looked more sympathetically on Bobby's personality and criticised his detractors

WSC No 188, October 2002

WHEN IT COMES TO THE CHARLTON BROTHERS, most people probably concur with the assessment Big Jack apparently delivered to Ron Atkinson: "Our kid was the better footballer, but I am the better bloke."

In this biography of the two very different Northumbrians, Leo McKinstry – a former Labour party activist and author of a well received book on Geoff Boycott – doesn't quite reverse that opinion, but he does present a much more sympathetic portrait of Bobby than has appeared in print for some while. At the same time he does little to discredit the view that in a world where every cynical poltroon lays claim to being courageously honest and free of bullshit, Jack is the genuine article. The result is a thoroughly entertaining and ultimately rather uplifting read.

As *Jack & Bobby* makes plain, the elder brother remains fiercely loyal to his younger sibling despite their falling out. The cause of that, as has been well documented, was Bobby's estrangement from their mother, Cissie. Cissie Charlton was a tough northern matriarch and plainly didn't much care for Bobby's wife, Norma. Maybe Norma's coolness was partly defensive. Because while everybody likes Jack (well, everybody except Eamon Dunphy and Roy Keane), Bobby, for all his gifts on the field, is a different kettle of cold fish – in Brian Labone's words "a bit of a sad sack".

Bobby was a natural conformist who paradoxically failed to fit in. As a consequence he was derided by team-mates like Denis Law (who caustically referred to him as "Sir Bobby" decades before that title was officially bestowed) and Paddy Crerand (who dubbed him "the imposter" because he thought his abilities so wildly over-rated). He was also mercilessly baited by George Best – asked to name the biggest influence on his career on a TV chat show, Best sarcastically replied "Cissie Charlton".

Despite that, McKinstry finds plenty of former players prepared to testify to Bobby's charm, kindness and the hilarity of his Ben Turpin impression. And it's hard to imagine that if he was really quite as aloof as has been alleged, Bill Shankly would frequently have called round at his house unannounced for tea, biscuits and hours of football talk. Despite all the glowing endorsements to his gentlemanliness McKinstry has accumulated, in the end perhaps the greatest testimony to Bobby's essential decency is the list of those who hate him. After all, anyone who's earned the enmity of Law, Crerand and Big Ron can't be all bad.

And then there is that other Charlton detester, Best. McKinstry doesn't have much time for "El Beatle" and delivers an impassioned diatribe about the injustice of the Irishman being more popular than his dedicated and well behaved team-mate that recalls the speech Anthony Hopkins delivers about John F Kennedy in the Oliver Stone movie *Nixon*.

In light of the apparently endless parade of lard-chopped middle-aged men who appear on our TV screens tittering about Besty's, y'know, way with "the ladies", it's hard not to sympathise with the author's position. As he says, Best treated United like dirt and short-changed the fans by his absences, while Charlton gave his life (almost literally) to the club and never offered less than total commitment. Yet who do the supporters at Old Trafford idolise? In the end, as with JFK, it all boils down to the power of looks and charm.

McKinstry makes his point well enough, but when it comes to swatting Georgie boy, Big Jack inevitably does it better. During a trip to Lisbon to play in Eusebio's testimonial, the Leeds centre-half meets up with Best and Tommy Docherty on the hotel terrace. For five minutes he listens to Best bellyaching about what he will and won't do until finally, he remarks: "I was so disgusted I got up and walked away. He was just a fat little fellah who had been wasting his time."

Those, like Best, who criticise Bobby for his reticence and distance rarely seem to consider the effect the Munich air crash might have had on him. As a United room-mate Ronnie Cope comments: "Bobby altered unbelievably after Munich. He never got back to being a joker, the Bobby Charlton I had known as a lad. He became withdrawn. Sometimes you'd ask him a question and it was like he just didn't hear."

Given that Charlton was just 21 at the time of Munich and was seriously injured, while many of his closest friends died, that seems entirely understandable. While he is undoubtedly deeply conservative, publicly awkward and may not have visited his mother as often he should have done, you come away from this book feeling that a little compassion might be in order. ○

Ivory Poachers

Dan Brennan described how England's two most successful clubs linked up with struggling Belgian outfits in order to get easy access to the African market

WSC No 188, October 2002

A COUNTRY THAT CONSISTENTLY MANAGES to field a team of thirty-something geriatrics in the World Cup wouldn't seem like the first place to go looking for young talent. On the face of it, in fact, the idea of a Belgian nursery club seems like a bit of a contradiction in terms. Odd then, perhaps, that England's top two clubs, Manchester United and Arsenal, with the world seemingly at their fingertips, should have got into bed with a pair of cash-strapped Flemish strugglers, Royal Antwerp and Beveren. Man Utd's link-up with Royal Antwerp is now into its fourth year, while Arsenal, having formed an informal alliance with Beveren a season ago, have just announced a five-year "technical relationship" with the Belgian club. At first glance, the benefits in both cases seem to be almost entirely in the Belgians' favour.

Last season Beveren were bottom of the Belgian league and on the verge of financial ruin. In fact, the club's officials say they would have gone under had the link-up with Arsenal not been secured. While there is no money changing hands, Beveren have benefited from access to Arsenal's talented youngsters, not to mention the odd cast-off such as the Greek-passport-toting Lithuanian, Tomas Danilevicius. Youth team players Graham Stack, Liam Chilvers and John Halls have crossed the Channel for the current season, and have gone straight into the Beveren first team. Similarly, with Man Utd and Antwerp the traffic so far has been all one-way, with the likes of Ronnie Wallwork, Danny Higginbotham, Luke Chadwick and Simon Colosimo having served time in Belgium (almost literally in Wallwork's case, who escaped a life ban after assaulting a referee while with Antwerp).

With handy extra revenue from friendlies and the opportunity to bask in the reflected glory of their English counterparts, it seems like a pretty cushy deal for the Belgians. So what exactly do Arsenal and Man Utd get out of it? True, they might be able to add a little bit to the future transfer values of their young charges, as United did with Wallwork, now at West

Brom. But if all the clubs wanted was a temporary playground-cum-shop window then what is wrong with Bournemouth or Burnley? Surely the possibility of discovering the next Gerard Sibon doesn't warrant the extra hassle and the outgoings on Eurostar tickets?

The truth is that these are merely fringe benefits. The main attraction of Belgium is that it offers a backdoor into other markets, particularly Africa. Belgian clubs, out of economic necessity and with the aid of liberal rules on overseas imports, have long been tapping into that continent's abundant pool of talent. By forming strategic alliances with Antwerp and Beveren, Man Utd and Arsenal are putting themselves in pole position to beat other top European clubs in the race to discover the next Aghahowas and Dioufs before they acquire seven-figure price tags.

Last month, Man Utd announced the signing of Henry Gomez, the 18-year-old prodigy of Gambian football, a player they have been tracking quietly for almost two years. Instead of coming straight to Old Trafford, however, he has been put on the books at Antwerp. This will offer him a softer landing into European football, and the chance to gain some experience. More importantly though, because Belgian rules on nationality are much more lax than those in the UK, after two years in Antwerp Gomez will be eligible for citizenship, making him an EU player and removing any work permit headaches he would certainly encounter by coming straight to Britain.

Ferguson, as he says, always gets his man. However, in this latest round of managerial oneupmanship, Wenger has so far managed to go one better. While Ferguson has taken four years to unearth one Gambian gem, Wenger has opened up a whole new pipeline into Africa's top youth academy. The relationship with Beveren is based on Wenger's long-standing friendship with his fellow Frenchman Jean-Marc Guillou, now the Belgian club's general manager. A former French footballer of the year and team-mate of Michel Platini in the national side, Guillou spent most of the Nineties working in the Ivory Coast. There he set up Sifco, a football academy attached to the country's top side, ASEC Mimosas.

Sifco was founded with financial support from Monaco, but is now entirely self-sufficient and has been hailed as the finest breeding ground for young talent in Africa. In 1998 ASEC won the African Champions League, which meant they qualified to meet the Tunisian giants Espérance in the CAF Super Cup (the equivalent of the European Super Cup). To the disbelief of African football observers and the club's own fans, they rested their entire first team and sent out a team made up

17-year-olds – the first batch of graduates from Guillou's academy. The Tunisians, with a team full of seasoned internationals, were taken apart 3-1 in a fearless and stylish display that has since written itself into the folklore of African football.

Beveren have already benefited hugely from Guillou's connections. Their squad this year includes no fewer than seven Ivory Coast players and the signs from early games are that they could make a dramatic difference to a team that only avoided relegation last season because two clubs that finished above them were demoted due to irregularities. What's good for Beveren will also be good for Arsenal. Not only do they get an option on any of the African players already at Beveren, but they also tap directly into ASEC Mimosas and Guillou's academy in Abidjan.

The strategy has already started to pay off with the signing of Kolo Touré. Touré's arrival from ASEC last February went largely unnoticed, but the 23-year-old captain of the Ivory Coast national side is already staking a claim for a regular first-team place. In Touré's case, because he has already played many times for his country, there was no problem with work permits. But as with Man Utd and Gomez, Arsenal will in future have the option of bringing players in from ASEC via Beveren to avoid problems with Home Office red tape.

In a manoeuvre that has left European bureaucrats and the FIFA rulemakers scratching their heads, England's two dominant clubs have demonstrated that they are mastering the rules of globalisation. The two are reminiscent of a pair of rival generals mapping out their campaigns for global domination. Early signs are that the battle on the Belgian-African front seems to have gone to Arsenal. But with United also exploring similar links in South America, south-east Asia and Australia, the war is yet to be won. ○

North by North-East

The North Korea team that took the 1966 World Cup by storm were about to return to England, as a new film documented their triumph. Harry Pearson had a preview

WSC No 189, November 2002

ON FRIDAY OCTOBER 25 a worker from a North Korean textbook factory will return to the scene of his greatest triumph. Pak Do Ik has not been back to Middlesbrough since his goal set up what remains arguably the greatest shock in World Cup history, his country's 1-0 win over Italy in 1966. Ayresome Park is now a housing estate. The Holgate End, where support for the North Korean outsiders was so vociferous it fused the press-box lights ("They've never cheered Middlesbrough like this for years," bellowed BBC commentator Frank Bough), is a communal garden. The area to the left of what was once the Holgate End penalty spot is somebody's front lawn. But if you look very carefully you will see in among the neatly clipped grass the bronze cast of the imprint of a football boot – a sculpture by the artist Neville Gabie – that marks the spot from which North Korea's No 7 struck his shot.

Pak Do Ik, along with the six other surviving members of that North Korea team, are coming to England for the first time since Eusebio's barnstorming display at Goodison Park in the quarter-final removed them from the tournament. Daniel Gordon and Nicholas Bonner have spent the past five years making a wonderfully entertaining and moving documentary, *The Game Of Their Lives*, which tells the story of the North Korea team at the World Cup. They are the first Westerners to have been given permission to meet and film the players who caused such a sensation 36 years ago and then, apparently, disappeared without trace.

David Lacey, Bernard Gent and a clutch of the Middlesbrough fans who idolised them also contribute, as do a couple of the vanquished Italians. Gianni Rivera, looking like a wealthy technocrat from a Fellini movie, is still pleasingly grumpy about the whole business, disdainfully dismissing the North Koreans as an inferior team, though his former team-mate Sandro Mazzola is altogether more engaging, merrily chuckling as he recalls the Italians' arrival back home to a hail of rotten fruit: "I didn't get hit by anything. I was quick in those days!"

The film effectively juxtaposes archive commentary from the BBC and previously unseen footage shot by the North Korean documentary crew that accompanied the team throughout the World Cup, with film shot in the People's Democratic Republic over the past few years. The latter varies from the spectacular, to the grim, to the downright eerie. Anyone who wonders what a team from east Asia would make of training at Billingham Synthonia should take a look at the playing surface at the Ryongsong Cigarette Factory, a ruckled mud-patch on which we see The Tobacconists doing battle with The Paper Rollers under the watchful if slightly rheumy eye of Pak Do Ik's old colleague, Yang Song Guk.

Most of the spookiness comes courtesy of Kim Il Sung, The Great Leader – a man so revered in North Korea that he remains head of state despite having been dead for eight years. At one point in the film the players in their medal-bedecked baggy suits and ill-fitting military uniforms (what has communism got against tailoring?) gather in the shadow of an enormous statue of Kim Il Sung and recall their meeting with him before they left for England. Suddenly one of them, the half-back Rim Jung Song, blurts out "I wish he was still alive!" and bursts into tears, sending several other team members into convulsive sobs. It is a moment at once touching and yet unnerving, like watching an elderly German weeping over his old comrades.

Kim Il Sung loomed large in thoughts of the players throughout the World Cup. Recalling a period of self-doubt before the qualifying game against Australia, centre-half Rim Jung Song says: "Then I remembered what The Great Leader had said to us, 'In order to be a good footballer you must run swiftly and pass the ball accurately.'" This suggests that had the bottom ever fallen out of the dictatorship market The Great Leader could have found gainful employment as an east Asian Trevor Brooking, yet such is the belief in his wisdom among North Koreans that this bland comment was enough to refire Rim Jung Song's belief in himself. The team thrashed Australia 9-2 on aggregate. Those games highlighted some of the problems surrounding the North Korean team. Since the end of the Korean War in 1953, the north had been completely isolated. As Australia and North Korea did not officially recognise each other, both games were played in the Cambodian capital Phnom Penh.

Similar troubles attended the trip to Britain. The foreign office thought of refusing visas, but that might have lead FIFA to move the World Cup, so instead they came up with a series of diplomatic compromises. The team would be called "North Korea", never the Democratic People's

Republic of Korea; the flag could be flown, but national anthems would be played only before the first match and the final – neither of which was expected to involve Pak Do Ik and his fellows.

And so the North Koreans arrived at London Airport and then trundled northwards on British Rail singing their patriotic songs ("Carrying the nation's honour on our shoulders" runs one) and signing autographs for ladies with beehive hair-dos and wing-tipped spectacles. In Middlesbrough, the mayor, mindful of the fact that many locals might be mistrustful of the visitors with whom this country had so recently been at war ("We were the enemy," Pak Do Ik observes candidly), made a whole-hearted effort to ensure the North Koreans were given a warm welcome. It succeeded beyond all hopes. "It remains a riddle to me," says Rim Jung Song. "The people of Middlesbrough supported us all the way through – I still don't know why."

One Boro fan who watched the games offers an explanation: "They were small for a start, which was a novelty. They were like a team of jockeys. But they moved the ball around. They played good football." The size thing (the average height of the team was just 5ft 5in) was indeed a factor. In their first game against the Soviet Union the North Koreans were knocked flying by their much larger opponents who, to use a technical term, simply kicked the shit out of them. As David Lacey says, it was the sight of small men being bullied that really awakened the sympathy of the crowd.

After that, North Korea became the home side at Ayresome Park and hundreds of people travelled from Teesside to Liverpool to watch them take on Portugal, where they amazingly took a 3-0 lead after 24 minutes, only to succumb 5-3 thanks to the brilliance of Eusebio. "His shooting was so accurate and so powerful. I was just not good enough to save it," recalls the goalkeeper Ri Chan Myong, with an honesty and frankness some Premiership net-minders might learn from.

In the end, though, the result was hardly the point: "The English people took us to their hearts and vice versa," says Pak Do Ik. "I learned that football is not about winning. Wherever we go... playing football can improve diplomatic relations and promote peace." The North Koreans' trip back to England this autumn should prove his point. O

Dun Ranting

Jim McLean finally quit Dundee United. Ken Gall said the man who made the club great was right about most things, even if he didn't always put it politely

WSC No 190, December 2002

WITH ALL FOUR SCOTTISH ENTRANTS for European club competition experiencing varying degrees of disappointment and humiliation, and Arsène Wenger openly scoffing at the notion of ever signing a Scottish player, one might imagine that the game north of the border could do with all the help it can get. How appropriate, then, that Jim McLean, one of the finest coaches of young players in Scottish football history and, perhaps, the last manager ever to take a Scottish club to a major European final, should choose to take his leave from the game now. Have the SFA called on the youth development expertise of the man who discovered, among dozens of others, Andy Gray, Richard Gough, Paul Sturrock and Duncan Ferguson? Was McLean asked to provide coaching assistance of any kind to wee Berti? Of course not – although anyone with even a cursory knowledge of McLean and his tempestuous career might understand why that was.

McLean's sale of his 40 per cent shareholding in Dundee United brought to an end a 31-year spell at Tannadice as coach, manager, director, chairman and dictator (sometimes benevolent, sometimes less so). His achievements do not pale beside those of Jock Stein, Bill Shankly, Matt Busby and his friend and contemporary, Alex Ferguson. But his real peer was Brian Clough, another man of, shall we say, idiosyncratic personality who took previously unheralded clubs to the upper reaches of European competition. It hardly needs adding that both Nottingham Forest and Dundee United have faded towards insignificance following their departure, with no subsequent manager capable of even approaching the glory days. (McLean even attempted a previously untried genetic experiment in management by appointing his own younger brother to the post, sadly without success.)

When McLean took over as United manager in 1971, the club had won no major honours. A dozen years later, United, as champions of Scotland, were a goal away from a European Cup final appearance against Liverpool in Rome. Three seasons on, they lost narrowly to Gothenburg in the UEFA Cup final, having beaten Barcelona home and away to get there. McLean took his team to a European final for an outlay of approximately £500,000 – something that the post-Souness Rangers have signally failed to do for, at the very least, 100 times that amount.

With a bad temper of world class proportions, McLean seemed to thrive on conflict and contrary behaviour. Many supposedly lifelong enemies were created within the club, the media and the football authorities, only for them to be welcomed back into the charmed circle at a later stage. Unsubstantiated tales of dressing-room punch-ups and shouting matches with agents, parents of young players and fans were common currency in Dundee for many years. The volcanic eruption of legend was finally seen in horrifying close-up in a celebrated post-match encounter with the BBC's unfortunate John Barnes, who chose to ask the wrong question at the wrong moment to an under-pressure United chairman.

McLean's sour-faced complaints were numerous and well rehearsed. "Agents are a cancer within the game." "Players with not enough ability want too much money." "Television is killing football." "The Old Firm are stifling the Scottish game." Lacking the acolytes in the press that automatically accompany a job at either Celtic or Rangers, McLean's rants were often greeted with a smirk of indifference by the media and the authorities. The utterances of Rangers' David Murray – a man whose talents as a coach were unproven at best – were, by contrast, treated with the utmost seriousness.

Yet, in retrospect, the prophecies of the Tannadice Cassandra were pretty close to the mark. Most of what he feared would happen to football – Scottish football in particular – has come to pass, and much of what he now suggests is ignored. As the balance of power shifted from clubs with authoritarian managers to whining brats and their vulgar agents, McLean's policies with regard to young players were condemned publicly as neo-Victorian. According to agents – men who, it should be recalled, stood to gain substantially from the transfer of such young players – McLean was only just stopping short of putting nails in the young lads' feet and sending them up the Tannadice chimney. United's policy was clear – long-term contracts for young players on low wages until they had developed, whereupon the club would accept a large transfer fee, which would be channelled back into youth development. With the financial structure of the Scottish game close to meltdown at present, one can look at that policy for some considerable time before finding fault with it.

But the infamous television bust-up, serious heart surgery and – it must be said – the awareness that his 40 per cent of Dundee United would soon be worth 40 per cent of hee-haw, led to McLean finally calling it a day. And here is an indicator of how Scottish football treats its most notable eminences. McLean's principal contribution to the game now is a weekly column in a tabloid paper entitled, with no apparent thought for the feelings of the aforementioned Mr Barnes, "The Column that Packs a Punch". O

Senior Citizens

The European Union was expanding as rapidly as the waistlines of retired footballers. Al Needham puzzled over an event that brought the two together

WSC No 190, December 2002

THE EUROPE UNITED MASTERS TOURNAMENT was held at the London Arena on a miserable October Sunday, wedged between the Disney Channel Kids Awards and *Beauty and the Beast On Ice*. It had a weird premise: the Foreign Office decided that the best way to mark the admission of ten new countries to the European Union was to organise a kickabout for retired footballers, some of them not exactly renowned for their Europhilia (one of the British Masters squad once said living in Italy was like being in a foreign country and another famously told Norway to "Fuck off"). Mind you, if you needed reminding that there have been worse ideas, we're only a stone's throw away from the Millennium Dome.

Although Masters football has a bit of a joke reputation, you can't deny it's an impressive turnout. There are four squads – British Masters and representatives (loosely defined) from northern, central and southern Europe, scattered with the aforementioned legends and lesser stars from Ireland to Slovenia. And I'm in the "press area", which is actually the empty end behind one of the goals on the carpeted-over hockey rink. As soon as I get there, I'm granted an interview with none other than Tony Banks. Crikey. "So, Tony, what's the appeal of retired footballers?" He looks back at me as if I've suggested that he'd been involved in threesomes with David Mellor and Stamford the Lion. "Well, you just wait until you see the skill level of these players," he asserts. "Gazza in particular, he's in outstanding condition. Masters Football does a lot of good work in showcasing the talents of former professionals, and remember that most of the players here are part of the last generation before the big money arrived, so they're entitled to it." Tony then goes on to describe the entertainment he organised for a selection of Leeds United Old Boys, and I depart with a nightmare image of him having a "Singalonga" with Paul Madeley, and Gary Sprake in a sequinned suit organising the tombola.

I'm now backstage, behind the curtains, witnessing a passing triangle between Gazza, Ally McCoist (who looks two stone heavier than he does on the telly) and Ray Wilkins. They tap the ball about with all the casual flair and nonchalance of the Four Tops hunkered round a brazier, and I'm desperate to lunge in and tonk it one like Peter Kay in the beer advert. But I can't. The main focus of today is Gazza's attempt to make one last comeback, and he appears to be taking it seriously. There's a tennis court off to the left. The Gazza of old would have been knackering himself out on it, but not today. Then he muscles the ball off Ally McCoist, blasts it miles, says "Have it! Hurr hurr! Off the advert, like!" and wanders over to the arena. There's a huge crowd of people roped off in the corner like the saddos in Leicester Square when there's a film premiere, not even watching the games, brandishing autograph books the size of the Yellow Pages, desperate for his attention. In the most telling moment of the day, Sebastiano Nela (Italy squad, 1986 World Cup) pushes a camera into the hand of Moreno Manini (Sampdoria and Forest), shyly taps Gazza on the back and poses for a photo with him.

The games themselves. Well. "Interesting." Rather like those episodes of *Roy of the Rovers* in the late 1970s when the NASL looked esoteric and threatening. The main concern for the audience was what shape the heroes of old were in. Gazza – fit. Ian Rush – leaner than ever (possibly because his tache has gone). Liam Brady – very dad-like. Neville Southall? Ted Bovis. From close up, the entire skill set is still in place and at times you forget that these players are pros no more (Amara Simba, for example – surely he could do a job for a club a few rungs up the ladder from Clacton). But it's weird. The *Gladiators*-like presentation detracts from it. You can't really believe it when the announcer screams: "Boncho Genchev, who absolutely shone for Sporting Lisbon – and Carshalton Athletic", or: "We need a hero! We need Henry IV! We need Winston Churchill! We need... Michael Thomas!" Tellingly, most of the kids are looking up at the TV screens built into the ice hockey scoreboard, just like *Top of the Pops* audiences, and slope off during the games not involving Britain (who don't make the final, putting a bit of a damp squib on things – the South beat the North 6-2, incidentally).

When it was all over, I hit the door wondering what the point was of seeing past-their prime-players. And then I saw a billboard for forthcoming attractions at the London Arena: Madness, Dollar, Five Star, Visage, for Christ's sake. And the scales dropped from my eyes. We live in an age when audiences reject the new for the old, and if bands who haven't had a hit for nearly two decades are entitled to be on stage and earn a pension, then why not Paul Walsh, Bernie Slaven and Owen Coyle too?

This time next year, some entrepreneur will take the phenomenon to its logical conclusion and form lookalike "tribute" teams. You'll be able to see Boys Of '66, The Perma-Wave (Liverpool 1977), Spirit Of '76 (Czechoslovakia's European Championship squad) and the '48 Crash (Blackpool's FA Cup-losing squad, for the purists). I guarantee it. ○

Frayed in Wales

Fierce rivalry is one thing, but Swansea and Cardiff had become a poisonous affair in recent years. It wasn't always that way, explained Huw Richards

WSC No 190, December 2002

GAVIN GORDON OF OXFORD UNITED probably did not enjoy playing against Swansea in October. He got the reception George Bush might expect at a peace rally, was booed unceasingly and went off injured after about 20 minutes. Swans fans enjoyed the game even less, mind you, going bottom of the league for the second time after a 1-0 defeat. The abuse of Gordon was not racist in intent, although the Swans following is not free of that poison. Gordon's crime was not that he is black, but that he was a Bluebird. That's all it takes.

The relationship between Swansea and Cardiff combines standard intercity venom with strictly local idiosyncrasies. Unwillingness to unite in the national cause is one. And where most vicious rivalries gather fresh momentum from frequent meetings, Swansea and Cardiff don't play that often – only 48 league meetings in more than 80 years (concern for balance forces me to add that the Swans lead 18-16), although the Welsh Cup (Cardiff lead 18-7) has provided 33 more opportunities for mutual revilement.

The violence pervading these games is generally more of atmosphere than commission. Many were played on Boxing Day morning with spectators (and players, to judge by the quality of the football) too hungover to do more than make rude gestures. We should, however, acknowledge the genius of the South Wales Police who, irked by holiday overtime payments, insisted on Cardiff's 1993-94 home game being moved to the evening of Wednesday, December 22 and were surprised when fans took the chance to get tanked up before spreading alarm and despondency among city centre shoppers. As well, too, that Cardiff lost their Third Division semi-final play-off in 1997. A Wembley meeting might have got demolition work off to a flying start, but militarising the entire M4 would have been challenging.

It wasn't always like this. News of Swansea Town's Second Division survival in 1952 reportedly inspired one of the "biggest cheers" at Ninian Park. Martin Johnes's excellent *Soccer and Society: Wales 1900-39* records that 25 years earlier Cardiff City's FA Cup winners were supported by a trainload of fans from Swansea and exultant coverage in Swansea papers. What has changed since then is the relationship between the cities, as well as the football clubs. If Cardiff was always a little larger, wealthier, closer to England and more football-minded – its Valleys hinterland is predominantly football territory while Swansea is ringed with rugby towns like Neath and Llanelli – these were differences of degree. This changed in 1954 when Cardiff was declared the capital of Wales and, after 70 years of equal sharing, rugby internationals were taken away from Swansea.

This created a pattern, maintained since – the Opera House, Millennium Stadium, county cricket and the Welsh Assembly are only the most recent prizes bestowed on Cardiff – which has fed Swansea's sense of grievance and Cardiff's of superiority. True, the average North Banker setting upon his Grange End counterpart is not thinking about the opera, or consciously avenging the decision to locate the Assembly in a city which voted against its creation. But there is a general resentment, crisply if inelegantly summarised by the Swansea *Evening Post*'s description of our capital as "a greedy city with a big mouth". It is deepened when the Cardiff-based media echoes Sam Hammam's belief that Cardiff City represent the whole of Wales – the equivalent of suggesting all Lancastrians support Man Utd while Londoners follow Arsenal. It adds edge to Cardiff chants of "We won't play you again" – football's equivalent of Metropolitan policemen waving their wage packets at striking miners – at last season's FAW Premier Cup final.

Yet we have a great deal in common. Large numbers of our greatest players have played for both sides. The poet Danny Abse recounted how he would while away sleepless hours with a litany of Cardiff heroes: "Trevor Ford, John Charles, Mel Charles, Ivor Allchurch". All four came from Swansea and started with the Swans, although John Toshack, perhaps the most significant of the shared careers, made the opposite journey. Cardiff admittedly have the edge in literary support – Abse planned poetry readings around their fixture list, while Dylan Thomas's sole acknowledgement of his home town club was the question debated by two schoolboys in an autobiographical story: "Would the Swans beat the Spurs?" (Thomas does not tell us, but of course they didn't.) But Abse's litany also underlines decline. Will any of us ever while away insomnia by summoning images of recent players, such as the obscure centre-forward and notorious hooligan Dai Thomas, or even useful performers like Andy Legg and Jason Bowen?

All 28 of the league derbies up to 1983-84 were played in the old Second Division. All 20 since have been lower. Cardiff's ten-year average is 69th out of 92, and Swansea's 72nd. So the answer to the endless, futile debate about Wales's top club is, of course, Wrexham (58th). As Cardiff rise, we fear that our next derby will be with Newport County or, worse still, Afan Lido. This induces envy – we'd like owners with the money and drive of Hammam, or before him Rick Wright. There's amusement when they screw up in the play-offs, irritation at delusional "sleeping giant" guff related to a club of such minimal recent achievement and frank amazement at protestations of injured innocence following the Leeds riot last year. A vile reputation in every town in the lower divisions (no, we're no angels either) hasn't happened by accident. But it is frankly tedious – as well as taking them at their inflated self-valuation – to chant "We Hate Cardiff" when playing Oxford or Darlington. Add in chants of "England's full of shit", and hating 90 out of 91 possible league opponents (not that we're keen on Wrexham, mind), seems a touch misanthropic.

There are some signs of change. Jackarmy.net, a Swans website, has initiated a series of matches against Cardiff fans. Cardiff voices were prominent in support of the Swansea campaign to eject the despised Tony Petty last year – and we will happily reciprocate should their Hammam adventure end, as it may well, in fresh disappointment.

So perhaps the Cardiff media folk who say we should welcome their success as good news for Welsh football (although I don't remember Swansea's Toshack-era rise being seen in this light) are right. I can buy that, just as I accept that Conservative governments are the price of democracy and that England have the most exciting rugby team in Europe. Realities all. But who says you have to like reality ? ○

2003

Star Mistreatment

Sergei Rebrov was off to Istanbul. His former translator, Dan Brennan, hoped the Ukrainian would be better looked after at Fenerbahce than at Tottenham

WSC No 193, March 2003

AND SO, FINALLY, the Sergei Rebrov saga has drawn to a close. Just as it seemed he would be playing his football in west London, he has bid the Premiership a sad farewell and opted for Istanbul. It has been two wasted years for the player, and an opportunity missed for Spurs and English football.

Disentangling the web of intrigue surrounding the Ukrainian over the last few months has become, even for the most ardent Rebrov watchers, a tricky business. I should first declare my interest. I worked with Sergei during his initial season at Spurs, in a role which officially embraced English teaching and interpreting. Unofficially, it involved everything from assembling Ikea furniture to providing conflict resolution services – appeasing his Chigwell neighbours whose alarm systems were constantly being triggered by his nocturnal ham radio signals – and fielding calls on Christmas day about seasonal opening hours. Although we parted company after a year, I have continued to follow his career with more than passing curiosity.

As an Arsenal supporter, it was an odd situation to be in. I had watched him grab a last-minute Champions League equaliser against us for Dinamo Kiev and thought he'd be a great player to have. Arsène Wenger even made a £7 million bid. But doing my best to put partisanship aside, I became very fond of Rebrov – a good thing, really, as we spent a lot of time together. I think many people – those at football clubs included – underestimate just how much support a foreign player and his family need when they first arrive in a new country. I even found myself cheering from the stands when he scored in a derby at White Hart Lane – in mitigation I should say that he'd got me the ticket for my birthday, so it would have been bad manners not to.

Soon after his goal, with ten minutes to go, having worked his socks off, Rebrov was substituted. It was clear as he trundled off that, like the crowd, he could not understand why. Arsenal equalised at the death. I think that game was typical of his predicament at Spurs. It was pearls to swine. The fans clearly knew a good thing when they saw it, but neither George Graham nor Glenn Hoddle seemed to. The club failed to make him feel appreciated. That they managed to reduce one of Europe's biggest talents to a self-doubting benchwarmer in a couple of years will go down, in my view, as one of the great feats of football mismanagement; and in Hoddle's case it leaves an even more indelible question mark against his interpersonal skills than his inept handling of Paul Gascoigne.

Rebrov is, by nature, reticent and retiring – he is certainly not the prima donna sort who goes crying to the tabloids at the first hint of a problem. For the most part he let his agent do the talking (some would say more than enough for both of them) and when he did speak about his situation at Spurs he always showed remarkable restraint and decorum. But in his final few days, as his transfer stalled for the umpteenth time, he made a rare outburst. Having been made to wait for over three hours at the club outside the directors' office as his future was discussed – like a naughty schoolboy awaiting punishment from the headmaster – he told me, in a mixture of anger and disbelief: "It is one thing not to be played, but to be treated the way that Daniel Levy has treated me – like a piece of meat, not as part of the club – is just lacking in human decency. He didn't even say hello to me, or offer me a cup of tea. This would never have happened in Kiev."

Widely reported as the reason for the late collapse of a move to

Fulham was the player's worry that Jean Tigana would not be there next season: after his unhappy experience with Hoddle, the Ukrainian is understandably sensitive about finding a boss who will love him and be there for him. But the Tigana factor was also probably used to hide deeper concerns over the state of Fulham's finances. With Mohamed Fayed threatening to take away his ball, the Craven Cottage revamp in tatters, and the Marlet affair casting a pall over the club's transfer dealings and sowing seeds of mistrust within the club, it is quite possible that Rebrov and his agent, Sandor Varga, looked 12 months down the line and didn't like what they saw.

However, there are strong indications that having narrowly avoided a frying pan in Fulham, the ill-starred Ukrainian may just walk into a fire at Fenerbahce. Apart from the fact that carting all that ham radio paraphernalia across Europe will be one hell of a hassle, Fenerbahce does appear a more enticing option. He should renew his acquaintance with European football and maybe add to the 28 Champions League goals (including nine in qualifying) that make him one of the competition's all-time top scorers. He can link up with Argentina playmaker Ariel Ortega, as near to the antithesis of Steffen Freund as you can get and in fact just the sort of midfielder that Spurs have lacked since, oh irony of ironies, Hoddle the Player moved on. And of course being able to chew the fat with Russian international Vladimir Beschastnykh, whose claims, touchingly, that he "speaks the same language as Sergei on and off the field", will make a nice change from waving helplessly for the ball and exchanging grunts with Gary Doherty in the Spurs reserves. But not so fast – headlines pronouncing "Rebrov's Turkish Delight" could still be premature. Fenerbahce have big problems of their own.

First, let's deal with Beschastnykh. Although his contract with Spartak Moscow ostensibly ran out on December 31, the Russians insisted that he, or any club that signed him, must pay them $800,000. This was the mystery factor that scared off Bolton, after Beschastnykh impressed in a trial. The Turks thought they could tough it out and called Spartak's bluff. But the Russians kept knocking on their door – literally. Last month, after Beschastnykh had already signed a deal with Fenerbahce, Spartak were also in town for their winter training camp. Late one evening, two of the Russian club's senior directors, allegedly in a state of some inebriation, came to Beschastnykh's hotel room and told him he should pack his bags and go back to Moscow with them as Fenerbahce hadn't shown them the money and he was still their player.

It transpired that Spartak really were the aggrieved party. Back in August, young Vladimir, it seems, signed an extension with Spartak until 2005, then lost his copy of the agreement and "forgot" all about it. Fenerbahce made a last-ditch attempt to sign Kanu from Arsenal instead, just before the transfer window closed, but when this failed, in order to prevent further outrage among their supporters, found themselves with no choice but to cough up the money for Beschastnykh.

Several other Fenerbahce players are claiming they have not been paid for several months. The club's president and main source of funds is Aziz Yildirim, who is apparently more concerned about completing a couple of five-star hotel projects, for which he needs to find an extra $60m, than investing in the team. Meanwhile, one of their most popular players, the Israel midfielder Haim Revivo, has signed for city rivals Galatasaray. It's altogether not a happy scene. Rebrov's agent Varga has done business in Turkey before and he is a canny operator, so one would think they are not going into this one blind. I hope not – it's high time Rebrov got a lucky break. O

Pools unto Themselves

Every Saturday three men decide the results of postponed matches. Al Needham attempted to find out how they arrived at their decisions

WSC No 193, March 2003

WHENEVER I HAVE AN ARGUMENT with anyone about the innate superiority of British football over any other sporting entity in the world, I always keep one killer argument in reserve: the fact that we have a Pools Panel. It gives off the impression to foreigners that our game is so important that when matches can't be played, we actually have a platoon of experts who decide the result for us. Of course, they could counter this fact by pointing out that if every team in the country had the kind of facilities that they should have in the 21st century, there would be no need for a Pools Panel, but I counter that by stating that, even if there was a nuclear holocaust, the Pools Panel are probably on standby to decide entire seasons until civilisation recovered. That shuts them up a treat.

Like heaven, everyone has their own idea what the Pools Panel look like and how they go about deciding the results. I had this image of them loafing about like the Greek gods in *Jason and the Argonauts*, who would break off from lute-playing and grape-gorging every now and then to peer into a watery portal at us mere mortals. "Hmm... pestilence stalks the land... the blood is being returned to the fields... a home win for Scunthorpe." Sadly, that particular fantasy is about to be stomped upon, as I've been given the opportunity to meet them in the flesh – but before that a history lesson. If you think the weather has been particular grim this winter, you should have been around in 1963. I wasn't, but a cursory glance at the statistics (25-foot snowdrifts on Dartmoor, skating on the Mersey, a frozen seafront at Eastbourne, average wind speed of 99mph in Cumberland, etc) tells you that it must have been an absolute bastard. Not only was there the risk of death and a possible breakdown of society, the football season was well and truly knackered.

Take the 1963 FA Cup, for example. There have been Papal reigns that have been shorter than the third round. It lasted from January 5 until March 11, taking in 22 different match dates and 261 postponements. Bad enough if you're a fan, but even worse if you were depending on the pools to lift you out of your Steptoe-like existence. Obviously, something had to be done to prevent a revolt by housewives in beehives, and the Pools Panel came into effect on January 26, 1963.

The original panel was chaired by Sir Gerald Nabarro, a rather flamboyant Tory backbencher better known for being name-checked in a Monty Python sketch for having a pet prawn called Simon, and also for having a secretary called Christine Hamilton. But it was no faceless bureaucratic entity – the rest of the panel was packed with familiar and respected ex-pros who the public could rely on to play a straight bat (George Young, Ted Drake, Tommy Lawton and Tom Finney), as well as former ref Arthur Ellis, who went on to greater fame as the man in *It's a Knockout* who measured how much coloured water had been tipped into containers by bank clerks from Surbiton dressed as penguins.

The first meetings were held within the imposing confines of the Connaught Rooms in central London, and it was here that the current Panel – Gordon Banks, Roger Hunt and former Scotland and Newcastle midfielder Tony Green – convened for one day only to celebrate the body's 40th anniversary and offer the press a rare glimpse into their shadowy world, where – every Saturday between 2pm and 4pm – they control the footballing universe and decide whether or not your Auntie is going to chuck her job in at Kwik Save, get herself breast implants and run off with a "Fancy Man".

Back in the day, their decision was so important that the BBC would break into *Grandstand* with a televised announcement live from the Connaught Rooms, but these days the Panel spend their Saturday afternoons locked in a solicitors' office in Liverpool. I start the interview by pulling out the fixture list for that day, pointing to Nottingham Forest v Preston and demanding to know the result. They can't tell me. "We have access to years of statistics, form books and injury reports," says Roger Hunt, the chairman of the Panel. "And we don't discuss results until the meeting has begun," chips in Gordon Banks. Oh. All of them have been on the panel since the mid-1970s, and not only are they barred from playing the pools, so are their families. Two officials from the various pools companies are present at all times, and there's no outside communication allowed once the meeting begins.

Obviously, they're pretty tight-lipped about how precisely they go about their business, but from what I can gather, it's like a pub argument with instant access to a library of stats, and without the alcohol, shouting over each other and the potential threat of violence. "There's no set time for how long we decide a result," says Tony Green. "It all depends on the fixture. The average is about six or seven minutes, based on the information we have. If there's a difference of opinion, Roger has the casting vote. And club loyalties are checked in at the door."

Naturally, you can't just walk onto the panel. "They're all well respected, well known ex-pros who've been screened by Littlewoods, Vernons and Zetters. It's a very time-consuming job, and a very big responsibility," says Phil Watkins of Littlewoods. So why haven't they got round to just feeding the results into a computer? "Computers don't have gut feelings," says Phil. They're not bad at picking games, either. When the games are actually played, the Pools Panel have got it right 40 per cent of the time, which gives them a ten per cent edge over the pools predictors in the papers.

Although the pools have taken a bit of a knock since the National Lottery, the workload of the panel has increased. They only used to meet whenever 25 or more matches were called of, but these days they have to meet up whenever any Saturday game is cancelled – including the ones that have been moved by Sky. Factor in the Australian season, and it's virtually a full-time Saturday job. And although they're on a decent salary with full expenses, it can't be much fun having your shopping binge, quality time with grandkids or round of golf ruined because a groundskeeper's assistant in East Fife forgot to turn the hosepipe off, or there's been a monsoon in Tasmania.

So the next time the fixture list is decimated and you're staring in the shop window at Dixons for the results, spare a thought for three ex-pros trapped in an office. Personally, I'm going to stick with the *Jason and the Argonauts* fantasy, but that's just me. ○

Jimmy Riddle

Jimmy Hill comes across as a pointless relic, yet more than anyone else his life is the story of postwar football. In a series looking at influential figures in the game's history, Barney Ronay investigated the man behind the chin

WSC No 194, April 2003

PICTURE THE SCENE: four middle-aged men are seated around a mahogany-effect dining table. Beyond them a window looks out on to trees and green fields, but on inspection it turns out to be just a large photograph on the wall. One of the men has glasses and a protuberant chin; across the room from him a complacent-looking man with extravagantly bouffant hair says: "Well Jimmy. It's certainly been a busy weekend for referees." A deep lethargy descends.

This is *Jimmy Hill's Sunday Supplement*. Like a sporting Forrest Gump, Hill has been present at almost every major staging point in the evolution of English football during the last 40 years. Exorbitant wages, egotistical chairmen, backroom deals with television – only Jimmy can say: I was there at the start. One of the most influential figures in the history of the modern game is currently trapped within the flimsy chipboard walls of television purgatory. Where did it all go wrong?

By the time he retired from playing at the age of 33 after a serious knee injury, Hill had already embarked on the most significant achievement of his career. In his capacity as chairman of the players' union he initiated the strike action that would ultimately result in the abolition of the maximum wage for footballers. If anyone can claim to be the father of the modern Premiership player, it is Jimmy Hill. Without Jimmy, there would be no Beckingham Palace, no *Footballers' Wives* – maybe even no Jordan. Hill threatened to bring the game to a complete halt in the winter of 1961 unless the £20-a-week ceiling was abolished. Fulham team-mate Bobby Robson has described how the "very eloquent" young Hill managed to attract a 100 per cent ballot backing for the strike.

For the first time since the 19th century, players were free to earn whatever clubs were prepared to pay, and wages have increased steadily ever since. Last year the combined wage bill of Premiership players rose to £720 million, with top-flight clubs spending 75 per cent of their income on wages. Perhaps it would be overstatement to suggest that this is all Jimmy Hill's fault. But if ever a man left a trail of half-opened Pandora's boxes in his wake, it's Jimmy.

After a successful spell as manager of Coventry City, Hill left Highfield Road to begin his television career. As head of sport at London Weekend Television, and later ITV's deputy controller of programmes, he faced a mountainous task. When he started at LWT, commercial television had no broadcasting rights to live sport at all. ITV were desperate to compete and before long Hill was introducing the *World of Sport* to such televised treats as log-chopping and off-road cycling. In a groundbreaking piece of broadcasting, Jimmy then put together a legendary hand-picked panel for ITV's coverage of the 1970 World Cup. Through a haze of nylon-swathed, kipper-tied and faintly woozy footballing badinage, the likes of Brian Clough, Malcolm Allison and teen dreamboat Bob McNab took British television by storm. Almost single-handedly, Jimmy Hill had invented the Outspoken Punditry Panel. A fine achievement in itself, although the next time you wince as Ray Stubbs and the glassy-eyed "Lawro" mug pitifully for the cameras from their Saturday morning couch, you will know who to blame.

Buoyed by his World Cup coup, Hill soon had ITV wrangling with the BBC over the amounts paid to screen domestic football (which still totalled just half a million pounds as late as 1978), thereby helping to introduce the notion of competition among TV companies, producing an alternative – if unreliable – stream of revenue into the English game. Does any of this sound familiar? Fans of Leicester City, Derby County and any other club still reeling from the collapse of ITV Digital: if you have ever wondered where it might have all started, look no further. Jimmy knows.

Continuing on his odyssey of blazed trails and ticking time bombs, Hill returned to Coventry City in 1974. The nadir of Hill's spell as chairman of the Sky Blues came seven years later, when his attempt to make Highfield Road the country's first all-seat stadium ended in disaster, with hooligans ripping up the seats and using them as missiles. The terraces were restored and Hill left the club two years later. All the same, a seed had been planted and within 25 years of Hill's initiative standing terraces would vanish from the top flight of English football. The next time a steward tells you to sit down after your team have just scored, you will know the truth. It's all Jimmy Hill's fault.

So what else has he done? It's pretty simple really. When you're looking for something to pin on Jimmy Hill, just think of a problem and a route back to the man himself will always appear. Worried about sub-standard foreign players stifling home-grown British talent? During the Carlos Kickaball-friendly 1990s Jimmy Hill sat on the Football Work Permit Review Panel, a body charged with ruling which foreign players deserve a permit to play in the domestic leagues (in the panel's potted biographies Jimmy is described merely as "a respected football pundit"). Bothered by the current obsession with pubescent Premiership stars? Disturbed by the fact that Wayne Rooney won the BBC Young Sports Personality of the Year and has since been banned for violent conduct and scored just a single goal? Needless to say, Jimmy Hill ran the BBC *Sports Personality of the Year* programme during the 1970s, in the process helping to establish it as a national television event.

But this, of course, is all far too easy. Blaming Jimmy Hill for everything that has gone wrong in English football over the last 30 years is just a way of letting everyone else off the hook. In fact, like the man who split the atom, Jimmy merely gave us the chance to make choices; bad ones as it turned out. Abolishing the salary cap: obviously a good idea. As long as you don't go and spoil it by paying Benito Carbone £2m a year. TV companies competing to broadcast football: what could be better? Hardly Jimmy's fault they ruin everything 20 years down the line by overstretching their shallow-pocketed paymasters. As for running a club with unchecked ambition at the top – another excellent idea. Just try explaining that to a Leeds United fan right now.

What is certain is that Jimmy leaves a unique legacy to a game he has served uniquely – as player, union official, manager, chairman, pundit and even linesman (he once took up the flag in a league match at Arsenal after one of the officials had injured himself). And it's in this capacity, as a kind of footballing everyman, the hotdog seller in the background of all of football's biggest scenes, that Jimmy Hill will survive. We are

Jimmy; Jimmy is us. He showed us what could be done. His achievements, circumscribed by the kind of vanity that makes a man stick it out for over 600 appearances on *Match of the Day*, opened doors for others to tiptoe through – and then kick over a table or two once they're inside.

So let us leave him in his chipboard kitchen with its basket of plastic croissants. In a game saturated with players paid the millions he helped them to earn, fed by the mass media he helped to stoke up, perhaps Jimmy Hill has found a fitting resting place. Jaw-Jaw with Jimmy sounds a bit like the ultimate Sunday morning hangover. Ever the visionary, perhaps he's pointing the way once again for a game that has, of late, drunk rather too much champagne. ○

Broken Dreams

Tom Bower, who had previously investigated Robert Maxwell and Mohamed Fayed, turned to football in his award-winning book, *Broken Dreams*. It left Harry Pearson screaming

WSC No 194, April 2003

A DECADE OR SO AGO Paul Kimmage, who would later ghost Tony Cascarino's autobiography, wrote a book about his experiences as a professional cyclist. *A Rough Ride* told of systematic drug use by riders in races such as the Tour de France. In Britain, where bicycle racing ranks alongside clay-pigeon shooting, Kimmage was rewarded with the William Hill Sports Book of the Year award. In Europe, where cycling is big news and big business, however, he was denounced by everybody from fellow riders to sports journalists as a fantasist and an embittered loser. The Irishman had predicted this would happen. There existed, he said, a code of silence within the world of cycling when it came to drug taking, extending from the mechanics to the upper echelons of cycling's ruling bodies, from the team masseurs to all branches of the media.

Ten years after *A Rough Ride* was published, a Belgian named Willy Voet who worked for the Festina team, cycling's answer to Arsenal, was stopped by French customs officials. They found a stash of drugs that would have stunned Shaun Ryder. Within 12 months, cycling's silent conspirators were babbling away like budgerigars to the French police. Now the only charge that could be laid at Paul Kimmage's door is that he hadn't known the half of what was going on.

It would be nice to think that a few years from now something will occur to vindicate Tom Bower. His book about the shady finances of our national game, following acclaimed investigations into Robert Maxwell and Richard Branson among others, has certainly been greeted by football with a rare and intense silence. Bower is not a football fan and sometimes it shows in the spelling of players' names and the fact that he lets David Mellor pass through the chapters dealing with the Football Task Force without even once resorting to personal abuse, but he writes with great clarity and conciseness about murky business dealings. The result is a book that skewers the game's malfeasance with a precision and lucidity that even a fiscal-illiterate such as myself can easily comprehend.

Broken Dreams does not make happy reading. It conjures up a world in which greed, arrogance, stupidity, egomania and profligacy meet with stunning force. Underpinning it is a network of conflicting interests so complex it would make even the most dedicated Byzantine dizzy. In transfers, agents represent the player, but also the buying and selling clubs; FA officials own stadium seating companies; managers buy shares in players' agencies which also employ their sons ("Nepotism is not a crime," one agent opined recently. The idea that illegality and immorality may be separate issues has not penetrated football) and so it goes on.

Every few pages, as I read how Rune Hauge had somehow pocketed £600,000 for his part in the transfer of Rio Ferdinand from West Ham to Leeds despite the fact that he wasn't Ferdinand's agent and was in the middle of a FIFA-imposed ban at the time; or discovered the FA paid £103 million for Wembley despite their own independent valuation pricing it at £64m; or that Liverpool's Rick Parry, confronted with demands that the Premier League do something about the activities of agents, replied "We've got to leave it to FIFA" (ah yes, Sepp Blatter, the very man to root out fiscal malpractice); I had to stick my head out of the window, breath some fresh air and scream.

Despite griping about how they are being cheated, Premiership chairmen resist any attempt at regulation. It is tempting to suggest this is because a corrupt society inevitably favours the rich and the unscrupulous and there are plenty of people running football clubs who answer that description. (Unfortunately our libel laws also favour the rich and the unscrupulous, which may explain why occasionally Bower delivers non-sequiturs that require some interpretation.) Unwilling to rock the boat, especially one that guarantees them so many junkets around the globe, the FA seem as resistant to the idea of regulation as the chairmen.

The result is the FA Compliance Unit, an investigative body made up one man, former police detective Graham Bean, with limited legal and financial power. The Premier League chairmen deride the Yorkshireman with a wince-inducing snobbery ("Just another sergeant," says David Sheepshanks dismissively). It is like Dixon of Dock Green trying to take on the Russian mafia with a truncheon and a whistle.

To make Bean's task even more difficult, his employers are reluctant to act on any evidence he provides. The only action against a club the men from Lancaster Gate/Soho Square ever seem to have pursued with any vigour was against Tottenham. In that case, though, they were motivated less by a desire to clean up the game than to punish Alan Sugar for his "Cloughie likes a bung" affidavit (a document that had the unwelcome effect of compelling them to act) and the fact that his abrasive manner had offended the otiose Graham Kelly. Unfortunately when Bean has met with success, such as at Chesterfield, Hull City and Boston Utd, it has been turned into propaganda by the Premiership. To men like Ken Bates, recently heard on Channel 4 gallantly defending the Compliance Unit's record, Bean's success in the lower divisions is proof that no malfeasance is present at the upper end of the league.

Meanwhile, Labour politicians whose election manifesto promised to tackle problems within football seem more intent on proving Napoleon's maxim that "It is by titles and baubles that men are led". Any hope the Football Task Force had of reforming the game, or that Wembley had of being built for less than the gross national product of a cluster of emerging nations, are scuppered by battles between senior government figures, many of whom seem to enjoy the kind of relationship Roy Keane shares with Alf-Inge Haaland.

In the face of this mix of silence, incompetence, complaisance and petty vendettas it is hard to see how to rectify the situation. Certainly the chances of a Willy Voet moment are, as boxing promoter Don King is fond of remarking, slim to nil, with slim having just skipped town. Drugs are more easily tested for than corruption. And even when the latter is detected, people within the game seem unwilling to take any kind of moral stand. Switch on Sky and there are Frank McLintock, El Tel's delivery boy, and George Graham grinning out at you.

I have searched long and hard for a pithy summation of *Broken Dreams*. In the end the phrase that keeps bobbing into my head is the strapline on the posters for *Wayne's World*: "You'll laugh, you'll cry, you'll hurl." ○

North Terrace Orient

Tom Davies paid tribute to the quietest part of Brisbane Road, which was about to be knocked down as part of a ground redevelopment

WSC No 194, April 2003

THOSE WHO HAVE CAMPAIGNED for the retention or return of terracing at football have aimed their fire too narrowly. In highlighting the mystique of a terrace as a throbbing, heaving mass of partisan passion, they've missed what makes an awful lot of terraces – particularly a lot of those that still exist – special: their quiet, easy-going affability.

The place where I've stood for the last 16 years, Leyton Orient's North Terrace, is one such place. Not long for this world now, it won't be fondly remembered for singing, intimidation and rabid fans "sucking them in", but because it's none of those things. Sure, there are songs, but more often than not of the sarcastic *Send in the Clowns* variety; sure, there's passion, but it manifests itself as much in withering scorn against the team's deficiencies as in raucous encouragement. Above all, there's eccentricity and conviviality. People wander about, catch up with friends, sit down at half-time and read the Guardian. And, of course, they moan.

These things are as important to the terrace experience as the much-celebrated swaying masses. Third Division boredom can be alleviated by a quick stroll to see who's in today. And our cold open terrace – deprived of a roof to amplify any co-ordinated chanting – instead reverberates (if that's the appropriate word) to the contented and occasionally discontented burble of several hundred private conversations. Distilled, it might sound something like: "How's the family?" "Yeah, not too bad, keeping well yerself?" "All right... oh sort it out Brush you useless tosser!"

If the Kops and Holte Ends of old were wild, sweaty nightclubs, ends such as ours are cosy backstreet locals – friendly, in need of a lick of paint, with a quirky jukebox and an unshiftable collection of irascible old gits sat at the bar. And all the worthier of preservation because of that.

We like it that way, even if the club probably doesn't. Partly because of the acoustics problem, ours is the quietest part of Brisbane Road, and that's saying something – as anyone who's been part of a 50-strong away contingent that's out-sung the Os faithful could attest. This could be paranoia creeping in, but I've noticed the terrace's patrons are often the last to be applauded by the players. The noisier denizens of the small but modern South Stand, the decrepit West Stand and the durable old Main Stand are usually acknowledged before us. You can sense the team saying to themselves: "Oh well, better do these miserable sods too."

But they will not have to grudgingly put their hands together for much longer. The game on April 26 against Rushden & Diamonds – themselves an emblem of "modern football" – may well be the North Terrace's last. It is unlikely to be sent on its way with a big flag day or many, or even any, tears. Quite a number of Orient fans probably won't care, for the uncomfortable truth is that a whole new generation of fans is now growing up with no real awareness of what terracing meant, for good or ill.

In its place will be a small but perfectly formed all-seat number, part of redevelopment plans that involve the construction of blocks of flats by all four corners and more community facilities and "lettable areas" than you can shake a stick at. Oh, and some seats. There will be room amid all this for just 9,400 spectators. As recently as the late Eighties, around two-thirds of that number could squeeze on to the North Terrace alone (though they hardly ever did). All this may well secure the club's financial future, and that's not to be sniffed at, but one can't help feeling that as identikit ground facelift follows identikit new stadium development up and down the country, we're getting neither pumping, jumping nightclubs nor cosy locals, just a whole load of chain pubs. Is that a future worth drinking to? ○

Lights Out

Simon Inglis mourned the loss of traditional floodlights from the horizon following the changing trends in stadium construction

WSC No 196, June 2003

WE'VE ALL BEEN THERE. Driving to a game, negotiating the ring-roads and roundabouts of Awaysville, then growing hotter and more bothered as you realise the back streets in which you're mired are nowhere near the ground. What's worse is you've never had to look at a map before. All you've ever done was take more or less the right turn-off from the motorway and then drive blithely toward that distant set of floodlights on the horizon, like a moth homing in on a night light.

But now? Maybe no problem at Old Trafford, Elland Road or St James' Park (the larger of the two) where the sheer mass of the stadium makes it impossible to miss. But most other places, forget it. If the beacon-like pylons that once rendered map reading unnecessary haven't been replaced by discreet roof-mounted lights, the chances are they've transmuted into slender galvanised masts that are nigh impossible to make out against anything other than the bluest of skies. A proper football ground, I think we're all agreed, should have prominent floodlights. Or rather, it should have four prominent floodlight towers that clearly express from afar the rectangular shape of the pitch. Like the spire of a distant church, they should announce: "Local landmark. Place of worship."

Not that such obvious totems have always been foolproof. Before the JJB Stadium opened in Wigan, Springfield Park (round ball) and Central Park (oval) possessed uncannily similar pylons. That was my excuse for missing the kick-off, anyway. Maybe you too have been similarly lured into a wrong turn by the forests of pylons around Teesside or in parts of the east midlands coalfields. I walked for miles towards a quartet of floodlights in Sweden once, only to find them standing sentinel over, ahem, a motorway interchange.

This, of course, is a relatively modern dilemma. After the first experiments with floodlighting, starting famously at Bramall Lane in 1878, permanent floodlighting finally arrived in British football in the early 1950s. Even so this was 20 years after it had been introduced at various north and south American stadiums. (Baseball's first regular night games took place in 1930, spreading to the major leagues by 1935.) The Netherlands were pioneers also, thanks to the Philips Electrical Company of Eindhoven, who installed Europe's first floodlight towers at Amsterdam's Olympic Stadium in 1934. Mighty fine and futuristic they were too. Our own far-sighted FA, meanwhile, threatened to ban any club that played a floodlit game, despite the existence, after 1926, of floodlit greyhound tracks and two demonstrations at White City (of rugby league and football) in 1932-33. It'll never catch on, claimed a string of experts, the venerable Charles Buchan among them.

But there was no turning back (or off) after the Second World War. From 1949 telegraph poles started popping up along touchlines all over Britain to bear the new generation of improvised floodlights. Non-League South Liverpool were probably the first, at their Holly Park ground, in September 1949 (having been inspired during a visit to Holland the year before). A year later, Headington (now Oxford) United borrowed lamps from college buildings usually illuminated at night. Bristol City's, on removable poles, had to be switched on one by one. Even Spurs started off, in 1953, with the most basic of poles in each corner. As with Anfield's lights, installed also on poles in 1957, they barely rose above the roof lines of the stands. Also among the early birds in 1951, both Arsenal (who'd used basic lighting for training since 1936) and Southampton mounted floodlights on their stand roofs, as is the modern way. But the Saints and Gunners were the exception, each having stands of a similar height on either side of the pitch. Elsewhere, as poles soon proved inadequate – being too low and therefore dazzl-ing players and spectators alike – pylons took over.

It was also an era of austerity. Although floodit friendlies against exotic opposition were the decade's top draw – as seen most famously at Molineux with the visits of Honved, Moscow Dynamo and Spartak – a full set of pylons and lights was by no means cheap. Stockport County, then in the Third Division North, shelled out £17,000 for theirs in 1956, at a time when England's record transfer fee was just £34,500. A few months later Manchester United paid £40,000. Overall, two main designs dominated. The most common, supplied by GEC, was the tapering pylon with a rectangular gantry secured by angled tie rods at the top, holding a grid of, say, 6 x 8 or 6 x 9 lamps. Heights varied according to location from roughly 90 to 180 feet, but the lower half of struts always followed the same criss-cross pattern. Several survive, at Shrewsbury,

Orient, Fulham, Darlington, Cambridge United and Cardiff City, inter alia. Ones that have gone? Palace, Wrexham, Oxford United, Spurs, both Nottingham clubs, Stirling Albion, West Brom and Aston Villa (where, as an amusement to drivers crossing Spaghetti Junction during the 1970s, the lamps were arranged as an A and a V).

But my favourite, if one dares admit to it, was the style most frequently seen in Scotland, at, for example, Hampden, Celtic, Hearts and Hibs, but also, oddly, at Brighton. Called "Drenchliting" and supplied by Millers of Edinburgh, it had a fairly normal tapering pylon, but with a gantry at the top that consisted of open ended horizontal bars, angled down as if bowing in homage to the pitch. Newcastle, I believe, had the tallest such set, some 190 feet tall. Only a few survive, at Queen of the South and Dundee United, to my knowledge.

And what of today's floodlights? The majority of large stadiums now sport roof-mounted lights, which are easier to maintain and direct, while in smaller grounds, simple (ie bland) masts or columns are taking over. Some, as at Scunthorpe, Chester and Ross County, are on huge hinges, allowing the lights to be lowered and maintained. Some, as at Blackburn, Charlton and QPR, have a wider girth and a more continental air. Thankfully there are still some designers who make a feature of floodlights. Go to Bolton's Reebok Stadium, where the leaning, three-legged corner pylons form part of the roof structure and appear like inquisitive robot insects peering over the edge. Or to Hearts, Huddersfield, Preston, Watford or West Bromwich, where one-off designs add a real touch of class, or at least variety, to the overall look.

But if you're still feeling nostalgic, visit the excellent National Football Museum at Preston, where you can see old floodlights bulbs collected by Preston North End fan Mike Pye. My favourite is the one he rescued from Bradford Park Avenue; a two kilowatt monster version of an ordinary household bulb which looks like a prop from *Honey I Shrunk the Kids*. Mike sounds embarrassed when I ask him to explain his predilection. "I realise it's unusual," he replies, "but I suppose they're evocative of a golden era. When I was a kid I walked three miles to Deepdale, and it was just part of the build-up to the game, heading towards those pylons." Fear not Mike. We've all been there. ○

Grim Reep

Not all revolutionaries are fondly remembered. Barney Ronay examined the controversial legacy of Charles Reep, football's first tactical statistician

WSC No 196, June 2003

WING COMMANDER CHARLES REEP has been called many things. Twenty years ago the *Times* dubbed him "The Human Computer of the Fabled Fifties"; an obituary described him more simply as "a football analyst"; while a slightly empurpled Brain Glanville once declared him a member of FA coaching director Charles Hughes's "band of believers and acolytes", the archangel of "a fanatical credo, a pseudo-religion". Few figures in English football history have attracted as much vitriol or as much ideological zeal. The lothario of the long ball, Reep has remained unfathomably seductive to a roll-call of many of the most influential coaching figures in post-war domestic football. He is the national game's deep dark secret; we know he's bad for us, but we just can't help ourselves.

In fact, as the *Journal of Sports Sciences* remarked after his death last year, Reep was the first "professional performance analyst of football". His shorthand notes – details of nearly 2,500 matches survive – provided coaches with a comprehensive set of match data at least 20 years before any similar process emerged. But while Reep's obituary lists a medley of his greatest hits – "over 80 per cent of goals result from moves of three passes or less"; "60 per cent of all goalscoring moves begin 35 yards from an opponent's goal" – only brief mention is made of the vilification attracted by the various interpretations of "direct football" induced by his analysis.

Thorold Charles Reep was born in 1904 and joined the RAF at 24 after training as an accountant. It was in 1933, at a talk given by Arsenal captain Charles Jones, that he was captivated by a description of manager Herbert Chapman's use of statistics to orchestrate attacking play. Reep subsequently put into practice some of these theories with RAF teams, no doubt spurred on by the continued success of the Gunners in carrying out Chapman's mantra of "the shortest route to goal" and employing a revolutionary "static" central defender (insert Sol Campbell joke of your choice here). Like many great innovators, though, Chapman was frequently misunderstood. Bernard Joy heads one of the chapters of his classic, *Soccer Tactics*: "Imitation of Arsenal's Tactics Brings in Kick-And-Rush Football". Or as some might choose to put it, enter Charles Reep. He documented the exact time he first implemented his notational system at a professional match – 3.50pm on March 18, 1950, the moment a new method of rationalising the science of the game came into being, one that would intoxicate those at the highest level of the English game and lead a wild-eyed figure some 40 years distant, the initials GT at the breast of his tracksuit, to shout the words "Send it long Carlton!" into the warm Norwegian air. But a lot happened first.

In 1953 England suffered the greatest shock in its history, losing 6-3 at Wembley to an overwhelmingly superior Hungary side. The effects are hard to overstate. Reep shared the mood of national humiliation, but not the general prognosis that traditional English methods were outdated. Almost 30 years later Reep wrote an article in the *Times* entitled "The Great Magyar Myth Exploded", in which he claimed to have "all the relevant facts and figures" necessary to demystify the Hungarian team's apparent complete technical superiority.

The urge to debunk footballing complexities was a force behind much of Reep's work. Among his published articles are the jaunty "This Pattern-Weaving Talk Is All Bunk!" (1961), the po-faced "Skill And Chance In Association Football" (1968) and the downright aggrieved "Are We Getting Too Clever?" (1962). In this article Reep goes on to recount his first meeting with Wolves manager Stan Cullis, shortly after the Hungarian demolition in 1953. Cullis, perhaps impressed by Reep's work in helping Brentford avoid relegation in the spring of 1952, requested his assistance in devising a style of play that would borrow from the Magyars while reaffirming the "wholly English" principles of "direct passing".

The Cullis/Reep methodology met with immediate success as Wolves defeated Hungarian champions Honved 3-2 at Molineux in December 1954. Retiring from the RAF a year later, Reep spent three years working as a performance analyst for Sheffield Wednesday. But with the advent of the flair-friendly Sixties and against a background of World and European Cup triumphs there seemed little demand for a statistically robust analysis of why George Best really ought to stop holding on to the ball and – ideally – get his hair cut too. A series of articles for the *Daily Mail* assessing the performance of players – a kind of biro and notebook prototype of the current vogue for Opta-style statistics – was ridiculed by the sports editor of the *Times*, and Reep abruptly disappeared from the scene.

It took ten years of World Cup humiliation – and a crisis of confidence in its ability to coach a game that had suddenly become difficult – for English football to turn to Reep again. In 1980, sensing a sea-change in tactical thinking, Reep contacted Graham Taylor, then manager at Watford. Taylor would remark after England's World Cup exit in 1982 that "possession and patience are myths. Goals come from mistakes"; he was ripe for Reep, and before long the ex-Wing Commander was providing match-by-match performance analysis as Taylor's no-nonsense Hornets marched towards the top of the First Division.

Within six months Reep was working with Charles Hughes, soon to become FA director of coaching and the staunchest advocate of the "direct football" mantra of the time. To Hughes and his associates, football was most definitely a science, and the findings of Reep's 30 years of notebook-scribbling and calculator-bashing permeate both his FA coaching manual (reprinted 11 times since 1980; dedication page mentions Graham Taylor and Howard Wilkinson) and his more theoretical *Winning Formula* (1990). Hughes's FA manual contains seven pages under the heading "Passing Techniques – Lofted Passes", while what he describes as "Improvisation and Inventive Play" merit just two. Whether Reep intended to nurture such extremes of utilitarian football has never been clear, but the influence of his findings had never been so pervasive.

Reep's influence began to dwindle with the approach of the Premiership and the increasingly cosmopolitan nature of domestic players and coaches. English football was starting to feel good about itself again; sophisticated even. However, for Reep, at the age of 89 there would be a bizarre final call to arms. Performance analysis had been used in Norwegian football since the 1970s – pioneered by Egil Olsen – and in 1993 the octogenarian ex-Wing Commander was flown to Oslo as guest of honour of the Norwegian FA for a World Cup qualifier against Graham Taylor's England, thereby creating one of the most bizarre tableaux in the history of English international football. Reep watched from his box as Olsen's Norway, schooled in his long-ball theory, out-muscled an England XI marshalled by the man responsible for resur-recting his methods nearly 15 years earlier. But this was to be Reep's last stand. The man who had inadvertently given birth to such footballing catch-alls as "playing the percentage game", "putting it in the mixer" and the Sunday morning classic "just get rid of it" would have no further involvement in the professional game.

Although in many ways Charles Reep's influence at the highest level is as great as ever. Humiliating defeat at Euro 2000 led to perhaps the third great crisis of confidence in the recent history of English football. "I don't think you can question our commitment – but you can question our ability to pass a football," remarked national coach Kevin Keegan. And so English football did what it always does in times of crisis; when the game seems to have become mysterious, a confusing, foreign-accented thing that can no longer be mastered, it goes back to basics. "The continental teams have conned us into believing the way we play has no chance. They have made us ashamed of our own style," explained Graham Taylor during TV punditry duties in Belgium. Taylor knew what was coming.

In time for qualification for the 2002 World Cup the England team would be led by a Swedish pragmatist, who would announce at a press conference just three months before Charles Reep's death: "If you look at the statistics in big club games or internationals, more than 80 per cent of goals are scored with fewer than five passes." Now who does that sound like? ○

Twelfth Men

Thirty-seven years after Keith Peacock became the league's first substitute, Philip Cornwall traced the changing role of the sub with the help of the man himself

WSC No 196, June 2003

Once upon a time, there were no substitutes. None. By the time I started understanding football, the mid-1970s, they were such an established part of the game that there was an emerging player soon to be known to all as Super Sub, and the idea that football had once been just 11 against 11 was very difficult to get my head around.

It wasn't until I was given one of those football quiz books, which asked "Who was the first substitute in a Football League match?", that I even realised there was a time before 12th men. Astonishingly, the answer to the question – Keith Peacock of Charlton Athletic – was still Keith Peacock of Charlton Athletic then, a dozen or so years after his moment of history. As he is today, albeit as assistant manager and not as a player. The moment came at Bolton, on August 21, 1965. "I remember quite clearly I was disappointed at not playing," he recalls. "Before then a spare player had travelled, in case of illness, but not got changed. I still didn't expect to be involved – but after only a few minutes Mick Rose, our goalkeeper, had to come off. It was only on the train back from Manchester, from one of the evening papers, that I found out I had been the first." Charlton still had no proper keeper – Peacock wasn't that give that difficult task – and lost 4-2, but had done so with 11 men.

So what was life like, pre-Peacock? Another quiz book question is "Which pop star's uncle played in the 1959 FA Cup final?" As we all know, it was Roy Dwight, Elton John's uncle, and he broke his leg with an hour to go – but you rarely see the corollary of that fact, that his Nottingham Forest side were thereby reduced to ten men, only just hanging on to the lead Dwight had helped establish. A year later, Blackburn Rovers were less fortunate against Wolves, when Dave Whelan – now the owner of Wigan – suffered a similar fate to Dwight. (The injury ended Whelan's playing career; his £400 compensation was the beginning of his business career, which led all the way to JJB Sports.)

A solution was only a matter of time. Too much time, inevitably, and the change in the rule which gave Peacock his place in the history books was initially just for domestic games; as a result, Alf Ramsey was able to name just 11 men for the World Cup final at the end of that season and was denied the option to even choose Jimmy Greaves or anyone else as a replacement in the event of an injury. But the rules had changed completely by 1970, to allow Sir Alf to make tactical substitutions. "After a couple of seasons there were a number of dodgy substitutions," Peacock remembers, and so the rules were change and a new phrase was needed – the tactical substitution, a term which according to Peacock took a while to get used to. Players took it personally when taken off, as some still do today. Nonetheless, that transformed the rule and the game, giving David Fairclough his chance for peculiar fame.

Fairclough's initial substitute success came in the closing weeks of Liverpool's 1975-76 title run, when he grabbed a brace against Burnley and the only goal of a Merseyside derby. But it was the next season's European Cup quarter-final when, with Saint-Etienne ahead on away goals, he scored in the closing minutes to secure a 3-1 win, which made him the Super Sub of the 1970s, a tag which stuck and perhaps even held back his chances of gaining a regular place, but which assures him of lasting fame at Liverpool.

The initial change, to allow tactical substitutions, was one of the few examples of football changing into line with common sense – as happened again 30 years later, when the short-lived rule that one of the three substitutes allowed on the bench had to be a goalkeeper (1994) was altered to give the decision to the manager as to whether or not he wished to gamble and anyway to give him five to choose from (1995). But the changes, slow at first and then a flood in the last decade or so, have meant more than an increase in work for the Acme Dugout Company. In many ways, substitutions make management easier. Pre-Peacock, every injury from the first minute to the last could leave you a man short. With today's options, you have to lose two keepers, not one, before an outfielder goes in goal (meaning that the record of scoring a hat-trick and saving a penalty in the FA Cup final will probably remain unique to Roy Race).

And of course if things go wrong tactically you can try to fix them. In the old days you could only reorganise your men if one went off, then post-Peacock you had the one roll of the dice to repair – now you may have three more chances to get it right, or wrong. Graham Taylor, against Sweden at Euro 92, ended Gary Lineker's England career by pitching in Alan Smith for his swansong, rather than opting for Lineker's true international successor, Alan Shearer. It's also possible to make a mistake by not making a change – consider Bryan Robson in the closing moments of the 1997 League Cup final, not opting to disrupt Leicester's closing attacks, a decision which left the worldly wise Fabrizio Ravanelli shaking his head in disbelief when City equalised, denying Middlesbrough their first major trophy.

One thing that will never change is that it will always be the attacking substitutes who are remembered, rather than defenders sent on to close out a game. Sometimes it will be players who have been out through injury and cannot be risked as starters – remember Ian Wright, back from a broken leg at Wembley in 1990, coming on to save Crystal Palace and scoring twice to all but win them the FA Cup. Or the latter-day Faircloughs, such as Ole Gunnar Solskjaer who has surpassed any previous model with his efforts from the bench, most famously in Barcelona to win the 1999 European Cup.

Is the game fairer today, and better? Undoubtedly. But substitutions have created problems, too. "We can spend as long choosing the substitutes as we can the team," Peacock asserts. "It used to be that players were unhappy if they didn't make the team. Now, if they don't make the bench..." Omission from the 16 could be considered as saying someone isn't needed even in an emergency. At the same time, they drive towards ever bigger squads and therefore are very expensive. They hand an advantage to the richer teams. "You mark Thierry Henry for 75 minutes and then you see, say, Sylvain Wiltord come on."

When taken to extremes – as England fans saw at Upton Park in February, albeit in a friendly – substitutions damage the game, in that case by devaluing the fixture in the minds of one starting XI. With luck, Sven-Göran Eriksson's overkill will lead to a block on any increase, rather than a slide towards the American sporting system of free substitutions, players coming off for a rest and going back into the game.

Which makes me wary of rugby's move, to have "blood substitutes" so a team doesn't suffer while someone has stitches. How long before that drifts towards taking a break for other injuries, or just tiredness? But the good outweighs the bad by far, and more than anything else substitutes give hope. To the manager (and his assistant) and to the fans, the belief that if you can send on a Solskjaer rather than a Smith, a game which is slipping away can be turned around. There is still a sense of anticipation when the fourth official starts fiddling around. It didn't do Charlton much good that day when Peacock made history, but it is almost impossible to imagine the game without his successors. ○

The Fifth Column

Roger Titford asked whether the gradual rise in the status of the Conference was a good thing

WSC No 197, July 2003

FOOTBALL LEAGUE MEMBERSHIP HAS, I've always thought, been a very precious thing, a distinction that was historically conferred on a club by the existing members. That once huge distinction between League and non-League is suddenly getting very blurred. I feel there's a fifth column, literally, in our divisional tables now; someone else pretending to be part of the League family, creeping in bit by bit. Unfashionable though it may be to say so, I'm not sure I like what's happening any more.

You have to say the Conference has done a great job in the past 25 years. Against the grain of the usual reformist thinking in favour of part-time, regionalised football, it has succeeded in its prime objective of establishing its credibility as a kind of Division Five on a national basis, with many full-time clubs. Where once there was a chasm between the perception of League and non-League football, there may now be little difference in the minds of younger fans of bigger clubs. The Conference has the same sponsor as the Football League, its clubs seem to get more exposure on Sky than those in the Third Division, its results and tables often follow on the same page on Ceefax and are treated with equal emphasis in the Sunday papers. Some of its clubs compete with League clubs in the LDV Trophy, some have all-seater stadiums, others full-time staffs.

With two up, two down the exchange of clubs between Division Three and the Conference is likely to grow. Next season half the Conference clubs will be either ex-League clubs or from towns that used to have a League club, while there will be half a dozen "non-League names" in the Third. It's all being done softly, softly and around the edges without any objections. Well, here's a tiny one. The press reported that Doncaster owner John Ryan is now the oldest-ever player at 55, taking Neil McBain's record, set back in 1947. No! That's a League record and John Ryan has never (yet) played in the Football League. But that's what I mean about the distinctions being blurred – a non-League gimmick said to take the place of a League record. *Rothmans*, at least, is so far maintaining the distinction in its coverage.

There are a few other things that concern me about treating the Conference as if it were a Fifth Division. Clubs in it appear to be less stable – appearing out of nowhere (Rushden & Diamonds, Dagenham & Redbridge) or suddenly disappearing from national view (Enfield, Maidstone). That old non-League tendency of players suddenly marching off to follow a manager is still there (the Farnborough exodus to Stevenage this season). The crowds are not terrific – averaging about 1,600 versus Division Three's 4,450 this season, less than half as much.

The main impact the Conference has had on followers of League football is to give us some new clubs, though fewer than you might suspect since the introduction of automatic promotion in 1987. Scarborough, Maidstone and Barnet have come and gone, so the net effect is seven new clubs. All but two will be playing in the lowest League division next season and only one, Wycombe, has so far made a substantial impact in the Second Division.

It would be unthinkable to go back to the old process of re-election whereby the bottom four clubs were judged very largely by the votes of the top two divisions. The chairmen of Arsenal and Tottenham, for instance, had the same amount of say in whether Aberdare Athletic or New Brighton lived or, in 1927 and 1951 respectively, died as did all the clubs they played against those seasons. After the creation of the Fourth Division in 1958, only six clubs came into the Football League by that process: Peterborough, Oxford United, Cambridge United, Hereford, Wimbledon and Wigan – all of whom have now reached Division One level (at least) in their League history. In those days there was more to getting in than your playing record, though some of the decision-making looks to have been as arbitrary as a Roman Emperor's thumbs up or down.

For all its friendly media treatment, we should remember the Conference is not part of the Football League and promotion into the League is not solely and automatically on playing merit. Certain financial and stadium criteria have to be met. Kidderminster, Macclesfield and Stevenage have all failed at this hurdle, though the first two have subsequently jumped it. Boston's controversial promotion season left them with other obstacles to overcome. Yet I still have the nagging feeling that it has now become just a little too easy to make the jump, that half a season of terrific form can get you in, via the Conference play-offs, at the expense of a solid 80-year-old member of the League that has had a bad season.

Promotion and relegation is a two-way street, of course, and it is also easier for a relegated club to get back into the League. Halifax have been out, in and back out again within a decade and that example, in particular, gives League status at this level a temporary air. It is becoming disposable and retrievable, less of a precious distinction and more of a current situation. Faced with the growing status of European competition and the Premiership, perhaps we should worry more about this erosion of the central pillar of English football's architecture, membership of the Football League. O

Yesterday's Man

When Graham Taylor resigned as Aston Villa manager, David Wangerin looked back at the ups and downs of a man who more than once took a job too far

WSC No 197, July 2003

GRAHAM TAYLOR'S HASTY DEPARTURE from Aston Villa has in all likelihood ended a coaching career spanning five decades. To many, that career will live in a sort of infamy, largely due to the shortcomings he exhibited as England manager a decade ago which led to the team's failure to qualify for USA 94. But to others, his greatest blunder came not with the national teams he selected, the tactics he deployed, or even the results he failed to deliver, but in allowing himself to become the subject of that fly-on-the-wall television documentary for, as it turned out, the benefit of a rather bitter and recriminatory audience. Within a worryingly short time, "Do I not like that" became a kind of catchphrase for ineptitude, the TV programme an inadvertent testimonial for the Peter Principle of a man rising to the level of his own incompetence.

This wasn't the man Aston Villa fans recognised from only a few seasons earlier, the man who inherited a club in free fall and took it to the brink of the league championship in three years with players such as Kent Nielsen and Tony Cascarino. At Villa there had been Only One Graham Taylor; now he was Taylor the Turnip, capping Geoff Thomas, benching Gary Lineker and conceding a goal to San Marino before the national anthem had finished. Lacking the oleaginous glibness of a Venables or the inscrutability of an Eriksson, he, like Hoddle, Keegan and, lest we forget, Bobby Robson, since lifted to icon status, was pilloried, his pedigree swept away by the ever-ravenous British press.

Of course, it's not how you get knocked down, it's how you get up again. Resuscitated at struggling Wolves, he took them to within a whisker of the Premiership. Four managers would follow; none of them could do better. Number five, Dave Jones, took two-and-a-half years to get it right. Returning to Watford, tail between legs, Taylor seemed unlikely to deliver anything more than a season or two of mediocrity and a retirement speech. Instead, he took the club into the Premiership. Good grief, who else could have managed it?

The electric chair that passes for the manager's seat at Villa Park seemed comfortable enough for Taylor at first, but big-league football eventually played him offside. Premiership management was less about pumping up players for a game and increasingly about convincing boards to write off expensive contracts and cough up ludicrous amounts of money for squad fillers. Instead of galvanising the young aspirants from Hereford or Barnsley, there was now an international cadre of disillusioned millionaires to contend with, most of them coasting, wanting out, or both. The diplomatic yet incisive parting shots Taylor fired at the board on his last day rang true to many. Having dismissed ten managers since their European Cup triumph of 1981-82, and with just a meagre two League Cups to show for it, only Doug Ellis's staunchest allies can claim the Villa ship sails on an even keel. Whether David O'Leary, fresh from a £100 million spending spree at Elland Road, enters this lions' den with both eyes open is moot; Villa fans would do well to remember how quickly £100m of talent can shape itself into a noose.

Proponents of regime change, seeking the root-and-branch reform they so resolutely believe will catapult Villa into Champions League heaven, argue Taylor was forced to work with one hand tied behind his back. Perhaps he was; if so, he should have been in his element. With the playing stock of an entire nation at his disposal, and no reserve teams or balance sheets to weigh him down, he failed. With limited playing squads, kibitzing boards, restrictive budgets and contract negotiations to contend with, he succeeded. Time and time again. We will probably never see another club rise to runners-up in the top flight from runners-up a division down in just two seasons, as Villa did under Taylor 13 seasons ago. We will also probably never see an England manager picked largely on the strength of two such seasons.

Claret-and-blue fans still rhapsodise over Taylor's 1990 team, as superb an example as you'll find of a whole being greater than the sum of its parts. But today's top flight has little room for men whose talents lie in taking ordinary players to extraordinary heights. Taylor's final season at Villa was an embarrassment, his team lethargic, his selections often baffling, his signings worse than ever. Arriving at Villa Park in May 2001 as a non-executive board member, he claimed to be "yesterday's man". How right he proved himself to be. And how sad, too. O

Bottoming Out

Ken Sproat saw Newcastle inflict one of Stoke's 31 defeats of 1984-85 – a dark season for the game as well as the Potters. But looking he could see a new era was about to begin

WSC No 197, July 2003

A FOOTBALL TEAM cannot get much worse than Stoke City during the 1984-85 season. There, in the all-time records for being hopeless, they skulk alongside such Victorian disasters as Darwen, Loughborough Town and Glossop. The fewest points in a season (17), the fewest wins (three – all at home), the most defeats (31) and, with 24, the fewest goals (the leading scorer was Ian Painter with six, of which four were penalties). They failed to score in 25 of the 42 league matches. They suffered mathematically definite relegation with eight miserable matches still to play.

It seems somehow appropriate and indeed inevitable that this trough of performance should happen during football's darkest hour. Depressingly low attendances everywhere (over five per cent of top flight crowds were in four figures, and that was before Wimbledon got there), precious little enthusiasm for the game other than from the active supporters and, just weeks around the corner, the twin disasters of the Bradford fire and Heysel. I had no reason to hate or even mildly dislike Stoke City when I went to see my team Newcastle play at the Victoria Ground on May 4. In fact, I sort of liked them for being high-profile FA Cup victims of Blyth Spartans seven years earlier. Also, though looking pathetic compared to today's towering arenas, the aerial photo of the Victoria Ground in Simon Inglis's *Football Grounds of Britain* book impressed me no end.

Though my reasons for travel were a bit more esoteric than the norm, perhaps it was the chance to see Newcastle get a rare double that prompted so many others to travel down. Good job too. The crowd nudged over 7,000, whereas for the previous home match against Norwich, the first after relegation was confirmed, a mere 4,500 turned up. The Newcastle United of the era were hardly big box office. Managed by Jack Charlton and playing an austere long ball game that largely floated over the frustrated, soon-to-be-leaving Chris Waddle and the not-yet-fully-recognised talents of Peter Beardsley, Newcastle would just lamp the ball up to the "twin battering rams" of Tony Cunningham and George Reilly. Seeing as neither could hope to keep their first touch within five yards of themselves, and the midfield was "bossed" by Gary Megson, whom Brian Clough famously described as being unable to control a medicine ball, it is no surprise that the crowds at St James' Park had dwindled since the previous term's exciting promotion.

We arrived at the Victoria Ground and, after walking around it, I was struck that the general atmosphere seemed like a Newcastle reserve match. Such was the paucity of home support that it was easy to get into the Stoke club shop. How we laughed at the George Berry mirror.

In the ground, the Newcastle fans became quite exuberant, wedged into the terracing of the newish stand. Opposite, the home end had the population and appearance of a queue at a bus stop: bored looking, the odd person holding shopping bags, with an almost tangible wish to get home as quickly as possible. Knots of fans would occasionally draw the eye in the otherwise empty seats. Higher to our left, on seemingly warping wooden benches, was a small old man. Sitting by himself he remained a dignified spectator, as he probably had done on much better afternoons there watching Stanley Matthews and Gordon Banks. Now he had to be content with – and these were the better players – the zombie-haired Sammy McIlroy, Seventies "golden age" throwback Alan Hudson (though he was injured, or, rumour had it, pissed, for this game) the emerging Steve Bould and his partner in defensive crime, Paul Dyson. Incredibly, the next season, Dyson would return to another First Division relegation freakshow with the almost-as-bad-as-Stoke West Brom. I hope that the payment of his mortgage was not dependent on win bonuses.

Just for the old bloke, and for the faithful few who had crept into the ground, I secretly wished that Stoke would score, on the proviso that Newcastle secured an easy victory, of course. My wish only came half true, however, as Newcastle kept a clean sheet and didn't really look threatened by the lame Keith Bertschin or Painter. Newcastle won 1-0, though it took a Stoke player to slide it in from a corner for us. Who else but Dyson? How desperate it must have been for the Stoke fans to watch this sort of carry-on on a fortnightly basis as their team slipped out of the top league, so far never to return?

So we did our double over Stoke, like 11 other teams that season. An own-goal winner at their place, a penalty winner at ours – very fitting. Both games in the middle of two separate Stoke losing streaks of ten consecutive games. When Stoke scored at Newcastle on December 1, 1984, it was only their second away goal of the season. Two days after the return match, on May 6, Stoke were to score their first away goal of 1985 in losing 5-1 at Ipswich.

It occurred to me at the time that football would always be like this, that the crowds would get lower and lower till it became like watching a Sunday morning game. But this most pointless and torpid of matches had within it some important components of the forthcoming footballing big bang. Jack Charlton would leave Newcastle in a huff and ended up managing the Republic of Ireland. Waddle would move to Tottenham and his skills would soon make him a star in Europe. Peter Beardsley would play so well the following season even England couldn't ignore him. On the Newcastle bench, as a non-playing substitute yet to make his full debut, was a certain podgy thighed, curly haired kid – Paul Gascoigne.

Steve Bould would leave Stoke to become part of a legendary Arsenal back four. The Victoria Ground, like so many other decaying, inadequate stadiums, would disappear as new grounds, built with new money, would house bigger crowds. Stoke, even when playing in "the new Division Two", would often get twice as many in as they did for this match. You see, this apparently tepid non-event was actually a white hot crucible, where the catalysts for the explosion of the footballing interest of 1990 were being moulded. The basic elements were lying around here and there. It's just that people had forgotten. ○

Too Big for his Boots

From foresight to hindsight, sound judgements to naked prejudices, Joyce Woolridge sifted through the newspapers' assessment of David Beckham's departure from Man Utd

WSC No 198, August 2003

DAVID BECKHAM'S TRANSFER to Real Madrid has provided the press with a close-season story beyond its wildest imaginings. The amount of print dedicated to increasingly wild speculation about the sale of (variously) "The boy who got too big for his boots" or "An England hero" led

Beckham himself, according to the *Manchester Evening News*, to text his Dad in disbelief: "Can you believe all this **** in the papers?" Most of what was written was best described as **** flowing copiously on to the pages of broadsheet and tabloid.

Early reports contained a succinct and reasonably accurate picture of what would transpire. United's board had talked itself into the position that selling Beckham was "good business". Ferguson deemed him inessential. Beckham's agents had sounded out Real. United were contacted by two candidates from Barcelona's forthcoming presidential election. But this relatively sane and comprehensible version was to be buried under a welter of insinuations, opinions, moralising and, in the end, complete invention.

Harry Harris, the man with the "inside track" in his Harry's Game column in the *Sunday Express*, helpfully provided readers without a Media Studies GCSE with a quick guide to just how and why a story takes such a battering. One on-the-ball reporter (called Harry, no doubt) knows the truth, but is immediately rubbished by rivals because journalism is a world where envy rules. Managers and officials leak information, some of it inaccurate. Harry's predictions were spot on. Although Joan Laporta's use of Beckham's allure to bump him into top spot in the Barcelona presidential campaign briefly offered an interesting sideline, the chief concern of those commenting on the Beckham "saga" was not how he came to join Real, but why.

Already by June 9 the *Guardian* had decided that footballing reasons were largely unimportant. Beckham was simply "too sexy for his team", though, presumably because there is still some semblance of broad-sheet responsibility left in their *G2* tabloid, they could not really claim that David Beckham had allowed his "celebrity lifestyle" and "other activities" to distract him from the football field. As Sven-Göran Eriksson, quoted in the article, confirmed: "The ladies think he's a nice-looking young man... From what I have seen though, he has always lived perfectly."

It had also become time to take sides and deal in caricature, though who exactly was the villain, or villainess, was sometimes difficult to fathom. United's manager is a man who should never take his shirt off within 30 miles of a camera. Hence shots of him burning his pallid Glaswegian flesh made the perfect accompaniment to the outpourings of the anti-Ferguson brigade. By June 9 the *Sun's* back page screamed **United Treat Me Like a Piece of Meat** and the *Mirror* had the best advertisement for

Factor 40 ever with its Red Bully cover, where a "Sunburned Sir Alex smirks hours before 'selling' David Beckham, without even telling him. What a way to treat an England hero".

In G2, Tom Bower, the latest (not without justification) prophet of doom for English football, used language usually reserved for castigating First World War generals, to denounce the man from Govan's petty-minded machinations against the "best of British youth". "Ferguson is jealous if the spotlight or TV camera wavers from himself. Football is the vehicle for prima donnas and few are more self-preening than Ferguson." The FA "steeped in debt and managed by fools" lies powerless as graspers and chancers push football on its merry way to perdition.

But Diamond Dave was not having it all his own way. That expert on the *mores* of "the real working class", Julie Burchill, bored with touting David as modern man, pronounced the Beckhams the inferiors of her own mum and dad. Becks, she now understands, is "grotesquely, massively, pussy-whipped by his talentless, ambition-hound of a wife", whereas Julie's mum "did not seem intent on cutting my father's nuts off – either in the privacy of our own home or in front of the world's media", though how often the Burchill family found themselves before the latter is unclear. (Later Tony Parsons was to mount an heroic challenge to his ex-wife's attempt to monopolise the position of talking bollocks about the working class by seeing Beckham v Ferguson as "the old working class versus the new". Alex Ferguson, he tried to argue tortuously, was old working class, because he "knew his place"...)

The lugubrious James Lawton of the *Independent* invoked the all-powerful shade of the "late Bobby Moore" to blast the authorities for honouring with an OBE a limited footballer who has yet achieved little. Andrew Morton, like Burchill the author of an opportunist volume about the not-so-royal couple, strained the bounds of taste in the *Express* by comparing Beckham and Princess Diana, whose popularity may not have survived the move to another country and a new life. Stan Hey in the *Independent on Sunday* could not shake from his mind David's first act on the road to poseurdom, the sarong, nor the GQ cover which showed Beckham's "shirtless torso doused in baby-oil, fingernails painted dark purple". And neither, according to Stan, could Sir Alex, a man, one presumes, whose nails had known nothing more effeminate than Swarfega, to whom "it was a clear signal he had lost control of the man he had sheltered since he was a boy".

A frequent marker of the Beckhams' descent into an out-of-control celebrity lifestyle was that they were "close friends of Elton John", a line oft-repeated, but never elaborated, obviously sufficiently damning in itself. In fact, Sir Elton appeared to be one of the few people not actively involved in the transfer. The list of those who were grew longer and more bewildering every day, including "the genial Israeli agent" Pini Zahavi (whose geniality may have sprung from squeezing £58 million out of United for Ferdinand and Verón).

The business sections wheeled in consultants to talk vaguely about branding, endorsements and image rights, usually accompanied by "think of a number, double it and add ten noughts" financial analysis. Like Monty Python's Spiny Norman, the Beckhams' personal wealth grew or shrank according to the hysteria of the correspondent. Patrick Collins in the *Mail on Sunday* rubbished claims of shrewd business dealings at Old Trafford, describing Peter Kenyon as "woefully maladroit" and the sale to Madrid "a textbook case of how not to conduct a major transfer".

Overall Beckham was deemed more sinned against than sinning. Ferguson's bullying of the press has left him few defenders in the media. Though Victoria's skinny, fake-tanned body excites a torrent of misogyny, the dislike of Ferguson's attitude still overrides it. Vicky, as Oliver Holt in the *Mirror* pointed out, serves the same role for the media as Yoko Ono, and the papers largely agree that her encouragement of her husband to be an active parent and a tendency to express her own opinions could never be tolerated by the irascible Scot.

By the time Beckham was sold, few had managed to resist the temptation to drift into posturing. Henry Winter in the *Telegraph* oddly insisted on discussing the transfer as a football matter and wrote an intelligent and quietly funny tactical analysis of "Ferguson's adoption of a new doctrine", 4-2-3-1, which has led him to overate his own tactical acumen and underrate Beckham's capacity to become a midfield playmaker. Patrick Barclay probably had the best verdict, writing in his column for the *Sunday Telegraph* on June 15: "In an ideal world, big clubs should not sell home-grown heroes at their peak." Meanwhile, others were breathing insincere sighs of relief, such as Jeff Powell in the *Mail* writing: "This grotesque saga is now at an end."

As if any of us believe it – the media's most rhyming reporter, the *Sun's* "Dave Kidd in Madrid", was already embroiled in the jealousies in the Bernabéu dressing room and the rest were rubbing their hands at the prospect of the Beckhams either doing a "Rushie" and fleeing back home in tears, or picturing the look on Sir Alex's face as a gleeful Becks slots the winner past whoever ends up occupying United's goal next season in the Champions League final. Whether he dethrones Raúl to "reign in Spain" or not, David's beautiful face will go on regularly adorning the front and back pages, because there is no one else to replace him, in the English media, if not in English football. ○

Bye, Buy, Maine Road

Some Manchester City fans didn't want to let their old ground go, and spent a few hundred quid at auction to make sure they never had to, as Helen Duff reported

WSC No 199, September 2003

THOUGH THE WAKE for Maine Road was held on the last day of the season, the will reading had to wait until high summer. On a scorching Sunday morning in July, Manchester City fans converged for one final time on the stadium that had served their team through 80 turbulent years – to bid for its fixtures and fittings. The auction spelled a temporary change of emphasis for City, from eager anticipation of the future (this was the week in which an excited Kevin Keegan had taken custody of the keys to the club's sparkling new 48,000-seat stadium) to bittersweet retrospection.

Sombre thoughts were uppermost at the start of the day, with a minute's silence held in memory of Marc-Vivien Foé, before the auctioneer took his place on the overgrown pitch, tapped his microphone, raised his gavel and addressed a crowd of around 1,000 seated in the Main Stand. And so to business. Just about every vestige and trapping of Maine Road that hadn't been spirited away following the final game in May was up for grabs as a sentimental keepsake.

Bidders might not have been given an option on the kitchen sink, but they were offered both a basin from the gents toilets in the Main Stand (hot tap missing, in need of Vim – went for £45) and the enamel boot-bath from the home dressing room (highest bid: £310). Prized memorabilia on offer included the boardroom table (fetched £460), the gates from the players' tunnel (£40), the front doors to the stadium (£600), a mahogany treatment table dating from the 1930s (£130), the City squad's dressing-room door (£190) and the door to the manager's office (£70 – and not, as those who recall the exciting days of Alan Ball/Steve Coppell/ Frank Clark might have expected, revolving).

Some of the stadium signs being auctioned had amusing appeal as domestic decorations (what home wouldn't benefit from a "THANK YOU FOR NOT USING FOUL AND ABUSIVE LANGUAGE" warning? Yours for £60) but others were practical only if you fancied naming your house "CENTRE SEATS 26 – 41". Contenders for the least useful lot of the day included a plaque bearing the legend "ANYONE FOUND ALLOWING DOGS TO FOUL THE PAVED AREA AROUND THIS FOOTBALL GROUND WILL BE PROSECUTED JB HALFORD SECRETARY" and a replica City shirt slightly larger than the average roof, but both found loving homes (selling for £80 and £950 respectively). Turnstiles went for as little as £150 (plus £140 removal costs) and as much as £625 – the latter for an 1890s antique which had put in 30 years' service at City's Hyde Road ground before Maine Road was even constructed. Then again, as one bidding fan was heard to comment in a barbed mutter: "We've got goalkeepers older than that."

Predictions that the club's pre-eminent celebrity supporters, Noel and Liam, would be in attendance waggling wads proved unfounded; according to the auctioneers Smith Hodgkinson, no dealings were had with the Gallaghers. Nor were there any signs of the Blues' other famous fans: Stuart Hall, Bernard Manning, Jennifer Lopez (if you believe the rumours). There were, however, 630 registered bidders who bought more than 700 lots during the seven-plus hours of the auction, generating £40,000 on the day. Final takings are expected to top £100,000 once the sale of Maine Road's larger items – including floodlights, scoreboard and main banks of seating – has been completed by industry tender. All money raised is being donated to community projects in Manchester's Moss Side district: a parting gift to the neighbourhood City called home for generations.

But what was the steal of the day? A penalty spot due to have been auctioned off was withdrawn from the sale (having been damaged in an unspecified accident) as was the tactics board from the home dressing room (insert your own cruel joke here), but one lucky punter did go home with the players' ping-pong table for a tenner. Proof – if it were needed – that City fans are masochists came with the fact that a display board documenting the club's resurgence between 1998 and 2000 sold for less (£25) than one detailing the misery of the preceding period (£35) and, although there were no takers for 25 of the 26 colour televisions in the auction, the final lot – a framed oil painting of legendary goalkeeper Joe Corrigan – fetched an impressive £725.

Which just left time to lock up, leave a note out for the milkman and turn eyes and ambitions eastwards, towards the City of Manchester stadium. ○

Beyond our Ken

Chelsea fan Mike Ticher paid grudging and limited tribute to the man who had run the Blues for good or ill for the past 21 years – and wasn't going anywhere just yet

WSC No 199, September 2003

FOR MORE THAN 20 YEARS, Chelsea have been run by a man who has sailed close to the wind in his business dealings. Some of Ken Bates's closest associates have been in serious trouble with the law and the ownership of the controlling stake in Chelsea Village was officially a mystery for many years. Now the club is owned by Roman Abramovich, a man with an even more colourful business background, much more alarming connections (such as the fugitive tycoon Boris Berezovsky) and, of course, a whole lot more money. Predictably, the only thing that has interested most Chelsea fans so far is the size of that fortune and the quality of the players it might buy.

Bates and Abramovich have something else in common. Abramovich's vehicle for buying Chelsea Village, called Chelsea Limited, is ultimately owned by a company of which he is the sole shareholder, based in the British Virgin Islands. Among the still obscure companies (with addresses in tax shelters around the world) that have sold their shares to him is Bates's own Mayflower Securities – also based in the British Virgin Islands. Curiously, it was in those same islands that Bates made part of his fortune back in 1970, in an unusual land deal.

The extraordinary purchase of the club raises far more questions than can be satisfactorily answered at this stage. Nor is the Bates era entirely open for inspection yet, since it is not really over. Quite apart from his continued presence on the board, the circumstances of the sale mean the history of the club's finances is likely to be buried beyond reach before long. Abramovich intends to acquire enough shares to make Chelsea Village a private company, which means there will be even less chance of scrutiny. But, as London's *Evening Standard* commented, "with Abramovich's deep pockets behind the club, that will probably not matter". Just hold on to that "probably" for the time being.

Leaving aside the Village's massive debts and unorthodox financial structures, most fans would concede, with varying levels of reluctance, that Bates has some solid achievements to his name. The ground has been transformed, albeit not entirely to everyone's satisfaction, cups have been won and an array of (mostly) fantastic players has passed through since the mid-1990s.

You still have to remind yourself that in 1981-82, the season before Bates took over, Chelsea lost twice to Rotherham in the league (6-1 away, 4-0 at home) and 6,009 saw their penultimate home game, a 2-2 draw with Orient. The next year they almost went down to the Third Division. It would be easy, but wrong, to assume that the subsequent revival was inevitable. Chelsea might well have plumbed the depths of a Wolves or a Derby, or gone under altogether. Bates may not have "saved" the club in quite the manner he likes to portray it, but, by the standards of British football chairmanship, he certainly was not incompetent. So much for the plaudits. The most obvious charge against Bates is one of charmlessness combined with an infuriating habit of rewriting history. Most of his appointments as manager have changed almost overnight from being a genius to a dangerous wrecker, but somehow the buck for giving them a job in the first place never seemed to stop with Bates.

The latest, shameless, instance of retrospective blame concerns former managing director Colin Hutchinson, who has now become the official scapegoat for the financial mess of Chelsea Village, which is pretty close to being the opposite of the truth.

Bates's inability to do anything with grace or dignity has damaged the club's image immeasurably, though, again, few fans care as long as success comes on the field. Some, though, might have more than a twinge of regret at his other most glaring failure, the bankruptcy of the club's youth policy. Chelsea have not produced a goalkeeper since Steve Francis, whose last season as No 1 was 1982-83. No homegrown striker has scored more than 20 goals for the club (that's in a career, not a season) since Clive Walker. It was bad enough when young players got into the team, only to be found wanting or, in a few cases (such as Graeme Le

Saux and Muzzy Izzet) for the club to misjudge them. Now, of course, they rarely even make it that far. If Carlton Cole wants to play for England he would probably be well advised to fix up a move to somewhere such as Charlton or Southampton before it's too late.

Perhaps under Abramovich the long-promised academy will take shape and the embarrassingly basic training ground will find a new home. Although it seems unlikely this will be any more of a priority for him than it was for Bates. The attempt to buy success rather than nurture it is hardly likely to change.

In many ways the club's underlying situation has not really altered, either. It is still part of a loss-making group that would be on the verge of a debt crisis if it wasn't being supported by the massive wealth of one individual (who seems keen to commit the club to vast new liabilities in player contracts). "Probably" the cash will keep flowing, although being Chelsea you would be unwise to bet that it will bring the titles that some expect. On the other hand, if anything were to happen that prevented Abramovich from pumping that money in, the consequences do not bear thinking about. But in the stable and peaceful world of Russian big business, that's hardly likely, is it? O

Tat's Entertainment

**Footballers' autographs had become big business.
Al Needham went to an exhibition at the NEC to snub Jimmy
Greaves and see what an old Tony Woodcock would be worth**

WSC No 203, January 2004

THE FIRST AUTOGRAPH I ever got was a signed photo of Tony Woodcock kneeling behind the League Cup, in exchange for my Dad moving house for him. I would dig it out, but I chucked it away when he was transferred to Cologne. I filled up assorted notebooks with autographs purloined at the Nottingham Forest training ground and outside dressing rooms after matches. Brian Clough always wrote "Be good" after his name, Martin O'Neill always had a face like a smacked arse when he did his and John Robertson always said: "Jesus, not you again."

I'm not sure when I packed in hassling footballers to write their names on bits of paper – and I can't even remember the last time I asked a celebrity for an autograph – but what I do know is that I was an absolute moron for getting them to sign tatty notebooks in order to show off to my mates at school. What I should have been doing was getting them to sign 50 shirts in one go, which I then framed and locked away for 25 years.

As anyone who's ever seen the scooter hung from the ceiling in the Chelsea Megastore knows, the market for football tat has peaked and people want something more. Something personal. Something meaningful. Sadly, employing retired players as sex slaves is still frowned upon by society, so the next best thing is the booming market in football memorabilia. And if you needed an example – another example – as to how football has loosed itself from its traditional moorings and floated off into the realms of showbiz, you needed to have been at Memorabilia 2003 at the NEC. Billed as Europe's largest collectors' fair for the kind of things Comic Book Guy out of *The Simpsons* prizes above all else, it's the kind of event where you spend half your time tutting over the gullibility of a generation who want their second childhood about five minutes into their adulthood and the other half screaming: "£40 for a Six Million Dollar Man doll with a plastic engine? Please – take my credit card."

Like all conventions of this ilk, the main attraction is 100 or so celebrities who – at a price – will scribble their name on a photo. All the usual suspects are there – cast members of *Dr Who*, *Blakes 7* and *Lord Of The Rings*, and an entire row of middle-aged Bond girls. Plonked in the middle of this for the first time in its nine-year existence is a "Sporting Arena" filled with ex-footballers and very well known ones at that: Jimmy Greaves, Pat Jennings, Charlie George and Norman Whiteside, to name but a few. If you want a precise reading as to the state of British football on the national psyche, I can tell you unequivocally: you turn left at Kenny Baker (who was R2-D2) and it's just across the aisle from Tom Baker and next door to Jaws out of *Moonraker*.

After barging through a load of people dressed up as Cybermen and being seriously distracted by a full set of *Roy of the Rovers* annuals, I chance upon someone who looks like a clean-shaven Eight Ace from *Viz*, with a ponytail and shell-suit bottoms. By the name-tag on the table (next to a stack of photos and 1977 FA Cup final programmes) it's Stuart Pearson. Or Jimmy Greenhoff. Or maybe even Martin Buchan. I'd find out if he were actually signing anything, but there's no one about – they're all queuing up at the *Lord of the Rings* stall or trying to chat up Bond girls. I get really angry about this. Instead of pretending to hack at a man in an Orc costume or pretending to have sex with Roger Moore, Jimmy/Martin/Stuart actually achieved something in real life. I'd go over and talk to him, but he might charge me £15 for doing so.

Instead, I peruse the merchandise stalls, which are so festooned with Man United stuff that I feel like I'm at the most exclusive car-boot sale in Cheshire. You can't help but make comparisons between the football memorabilia and the more traditional items. A Topps bubblegum card with a tiny square of a match-worn Beckham shirt costs £45. Unless it's got a bit of his shirt number on, in which case the price doubles. This makes it £5 more expensive than a square inch of the carpet used on the set of the original *Star Trek*. Naturally, the serious money goes on England 1966 memorabilia – a Watney's Red Barrel pennant is on display without a price tag, which means you have to ask the dealer how much before having to sit down when he tells you.

Back at the stall, Greaves, Jennings and Chopper Harris sit about having a natter, waiting for someone to come over. It's Saturday afternoon, so they won't see much business until Sunday, a dealer tells me – and business will pick up when the secret special guest arrives (who turns out to be Geoff Hurst). In America, players hit the signing circuit the minute they retire and make an absolute packet by writing their names for hours at a time and refusing to indulge in small talk. There, elderly ex-players brought in for one-off appearances are cheerfully advertised as "dead signatures", but thankfully we're a long way from that. The old pros are happy to pose for photos and Greavsie even picks up a cuddly seal and runs through a group of people like a rugby player. I'd ask him how much he expected to earn from the weekend, but I refuse to do so after he accused Forest players of throwing a game in the early Sixties in his new book (£30 gold-embossed special edition, signed).

In any case, the real money in football autographs seems to be with current players, who are too busy playing the sport to sit around signing stuff. Sportizus is a chain of memorabilia shops across the country, which contains the usual stuff – signed glossies of Darth Maul, Ali's gloves etc – but their dealings in football-related merchandise have gone through the roof. Part shop, part museum, they offload anything David Beckham deigns to scribble upon the minute they get hold of it. "In the past five years, the value of football memorabilia has rocketed," says Mike McGee, manager of the Nottingham branch. "Since the Premiership boom, it's become much harder to approach players for autographs – you just don't get the access to players that you used to, which makes a ball signed on the training ground much more valuable than it used to be." It's a frighteningly watertight set-up – they don't do on-the-spot valuations on the premises and everything they sell has not one but three holograms – one on the back of the pic, one on the certificate of authentication and one that goes to their head office for tracking purposes.

The value of a signed glossy seems to be a combination of celebrity and rarity, but this goes out of the window with football signatures, which is a formulaic process which factors in how famous you are, what team you play for and if you're married to Posh Spice or not. There's no better time-killer than going on the Sportizus website (www.sportizus.com) and comparing autographs. Right now, a signed Beckham pic in Real kit goes for £325 – the combined total of Al Pacino, Sebastian Coe, Geoff Boycott, Margaret Thatcher and Arthur Scargill. Even Wayne Rooney – who, at the time of writing, has won precisely nothing – goes for £245 (or Kevin Costner and George Clooney).

In a list of the top 100 most valuable autographs (which is monitored with Stock Exchange-like precision), the England 1966 squad are the most valuable football-wise, with prices up to £3,500 for a full set (on a par with Judy Garland, Neil Armstrong and the Queen). Obviously, the most valuable single signature is Bobby Moore, what with him being a) the captain and b) the only dead one. Pelé is the top player, at £295 (on a par with Marc Bolan and Isambard Kingdom Brunel). Like Muhammad Ali, his value would be much higher if he wasn't still alive and signing everything put before him. According to McGee, you don't have to be a rocket scientist to predict which signatures from the current crop of players will be worth something in the future. "It's essential that the player has had a successful international career, or is iconic – Best, Moore, Pelé, etc. But it's all about publicity in the end. Vinnie Jones is a valuable autograph, and how many times did he play for Wales?"

One last tip – collectors go mental over anything signed on something unusual, such as a sardine tin signed by Eric Cantona, a kebab wrapper signed by Gazza or a sample bottle signed by Rio Ferdinand. And if you think all this is a sign that football has become blown out of all proportion, wait until George Best's old liver appears on eBay. ○

Vision Excess

Barney Ronay considered how a piece of squat, ugly technology, once a source of condescension, changed English football

WSC No 203, January 2004

DESPERATE TIMES call for desperate publicity stunts. In 1990, with the battle for control of the skies between BSB and Sky TV at its most feverish, camera-shy media mogul Rupert Murdoch took the unusual step of paying a surprise visit to the home of Sky's millionth UK subscriber. Awkwardly posed in raincoat and inch-thick specs, Murdoch smiled for the cameras with an arm around the shoulders of his hosts, a family of five torn from their expensively assembled tea-time viewing to stand outside in the cold next to a laconic billionaire.

Oddly, Murdoch's unlikely piece of doorstepping prefigures the frequent *deus ex machina* appearances of *The Simpsons'* Mr Burns in the cartoon that ultimately, along with football, would secure the survival of Sky's television service. However, the most significant presence at Murdoch's day out with the Cratchitts remains the large, round object cradled lovingly under his other arm. The satellite dish looks suitably bashful. Monstrously proportioned, gleaming white and emblazoned with the words "thanks a million", the dish also manages to obscure most of the lucky millionth family. This is fitting: over the next 13 years the satellite dish would become the central component in the transformation of football. Players, supporters, clubs and competitions have all found themselves refracted, magnified and distorted through its shiny concave surface. Recently Sky announced that it had signed up its seven millionth subscriber. The dish has reacted to its success in the way of most celebrities: with a makeover. Now a svelte, gun-metal grey size eight and almost unrecognisable from the stuttering wannabe goosed for the cameras by Mr Murdoch, the dish remains central to the most rapid of English football's many revolutions.

In 1979 Harold Wilson warned that the UK was about to be struck by "a foreign cultural invasion through the satellite". In fact it would be seven years before the battle began in earnest, when a newly formed company called British Satellite Broadcasting (BSB) secured the right to run five as-yet-unused domestic satellite frequencies. Within two years Murdoch had announced his intention to begin broadcasting his own unlicensed Sky service from the Luxembourg-based Astra satellite, transmitting on the widely disregarded Pal system, which allowed Sky to overcome reservations that Astra broadcasts would require an unmanageably huge dish in order to be received in the UK. BSB fought back, spending heavily on programming but crucially stopping just short of acquiring the rights to screen the Football League. By November 1990, with both companies losing huge amounts of money – Sky's £10 million weekly shortfall threatened the future of the entire News International operation – the two companies decided to cut their losses and merge to form British Sky Broadcasting, or BSkyB. Or, eventually, as a brand just Sky. In the event most BSB staff lost their jobs, the Sky dish prevailed and nearly all of BSB's programming was dropped.

Football and the newly launched Sky Sports channel were key to BSkyB's survival, although with a line-up comprising cast-offs from (the temporarily defunct) Eurosport and a handful of FA Cup matches, it was clear Sky had its eye on a larger footballing prize. Nevertheless its influence was already being felt, even by those without a three-foot wide chunk of heavy metal screwed to the side of their house. By February 1991, after the first significant rash of TV-scheduled fixture switches had angered Liverpool and Manchester United supporters, the *Independent* felt moved to exclaim: "The time has come to ask who runs English football: the game's authorities or the TV stations?"

For the Premier League and its nascent romance with satellite hardware, the big deal arrived in May 1992. Amstrad owner Alan Sugar's role in the seminal meeting of Premier League chairman at the Royal Lancaster Hotel in London on May 18 that year is hard to overstate. Faced with rival bids from ITV and BSkyB, the chairmen were meeting to vote on the destination of the new Premiership TV rights deal. On the morning of the meeting Sugar, in his capacity as Spurs chairman, was supplied with a sealed envelope containing the substance of ITV's offer. Swiftly donning his Amstrad hat, Sugar immediately phoned BSkyB executive Sam Chisholm from the lobby of the hotel to leak details of the £262m bid.

Witnesses are said to have overheard an excitable Sugar instructing Chisholm to "blow them out of the water". Why would Sugar do such a thing? Amstrad, under his guidance, were the main suppliers of dishes to BSkyB. Chisholm duly provided his counter-bid and in a moment of laughable propriety the Spurs chairman then offered not to vote on the deal, although it was subsequently agreed that he could do so. The Sky bid was accepted by 14 votes to six, Sugar's vote proving crucial in completing the required two-thirds majority. Amstrad's share value jumped by £7m on announcement of completion of the deal. A venture founded in football's urge to gorge itself on the TV revenue stream of satellite broadcasting; given shape by the self-serving machinations of a dish mogul with a foot in both camps; and destined to mortgage itself utterly to the demands and rewards of the schedulers: the Premiership launched three months later.

Soon Sky's hardware would become a modern urban phenomenon. Across inner cities the dishes spread like a fungus on the side of tower blocks and hung like inverted birdbaths from the stone cladding of the suburban villa. Football's booming popularity would service the monstrous expansion in Sky's audience during the 1990s. Sky Sports 2 was launched in 1994 followed by Sky Sports 3 two years later and BSkyB currently claims to have "more than 17 million viewers in seven million households". Despite the ham-fisted demise of ITV Digital and the generally slow uptake of digital subscription services, the government is planning to switch off analogue terrestrial in 2010. Victory for the dish – and the revolutionary symbiosis between subscription TV and British football – is almost complete.

At the same time, beyond the technical innovations and trailblazing corporate production style, Sky's coverage began to change the game fundamentally. Football was once an almost entirely inclusive activity. Watching a match involved seeking it out, braving crowds, negotiating various random and possibly unpleasant elements. Refracted through the continual access of the dish, the game now divides and alienates: watch it from your armchair, select your match, your camera view, your highlights package. The dish is the tool with which football, for millions of people, has been remade as a solitary experience. Television is not entirely to blame for this. A ticket to watch Queens Park Rangers in the Second Division now costs between £13 and £18, while a seat at Stamford Bridge retails at up to £40. If prices had kept in pace with inflation since 1991 the cheapest tickets to watch a match in any division would cost between £5 and £8. Little wonder the supporter unable to meet these prices chooses instead a whole month's subscription to Sky.

There is, of course, the ghastly bonhomie of the football pub, another satellite phenomenon. The technology was even unexpectedly subverted when Norwegian live satellite feeds picked up by English pubs provided live pirate broadcasts of 3 o'clock kick-offs on a Saturday afternoon. This loophole was swiftly stamped on by the Premier League and Sky, who had embraced the public screening of its sports services in pubs as part of its marketing campaign, but had no desire to allow landlords to show matches they hadn't paid for or divert potential subscribers.

Only 15 years into its lifetime, an Australian-owned tabloid-style TV service, broadcast via an unlicensed Luxembourg satellite, has utterly transformed the national game. Occasionally, among the mini-dishes and cable boxes that are now a standard British architectural folly, a few of the original white soup plate-shaped dishes remain rusting on their moorings, relics of the commercial football war of the early 1990s and, if we need one, something of a smoking gun. The game remains supremely vulnerable to the greed of a few individuals when the most profound transformation in its history has its roots in the cynical manoeuvres of a low-tech hardware retailer, the dubious screen presence of Richard Keys and the most visible application of space travel technology to emerge since man walked on the moon: the satellite dish. ○

It was my Agent's Idea

Though far from ever-present, agents have been around longer than you might think. John Harding charted their changing role back to the days when they built whole teams

WSC No 204, February 2004

THE TERM "FOOTBALL AGENT" first entered the language in the 1890s, as the professional game began to expand. The purpose of the agent was to place players with clubs. For a time, they did good business: in 1893, Middlesbrough Ironopolis had its playing strength built up from scratch in about three days by one unnamed agent. But clubs soon became suspicious of the ties developing between players and "outsiders". Control was all-important and, once the maximum wage was instituted in 1900, along with the contractual straitjacket of the retain-and-transfer system, agents faded away. The scout was soon providing clubs with as many players as they needed for a fraction of the cost.

For the next 50 years or so, players' earnings would be controlled to the penny. When agents did appear, it was always from abroad. In the 1920s, North American soccer clubs employed them to lure away players, such as Scotland's Alex Jackson, as did certain French clubs in the 1930s. Between the wars, little money could be made via endorsements, but that changed soon after the Second World War. Denis Compton approached journalist Reg Hayter in 1949 for help in organising his chaotic postbag. When Hayter discovered lucrative newspaper offers Compton had failed to spot, he introduced Arsenal's glamour boy to Bagenal Harvey, who became Britain's first sportsman's agent, setting up the famous deal in which Compton slicked down his hair and became forever identified with Brylcreem.

The transfer of top British players to Italy in the Fifties and Sixties saw agents become ever more closely embroiled in player/club negotiations. John Charles's move to Juventus in 1957 was notable for the intervention of Teddy Sommerfield, whose regular clients included TV celebrities such as Eamonn Andrews. It was the first time a British player had employed an agent to hammer out a transfer deal, but Charles was moving abroad. The involvement of agents in domestic transfers and wage deals was still a long way off.

England's 1966 World Cup stars Bobby Moore and Geoff Hurst, for instance, shunned offers to join Mark McCormack's international organisation, preferring instead the services of a loyal West Ham club servant, Jack Turner, whose principal expertise was buying and selling houses. Although Turner formed Bobby Moore Ltd with himself as a director, he later admitted: "Moore should have got away from me and been handled by someone like McCormack." Hurst was frightened off by the American's 20 per cent fee. George Best, meanwhile, employed Denis Law's agent, Ken Stanley, who worked from a couple of rooms in an office in Huddersfield. Stanley had originally run a table tennis hall in Burnley before joining the sportswear firm Mitre. Although Best claimed to be happy with Stanley, one senses that ads for Irish sausages and modelling assignments for the Great Universal Stories catalogue were hardly appropriate for the game's first international superstar.

By the late 1970s, with firms looking increasingly at global markets, players such as Trevor Francis, Britain's first £1 million player, were marketable beyond these shores, giving agents such as Francis's Dennis Roach a deal more to exploit. Roach explained: "The tag of being the first £1m player opened up avenues not previously available to footballers."

The next couple of decades saw a gradual loosening of the tight contractual grip clubs exercised, climaxing in the Bosman ruling of 1995, which saw complete freedom for players once their contracts expired. Now clubs had to deal face to face with players' representatives, intent on negotiating the best possible contracts for their clients as well as for themselves. British agents came into the business from many directions. There was Hayter, a sports journalist; Roach, at one time the most powerful and well connected agent in Europe, got into the business after meeting Johan Cruyff on a family seaside holiday; Eric Hall crossed over from showbiz; and Barry Silkman, one of the busiest of a more recent generation, was a player with Crystal Palace and Manchester City.

In 1989, as a response to complaints about agents' unscrupulous ways and lack of accountability, FIFA proposed a code of conduct, while the Professional Footballers' Association offered a service for players at a fraction of the cost agents charged. (Nigel Martyn, the first £1m goalkeeper, paid just £200 to arrange his move from Bristol Rovers to Crystal Palace.) Soon operators such as Jon Holmes claimed they were no longer interested in just hawking their men around for the highest price. "I wanted to follow [Mark] McCormack and be a manager and exploiter of talent, not some middleman trying to broker transfers and chivvy a few quid. The development of the client is what we're interested in. That's where you maximise earning potential, not through moves."

The influence of the agent is, perhaps, waning. Top legal firms now pick up the biggest deals, while the new transfer windows, the demise of ITV Digital, the halving of player values and the rapid increase in player unemployment have seen a substantial slump in the share value of many agencies. Some have already gone out of business. Others have changed direction entirely. Roach became almost "establishment" as president of the FIFA-recognised International Association of Football Agents; Tony Stephens, agent for players such as David Platt, Alan Shearer, David Beckham and Michael Owen, edged away from transfer dealing to sponsorship creation; and Holmes, friend and manager of Gary Lineker, put his agent's licence on ice to chair the consortium seeking to bring Leicester City back from the brink of financial disaster.

However, agents are here to stay. As Tommaso Angelini, a Scottish-based Italian agent, says: "Everyone in football has a specific job: director, administrator, manager, player. But since they are public figures, they need someone who can work out of sight. That's the essential job of the agent. Without us, it couldn't work." O

Boarding Party

The internet has its critics, but after using it to spend his money on football games to make up for his deprived childhood, Harry Pearson certainly wasn't one of them

WSC No 204, February 2004

MY CHILDHOOD CONTACT with football board games was confined to gazing wistfully at the adverts in *Jimmy Hill's Football Weekly*. They promised so much delight. Wembley was based on "The English Football Association Challenge Cup Competition" and boasted "the most gripping features and exciting uncertainties" recreated "with vivid and amazing fidelity". Soccerama, meanwhile was thrillingly endorsed by England World Cup star Alan Ball.

But I was an only child and the Second World War had given my parents an aversion to board games that was exceeded only by their loathing for German aeroplanes and tinned fish. "If you'd played as much Monopoly in air raid shelters as I have you'd never want to shake a dice again," my mother would say as I attempted to persuade her of the joyful family evenings we could spend playing Soccerboss ("Buy to strengthen your team") or League Championship ("Exciting action every second", according to Gordon Banks).

But you didn't win the war by giving in to whining, so I never got to own a football board game. Well, not back then anyway. Thirty years later and thanks to the internet auction site eBay my house is bulging with them. Soccerboss, Wembley, Soccerama, Forecast ("The football game of the 90s") Emlyn Hughes' Team Tactix ("90 minutes to compile England's greatest team") Kevin Keegan's Matchday, Billy Hamilton's Football Academy, Bryan Robson's 90 Minutes and Pepys' Penalty all now take up space that might otherwise be filled with something culturally uplifting, such as a piano or a life-size wax model of Peter Schmeichel.

I should stress that I am not talking about action games. Not Waddington's Table Soccer (played with a tiddlywink), games in which spring-loaded players are operated by levers (Chad Valley Soccer, Campioni), moved around with magnets (Super Soccer) or twiddled using knobs (Casdon's Soccer Game – endorsed by Bobby Charlton and later by Kenny Dalglish), or where they kick the ball when you push their heads down (the 1960s German game Tippkick and its successors such as Striker) have no place in My Collection. Dice, spinners and cards marked with instructions such as "strong wind favours home team add two to their score" control these games. And I have persuaded a few like-minded individuals (or sad middle-aged losers as we prefer to think of ourselves) into playing, too. Results have been mixed in more ways than one.

"The best game I've ever played!" Alan Ball says on the lid of ASL's Soccerama. If this is true all I can say is Ball should have stayed in more. Soccerama has low production values and the same relationship to football as that line of hair on Gary Neville's top lip has to a moustache. The game's one endearing feature is the board. Made from extruded polythene ("stain resistant to hot and cold liquids") it features drawings of rear views of footballers, many of whom seem to be executing the sort of dance moves Dick Shawn demonstrates in the 1960s comedy epic *It's A Mad, Mad, Mad, Mad, World*. The effect is given a Michael Clarke-ish tinge by the fact that the No 6 is apparently wearing a G-string, while the centre-forward is plainly naked from the waist down. Ball's World Cup team-mate Gordon Banks's game League Championship is little better in terms of realism and lower on latent homoeroticism, but at least the winner gets to wave a two-inch high replica of the League trophy.

Wembley and Soccerboss were made by Ariel, an upmarket company that specialised in complex strategy games such as Kingmaker that locked teenage boys (or fat men with beards and Metallica T-shirts) in a room for several days without producing any tangible result other than a collective headache and a refulgent pong. Their two football games are, quite literally, heavy in comparison to their rivals. Soccerboss, for instance, outweighs Kevin Keegan's Matchday by close to a kilo. Wembley, which first appeared just after the Second World War ("Like all Ariel games it is British in conception, in its intelligent construction, universality of appeal, as well as in the unrivalled quality of its manufacture," says the introduction with the same complacency that led the England international team to unravel) could be played by between three and 12 players. In the opening, Monopoly-style, stages players accumulate money that will allow them to buy teams. The better the team the more they cost. The fact that Spurs are valued at 50 per cent more than Manchester United will be a source of amusement, or pathos depending on your point of view. When "The Cup" begins results are determined by die rolls – the better teams getting to throw dice with higher numbers on them. Inevitably in my experience the game ends with one player having all the semi-finalists while the others look on sourly and pretend to take an interest.

Soccerboss billed itself as "The Exciting Game That Puts You In The Manager's Hot Seat" (if the cover shot is anything to go on, in those days that gave you access to a big telephone, an in-tray and a cinema screen showing Leeds v Wolves). It has a lot going for it. There are hundreds of brightly coloured little footballers which slot into your team board, an injury and suspension chart and rules that come in the form of a mocked up newspaper with headlines reading "Italians in £400,000 swoop for United Trio" and so on. The focus of Soccerboss is a truncated Division One, which mysteriously includes Celtic and Rangers as well as Manchester United, Liverpool and Nottingham Forest (though as the rules point out, these names can easily be replaced with your own favourite team – charmingly the example given is Bishop Auckland). The same dice used in Wembley determine who wins fixtures and at the end the person who has accrued the most points from winning the league, Cup or accumulating the most money is crowned manager of the year. This takes a very long time. If a full complement of eight people is playing, by the halfway point even hard-bitten traditionalists may find themselves joining Arsène Wenger in appealing for a winter break.

Billy Hamilton's Football Academy is "The game designed by a professional footballer" and since the copyright is in his name you suspect that for once this may be true. The usual mad randomness prevails (clearly even pros believe the game to be completely controlled by fate), though Football Academy at least takes a different approach to the usual with each player serving a three-year apprenticeship before being let loose in the professional game. During their apprenticeship players win effort and skill tokens by landing on squares that say things such as "Your leg hurts in training but you play on. Pick up 2 effort tokens". Effort tokens are aspirin-sized, blue and marked with the letter E. Those were more innocent times.

Bryan Robson endorses 90 Minutes with the words "It's a winner" (this is clearly a truncated version of what Bryan really said which was, of course, "As I said earlier, it's a winner"). 90 Minutes takes place on a pitch, the movement of the ball controlled by dice and the picking up of action cards featuring photographs of two very unathletic looking men in football kits posed against a mocked-up crowd. In many ways the game perfectly recreates the feeling of being a football fan since what is happening on the field is completely out of your control. I played 90 Minutes on my own and after a quarter of an hour was yelling "Stop passing it backwards, you morons", just like at a real game.

I could go on about luxury stand cards, the Central Authority Pool and the painting of Malcolm Macdonald on the front of Palitoy's Superstars, but I wouldn't want to sound like an obsessive geek. And besides, the auction on a 1920s edition of Car-Soc ("Incorporates every move in football") ends in 15 minutes and there's no way I'm missing out on that. ○

A Different League

WSC greeted the corporate rebranding of the three divisions below the Premiership with a mixture of bewilderment, anger and disbelief

WSC No 205, March 2004 ~ Editorial

THREE YEARS AGO, we suggested that if a marketing company were ever presented with the task of revamping football they might suggest renaming it Krazy Kick, or Leggy Fun. In fact, 13 years ago we speculated that soon we would be reading about "the Hyper League or the Supreme Set-up or the Utter Division". We're horrified to discover that the Football League are entertaining similar thoughts, only they appear to be serious. It has recently been revealed that the First Division may be renamed "The Football League Championship" from next season, with the lower levels renamed, astonishingly, the First and Second Division. This brilliant scheme is one of a series of proposals developed by an agency called TBWA, previously responsible for the "acclaimed" (it says here) Wonderbra and FCUK campaigns. Club chairmen are to discuss the agency's ideas in April and will put them to a vote in June.

Reports of the planned "rebranding" suggest that it has the support of those who lobbied for the removal of the previous League chairman, David Burns, over the ITV Digital fiasco. Take a bow, Millwall chairman Theo Paphitis and the bumptious Simon Jordan of Crystal Palace (the man who wouldn't even contemplate taking part in the play-offs this season – only automatic promotion was good enough). One has to have some sympathy for the League's staff – it can't be easy having people like these constantly breathing down your necks, though the promotion of Birmingham in 2002 did at least provide some respite from the incessant scheming of Karren Brady and the porn barons.

The problem is, those who agitate for changes to the First Division don't actually want to be members of it; they want to be in the Premier League. And if they can't achieve that, they want to kid themselves they have the next best thing, Premier League II (a concept last floated two years ago when various chairmen, led by the subsequently disgraced Geoffrey Richmond of Bradford City, tried to invite Rangers and Celtic to join them) or at the very least a competition that sounds a bit more like the Premiership. It's as if the Football League was some generic brand of gin hoping to fool the absent-minded punter by sticking itself in a green bottle and calling itself "Gordans".

But why does the product need rebranding at all? Half a million people watched Nationwide games on the last weekend in January – more than went to the theatre. It already has a big audience. These people shouldn't be patronised, nor will they be conned into thinking that what they pay to see each week has been magically transformed by a change of wording and a swish new logo. The whole idea of "Premier II" is based on a false premise: that the success of the Premiership was based on the name rather than the relentless promotion by Sky and the Murdoch press, catching a wave of popularity after Italia 90, combined with the money that was coming into the game from a variety of sources improving the quality at the top end and the facilities pretty much everywhere. Crass marketing scams – giant inflatable wrestlers, bands at half-time – got precisely nowhere and the ill-judged fireworks at Wolves v Newcastle have surely put an end to such needless sideshows.

In the absence of a major rival to the world's most famous Australian-American tycoon, it's hard to imagine anyone is going to do the same for Division One no matter what they call it – in fact the ITV Digital debacle was precisely a failed attempt to pull this trick off. If name changes really matter why don't the club chairmen go the way of their rugby league counterparts – Cardiff Crusaders, Selhurst Park Patriots etc? But we don't want to put more ideas in their heads.

No, we would rather remind them what a phenomenally successful product they have. In 1991-92, the turnstiles racked up 5.8 million people watching the 24 teams in what was then Division Two. Last season, you could reverse those figures: 8.5m watched Division One games. The third tier is up from a fraction under 3m to 3.9m, while the bottom rung – though effectively only 22 teams back in 1992 – is up close to 50 per cent, from 1.7m to nearly 2.5m. League football, whatever you call it, is incredibly popular. In the hands of responsible businessmen these would be recognised as boom years – not the time to make pointless ego-boosting changes that can only devalue the product. ○

The Great Orator

Bill Shankly was not just a football manager: he was a communicator. Barney Ronay listened to his words come to life and was reminded of a thousand pale imitations

WSC No 205, March 2004

IN 1997 A PLAQUE was unveiled in Glenbuck commemorating the 55 professional footballers the Scottish mining village produced during the last century. Among them was Bill Shankly accompanied, even here, by what have become his defining epithets: "the legend, the genius, the man". This seems to be more than just a localised view. "I watched his genius unfold," wrote Tom Finney in 1993. "A great man, a great manager and a great psychologist," enthused Kevin Keegan. No mention of Shankly, it seems, is complete without a magisterial turn of phrase. The legend, the greatest, the granditudelissimus – when it comes to Shankly we all turn into Don King.

Shankly's achievements as a manager were undoubtedly great. Between 1959 and 1974 Liverpool won the League three times, the UEFA Cup once and the FA Cup twice, success achieved by reconstructing the club from within. When he was appointed Liverpool had spent the past five seasons in Division Two and, in his own words, "the place was a shambles". Shankly released 24 players in his first two years, but kept hold of the boot-room personnel – Joe Fagan, Bob Paisley and Reuben Bennett – who would remain at the club throughout its subsequent success. By the time he retired, Shankly had laid the foundations for 15 years of domestic and European domination. Great, but not unique. His record is similar to that of Don Revie at Leeds over the same period.

Revie also took a struggling club into Division One, building a team and a way of playing that brought two League titles, European success and a certain era-defining swagger. Similarly, Herbert Chapman turned his Huddersfield Town side into the most successful team in the country during four mercurial years in the 1920s. Yet few outside Elland Road make a habit of hailing Revie's genius, while the Terriers similarly failed to implant themselves in the consciousness.

Shankly's genius exists outside his bare achievements. He remains a footballing archetype: an arresting, vivid, revolutionary voice. And one that refuses to die: at times it seems what survives of Shankly is a zombified anthology of quips, aphorisms and gags, still staggering from biography to website to after-dinner speech after all these years. Everybody knows the quotes. "I want to build a team that's invincible, so they'll have to send a team from Mars to beat us." "Me having no education, I had to use my brains." "I don't drop players, I make changes." What was once fresh and startling has become fogged by layer upon layer of repetition. Was Shankly actually funny? Or just a compulsively wisecracking boss: a footballing David Brent, with Tommy Docherty as his Finchy?

Take this, for example: Docherty: "You have to say Tony Hateley's good in the air." Shankly: "Aye, so was Douglas Bader... and he had a wooden leg." Or this: "If he had gunpowder for brains he couldn't blow his cap off." Shankly, like anyone, could be boorish: "The trouble with referees is they know the rules, but they do not know the game." Or platitudinous: "If you are first you are first. If you are second you are nothing." For the post-Shankly generation it is tempting to ask exactly why quotations such as these have been feverishly transcribed for the past 30 years. Shankly's genius, on the cold hard page, eludes us. What we need is Shankly the voice. And fortunately, the voice still exists – in the form of the gatefold double album *Shankly Speaks*.

Billed as "a feast of a listening experience", *Shankly Speaks* showcases a lengthy interview recorded over two days at the Adelphi Hotel in Liverpool in 1981. There is no preamble: as soon as the needle touches the record Shankly speaks, holding forth on what the sleeve notes describe as "producing great teams". The voice is a nimble baritone, rapid but still languid. In fact Shankly's sentences have a distinct dramatic rhythm, which the voice seems to reach for instinctively. Talking about "the Liverpool system", he says: "You need options, two people to take it off you. Three. Choices," and it's as though he's outlining some magical formula. Pressed on the funniest moments during his time in the game,

Shankly describes the older players at Glenbuck telling "exaggerated tales" to "lift away the gloom" and he laughs, a surprisingly childish gurgle. It's a sound you want to hear again: conspiratorial and unselfconscious; in the laugh you catch a glimpse of Shankly's talent for inspiring deep affection in those around him. Later, talking of the need to drum instructions into players, he recalls, as he does elsewhere, a recorded message in a New York lift repeating the words "mind the stairs". On paper the story doesn't register; told in Shankly's urgent tones, it seems keenly observed and startlingly relevant.

Shankly Speaks does exactly what it promises: Shankly does indeed speak. But rather than the trumpeted "insights", what stays with you are the quality and rhythm of the voice. More than just a silvery phrase-maker, Shankly communicated a passion for the game, for a club and for a region never before expressed through the media. He spoke directly to the support of his own and every club, using not quite the language of the terrace but a hybrid of everyday speech and the wisecracking theatricals of a movie gangster. Thus Shankly gave the manager his voice, creating a template for all the messianic Big Mals, Big Rons, Old Big 'Eads and Little Kevs that would follow, mostly limply, in his shadow. People didn't talk about the game like Shankly before Shankly. After Shankly, everybody did, or could, or wanted to.

Genius is a difficult concept in sport. In his essay on the cricketer Garry Sobers, A Representative Man, CLR James provides a working definition of the word in a sporting context: "Geniuses are merely individuals who carry to a definitive extreme the characteristics of the special act or function which they express." The influences that found such vivid expression in Shankly are easy to trace. As a manager he was belligerent, tyrannical, wisecracking, but always affectionate – a Scots James Cagney or a South Ayrshire Philip Marlowe. Of his own upbringing in Glenbuck during the inter-war years, Shankly said: "There were only two things in Scotland in those days: the pit and football. Football was better," and like many of his generation Shankly had grown up watching depression era and wartime films from the US. All of this would be reflected in his own public persona: the bluff façade of Cagney mixed with the wise-guy patter of Jack Benny or even, occasionally, Groucho Marx ("Just tell them I completely disagree with everything they say" – Shankly; "Whatever it is, I'm against it!" – Marx).

Like Benny, Shankly instinctively reached for a straight man. Hence his continual sparring with Everton. "This city has two great teams

– Liverpool and Liverpool reserves," Shankly quipped, putting an arm around the shoulder of his blue-shirted stooge and lighting a match off the back of his neck. "If Everton were playing down at the bottom of my garden I'd draw the curtains," he cracked – and yet Shankly ended up coaching an Everton boys team; the relationship never soured, remaining an affectionately rivalrous double act. It seems appropriate that his most celebrated quip was borrowed from an American. When Shankly said, in jest: "Some people say football is a matter of life and death. I'm very disappointed with that attitude. It's much more important than that," he was quoting Green Bay Packers coach Vince Lombardi. Shankly brought a US-style democratisation to the language of football. Where the pre-Shankly English manager was a mute, faux BBC-accented stammerer of platitudes, American sportsmen had a voice of their own and Shankly, by design or historical accident, brought this vernacular to football.

Shankly survives as the most living of dead managers. Matt Busby seems, for subsequent generations, a remote, slightly vicar-ish figure; but Shankly is vibrantly still with us. Titles and cups will always be won, but football's most lyrical icon, whether on vinyl, in the Chinese whispering of a fan website, or in the post-match posturing of a Shankly-ite managerial descendant, will continue to speak. ○

Hard Copy

Should books about football violence be on the top shelf? Rob Chapman believed the success of "hoolie porn" is due to some men's rather odd obsession with crime

WSC No 205, March 2004

ABOUT 20 YEARS AGO I used to work in one of Britain's hardest and most dangerous borstals. I mentioned this fact to the husband of my cousin one day at a family get-together. "Oh good, tell me more," he said, fetching me another drink. "I love villainy tales. They give me an erection." Yes, that's what he said. These people do exist. He wasn't the least bit discouraged when I told him that all I did was teach remedial English to a standard whereby the average semi-literate car thief or burglar might at least be able to grasp the rudiments of a *Sun* editorial. I haven't seen him for years but I bet he reads hoolie-books. I imagine most of the commissioning editors who publish the stuff are a bit like him, too. They love a bit of rough and they've created a veritable industry out of "literature" that documents the exploits of former, and in some cases not so former, football hooligans.

Type "hooligan books" into Google and the search will lead you to provocative titles such as *Want Some Aggro?*, *Who Wants It?*, *Bovver* and *Steaming In.* They range in quality and emphasis from *Saturday Is Service Day*, Callum Bell's breathless, hastily penned account of a Motherwell "crew" that punched above its weight among the Glasgow big boys, to *Naughty*, Stoke fan Mark Chester's disturbed and sometimes disturbing portrayal of a broken home and a brutalised youth. There are Dougie and Eddie Brimson's ethnographies of violence and mayhem in Europe (*Everywhere We Go, England My England*). There are tales from the post-industrial front line in Cardiff (*Soul Crew* – David Jones & Tony Rivers), Hull (*City Psychos* – Shaun Tordoff) and all points beyond. And they all tell the same story.

There's usually a bit about the casuals (rarely developed beyond an arbitrary list of bands and brands), a smidgen of cod-sociology about alienated yoof and sink estates, and tons about rucking. It's hoolie-porn and the publishers want the money shot every few pages. And that's exactly what you get. One long tedious litany of 'aving it and mixing it and calling cards and gaining prestige and status by running the opposition off New Street station – or, in one memorable moment from Tordoff's *City Psychos*, by commandeering the carriage next to the buffet car "and threatening anyone trying to wander through". "They defended this carriage as though it was a section of terracing," says Tordoff, "and found no one willing to take them on." Hardly the Battle of the Boyne or Culloden is it? Although in the minds of the participants you suspect that it is.

There's a certain kind of academic who loves this stuff of course. Puffed up on professorial salaries and usually found lecturing in Mickey Mouse Studies at one of Britain's many pretend universities, they talk of how "empowered" the participants feel as they assert their traditional masculine roles by taking over stadiums and staving in pub windows. The dons, of course, prefer to gain "empowerment" by buying houses in leafy suburbs and going on conference junkets to Mexico City or Stockholm. The hoolies have to make do with bawling "No Surrender!" at bemused foreigners.

Ironically, the interesting stuff in these books is often in the incidentals. Bell tells a touchingly familiar tale of going shopping as a novice casual, buying all the wrong gear, so having to replace it the following week. Chester tells a far more poignant tale of dead or drug-addicted friends and failed relationships. The most recent one was with his fiancée who finds her supposedly reformed forty-something future spouse "fronting up" in the bedroom mirror and calls the marriage off. It's a telling image and it lingers in the reader's mind long after the routine reminiscences of high-street rucks and back-alley beatings.

The music writer Nick Tosches recently made the controversial point that rap music is the new minstrelsy. In its exaggerated depictions of masculinity and ethnic identity he saw the same grotesque distortions that "blackface" singers portrayed, and perpetuated, a hundred years ago. There's something similar going on here with the post-industrial underclass and those Quintins and Pippas at the pulp end of publishing can't get enough of it. Dig deeper, though, and it's hard not to detect an undercurrent of poignancy in many of these books. Like those Seventies kids who once backflipped to Frankie Beverley or Dean Parrish at Wigan Casino or those Eighties kids who could bring an entire housing estate to a standstill with a beatbox and some breakdancing, many of the – now middle-aged – hoolies realise that this was their finest hour. The sheer number of RIPs in the acknowledgment sections tell another story, of course. Oh, and if any of you are still wondering why so many young recruits seem to be mysteriously committing suicide in the British armed forces, just read Chester's account of his time with the troops.

There's a key moment in *Style Wars*, Tony Silver's 1983 documentary about hip-hop culture, that goes to the very heart of what we're talking about here. Some of the film's best insights are provided by the exchanges between an African-American mother and her teenage son graffiti artist. The mother listens with increasingly weary resignation as her son relates his subway train- spraying exploits. "Listen to them talk," she sighs. "They sound absolutely ridiculous. 'I'm king of the yakety-yak yard.' Who died and left you king of the yard? He owns NOTHING in the subway." Then comes the devastating pay-off: "What you've got here is a whole miserable sub-culture." And then some.

Maybe what we need next is a new genre catering for the hoolies' long-suffering mums. Books with titles like *If Simmo Told You To Stick Your Head In The Fire, Would You?* And its best selling follow-up, *Well? Would You?* As Bell concludes yet another tediously identical description of a town-centre ruck, he mentions that the damage was restricted to "mainly bus shelters". It would make a good generic title for most of these tales. *Bus Shelters And Buffet Cars: My Life As A Frontline Hoolie.*

From the photographic evidence on display most of the authors and their mates still look pretty handy. You wouldn't want to spill their pint or call their lurcher a poof. You still see them at the match occasionally. Neck muscles bulging. Eyes swivelling and mobiles twitching. They can hear an away supporter rustling a sweet wrapper at 400 paces. There's fewer of them than there used to be, of course. After all, most of them are at home scribbling their memoirs. ○

Noise Annoys

After a historic win was consistently interrupted by pointless interventions from a self-important stadium DJ, Jon Driscoll finally snapped

WSC No 207, May 2004

"LADIES AND GENTLEMEN: The Carling Cup!" Exactly what we were supposed to do at this point wasn't entirely clear. Were we meant to cheer it or chant its name? Maybe they thought we had forgotten what it was. Or maybe this announcement at the Millennium Stadium after Boro had beaten Bolton was completely and utterly surplus to requirements.

I had been to the semi, I had asked for favours and shelled out hard cash to buy the tickets and then fought my way through the Cardiff traffic – I knew what I was there to see. Nothing, absolutely nothing, would have been lost if that announcement had not been made. In the unlikely event of there being a mass desire to applaud a man carrying a cup, surely it would have been better had it happened spontaneously? You may ask was there any harm in a man announcing the Carling Cup as if it was a guest at a posh dinner. Well, it got on my nerves and they had been through the shredder enough times that day. It interrupted rather than added to the noise level. After all, it is not as though the Boro fans who had witnessed their team win something proper for the first time were waiting silently to be told what they could and could not cheer.

The public address system at the modern football ground is one of the most irritating aspects of following the game and is getting worse. It has its uses, but these should be strictly limited. Teams need to be announced, goalscorers identified and away fans kept behind for 15 minutes (just for fun), but after that a little bit of background music at reasonable volume is all that is justified. Every club now seems to have its own special prematch routine. If there is a special piece of music by all means play it, but keep it short, keep the volume manageable and then shut up. It is not many years since PA systems didn't work and people would joke about not understanding what announcements at railway stations said – but no more. The technology now exists for a geek in a box to dominate the whole build-up and half-time at a football match and that is a backward step.

My first experience of the new beefed-up PA with enforced entertainment came at Sunderland's Stadium of Light. The resident DJ started to play Prokofiev's *Dance of the Knights* segued with Republica's *Ready To Go*. It went down well until success went to his head and he found the volume switch. It is in the blood of all DJs to go too far whenever they get a sniff of something working. But credit where it is due: Sunderland do it much better than Newcastle, where the players are welcomed with a pale imitation of what happens down the A19. At St James' Park they mix from Carl Orff's *Carmina Burana* to Mark Knopfler's *Local Hero*. Not only do you have to listen to the jarring change but it comes at earsplitting volume that would deafen sheep on the Northumberland hills. And worse still it lasts for what seems like an hour. It is a great way to destroy an atmosphere. I would actually go as far as to say this awful noise is one reason why St James' Park ain't what it used to be.

This is not just a north-east phenomenon. I went to a pre-season game at Bramall Lane with some friends but we barely spoke a word before the match or at half-time because it was too much of a battle against the Sugababes CD and the loud speaker. You wouldn't put up with it on a train or a tube, but at football we have no choice. This situation is getting rapidly worse and I wonder whether it is just down to the technology or whether there is a more sinister force at work. When things change for the more annoying there is usually someone making a quick buck out of it. Certainly one side-effect of the ridiculous noise levels at the Millennium Stadium is that it was impossible to ignore the adverts running on the big screens. Remember FIFA has recently floated the idea of a 20-minute half-time so we may soon have to endure an elongated break filled with adverts for mobile phones and double glazing.

But there is also an increasing tendency to control-freakery among football clubs. As the announcer is turned up, the club controls what is said at games and dominates the agenda. Less time, then, for unwelcome criticism and discussion among fans. Of course this conspiracy theorising could be missing a *coup d'état* of geeks. Inept DJs who can't command an audience on local radio are seizing a chance to torment a captive audience. Like the wedding DJ who turns down the music on *YMCA* and instructs everyone to join in, they don't understand that they are not the centre of attention and that nobody has come for them. Only in Wolverhampton is such behaviour considered cool. It really is an audio experience to behold when they turn down the music during Jeff Beck's *Hi Ho Silver Lining* and instead of "Silver Lining" all the Wolves fan sing "Wolverhampton". But as far as I can tell this is an exception and such intrusion is generally not welcome. Most clubs think a spod with a biscuit-tin full of Now That's What I Call Music CDs is more important than songs that have been developed over many decades.

I firmly believe there is a silent, deafened minority who regard this as a blight that is harming the sport. I'm not so grumpy that I allowed Boro winning the Carling Cup to be ruined by the PA, it's just that it poked at an already open sore. After all, what is the point of saying "Ladies and gentlemen, Middlesbrough and Boltoooonnnnn" at the end of the match. This guy was just thinking of things to say for the sake of it. I already knew who was playing and this added nothing. With the atmosphere at all-seat stadiums not as lively as when we could stand up and chant obscenities, the last thing we need is another blow. The message to the man in the box is simple: 1. Give out the team news; 2. Say who scored; 3. Tell me if my car is about to be towed away; 4. Turn the music down; and 5. Shut up. ○

Picking the Ron Moment

Al Needham reflected on a notorious racist outburst and wondered whether Ron Atkinson's fate revealed more about prevailing attitudes than the fall from grace itself

WSC No 208, June 2004

IN THE END, after all the finger-pointing, hair-shirt wearing, editorials and think-pieces, the only truly shocking thing about what Ron Atkinson said was that, for pretty much the first time in his public life, he came out with a phrase that came frighteningly close to plain English. He didn't describe Marcel Desailly as "totally nigmatic with his workrate, to be enocular". He refrained from mentioning that the Chelsea defender had been "giving it big lips all game". He didn't even advocate giving minorities the full gun, or bunging them in the mixer.

What he said was... well; you know what he said, because for a couple of days in April the media deemed it more important than Iraq, the European referendum and even the contents of Rebecca Loos's inbox. With one comment picked up by an abandoned microphone in Monaco, Ron – the former gaudy hunk of gold in the crown of ITV Sport, now known in some schools as a fucking ignorant orange bigot – put the ultimate reducer on his income, losing his TV contract, his column in the *Guardian* and four sponsorship deals.

We already had our doubts about the man. The Italia 90 quarter-final where he described a Cameroon player on-air as "absolutely brainless" then stated off-air that "I'll only get into trouble if his mother's back home watching the game sitting up a tree". His whispered notoriety in the football world for casual racism. Describing Cyrille Regis in Wolves kit as "looking like a bruised banana", and his appearance that very night on *Room 101*, where he displayed attitudes to women not seen on BBC2 since the last *Newsnight* feature on the Taliban (thankfully for all concerned, Roger Mellie had already selected "the blacks" in last month's issue of *Viz*). But this was the real deal. Ron – cuddly, avuncular, larger-than-life Ron – had dropped the N-bomb, the term coined by rednecks who are too stupid and slack-jawed to be able to pronounce "negro".

The following day, while Photoshopped images of Ron hanging out with the Klan zipped around the internet, came the fallout of said bomb, the highlight of which was his live appearance on Sky News. At the beginning, sporting an expression of sheepish penitence, he claimed: "I was talking to myself," although listening to the remark on the internet proves that he was in conversation with Clive Tyldesley (and even if he was talking to himself, he must be suffering a level of tinnitus usually attained by Who roadies). Then he almost lost his rag again when he got tired of the prodding and snapped: "How many times do I have to tell you? I was totally out of order. I don't think we need to go down that line. I'm one of those who has worked harder and longer with black players than anybody."

Ah, yes. Ron and his legions of supporters in the media have taken great pains to point out that while his words are inexcusable, his deeds – namely, his laudable managerial record with black players – are far more important. Back in the 1970s, you see, all gentlemen of colour who weren't in the 1970 Brazil squad were seen as rubbish at football, until Ron, the Great Emancipator, gave them 40 acres of grass and a ball. Ron is "a caring man" according to his colleague Tyldesley. "Genuine and generous and, above all, fun-loving. Mischief and mirth are his hobbies. He is an optimist. Live life to the full and to hell with the consequences." Simon Barnes of the *Times* went so far as to urge Tony Blair to reward him for his integrationalist policies. "Arise Sir Ron, knight of the new society, hero of the fight against racism, a man who staked his job and his reputation on the belief that black folk are as good as white folk."

Before the empty column of Trafalgar Square is filled with a statue of Ron sat in an armchair wearing a stovepipe hat is commissioned, however, it's worth remembering that Laurie Cunningham and Regis had already been signed to West Brom by previous manager Johnny Giles and that Atkinson's reputation pretty much rests upon his signing of Brendon Batson and forming – cringe – the "Three Degrees". Yes, he helped smash the myth that black players were all flair and no grit by championing Remi Moses, but Brian Clough was doing the same thing with Viv Anderson. And as Justin Fashanu would have told you, Cloughie was far from right-on.

But the speculation of pundits (this writer included) means nothing in comparison to the reaction of black players. Anderson, the man who broke England's colour bar, said he would never dream of branding him as a racist. Batson declared him a "supporter of the black cause", which brings to mind alarming images of Ron raising his jewel-encrusted fist outside the South African embassy whenever Manchester United played in London. "I've known Ron since I was 16, I've been on holiday with his family, my children have been sick on him," said Carlton Palmer. "No way is he a racist." Compare the above with the reaction of Ian Wright, however. "Lazy nigger? That's like a plantation vibe. What's that all about? What really gets me is that I have heard his interviews about this and he says that he has taken his mike off and his headphones off before he says it. Does that make it any better?"

It's worth remembering that the older pros are the second generation of the Windrush, who are willing to forgive because at least they were given the chance to play in an era when the National Front were recruiting supporters at grounds, monkey chants were heard on *Match of the Day* every week and workplace racism was dismissed as a harmless bit of fun. And that Wright is from the next generation who won't forgive because they know they have earned the right to play on their own merits and refuse to take the abuse their parents suffered. Who's right on Ron? I guess they all are.

In the most surreal moment of the week, the *Observer* set up a summit between Ron and Michael Eboda of the *New Nation*, in order to heal the wound. "Don't forget, I was brought up... look, I've had pairs of shoes that have been nigger brown, that's what they used to say," says Ron. Then, there's a conversation about the hip-hop usage of the word "Nigga" and why some homosexuals call themselves "Queer", which would have made an excellent out-take for *Brass Eye*. Finally, Ron asks the editor of the black community's leading publication to tell him if he actually is a racist. "No, you don't see colour when you are giving a person a job... but you come from an era when certain things were acceptable... I think that in the instant that you used the term 'Nigger' you were a racist." Sadly, they didn't go on to break out the guitars and sing *The Ink is Black*, but at least something vaguely resembling a line was drawn under the affair.

So what now? Ron's career might be in tatters at the moment, but – yes! – it's early doors. Being a "character" (or "an easily-caricatured two-dimensional cliche-monger of the highest order", depending on your point of view), Ron is an absolutely indispensable vehicle for selling football to the fledgling middle-class fan who actually takes an interest in the car adverts on ITV's sports coverage and reads newspapers such as the *Guardian*. He's always good for a "water-cooler moment" in the office and, when you think about it, he's just like Ron Manager in *The Fast Show*, isn't he?

Instead of feeling sorry for himself, Ron should consider himself lucky that he worked in the UK and was given the opportunity to resign. To paraphrase Linford Christie, Ron would have met career death on the "r" of the "ger" if he had come out with what he said in America. His nearest broadcasting equivalent, Jimmy "The Greek" Snyder, was canned for his on-air beliefs that the superiority of black athletes had something to do with the breeding techniques of slave owners. Rush Limbaugh lost his job on an NFL pregame show when he criticised a black quarterback and claimed that he was being hyped up by a liberal media. While being unbelievably crass, neither statement was as offensive as Atkinson's.

It would be easy to say that Ron Atkinson opened a can of worms marked "racism" last month, but we all know he merely pulled back the cling-film on a Tupperware container of wiggly bigotry. The best thing to come out of the fall of "Bigot Ron" (©the *Sun*) was a sense of perspective on past and present. Nobody is calling Patrick Vieira, Sylvain Wiltord and Sol Campbell "Mis-Teeq". Arsenal are renowned for having the best team in the country, not the team with all the black players, and when women make cooing noises at Thierry Henry, men generally understand. No one bats an eyelid when a black player manages to play 90 minutes in Grimsby on a Wednesday night in January, and racism is officially bad according to the *Sun*.

Ron seems to be making an effort to understand why he's let down so many people and he isn't pitching himself as a crusader against the forces of political correctness (or at least someone is advising him not to). That's why you can safely expect him to get his feet back under the table by the time Germany 2006 rolls round. Whether he can keep them out of his mouth will be another matter entirely. ○

Man Marketing

Cameron Carter traced the evolution of footballers'
endorsements from cigarettes to male grooming products

WSC No 208, June 2004

BEFORE THE CURRENT ERA of personal branding, footballers were placed
in front of the camera merely as celebrated tradesmen whose fame, as
a result of mastery of their craft, was viewed as sufficient reason for the
impressionable viewer to go out and buy the very latest hair lacquer.

No one looking upon the photographs of Dixie Dean sucking moodily
upon a Carreras Club cigarette ("the cigarette with a kick in them")
would have expected to gain an insight into the Dean personality. He
looked a bit like he'd just given his wife one last chance to stop talking
but he might just as well have been under the hypnotic spell of the insin-
uating weed (five for tuppence). Dean wasn't being cute, or funny, or
rebranding himself; he was simply being that fellow who scores loads
of goals for Everton. Stanley Matthews' image was used as an oblique
reference in another early advertising campaign, suggesting the quality
of smoothness shared between Craven A cigarettes and Matthews' ball
control. All you could possibly glean from this promotion was Matthews'
profession – there could not even be a direct link between player and
product as Stanley was a devout non-smoker. Similarly, Denis Compton's
famous Brylcreem advertisement intimated only that Denis knew how to
keep his hair simple for the big game, not that he was a mover in squeaky
dance halls and certainly not that he used the product because he was
worth it. Perhaps Sixties star George Cohen gave away a little more when
stating that Elliman's Athletic Rub was "both vital and stimulating for
my legs" but, for the most part, good, sturdy endorsement was all that
was necessary in this golden age.

Little had changed by the 1970s when Pat Jennings flung himself
around a muddy goalmouth demonstrating the goalkeeper's generic
similarity to an oil filter while a highly stimulated crowd chanted
"Unipart" until the word became almost meaningless. Pat was definitely
not being iconic here. He was being a goalkeeper, like it said in the script.
George Best appeared on Ulster TV in his "El Beatle" period with a
Cookstown sausage on his fork and a sultry come-to-pub look in his eyes.

Clearly, a link between the player's perceived image and the product he recommended was not yet thought vital. Kevin Keegan started the acting malarkey when he emerged from the steam of a highly charged dressing room to be matey with Henry Cooper about their shared aftershave. Apart from dully wondering how these two coincided at the communal showers unless they arranged to meet there, the viewer was led to believe for the first time that life went on for the professional footballer after he left the pitch. Perhaps he talked rather like a robot recovering from a stroke, but Keegan appeared to have a civilian existence and something approaching a personality to go with it.

John Barnes took us backstage again in a Lucozade Sport commercial, in which we saw our hero solitary, drained and spent "after 90 minutes of sheer hell". One had always assumed that Barnes enjoyed playing football to some extent but, no, every game was infernal to him. This was an insight into the man and would explain why, a decade and a half later, he looks like he would rather be absolutely anywhere else when he hosts matches on Five.

Joe Jordan's toothless Heineken advert we can dismiss as diverting slapstick but, as television's relationship with football became mature and serious, image-building entered the equation. With the exception of Jason McAteer's anti-dandruff shampoo commercial (despite lathering himself heavily, Jason aroused little erotic reaction unless you count sexual swear words), the modern football advertisement picks out the selling strength in each player. David Ginola was scented and flowing in his L'Oreal ad (not, however, doing much to dispel the idea that Frenchmen are essentially women with mistresses). Reebok, giving us Peter Schmeichel in his parallel universe career as a Danish pig farmer, sold us the scream-faced fanatic as a humble, honest labourer. Alan Shearer, signing autographs ceaselessly in a McDonald's ad, is a solid man of the people. Michael Owen, turning out for Daz Automatic, loves his mother (Walkers crisps dropped Owen from their recent campaign because his image was too clean-living for the target audience of pub-goers). David Beckham, through mostly keeping his mouth shut on screen, has developed the presence of a simpleton minor deity, which makes life easy for him and the copywriters.

And now we're stuck for the foreseeable future with big Nike/Pepsi productions with casts of thousands, which may soon become pay-per-view. They're skilfully done and even old Ronaldinho looks like he could get away with a short film career, but the contemporary player is now noticeably pulling out of tackles and heading the ball less so as not to jeopardise his midweek close-up. Playing football is not enough for them these days. I ask you to find absolutely any picture of Dixie Dean and imagine what he would have thought of this. ○

Usual Suspects

It was quite a coincidence – a film about hooliganism had come out just before Euro 2004. David Stubbs found barely a redeeming feature in people who really should know better

WSC No 209, July 2004

As EVIDENCE OF THE MINDSET of fevered gormlessness in which this film was forged, director Nick Love says he wanted to make a film about the white working-class men "who make up 70 per cent of this country". That demographic howler speaks more about a disproportionate fascination with hooliganism, its camaraderie, its violence, its blood and honour, than about reality, about which *The Football Factory* proudly says next to nothing. There may be some who find authenticity in this film, but the "truth" about hooliganism is in flux. To say it's a thing of the past is complacent, to say it's as prevalent as ever is alarmist. It recrudesces, dies down, is displaced. Its sociology has been raked over hundreds of times, often by writers concealing their hard-ons beneath the baggy trousers of academic rhetoric. Even those who didn't particularly want to know about hooliganism probably know all they need to by now.

The Football Factory bristles with bravado, imagines it's revealing ugly truths, breezing up the skirts of the prissy liberals. But it's set in concrete cliche. You're shocked, but only that the film-makers imagine they're doing anything new. The narrative voiceover, the freezeframe when introducing characters, filch directly from *Lock, Stock...* and *Trainspotting*. An early wind-up scene is a straight steal from *Goodfellas*. Still, they do arrive, like Livingstone at the Victoria Falls, upon one startling observation. The hoolies do it, apparently, for "the buzz". Oh, yes.

The Football Factory, however, has all the buzz of a dead wasp in an ancient jam jar. Based on John King's novel, it's about a Chelsea firm gearing up for a ruck with their Millwall counterparts and the crisis of one of its younger members, who has a premonition of death. There's one solid performance, that of Frank Harper as the Tony Soprano-esque Billy Bright, albeit with bone in lieu of psychological complexity. The rest of the cast, however, come on like an assortment of Rada students doing "cockney" and old-timers grateful for work. You expect from Danny Dyer's Tommy Johnson, the narrator, some semblance of humanity, some longing to break out of the hoolie syndrome. "You're bright," urges an older, ex-firm member. "Think about it." But he isn't. He's a pudgy-faced, zero-dimensional, obnoxious, self-pitying, lairy shit, not unlike the film's target audience. You realise his narrative isn't a moral torch-light, but a means of filling what might otherwise be reflective silences. Which wouldn't be so bad if the script sparkled – but this is the witless braying out to the witless. After a flashback to Billy's dad chasing off new Asian neighbours, Johnson narrates: "With parents like this he were never gonna end up in Greenpeace!" The rising sneer invites the response: "Wahey, I should facking coco. Greenpeace? Wankahs!"

The makers claim *The Football Factory* is "moral", but that's belied by the marketing (the director gurgling about how well screenings went down with Cardiff's Soul Crew) and the timing of its release, prior to Euro 2004. It's also belied by the conclusion, in which only a copper-bottomed tosser could take satisfaction. No pulpit hysteria here – this film will have no bearing on levels of violence in Portugal. Still, it doesn't help. Nor is it helpful that the film provides no sense of the peaceable majority, passionate about football but wanting absolutely rid of these over-romanticised boneheads. The action takes place in a south London vacuum, as if the characters are invisible to the wider community.

One could wish that *The Football Factory* had been a different sort of film, except that its makers shouldn't be making films at all. Every plot device is tediously predictable, contrived or implausible. Characters such as Jamie Foreman's bigoted cab driver (whom the hoolies eschew, in a strange, cack-handed attempt to establish politically correct brownie points for the film) are pitifully stereotypical. As are the middle-class potential in-laws, who might as well be pinstriped cardboard cut-outs, to whom a lead character makes the film's keynote speech, deriding "desperate suburban lives" against which, apparently, hooliganism is a glorious, Betjemanesque rebellion. This drivel would never emerge from the mouth of a hooligan, to whom cocking a snook at Acacia Avenue is not an uppermost priority, but would from a self-loathing, hooligan-fetishising middle-class type.

It adds further grist to the feeling that this film was made amid the whiff of takeaway cappuccinos, drawn from that contemporary generation of "geezers" who "should know better" who, depressingly, line up voluntarily alongside those who don't know better. Love brags that this film will "disturb" *Guardian-* and *Independent-*reading types. Well, I'm a *Guardian-* and *Independent-*reading type. Why? Because I don't want to stay stupid. The kind of stupid person that would either make, or be thrilled by, a wretched film such as this. ◯

Flags of Convenience

Al Needham sifted through the plastic flagpoles discarded in the wake of Euro 2004 and wondered where all those crosses of St George came from

WSC No 210, August 2004

IT'S GOOD FOR A COUNTRY and its people to take stock and re-evaluate its sense of identity every now and then, and I did just that in a bus shelter last month, sitting next to an elderly Jamaican woman, watching the endless procession of cars with plastic white flags with red crosses clipped to their windows. Where had they come from? Had a giant sandcastle firm been made bankrupt, or something? Was it just a local thing? And what did it all mean? "Look at these fools," said the Jamaican woman, all of a sudden. "They don't know what it means to be patriotic. In Jamaica, we have the flag up all year round, not for some... pussyclaat football game." Then she sucked her teeth. For a very long time.

Yes, just like everywhere else in the country (apart from Scotland, Wales and Northern Ireland) Nottingham was well and truly under the spell of Eng-er-land mania by the end of May and we're still trying to decide what it all meant. Was it – boo! – a portent of doom, ushering in a sinister rebirth of nationalism not seen since the National Front used the Union Jack in the mid-1970s? Was it – rayyy! – good old salt-of-the-earth Johnny England feeling at ease with his national identity once more and taking back the flag from the forces of darkness? Or could it be – strokes chin, raises eyebrow – a bunch of knob-ends in white vans showing off a bit?

As it turned out, it wasn't a local quirk. It was happening all over the country. A couple of days later, a friend in London excitedly rang from a garage to tell me he had just been overtaken by a car sporting a flag in each window, two mounted on broomsticks thrust through the sunroof and a massive Three Lions badge on the bonnet. He didn't know who the car belonged to, but he had a suspicion it might have something to do with the bloke on his estate who had painted his roof – and his lawn – with the cross of St George. Next thing you knew, Bobby Charlton was standing on a bridge on the telly, beaming with glee as an army of zombies with red and white faces lumbered about in a compulsive lust to buy England cakes with their credit cards.

Naturally, newspaper columnists and their ilk were parachuted in to tell us what it all really meant. And it wasn't only the *Sun* who put out the obligatory space-filling England flag centrespread – even the *Guardian* got stuck in with one of their own, albeit with a series of small-print caveats – "By wearing this flag I would like to show my support for the England team but: 1. Wholeheartedly reject any connotations of xenophobic nationalism; 2. Dissociate myself from anyone who removes his shirt in public; 3. Salute the rich contribution made by my Celtic cousins to British life; 4. Reaffirm my commitment to the European Social Chapter."

On a more poignant note, Sarfraz Manzoor wrote about how it took him 30 years to be able to buy an England T-shirt without fear of resentment or mockery, after the Argentina game in 2002. "That night, as Asians, blacks and whites joined together... I remember thinking: this is what patriotism could be like if we could defang it of its nastier elements... But I also remember an Asian friend laughing at the sight of us all singing for England. When I asked him what he found funny, he replied: 'It's as if, by wearing the flag, we're saying, "See, we're not that different from you, please don't beat us up".'"

The Tory papers were even more chuffed. "Something remarkable is happening. The reticent English middle classes, having long been queasy about flag-waving, are rediscovering – reclaiming – their national flag," wrote Quentin Letts of the *Sunday Telegraph*, who has obviously never been to see Tim Henman at Wimbledon or heard about the Last Night of the Proms, on the eve of the France game. Still, it's a lot more savoury than the bad old days, when "rat-faced youths with swastika armbands and skinheads would stick flags on the walls of provincial lock-up garages and strike clenched-fist poses". More amazingly, there was a distinct absence of stories about loony left councils banning the flag for fear of drivers blinded by aggressively nationalist symbols running into bus queues – the only note of caution struck throughout the month came from *Top Gear* magazine, which pointed out that English motorists were wasting 4.5 million gallons of petrol through the drag caused by flags.

If all this is a sign of Albion arising once more, it has to be said that we made a right pig's arse of it. For starters, flags should be attached to flagpoles and not bamboo canes purloined from the garden. And they most definitely shouldn't be trapped in someone's upstairs window. Do the Americans sing "O say does that star-spangled banner yet hang out of Dave's back bedroom"? No, they don't. Secondly, why did most of them need to have ENGLAND printed on them? Are the English that ignorant of their own national flag? Have you ever seen a maple leaf flag with CANADA written on it? Or a swastika bearing the legend THE NAZIS? Were we going to assume otherwise that the Red Cross had organised a flag day for cars?

It seems that everyone has their own theory about the proliferation of England flags at football tournaments, so here's mine: ever since the decline of the druids, the British have consistently received the fly-encrusted, smelly end of the stick when it comes to summer celebrations. While the Americans and French put aside a special day to let off fireworks and wave the flag, all we get is a barbecue in the rain and Wimbledon. However, every two years there's an international football tournament and England are usually in it. You only have to look at what happened to the national rugby side last year to work out what would happen if the football team won something. As we all know, though, England are the original Little Boys That Santa Claus Forgot. So what do we do? We have our celebrations in advance, adopting the triumphalism of post-match celebrations in Italy, Argentina and Brazil, without ever needing to win anything. It's probably the only legacy Ally McLeod has bestowed on British football. See the bloke on your street who put three England flags up? He's probably the same one who sticks a 12-foot inflatable snowman on his garage roof at Christmas.

Of course, after England lost their quarter-final to Portugal, the vast majority of flags were wrenched from their moorings long before Tim Henman had a chance to get knocked out of Wimbledon and the ones that remain hang limp in the rain like condoms thrown into a bush. The extreme right have approximately two years to reclaim it, but I don't fancy their chances that much. The next time I get a BNP pamphlet through the door and see it festooned with the cross of St George, I won't be wondering if you can be truly patriotic without being a moron – I'll be thinking of my three-year-old nephew on the bus, pointing at hunks of plastic attached to cars and bellowing "Football flag! ROOOOO-NEEEE!" while everyone else falls about laughing, as I chuck it in the bin. ○

Strange Case of Sonny Pike

He had been trumpeted as a star at ten, but was drifting around the Ryman League by the age of 20. Gavin Willacy charted the career of a player for whom it all happened way, way too soon

WSC No 210, August 2004

ON A FANS' INTERNET FORUM last November, someone calling themself Spankyplugs posed the question: "Sonny Pike – anyone remember him? Some little kid with an afro; they would periodically have him on *Blue Peter* or *The Big Breakfast* and yap on about how he will play for England, just because he was in the Ajax youth team. He must be old enough now, so where is he?" None of Spankyplugs' fellow web chatters could help. Nor could *Guardian* readers when the question was posed two years ago. Some, quite reasonably, asked who on earth was Sonny Pike anyway, apart from sounding like a keen angler from *Miami Vice*.

A decade ago, Pike was one of the best known young footballers in Britain. And we're talking young here. Still in junior school, the ten-year-old was a mass of Leo Sayer curls, Donny Osmond smiles and Johan Cruyff turns as he weaved his way around his school playground in north London. How do we know? Well the TV cameras were following him. Why? Because someone was encouraging them to. Why? Because we live in a crazy, sad world.

Just as Sky were taking over the English game and transforming it into a riot of fireworks, dancing girls and *Monday Night Football*, Sonny Pike was showing himself to be an extremely gifted little boy. His dad, Mickey, was so infatuated with the possibilities his son's skills offered that he got him a high-profile agent and allowed his boy to be touted around the media, relishing in him being courted as England's No 10 in waiting: the next Maradona. Or, more appropriately, Gazza. The boy was good, but he was ten years old. Originally on Leyton Orient's books, he was – controversially – filmed training with Chelsea. Then there was the Ajax episode, when Sonny was supposedly being flown there to train every week – a period of his life he is reluctant to talk about now.

It isn't every day that a British player is wanted by one of Europe's finest, let alone a prepubescent, so the media lapped it up. The BBC did a series on child prodigies, *Touched With Fire*, featuring a 13-year-old Pike in Amsterdam; he appeared as a special guest on stage at Sky's *nouveau riche*-fest of an awards night, with Ian Wright, and he was the talk of every football magazine and tabloid.

There were issues of child protection, let alone educational welfare. Pike, never the brightest academically but a nice enough lad according to his teachers in Enfield, was not gaining many positive experiences. Home life became extremely unsettled as little Pike became a rather large fish in a minuscule pond – and a former class-mate recalls that he wasn't even the best player in the school team.

Ninety-odd per cent of English boys get released by pro clubs before they can sign scholarship forms at 16. Pike was one of them. Four years after being with Ajax, he was training with a college academy in north London. Dealing with the drop in status from famous footballer to everyman is tough enough in your 30s, let alone as a teenager, especially without wealth, illustrious colleagues or glorious memories to fall back on. Every day Pike is having to come to terms with the reality that he is almost certainly not going to make it as a professional player and that he needs to find another avenue in life. He still had skill and relished being the star turn in games, but then again he was playing for London Colney reserves. "He had a lot of skill, could pass it and was a nice player, but he lacked pace," said a former coach. "He was a yard too slow." That's something difficult to foresee in a ten-year-old.

Now a tall, athletic 20-year-old, Pike spent some of last season playing with a former Chelsea striker, another from Fulham, an ex-Newcastle United midfielder and defenders from Spurs and Charlton. But you almost certainly won't have seen him in action because after brief spells with Stevenage Borough, Barnet and Enfield, Pike had signed for local club Waltham Forest, of the Ryman League Division One North. Now he's left there too, but he's keeping his next port of call under wraps. Not that

Ryman League fans, used to the mighty falling onto their patch, would have even realised they had a Nineties TV star in their midst. Sonny has changed his name too. Being Luke Pike is unlikely to draw too much attention from opposing centre-backs, especially in the reserves. ○

Words from our Sponsors

David Wangerin traced the history of kit advertising from Kettering Tyres to Spiderman 2 and wondered if club identity had been lost along the way

WSC No 211, September 2004

LOOK AT ANY FOOTBALL PHOTOGRAPH from the mid-Seventies. The glue-pot pitch, the plain white ball and the wild sideburns of some of the players certainly call to mind an almost primitive era, as does the enormous terrace of fans crammed into the background. Yet one anachronism in particular reveals just how the visual elements of British football have changed: the remarkable austerity of the playing strips. There are no manufacturer trademarks and no league logos or appeals for fair play on the sleeves. Most conspicuously of all, nothing is displayed across the chest. It's undeniably an outdated image, yet one that happily draws the eye closer to the tiny club crest, instead of toward some gargantuan commercial message. An age of marketing innocence, some will bewail, but one certainly to be admired for its aesthetic appeal, to say nothing of its integrity.

It is apparently now 25 years since the Football Association first permitted shirt advertising, bending to pressures that their French, Austrian and Swiss equivalents had acceded to a decade earlier. Cash-starved teams wasted little time in transforming themselves into ambulatory billboards, soon to promote all manner of breweries, electronics firms, airlines, building societies, fast-food restaurants, online casinos, anti-smoking initiatives and the odd garden centre. So ingrained has it all become that it now seems strange whenever a club happens to play in a strip devoid of such graffiti: one becomes suspicious that the commercial department has not got its act together, or that the "brand" lacks sufficient appeal to the commercial world.

While Liverpool are widely regarded to have been the pioneers of this movement, splattering Hitachi across their collective selves in 1979, strictly speaking they weren't the first British club to compromise themselves in this way. A few years earlier, Kettering Town had tested the FA's resolve by turning out in jerseys promoting Kettering Tyres. The club's chief executive, none other than Derek Dougan, claimed the advertising ban had never been put in writing; when the FA ordered him to desist, he craftily truncated the message to a more ambiguous "Kettering T" – in vain, as it turned out: under the threat of a crippling fine, the remaining letters disappeared a few months later.

No such fate awaited the Anfield Reds and their Japanese suitors, who were given a statutory 16 square inches of space to sell, in letters no more than two inches high (a regulation that would land Aston Villa in hot water a few years later when they exclaimed "Mita" a little too loudly). Others would follow in rapid succession – not in front of the television cameras, mind; another decade would pass before that barrier fell – and soon companies such as Hafnia and Talbot found themselves as prominent, and unwanted, a part of the game as the professional foul and the offside trap.

The landscape of the time was rather more barren – particularly at the top: for all their domestic and European glory, Liverpool's chairman claimed his club had made a profit of just £71,000 in their last season of unadorned attire. Today, of course, such a figure is so inconsequential as to scarcely warrant attention at a club of such stature. English football had still to encounter the penury of the Eighties: one need only thumb through the diary section of the day's *Rothmans* to realise just how hard-up even the title contenders were in the years before the television monster was unleashed. However laughable those first shirt deals may seem in comparison with today's arrangements (typically, a few hundred thousand stretched over two or three years – for the bigger clubs), there was at least something of a financial case for them. Today, leagues such as the Premiership advance the case in tiresomely familiar rhetoric: shirt sponsorship is no longer a financial lifeline, just another attractive revenue stream.

For some, of course, it is far more attractive than others. Those clubs distant of Vodafone United or the O2 Gunners may think shirt deals enhance their competitiveness; they would be wise to think again. The space on a Charlton Athletic or Blackburn Rovers chest will only ever earn a fraction of the £30-odd million Manchester United are said to command for theirs. Denying top-division clubs the opportunity to rent out this space would remove some of the tilt from an already heavily sloped playing field. But, like penalty shoot-outs and promotion play-offs, it's almost as if football can't remember coping without it.

So it has come to pass that thousands upon thousands of fans parade through the streets of Britain in outfits which promote a brand of lager or a telecom firm just as loudly as their football team; it is impossible not to pay as much attention to these "messages" as to the few square inches clubs keeps for themselves. In an age when shirts of any type tend to be worn not so much for colour or style as the words that appear on them, this is perhaps not too surprising. For the reactionaries opting out of this game, there is always the retro jersey, far better value and less likely to end up at Oxfam. But it is not nearly as easy to assert one's loyalties in a somewhat ambiguous, if cotton-rich, shirt – not when a sponsor's name can amplify the identity so markedly. For years, JVC were just as Arsenal as the club crest, Brother as much a part of Manchester City as sky blue; it just wasn't discussed in polite company. The purpose of retaining the club crest, and keeping it so inconspicuously tucked into a corner, seems largely cosmetic, perhaps even defensive.

Yet wear a replica strip in those parts of North America that still live in ignorance of international football and you are likely to be met with comments like "Northern Rock? What team is that?" or "That striped shirt is cool, but why does it say 'Churchill' on it?" These are not stupid questions. To the uninitiated, Bolton are not playing Chelsea so much as Reebok are playing Fly Emirates. I for one can scarcely think of Brighton & Hove Albion without recalling Nobo, the firm that once loomed so large across their stripes.

This begs the question: in an age when clubs seem to speak as much of brand awareness as back fours, shouldn't they be more concerned with the mixed messages of their kit? Sponsor colours and names often clash violently with those of the club: not long ago Aston Villa fans saw their claret and blue competing with the bright purple and lime green of their sponsor, creating a colour combination rarely seen outside infant school art class. Playing in shirts labelled "Friends Provident" cannot strike much fear into the opponents of Southampton; neither can the cuddly heart on Portsmouth's chest or the wry smile on Tottenham's. Cardiff City – the Bluebirds – have now struck a deal with a building firm named Redrow. These and other arrangements (how the more corpulent fans of Grimsby Town must have enjoyed wearing a replica strip bearing the phrase "Food Giant") seem risibly ill-advised, given the ferocity with which clubs now guard their "image". Surely in time Manchester United will come to realise their most appropriate shirt sponsor is Manchester United plc. Yet the future points away from this, toward an environment where the lines between club and sponsor blur – particularly if recent developments in Madrid are anything to go by.

Atlético's red-and-white striped shirts seem to have been forsaken for ones of navy blue; these, apparently, offer a more suitable backdrop for Atlético's latest sponsor, the film Spiderman 2, whose webbed imagery all but chokes the life out of the club's own identity. This "innovation", which if nothing else will excite the 13-year-old in your life, seems to have aggravated UEFA, but it's hard to imagine administrators standing in the way of the marketers for long. After all, it's fewer than ten years since jerseys with advertising were first seen at a European Cup final.

If that's not frightening enough, a quick trawl of the internet reveals that some poor soul at Leeds University business school has managed to segment football shirt sponsors into groups, concocting labels such as "Carers and Communals" and "Calculators and Commercials" to describe their behaviour. Apparently "clubs and sponsors are starting to recognise the need to take a different view of the way in which they manage their relationship", don't you know.

It's perhaps too much to expect clubs to reclaim their own jerseys; you just can't keep a good revenue stream down. And as the distinction between acceptable and unacceptable levels of commercialism is wholly subjective – and still evolving – we're far more likely to see new sources of income being tapped into: shorts and hosiery, perhaps, or the soles of boots. Goalkeepers might even be encouraged to wear a baseball cap on the cloudiest of days. If it all seems rather preposterous, it might be worth remembering that only a few decades ago the thought of a football team turning out in a strip bearing the message "Fly Virgin" was equally as absurd. ○

No Talking Back

Philip Cornwall wasn't sure why England's players refused to speak to the media after an international match. But having read the papers he found plenty of good reasons

WSC No 213, November 2004

Stood in the corner towards which Jermain Defoe ran to celebrate his first England goal, it was obvious the team wished to thank their fans for their support in Chorzow. It had been a fraught few days, a cold night and an at times awkward 90 minutes, during which, for the most part, we had kept the faith. The previous Saturday, David James had received a post-match reception that could scarcely be called mixed. But the whole team, following the example set by David Beckham when he was substituted, came over to thank us again. And we thanked them.

What many there didn't know till much later was that this was the team's last attempt at communication that evening. Sven-Göran Eriksson spoke, but the team did not, to the outrage of those who a) hang on their every word and b) complain about how little of interest they usually say. "And now for the bad news," wrote Jeff Powell in the *Daily Mail*. "England's footballers are threatening to resume talking next month."

The players did not even give a direct indication of why they had chosen to let their football do the talking. Which quickly emerged, alas, as a mistake, because it allowed the media to tell us what they took to be the reason. Some reporters may have been right. Paul Hayward in the Telegraph wrote: "An educated guess is that the boycott stemmed not only from the David James lampoon but from the willingness of some experts to argue that David Beckham should also have been dropped." If this was true – that the team regarded themselves as above criticism as well as objecting to ridicule – then they were wrong. But the media coverage of the media boycott did inadvertently give some hint that there was more at work than donkeys or egos.

For a start, there is the failure of the journalists to do their jobs professionally when England play. John Rawling in the *Guardian* (for me an increasingly reliable inverse barometer) wrote: "Whatever... the rights and wrongs of placing donkey ears on David James in the *Sun* (it made me chuckle), it was only a visual representation of the emotions felt by millions of England fans." True. But the problem was that journalists are paid to be journalists, not to be fans.

Worse, as a donkey was taken to Chorzow, what we say in the pub or in the stands in the heat of the moment was translated, cold bloodedly, into a vindictive campaign against someone who was only an injury away from once more being England's No 1. But in the absence of a clear statement of the reasons for the boycott, papers could dismiss a key element. After a few words from Graham Taylor, Shaun Custis in the *Sun* was able to ask sarcastically: "So criticism is fine as long as it is not harsh and does not upset people."

The reports that tried to tell us what to think gave away more than they intended. Philip Whiteside's report on the "news" pages of the *Mail* began: "England's pampered and overpaid footballers were accused of betraying the fans last night." Such prejudicial adjectives should not be in the first paragraph of a news story. Yes, you could make a case that England players are "pampered" (I agree, but so are journalists) and overpaid (I disagree – overpaid players are club benchwarmers rather than national-team stars). But Whiteside's article opens with a simple prejudice – encouraged, enforced or emboldened by his editors – that means that it has no place on a news page.

Whiteside is also striking another theme – journalistic jealousy, or at least a willingness to play on readers' jealousy, of "common" footballers being paid for their talents. In an otherwise irrelevant aside, he added: "James... earns £25,000 a week with Manchester City. Several of his colleagues earn £100,000 a week." He attempted to connect this to the poor supporters, deprived of post-match interviews. Their salaries are "paid for by fans buying match tickets, by TV rights and by sponsorship". But it's not the taking part in post-match interviews that bother us, it's the winning or the losing – and those who paid for their match tickets, like me, were thanked. Week in, week out, we watch club matches and then happily read reports in which the only people quoted are the managers. Nor on this occasion did Sky or the sponsors have grounds to complain: this was an overseas international and, while press conferences are an obligation when England play at home, this was not the case in Poland.

Of course, the *Daily Mail* often gets things wrong. Back during Fariagate, their "news" pages ran coupons for readers to put in their windows, demanding the sacking of the manager, under the headline If not now, Sven. The back of the paper screamed **Dead Man Walking** and **No Escape Now** for cornered Eriksson. Such bias colours theirs and others' coverage; it would not be a surprise if sympathy with the manager over a witch hunt had something to do with the boycott.

There is also the extent to which the focus on sport for patriotic pride makes incredible demands. England have four points from two away games, a total most sides around Europe would be delighted with, and in Portugal this summer for the first time the team escaped their group in a European Championship outside England; we have had a lot worse teams. For Powell, "every player honoured by selection has a duty to the nation", which clearly includes answering questions so that he can later ridicule the answers, rather than simply performing as well as they can.

The England team are not the only sportspeople to embrace silence lately. Tim Henman refused all non-contractual interviews on his way to the US Open semi-final – his second in a grand slam event this year – fed up of being labelled a failure when he is our most successful tennis player for decades. The best responsible, intelligent, balanced writing about the England team, containing plenty of criticism, is often the work of journalists who for reasons of culture or background are not actually football or sporting English patriots.

Paula Radcliffe, who went from hero to zero in a couple of hours in Athens, said that she was used to the sports journalists – the ones who understood and cared about what she did – writing about her, but found the attention of the front of the papers hard to take. The *Sun*'s donkey campaign, according to the media diaries of other papers and *Private Eye*, was the "brain" child of Dominic Mohan, the former showbiz writer who is now an associate editor of the paper. He was responsible for "the sneers" and "widespread vilification" – as Steve Brenner, seemingly forgetting which paper he was talking about or writing for, put it in the *Sun*'s sports pages once the fuss had died down.

There are some people that the *Sun* believes are too delicate to take flak. The actor Ross Kemp, for instance, whose post-*EastEnders* work has been widely criticised or else ignored, except by the Currant Bun, where it is often described as the highlight of a day's viewing. He is, of course, married to its editor, Rebekah Wade. Perhaps the only way to make Wade and Mohan realise that criticism can go too far is if a man dressed as a giant potato picketed all of Kemp's film sets, day in, day out, demanding a chance to prove it could do a better job. Vans with "Give Kemp His Chips" banners could drive round past Wade and Kemp's house.

With England playing twice in the week after this article goes to press, I don't know if the players will now explain their boycott. But they could say that they fully accept that they will be criticised if they fail, but that they are the targets of biased "news" journalism; that they are abused by journalists who are not really that bothered about sport; that xenophobic anti-Eriksson bile plays its part; and that they are being called unprofessional by people who are ostensibly football journalists but become fans rather than pros the moment the England team are involved. O

North-East of Eden

While the East Midlands mourned a great manager on Brian Clough's death, his native region had lost a great player. Harry Pearson traced a legend's goalscoring career

WSC No 213, November 2004

IT WAS DURING THE 1986 WORLD CUP. England had got off to a pathetic start and in the ITV studio Mick Channon was lamenting the inability of English players to "get by people". "The Brazilians do it," he burbled. "The French do it. The Danes do it…" From off camera came an unmistakable whine: "Even educated fleas do it." Brian Clough may have won titles and European Cups, but the queasy, humiliated expression that remark put on Channon's medieval mug will likely live longer in my memory than any of them. To anyone who grew up on Teesside the tone, if not the accent (Clough's peculiar vocal style was all his own) was unmistakable. Funny undoubtedly, but also scornful, the humorous equivalent of a slap in the face.

Born and brought up in the Grove Hill area of Middlesbrough, Clough must have had plenty of chance to practise those withering put-downs, if only in self-defence. Nowadays cockiness is seen as a not-entirely-negative trait; some even view it as a prerequisite to sporting success. But back then self-regard was a mortal sin. The slightest sign of confidence was mercilessly crushed. Nobody liked a bighead. And Clough was by all accounts a monstrous egotist right from the start. A schoolmate of my father had been goalkeeper in our village team. One Saturday in the 1950s they had played a Great Broughton side featuring a teenage centre-forward – Clough. The adolescent had scored three times and, at the end of the game, gone over to my mate's father, given him a consoling pat on the shoulder and said: "Don't worry, one day you'll be telling your mates Brian Clough put a hat-trick past you." Which was true as it turned out, though it's hard to imagine anyone was impressed at the time.

Clough signed for Middlesbrough – the team he had supported since boyhood – from Great Broughton in 1955. Photos show a sharp-featured face beneath a Woody Woodpecker quiff. His skin is so pale it looks as if he has lain under a sun lamp switched to "suck" and his dark eyes are shiny with energy. His scoring record for Boro was extraordinary. In his five full seasons at Ayresome Park his lowest tally was 36. Yet he was never popular with his team-mates. His quest for goals was said to have been so single-minded he shoved better-placed colleagues out of the way so he could score himself. He allegedly sulked after defeats and criticised others on the field of play; he was accused of being arrogant, scathing and combative. Clough hit back with accusations of his own, more serious ones. Boro were mired in the old Second Division and apparently incapable of escape no matter how many times their centre-forward found the net. Clough believed there was something more sinister behind the situation than mere mediocrity. He went public, alleging his team-mates had a habit of betting on themselves to lose, then ensuring they did so by deliberately conceding goals. The accusations led to fisticuffs in the dressing room and when Clough was made captain nine players signed a round-robin letter to the directors asking for him to be removed.

The Boro crowd took the majority view (though few supporters these days doubt Clough's version) and in the next home game barracked the skipper from the kick-off. He responded in typical style – scoring a hat-trick, all with shots from outside the area. That his swagger survived in the venomous atmosphere at Ayresome is an extraordinary testimony to his toughness, mental and physical. In the end you suspect the boasting was more about challenging doubters than an act of self-promotion. While at Boro, Clough had put in transfer requests every season without fail. He was linked with Everton and Birmingham, but eventually went to Sunderland for £55,000. He liked it much better at Roker Park and hit 63 goals in 74 appearances, before a collision with Bury goalkeeper Chris Harker smashed his knee. He struggled gamely to recover. But though 20,000 turned out at Roker Park to watch his comeback for the reserves, he made only three more appearances for the first team before being forced to quit. He was 29.

It is hard now to see Clough's playing days as anything but a prologue to his brilliant management career, but in many ways it was his time at Middlesbrough and Sunderland that formed him as a man. He was bright, brash and outspoken before he arrived at Ayresome Park, but his experiences with his hometown club stirred bitterness and frustration into the mix. It was there, too, that he met Peter Taylor, while the injury at Sunderland led to his first prolonged bout of drinking. His strong sense of right and wrong (evinced by his teams' excellent disciplinary records and his hatred of gamesmanship) was affronted by Boro's habit of frittering away matches for financial gain; the fact that the board turned a blind-eye added a mistrust of authority that would be vindicated years later at the Baseball Ground. The thwarted ambition, the back-stabbing and the sense of injustice made him what he sometimes was – particularly during the "Mike Yarwood" years at Derby, Brighton and Leeds: awkward, confrontational and belligerent, a man determined that no one should get by him again. ○

Independent's Day

For a fleeting moment in 2001, The Premiership usurped Blind Date from ITV's prime slot on Saturday evenings. Barney Ronay had a clear recollection of what it was like – after all, he worked in the Tactics Truck

WSC No 213, November 2004 ~ Football on TV Special

"FOOTBALL IS NOT FAMILY ENTERTAINMENT," Cilla Black insisted shortly after *Blind Date* had been shunted out of its Saturday evening slot to make way for ITV's new football highlights programme, *The Premiership*. To the relief of everyone but a small group of soon-to-be-downsized marketing executives, Cilla was right: within weeks *The Premiership* had become the most unpopular programme in the history of televised football. Quite how an hour of football highlights could become the subject of mass ridicule, scorn and apparently genuine bile is open to question. The switch to a prime-time viewing slot seems to have been the key. It certainly spooked the production team, as various gimmicky presentation "ideas" were nervously unveiled during the show's opening episode. Terry Venables was given free rein to bark tactical instructions across the family sofa with the help of some very tedious ProZone statistics. And the debut appearance of Andy Townsend's Tactics Truck provided a moment of iconically awful live television: a freshly showered Ugo Ehiogu watching in wide-eyed disbelief as Townsend demonstrated exactly why it was his fault ("I've got to say Ugo you needed to be much tighter there") that his team had just conceded a late winning goal.

The prime-time *Premiership* was more than just a bad programme. It was a very bad programme and also very weird – football dressed up like Ant 'n' Dec, holding its stomach in and hoping the overhead lights aren't too bright. At this point I must declare an interest. I have been inside the belly of the beast. In fact, I've been inside the belly of the Tactics Truck. In my role as journalist on the ITV Football website (launched at the same time as *The Premiership*) I was dispatched to report from the outside-broadcast truck at Loftus Road while Fulham were playing Liverpool. In fact, by this stage the Tactics Truck had been shunted off the road – and probably torched and dumped in a lay-by for good measure. This was just a dark and very clammy van. Inside it five men sat staring at a bank of small screens. Another man pressed buttons and swore quietly to himself while Clive Tyldesley's voice droned through a small speaker next to my head.

Every few seconds Clive's face – complete with a large clump of mud on his microphone – would appear on an overhead screen like an apparition of Stalin. It's hard not to feel some affection for a programme when you've watched its director hunkered over his console like an MC at the World Speed Bingo Championships saying things like: "Ready seven, hold it eight, three thanks hold it two. Six. Fucking six!" and heard Tyldesley complain about the contents of his sandwich, not just once, but three times.

The unpopularity of *The Premiership* stemmed from beyond the Tactics Truck, beyond the eviction of *Blind Date* and beyond even Des and Terry – who still sound like a tropical disease – back in the studio. It was the sheer, blatant avarice of the whole exercise that invited misgivings. ITV's interest in football was entirely expansionist. *The Premiership* was the big idea that would drive its push into subscription television via, chiefly, the ITV Sport Channel. To Granada, football was a light-entertainment product that could be disseminated across a number of platforms. Marketeers, advertisers and focus group wonks were set to work. A great many meetings were held with a great many sponsors, involving expert use of the overhead projector and lots of clear-blue-sky thinking outside the envelope. *The Premiership* was an hour of football held aloft on a Tower of Babel of brand management and marketing chunter.

Even on the website it was made clear to us that we were a small part of a shining vision of a new hope of a brighter day of a better tomorrow where the sun only rises and everybody gets to watch football (and drink Coca-Cola) all the time. Parts of the job were fun. For sound-bite purposes, we were issued with a list of mobile numbers for *The Premiership* pundits (with the proviso that "under no circumstances" should we try to contact Ally McCoist). Andy Townsend turned out to have a regular trick of telling you he was just driving his car, then turning his phone off for the rest of the day. John Barnes proved to be spectacularly helpful, to the point where you wished he would just stop talking so you could get on with your 200-word Barnes Backs Becks article. And Des Lynam was reported to spend his Saturday afternoons tanking up with *nouvelle cuisine* in the Oxo Tower next door before wandering across to raise an eyebrow for the camera.

ITV's optimism proved to be as plastic as one of its strobe-lit coffee tables. The forcible removal of *The Premiership* from its 7.30pm slot was first touted in the office the day after the Al-Qaeda attacks on New York and Washington. No one, as far as I know, drew an explicit parallel between the two events; but these were still heady times at LWT tower. Soon ITV Digital would be tottering under the weight of its own miserably over-extended expectations. The contract with the Football League would be cancelled, leaving many clubs in financial peril. And a troupe of irate Gillingham fans would mysteriously receive precise directions to the correct building to accost chief executive Charles Allen (I'm probably safe now: it was me).

There was widespread relief when the final season of *The Premiership* ended. *Match of the Day* would be returning, along with Gary, Jocky, Lawro, Schmeichely and that creepingly supercilious sense of its own popularity. However, *The Premiership* did have a sting in its tail. Unexpectedly, by the end it was actually quite good. With nobody really watching, it had calmed down and streamlined itself to just two pundits and a semi-retired anchorman who was almost visibly looking at his watch.

The extended highlights were more evenly divided between different teams from week to week. Goals from games involving less popular teams weren't left right until the end (because of this policy we used to receive regular emails headed with things such as "YOU FUCKING

WANKERS") and the theme tune was still much better than on the BBC. Best of all, nobody felt very proud of themselves. Towards the end, *The Premiership* crept on to your screen in chastened mood, hoping you wouldn't mind if it just hung around for a little while. It had an anti-smugness, where *Match of the Day* currently seems about to explode under the weight of its own self-regard.

Having been badly bitten, ITV won't be back for a long time. If only as a counterpoint to the BBC, it will be missed. Like Sky and its subscription service, the BBC now have an effective monopoly. Gary Lineker introduced the new season with a ghastly close-up of his face mouthing some scripted remarks about having been rudely interrupted. Settle back if you can, because Gary's going to be with us for a long while yet. ○

Doing the Ground Work

Jon Driscoll's job as a TV reporter on football took him to all manner of glamorous locations, including the bracing seafront at Southend

WSC No 213, November 2004 ~ Football on TV Special

WHEN YOU'VE GONE TO WATCH Southend United train on a pitch at the back of a nightclub and the sky opens leaving you stranded 300 yards from your car, being a TV reporter doesn't seem too glamorous. But then Southend and glamorous rarely appear in the same sentence.

Perhaps oddly, there are two TV crews at the Boots & Laces training ground on a Monday morning. You are often on your own at a lower division club, but this is the day before they play local big boys West Ham in the Carling Cup. A cameraman and I are working for Sky Sports News and there's an ITV team there as well. It won't come as a great surprise to learn that Boots & Laces is a metaphorical million miles away from more famous places such as Arsenal's London Colney training complex. There are no security gates keeping out the common herd and reporters are allowed to mingle freely with players. I would if only I recognised any of them. They don't seem to have a nutritional specialist at Southend. When we get inside there is an intriguing pile of bread rolls on the table and I wonder what's going to arrive to accompany them – soup, salad buffet, hi-carb pasta meal? None of that – instead there's a jar of pickle and each player spoons some into his cheese sandwich: two cheese and pickle rolls a man and a glass of orange squash.

Today's task is to persuade Paul Brush – formerly of West Ham and now Southend's number two – to join us on the seafront for a colourful if cliched Britain-by-the-sea piece. We get off to a bad start. Sky's planning desk asked the Southend press officer to mention to Paul that we wanted to do this rather than the run-of-the-mill two-minute interview by the training pitch. He hasn't bothered. Southend had lost at the weekend and he thought they might be in a bad mood. He says he'll do it now but buggers off without breathing a word to Brush. So I approach Paul and manager Steve Tilson while they're tucking into their cheese and pickle rolls and raise the idea. Steve laughs. Paul screws up his face as, I suspect, he tries to quickly think of a reason to say no, but he runs out of time. "Go on then, after I've eaten." You've got to be careful of that one. Many a time as a young reporter I was left hanging around training grounds for players who had used that line then sneaked off out of another entrance or, in Ruud Gullit's case, gone for an hour-long massage.

Thankfully Brush is a decent man and gets in the car with us before directing us to what he describes as "a posh bit of the seafront". He warms up once we're underway and remains patient as we reposition ourselves a number of times to escape the whipping wind. Interview done and reminiscences made, Paul thinks he's done. But then there are the set-up shots. Watch out for set-up shots next time you're watching Sky Sports News or the regular news – they're the five- or ten-second bits which give you time to introduce whoever is going to speak. If the interviewee hasn't played along they'll be shots of a radio reporter interviewing the same person and if it's been a real struggle they'll be arty shots of a press-conference platform. It's worse in politics where you still see the 1970s-style "walk five yards for no particular reason please, minister" set-up. Luckily for us Paul wants to go for a run so we film that and there's the few seconds we need to explain who he is and why we interviewed him sitting in front of a beach hut.

We drop Brush at the training ground and head to Roots Hall to meet Brian Dear – the former West Ham striker who now runs the bars and catering at Southend. His set-up shot involves him pulling a pint. Trouble is he clearly never does it and gets 80 per cent head every time we try. We have about four goes at it and each time Brian looks at the camera and says: "Is that what you're after lads?"

Still, they're not actors and getting someone from a top club to do anything beyond a short interview in front of a sponsor's board is difficult. Clubs point to the number of media outlets there are now as a reason why they can't give more of their time and indeed there can be around a dozen camera crews when Arsenal or Manchester United hold a Champions League press conference. Sky's money buys certain things, but not as much as you might think. When I was working as a local radio reporter my naive producer told me to get Kevin Keegan on before Sky did. He might as well have told me to stop a charging rhinoceros as the then Newcastle manager was marched to their interview point by a team of men in suits speaking into walkie-talkies. But working as a freelancer I see that Sky Sports reporters don't get much access that others don't. They generally get to go first and after matches having a place in the tunnel makes life a lot easier. But in terms of time, an average manager devotes more attention to newspapers in their various packs (Sundays, Mondays and evenings) than doing TV interviews. And clubs almost always limit access to the day before a game and post-match interviews.

The general view in football is that TV is a once- or twice-a-week duty rather than something they might embrace with enthusiasm. To me that seems the minimum when you consider that it's TV money that keeps Premiership stars in Ferraris and Southend players in Branston. ○

Named and Shamed

Arsenal announced that they were calling their new home the Emirates Stadium. Neville Hadsley looked at the bleak future offered by naming rights

WSC No 214, December 2004

MANY PEOPLE CAN RECALL where they were when they heard that John Lennon had been shot. I can't. But I can remember exactly where I was when word came through that Bradford City's ground had been renamed The Bradford And Bingley Building Society Stadium. I was in the offices of the Bradford *Telegraph & Argus* where, at the time, I was employed on the sports desk. The news did not impress the then-sports editor who, in a rare moment of decisiveness, said that we would continue to call the ground Valley Parade. Unsurprisingly, the Bradford supporters opted to stick with Valley Parade as well. It's tradition – you can't change it just by handing over a wad of cash, can you?

Not far south, it's a different story. Since moving from their old Leeds Road ground in 1994, Huddersfield Town have played at the McAlpine Stadium, named after the people who built it. Except, they don't any more. This year the naming sponsorship expired and they now play at The Galpharm Stadium. Same place, different name. The sponsorship with McAlpine expired and the power of cash is such that alternatives that reflect the club's tradition have been ditched in favour of a name determined by the size of the brown envelope. Many Town fans resented the change, but what could they do? As the ground had no other name than a corporate one, they found themselves at the whim of the club who, in turn, needed the money and so would probably always auction the name to the highest bidder. A nightmare vision of the future emerges where clubs such as Huddersfield are driven by market forces to give their stadiums sillier and more demeaning names just to satisfy the banks. What will it be next time? The Bargain Booze Stadium? Don't laugh – it's already been tried: Witton Albion's Wincham Park was called that for a couple of seasons.

Clubs, you see, have no shame. That's why – at the other end of the scale – Arsenal were happy to name their new stadium at Ashburton Grove "the Emirates Stadium", even though the word Emirates relates to a land far off and for the past few years has been associated with London rivals Chelsea (and will be on the Blues' shirts until the end of the season). The fact that something as important as the stadium name can be sold off, as a result having no local, community or club resonance, shows that the clubs now feel totally immune to fan power. The boards of clubs always had the upper hand. Now they know they can operate with impunity. Some might say that the clubs need the money to compete in football today. But, to take Arsenal's case, the club are already wealthy and will, as a result of the new stadium, almost double their gate income. So there was surely room to insert something into the title of the stadium – as Southampton did in the case of St Mary's – that could act as connection to the community and continuity when the 15-year deal expires and the stadium is given another name.

My club, Coventry City, is due to move into a new stadium next year. Most Sky Blues supporters were resigned to corporate naming for the new arena, as it is known. So when it was announced that it was to be the Jaguar Arena there was a sense of relief – a dignified name, thanks to sponsorship by a local firm with historic links. Jaguar have been building prestige cars in Coventry since 1928 and the deal seemed to quash the recurring rumours that the company was about to cut its links with the city. But the honeymoon did not last long. Just a few weeks after the announcement, Jaguar announced that they were, effectively, cutting their links with the city by sacking 1,000 workers and reducing their main production plant at Browns Lane to little more than a branch office. That it did not close Browns Lane altogether was surely a piece of local politicking. In the light of spending £7 million on naming the arena for ten years, it had to keep a token presence in the city. And so, my club has become just a pawn in a public-relations game on a grander scale. Many fans would have preferred to see our team play at the Kwik Save Stadium if Jaguar would spend that £7m on reinvesting in production in their home city.

Soon Liverpool fans will start to play this little game. What was once the mighty and proud Anfield will become, well what? A sign in the tunnel saying "This is the Carlsberg Stadium" is not going to intimidate anyone, is it? ○

2005

Wrong End of the Stick

Millwall supporters were used to negative portrayals in the media, said fanzine editor Paul Casella, but an article in the *Sun* took the misrepresentation to new levels

WSC No 216, February 2005

AS THE NEAREST CLUB TO WAPPING, a disproportionate amount of senior newspaper journalists visit The Den on a regular basis. It is not rare for the press box to see stars of stage and screen; or at least, stars of *Jimmy Hill's Sunday Supplement*. Indeed, judging by the amount of media coverage, Millwall are by far and away the "biggest" club that has 10,000 fans in the country. Hence perhaps, what has become MFC's own football philosophy T-shirt quotation, by former chairman Reg Burr, who said in 1993: "We are a convenient coat-peg upon which football hangs all its evils." However, the difference between what has gone before and the latest groundless nonsense is stark, and quite remarkable for at least one thing: the *Sun* has apologised for a stunningly ill-conceived article by *New Nation* sports editor Raymond Enisuoh.

Monkey chants and Sieg Heils screamed the headline. After reading this, anyone with any knowledge of English football would know that what might follow could only possibly be twisted fiction. And it was. Sent to watch a Millwall game, Enisuoh took a seat in the Cold Blow Lane stand and claimed: "No one actually sat directly next to me." A picture was included of someone sitting next to him. "A miskick from Millwall's black player Barry Hayles was met with some disturbing jeers. 'You fucking animal!' shouted someone to the top left of me." Enisuoh was referring to a first-half foul on Hayles and the subsequent abuse directed at a Brighton player. "Just minutes later I could distinctly hear monkey-grunting noises... The mood was beginning to grow ugly." Of course no one else heard this, although it could have been snoring. The mood, as at many mid-table clubs' grounds, was silent apathy. "After the final whistle, the photographer who accompanied me said he'd seen the section in the stand above me unfurl a racist banner." What a perfect opportunity for a photograph to support an article, but there was no banner and there was no photo.

There was of course much more nonsense in the two page article, but saving the best for last, Enisuoh wrote: "'Sieg heil. Sieg heil,' (German for 'hail victory') was being chanted by some fans and it was increasing in volume." Even if all the rest of the report had been accurate this was so obviously Brighton fans, chanting "Seagulls, Seagulls", that it made a complete mockery of the Sun's agenda.

The Sun once ran a two-page story claiming that Millwall supporters had hatched an evil plot to steal the famous Highbury clock before a cup-tie. Rupert Murdoch's most profitable newspaper also memorably included a full-page story about a Millwall follower who threw a meat pie on the pitch, after coin throwing became a popular tabloid topic. News, especially football news, goes in cycles and Millwall fans have grown used to their club being the easiest target, until the headlines move on, and the latest hot topic is racism.

Millwall have a "Zero tolerance to racism" policy that has seen the club ban more people than any other League member. It also proudly boasts that it has achieved more racism-related convictions than any other. The media is fully aware that this is not because Millwall have more racists than any other club, but because Millwall have done more than anyone else to combat racism. It had to, otherwise they faced the severe possibility of being refused a safety certificate by the police after a play-off defeat to Birmingham saw a riot two seasons ago.

Millwall's outspoken chairman, Theo Paphitis, has since reinvented the notion of a self-policing club and recent arrest and banning-order figures speak for themselves. Cardiff and Stoke followed Millwall's lead; admitting they also have problems with trouble-makers, by implementing similarly successful away travel membership schemes. But the Football Association steadfastly refuses to accept they, too, have problems, with the national team's following.

It is perhaps partly because of this that Millwall will never gain favour in the appropriate circles. A good example being the racism charge that sparked Enisuoh's article: alleged taunting of Liverpool's Djimi Traoré during a recent cup tie. Paphitis immediately issued a statement: "I just find the whole thing staggering. It seems like the FA is a rudderless ship and are seeking publicity for their own aim. Racism is too an important subject to use to point score. The charges are completely ridiculous."

Articles such as Enisuoh's are water off a duck's back to Millwall fans, but the glib approach of the media and the football authorities to tackling racism undermines the work of the Kick It Out campaign. Two days after Enisuoh's article, the *Sun* included a full page of readers' letters condemning the piece. It also included a half-page right of reply by self-appointed Millwall fan spokesman Frank Maloney in the main editorial spot, which is usually reserved for the *Sun* to have a go at "scrounging" asylum seekers. Although they will undoubtedly miss this particular irony, they will presumably wheel out their offer of a right of reply in the libel courts when defending Millwall's forthcoming action. O

Losing County

The oldest club in the League had never been in the Premiership and probably never will be, so the 1991-92 season was one for Martin Naylor to savour

WSC No 216, February 2005

ON HEARING THE WORDS "Neil" and "Warnock" a decent percentage of football fans would grimace and mutter an obscenity. But the current Sheffield United manager is remembered with fondness by Notts County supporters for the back-to-back play-off wins that took us into the top division for what will surely be the last time in our long history. At Wembley in May 1991 Brighton fans taunted us with chants of "Neil

Warnock's Chelsea Army" as it was rumoured that the big-nosed chirop-odist was to jump ship to see how best he could turn Joe Allon into Peter Osgood. Notts had the last laugh, however, as a 3-1 victory left us antici-pating the First Division fixture list. "We've only got Man U away first game," came the voice down my student-friendly incoming-calls-only phone. "And Forest at home the following Saturday." The excitement came from a friend who had flown back from Germany to spend the season following Notts around, having given up a £30,000-a-year job.

Not even the most partisan Magpie expected much of us that season: having announced that he was staying at Meadow Lane, Warnock insisted he would stick with the same bunch of thrown-together youngsters and journeymen that had been hammered 5-2 in front of 4,625 rain-soaked fans two years previously at Craven Cottage, in Division Three. "We're 250-1 for the title, which is rock bottom, so if we finish fourth from bottom, then it will have been a successful season," he told the local BBC news. The pace and eagerness of the 20-year-old Tommy Johnson and the sublime skills of his best mate Mark Draper would be complemented by the centre-half partnership of self-described "Dolly and Daisy", Craig Short and Dean Yates ("Deano and I would have competitions each game to see who could kick it furthest into the stands," Short would later admit). Former brickie Paul Harding, plucked from non-League football, would add bite to the centre of midfield and, as we rubbed our eyes at Old Trafford on August 17, we looked forward to seeing how Alan Paris would cope with the pace and trickery of Andrei Kanchelskis (for the record, he didn't).

The 2-0 defeat at Old Trafford didn't set alarm bells ringing – that came after a 4-0 home defeat to our neighbours across the Trent. By the end of September Paul Rideout was signed from Southampton for £250,000. When he got a debut goal at what turned out to be our best performance of the season, a 3-1 win at Bramall Lane, and another in the next game (a 2-2 draw with Norwich), the more attacking style of play led us to believe we were on the up. Three successive 1-0 defeats put paid to that. Although we enjoyed a successful Christmas, with a Boxing Day 2-0 win at home to Chelsea (when away fans turned their backs on the pitch as the second half kicked off, preferring to spend 45 minutes staring at an incinerator) and 3-0 against West Ham, a New Year's Day defeat at Selhurst Park proved to be Rideout's last game. With mutterings behind the scenes about the way the deal was done, he was shipped to Rangers for twice his original fee. Warnock spent the rest of the season bemoaning Rideout's loss and three months on used the March transfer deadline to take a swipe at chairman Derek Pavis's decision to sell, saying to the local press: "If I could buy back Paul Rideout from Rangers for half a million quid, then I certainly would."

A club record fee of £750,000 back in November had brought in Tony Agana from Sheffield United, but he hadn't scored until that win over the Hammers (a scuffed shot that trickled over the line after almost getting stuck in the mud) and didn't manage to find the net again all season. No one else was scoring, either: club stalwart Gary Lund and the pacy but limited Kevin Bartlett (runner-up in the Rumbelows Sprint Challenge before that year's League Cup final) failed to set Anfield et al alight, while Johnson was loaned and subsequently sold to Derby County. This transfer freed finance for a £5 million redevelopment of the decrepit Meadow Lane stadium. As Pavis claimed: "We have two pots, one for the players and one for the stadium. You don't mix the sugar with the sand."

The first win of 1992 didn't arrive until mid-April, when a Kenny Sansom own goal in front of just over 6,500 was enough to see off Coventry City, though we had at least scraped a draw at the City Ground where a black-and-white windmill bounced joyously among the Forest faithful ("I lost count of the amount of times I was told to stick it up my arse," admitted the protagonist) and Manchester United fought back to get a draw at Meadow Lane. This was the game where an ineffectual Ryan Giggs retorted "I doubt that very much" to his marker Chris Short's dig that "you did nowt this afternoon, son, see you next season", as he was substituted. By February, the press had decided that Warnock was the only man fit for the now vacant Sunderland job. "Is Warnock the man to put the roar back into Roker?" they screamed, even after watching David Batty run 80 yards with the ball to score only his third goal in five seasons as Notts crashed 3-0 at Elland Road.

With the transfer deadline looming and Swindon's free-scoring Duncan Shearer having opted for Ewood Park rather than Meadow Lane, there was a flurry of signings, including Kevin Wilson ("It's a difficult move") for £225,000 from Chelsea, future Australia coach Frank Farina on loan from Bari and Rob Matthews, a Loughborough University student. They failed to keep us up, but the fact that Matthews bagged three goals from one start and four substitute appearances at the end did lead me to think that his pace would set Division Two alight the following season (for the record, it didn't). Luton came down with West

Ham and ourselves on the final day of the season and the Premiership arrived over the summer. At time of writing, we lie 20th in the basement division, trying to survive on crowds of 5,000 and having come through a record time in administration. The plus side is that the supporters' trust currently own 30.2 per cent of the club and have a representative on the board of directors.

Warnock moved on from club to club, upsetting all and sundry before settling in at Bramall Lane. But there's still a small pocket in the East Midlands that follow his fortunes with a half smile, remembering a cold January afternoon when the half-time scoreline read "Notts County 1, Manchester United 0". Would Ken give up a £30,000 job in Germany to do it all again? "Of course I bloody would." ○

Blyth Spirit

The greatest non-League FA Cup run of the past 100 years could have been even better. Ken Sproat remembered when a floppy corner flag robbed Blyth Spartans of more glory

WSC No 218, April 2005

WHEN YOU SUPPORT a non-League team it can feel enough, and be a matter of quiet pride, that the club is known and respected in its own town. This has largely been the case in the Northumberland port of Blyth for generations, but in 1978 the town's team transcended their apparent lot completely. Blyth Spartans became one of the most famous teams in the entire football-speaking world.

The 1977-78 FA Cup run began ordinarily enough with a qualifying-round schedule that saw four local sides beaten, followed by another team of part-timers, Burscough, in the first-round proper. Third Division Chesterfield were next up at Croft Park. Blyth won 1-0, a superb result but not beyond recent experience because both Crewe and Stockport had been beaten in 1971-72. The third-round draw was both disappointing and brilliant. Home again, but to another non-League club: Enfield. No glamour, but Blyth took the opportunity, squeezing through. The reward for Alan Shoulder's header was a trip to Second Division Stoke City.

This was a bad winter for weather and the Stoke tie was called off twice. Fans who couldn't get down to the Midlands for a third time were to curse the postponements – they lost out on seeing one of the biggest Cup shocks in English football history. Stoke were a recent top-flight team, had won the League Cup six years earlier and had Howard Kendall, Terry Conroy, Alec Lindsay, former Newcastle striker Viv Busby (he was playing when Hereford's Ronnie Radford scored that goal) and a young Garth Crooks. By now the draw for the fifth round had been made. If, by a miracle, Stoke could be defeated, then the reward would be a trip to Newcastle (once they had disposed of Wrexham).

Spartans took a tenth-minute lead when Terry Johnson slid in a spilled corner, but two Stoke goals fairly soon after the break appeared to settle it. With ten minutes left, though, a Ron Guthrie free-kick spun off the wall at a daft angle and bobbled against the left post. Blyth forwards charged at the loose ball and Shoulder headed it against the opposite one. Steve Carney was standing in the right place to lash in the equaliser. Incredibly, and it seems even more incredible now than it did then, Blyth scored a last-minute winner, from another free-kick. This time it seemed to be overhit, but the ball found its way back into the danger area and Terry Johnson rammed it in.

But at Wrexham, Newcastle suffered a 4-1 stuffing. So Blyth fans were denied a chance to witness what would have been the most glorious of days at St James' Park. Still, the Stoke result made Spartans a nationally supported underdog. Blyth had it all – a great and unusual name, an odd strip, a solid history to show they were no mere fly-by-nights, eccentrics in the dressing room (cue excruciating footage of the players singing Zip-a-de-doo-dah), the de facto support of Newcastle and Sunderland fans, and for the papers an easy headline – Blyth Spirit.

Coach Jackie Marks handled the publicity duties. Of solid north-east non-League credentials, he imbued Spartans with team spirit, tactics and, to media delight, "speed oil", a special pre-match drink to release of tension and build courage. That Blyth were so good in this period was no fluke – the squad had been assembled and improved upon for about ten years. Having a relatively large support meant that they were able to attract the cream of north-east non-League talent – Dave Clarke, for instance, was considered the best semi-pro keeper in the country. Full-back Guthrie had played in that other great north-east Cup adventure, for Sunderland when they beat Leeds in the 1973 final. A key signing that season was a League journeyman fed up with slogging it around the motorways, former Brentford and Southend striker Terry Johnson.

In that era, being on *Match of the Day* was an event of note for the fans of any club, even those of Liverpool or Arsenal. The sudden prominence of Spartans meant it inevitable that the fifth-round match at Wrexham would be featured. The nation could therefore witness how close Blyth came to reaching the quarter-finals and how cruelly they were denied.

The pitch, as they say all too often, is the same for both sides. However, it is not the same for forwards and defenders. As the Wrexham back line tottered around on the frozen, bone-hard surface, full-back Alan Hill opted for a safety-first back pass to keeper Dai Davies. It was weakly hit and Terry Johnson was on to it before most of the crowd realised the error. He found the net easily, wheeling away with a knowing smile.

Blyth were on their way. Frustrating Wrexham, the semi-pros scrapped it out. With the end in sight, another home attack floundered against green-socked shins. Although the ball had clearly gone behind via a Wrexham player's foot, referee Alf Grey gave a corner. To give himself more room, midfielder Les Cartwright moved the corner flag so that it stood at an angle. As Clarke in the Blyth goal collected comfortably, Grey noticed the flag had fallen completely over. He ordered a retake and the flag was balanced into its frozen hole for Cartwright to swing the corner over again. Once more the defence repelled the threat but, incredibly, the flag had fallen over again. Another retake. This time the arc of the cross caught out the Blyth defence and Dixie McNeil managed to force it over the line at the back post. It was the final minute. Blyth had been denied in the harshest of ways. The sense of injustice was tangible. It still is. But Blyth were in the sixth-round draw – Arsenal at home – and there was a belief that we would surely win the replay, and perhaps even the Cup.

Despite being denied a trip to St James' Park by Newcastle's ineptitude, the town of Blyth could have its big night out at the "Toon" anyway: police pressure meant the replay would take place at St James' Park. Long before kick-off the turnstiles were closing one by one, causing people to roam round in ever increasing packs in search of a chance to gain entry. Thousands were locked out and the game started in front of the incredible noise generated by 42,000 cheering as if the world depended on it. Though Blyth didn't play badly, Wrexham established a 2-0 lead by the 20th minute. No one gave up, though, not on the terraces, nor on the pitch; with eight minutes left Terry Johnson blasted in a volley. But despite some close calls, the equaliser would not come.

The knowledge of what could have been if things had happened correctly was an impossible legacy for subsequent Spartans team to

live with. Current matches at Croft Park involve a Blyth team struggling apparently in perpetuity in front of a few hundred regulars. One
of these is Jackie Marks, dispenser of the "speed oil" and, if you stand
within earshot, an accurate summariser of modern players' weaknesses.
The £7-a-week part-time players each received £350 worth of bedroom
furniture from a local business. Two of them transferred to Newcastle:
Steve Carney, a central defender, and more famously Alan Shoulder, who
adapted to life away from the Northern League superbly. Terry Johnson,
goal poacher supreme, the man who nearly put Spartans into the FA
Cup quarter-finals, can still be found every Saturday afternoon in Blyth
– Blyth market that is. The fruit and veg sold at his stall has a special aura
to a certain generation.

No other non-League team has been this far in the FA Cup since before
the First World War. An FA Cup fifth-round replay is not only as good as
it got for Blyth Spartans, but for every non-League team. ○

Underneath the Archie

Simon Inglis, the acclaimed writer on football grounds,
turned his attention in a new biography to the long-forgotten
Scot who designed so much we took for granted

WSC No 219, May 2005

EVERY FOOTBALL WRITER ends up becoming a bore on at least one pet
subject, and I'm no different. Indeed there have been times when
I've embarrassed even myself by rattling on about Archibald Leitch,
the Scottish engineer whose football ground designs dominated the
landscape of British football for most of the 20th century. And now I
have written a whole book on Archie, as part of a new English Heritage
series called Played in Britain, which seeks to put the study of sporting
heritage on the same footing as that of other areas of popular architecture
(cinemas, housing, retail, industrial and so on). And quite right too.

Yet oddly enough it was only halfway through writing the book that I
really appreciated just how important Leitch had been and how intimately
my own life in football had been intertwined with his. When I first
started out on my journey around the football grounds of Britain in the

early 1980s, I had never heard of the man. Nor, seemingly, had anyone else. But the more I was able to identify the stylistic similarities – the criss-cross steelwork balconies of Roker, Goodison, Ibrox, Fratton et al, and the roof-top gables of Hillsborough, Craven Cottage and Ayresome Park – the more I sensed a common thread. Delving further into club histories, few of which even mentioned ground developments, Leitch's name started to crop up, here and there. I particularly recall spotting a tiny sepia portrait of Archie glued into the panelling of Roker Park's main stand. Building records and club minutes added to the evidence, until eventually, in 1983, I was able to build up a list. Even if not comprehensive, I thought it might form the basis for later research. If, that is, anyone was interested.

As it transpired, football fans were more interested than I could ever have dreamed. In time, as my postbag revealed, Archie even emerged as something of a minor cult figure. In 1987 his two buildings at Craven Cottage and the south stand at Ibrox were listed. Around the same time, to my huge delight, I was able to confirm that Archie had designed the Trinity Road stand at Villa Park. This was the magnificent redbrick stand in which I now had a season ticket and in which I had watched my first ever football match, in April 1962. The stand then was 40 years old. I was but seven. Whether the majesty of the Trinity Road stand was, subconsciously, the reason why Aston Villa became my team thereafter, I cannot honestly say. It can't have been the team's performances. They were in the Third Division by the time I became a regular.

Years later, the 1989 Hillsborough disaster and the subsequent Taylor Report changed everything and in the 1990s I found myself working with architects, engineers, civil servants and safety experts, drawing up design guidelines for the new, tougher era of ground regulation. In 1996-97 our research culminated in a review of the *Guide to Safety at Sports Grounds*, itself first published in response to the Ibrox disaster of 1971. As editor of the revised Guide, one of my tasks was to follow the paper trail back to that first edition to come to an understanding of what the standards were and how they had been formulated. A pattern quickly emerged. Much of what been considered as best practice, it turned out, had been based on the work of Leitch: almost unwittingly, I have spent much of the past two decades on the man's trail.

Not that Archie was perfect. As chief engineer to Rangers at the turn of the 20th century, he was heavily implicated in the causes of the first Ibrox disaster, in 1902, a disaster he witnessed and that surely haunted the rest of his days. He might easily have walked away from football at that moment. He was, after all, a factory architect, first and foremost. But Archie was also a practical man, the son of a blacksmith, raised in a tough part of Glasgow. Engineers don't walk away from problems. They tackle them. The good ones do, anyway. I am also convinced that Archie loved the game. He had to, to put up with all those clashing egos, the Ken Bates and Mohamed Fayeds of his day. So Archie stayed the course. After 1902 he went on to design grounds and grandstands for Middlesbrough, Chelsea, Fulham, Blackburn, Liverpool, Everton, Manchester United, Arsenal, Sunderland, Hearts... There are 29 grounds featured in the book and those are only his major commissions.

That much we already knew, however. What has emerged from my later research is that, as another consequence of the 1902 disaster, Leitch also designed the standard, 20th-century football terraces we knew between 1902 and the Hillsborough disaster. Every dimension of tread and riser, the sinking of lateral gangways, the provision of barrier configurations, the lowering of the first row to improve the sightlines... all these basic design parameters were drawn up by Archie, making their debut at Craven Cottage and Stamford Bridge in September 1905. If you ever stood on terracing, it is highly likely that at one time or another you have leant against a patented Leitch crush barrier. Leitch barriers were just part and parcel of the football scene, like Oxo ads or fat policemen.

Twickenham, as it was before 1990, was a definite Leitch creation, but, contrary to received wisdom, he had no hand in Celtic Park. Archie, it turns out, was a Rangers man and freemason through and through, a typical late Victorian Scottish Protestant professional. He did get involved with Hampden Park about 1927, but from the papers of a 1924 government working-party report I have also been able to discover why Wembley Stadium was such a dreadful place to watch football. I looked up the papers on the assumption that Archie would have been consulted. But he wasn't, which turns out to have been part of the problem. The report, reproduced in the book, is chilling reading.

Another revelation has been the discovery of Archie's only known surviving factory: the Sentinel Works in Glasgow, built 1903-04. This turns out to have been the first reinforced concrete construction in Scotland and is now a Grade A listed building. If you are into the aesthetics of stripped early 20th-century concrete, it is a gem, uncannily like a 1930s grandstand without the seats. Alas, it is also derelict. Even so, *Engineering Archie* is no attempt to turn Leitch into some kind of forgotten genius. Villa Park, Craven Cottage and Ibrox Park aside, the majority of his designs were otherwise quite utilitarian. He put function before form every time, which is why so many of his stands and terraces looked so similar. And you thought only modern grounds all looked the same.

Archie the engineer we know a great deal about from his stands and terraces. Of his character and personality – apparently a lively chappie with a keen sense of humour – all we have to go on are snippets extracted from newspaper reports, some letters, and a few, precious family records and reminiscences from his two grandchildren. The book's title, *Engineering Archie*, thus bears a double meaning. In engineering Archie, as it were, from these few precious sources, I hope to have come close to an estimation of the real Archibald Leitch and the football world in which he operated. It is not so different from that of today, even if no current architects dominate the scene quite as Leitch did.

If I am honest I guess I also wanted the book to honour the memory of the Trinity Road stand, in which I sat for so many years. Five years ago the philistines at Villa Park tore it down and put up a dreadful replacement. Pathetic as it may seem, I haven't felt the same about football since then. It was the Archie look I liked. O

The Retiring Type

Good news for Swedish oenophiles: Anders Frisk had opened a wine business. Marcus Christenson reported on other reactions to the referee's sudden retirement

WSC No 219, May 2005

"FRISK" MEANS HEALTHY in Swedish and for many years fans amused themselves by singing "Frisk, Frisk, Frisk, you must be ill" when the now world-famous referee was having a bad game. No one thinks it is that funny any more. On March 11, Anders Frisk retired from football after he and his family had received death threats following Chelsea's game at Barcelona. Frisk's life had been made hell – and he couldn't understand why. "I was quite happy after the game," Frisk told the *Sportbladet* newspaper. "I could never have imagined that it would turn out like this. It feels like I've been part of a reality show." The Swedish public was divided. Some argued that Frisk had lost his focus and that his unashamed love and admiration for himself had become an obstacle. Others said that, while he may have liked to lie on a sunbed every now and then, he was still one of the best international referees around.

Sweden is a small country and people are therefore proud of people who achieve worldwide recognition, such as Ace of Base, Ikea founder Ingvar Kamprad, Hans Blix, Björn Borg and, yes, even Anders Frisk. Everyone agreed, however, that the 2004-05 season had not been a good one for Frisk. He was hit by a coin during Roma's match with Dynamo Kiev and Claudio Ranieri then said that he understood "why they cut his head in Rome" after Frisk sent off Valencia's Miguel Angel Angulo against Werder Bremen.

And after the Chelsea game, *Expressen* columnist Hans Linne wrote: "Frisk is still a referee of the highest standard, one of the best in the world, but when a referee is in the spotlight too often in big games then there is a risk that a feeling of hate will spread." And that was before José Mourinho made his accusations about the now infamous game. Frisk, meanwhile, could not understand what he had done wrong. "The home team's coach [Frank Rijkaard] came up to me at half-time and apologised for not saying hello before the game, that was all there was to it," he said. "But Mourinho shook my hand before the game and I spoke with him. Isn't that wrong as well, then? If you are brought up in a Swedish way and told to look after relationships, then it is right to shake someone's hand when they come up to you. I also think we had a good game. Apart from the sending-off I don't think we were that noticeable."

Frisk decided to retire after the threats started to come through on his secret home phone number. He is, understandably, bitter about Mourinho's comments. Partly because he has followed Chelsea since he was a kid, but also his integrity was questioned. "Being impartial is so important in refereeing. It is important to me and it always has been, in my life and in my upbringing. I have been a referee for 26 years now and when someone says something like that it does hurt."

Frisk has been a well known figure in Sweden since 1995 when a Djurgårdens supporter ran on to the pitch and attacked him with a kung-fu kick. In 2002, Malmö chairman Bengt Madsen accused Frisk of ruining "everything" just because he wanted to be "the centre of attention". But *Sportbladet* recently asked 152 Swedish players who they thought was the best official in the country and Frisk finished second behind another FIFA official, Peter Fröjdfeldt. He was, however, also the person some of the players liked the least. "He has got a lot better the last few years," said Helsingborgs captain Jesper Jansson. Djurgårdens' Matias Concha was not impressed: "He does whatever he fancies and is impossible to talk to. A good referee is someone you don't notice and he is always looking to play the lead role."

Swedish journalists, meanwhile, suddenly had to defend an official they had often castigated. "Frisk may look like a peacock when he runs around and God knows that I have sworn many a time over his exhibitionism, but he is one of the best [in the world]," *Sportbladet*'s Simon Bank offered. Lasse Anrell at the same paper wrote: "I mourn Frisk. You can say a lot about him but there is no doubt that he has been the most successful Swede on a football pitch in the past few years. Sorry, Zlatan. Sorry, Brolin. Sorry, Ljungberg. It is good that Swedish fans have learned to differentiate between the person he is and how he referees. Other [people abroad] were too stupid to do that."

And so life as an ex-referee has started for Frisk. But, as a father of three, a full-time insurance agent and in charge of two cinemas, the 42-year-old is unlikely to grow restless. Since retiring, he has started a wine company called 3 Amigos, with his assistant referees Kenneth Petersson and Peter Ekström. José Mourinho, despite being a well known wine aficionado, is unlikely to get a discount. O

Wrong Time, Wrong Place

The death of 39 fans at the 1985 European Cup final was the culmination of an era when, as Mike Ticher recalled, English football appeared to be in terminal decline

WSC No 219, May 2005

IT'S THE TIMEWORN RIGHT of each generation to complain that things are not what they used to be. In 1983, Geoffrey Pearson's classic work *Hooligan: A History of Respectable Fears* showed how at any given point in the past 150 years public opinion held firmly that society's current state of violence and mayhem contrasted with a peaceful "golden age", consistently located about 20 years previously. Oddly, the very time he was writing has proved the exception to his rule. In football at least, no one in their right mind would want to risk a return to the mid-1980s. Football now has diseases of affluence: too much money, too much TV, too much sitting down. It has become common to use words such as "bloated" to describe it. We have got so used to the excesses of the long Premiership boom that it is sometimes hard to believe that in the 1980s intelligent observers doubted whether the game could survive in a recognisable form. Surely they were scare-mongering, victims of the "golden age" syndrome. Could things really have been that bad? Actually, they were.

In his 1986 edition of *The People's Game*, the social historian James Walvin pointed out the "temptation – to which most observers succumbed – to impose on [Bradford and Heysel] an inexorable inevitability; to see the disasters of 1985 as the unfolding of irresistibly long-term trends". It certainly wasn't inevitable that they would happen exactly when, where and how they did. But there were at least two good reasons in the early Eighties to sense that something apocalyptic was around the corner.

First, the long-term decline in attendances took a sudden lurch for the worse. In 1977 an aggregate of 26 million people watched league football, only slightly fewer than in the early Sixties. But the total fell gradually, then shockingly. By 1982-83 the figure was down to 18.8 million – football lost almost a quarter of its paying public in just three seasons. The reasons seemed obvious. On the one hand leisure patterns were changing drastically, made possible above all by cars and television. The editorial for the 1983-84 *Playfair Football Annual*, pondering gloomily on the figures, noted that television sets were now "as common as teapots" in British homes. Perhaps more potent (especially with hindsight) was the "push factor" of seemingly untameable hooliganism, with all its associated aggro of heavyweight policing, primitive conditions on the terraces and the poisonous atmosphere inside grounds. *Playfair*'s editors concluded: "It is extremely unlikely that 25 million people, let alone 30 million, will ever pass through the turnstiles in a single league season again." (In 2003-04, 29.1 million did just that.)

The second cause of nightmarish premonitions was the political climate of the early Thatcher years. The economic destruction of the old industrial areas seemed to mimic the failure of their struggling clubs. In 1988 the *Guardian* ran a series called "Fourth Division England" on what Matthew Engel called "the sad-sounding towns of uttermost England. The Fourth Division of the Football League has come to seem like a repository of the Britain left behind in the 1980s: uneconomic, dated, provincial and kept going out of unfashionable sentiment." Thatcher herself complained immediately after Heysel that "we have far too many football clubs – in any other industry the inefficient would have gone to the wall years ago".

In tandem with the raw economic winds that suggested football itself was ripe for closure came alarming political violence, such as the 1981 riots in Brixton and elsewhere, and the miners' strike of 1984-85. Fighting also raged across youth and music cultures that had become explicitly political, overlapping with football primarily through the enduring skinhead cult – when the Specials got to number one with *Ghost Town* in 1981, "all the clubs are being closed down" seemed like a prediction for football as well as music. Britain was deeply uneasy with itself, divided along old and new fault lines, and increasingly resigned to violence and decay. It was hardly surprising that football became infected with profound pessimism and helplessness. When the first post-Heysel season began with a five-month TV blackout, it seemed as though the game was slipping entirely from mainstream consciousness, except as a venue for death and destruction. Even Simon Inglis, in the first edition of *The Football Grounds of England and Wales* (1983), wondered whether "football could become as much a curiosity of the past as those gladiators in the Colosseum".

The 1984-85 season might have begun refreshed by the wonderful matches at the 1984 European Championship in France, but instead British writers drew the conclusion that both the atmosphere and the football there – not shown live on UK TV – had benefited enormously from England's absence. What followed was a familiar pattern of clubs teetering on the brink of collapse (notably Wolves), unwanted attendance records and constant outbreaks of hooliganism. The 2,976 who watched Cardiff play Wimbledon was the smallest crowd at Ninian Park for more than 50 years. Only 890 made it to Halifax v Torquay. Current Premiership contenders Charlton, Middlesbrough (both then in the Second Division) and Bolton (Third) were well and truly in the ranks of the "inefficient", all struggling to draw an average of 5,000.

Serious violence broke out at games as diverse as Celtic's troubled Cup-Winners Cup tie with Rapid Vienna (goalkeeper attacked by fan), Man City's defeat at Coventry (500 seats ripped out), the Cup tie between Burton Albion and Leicester (replayed behind closed doors) and the Milk Cup semi-final between Chelsea and Sunderland (Clive Walker dodged police horses to lay on the winner). That game led to the famous dispute over electrified fences at Stamford Bridge, while the even more notorious riot by Millwall fans at Luton in March 1985 prompted Thatcher to take a keener interest in football's crisis.

The violent disaster that football had been half expecting came on May 11, when a boy was killed and nearly 100 police injured as Leeds fans rioted at St Andrew's, though it was almost totally overshadowed by the Bradford fire on the same day. Heysel, 18 days later, was a numbing shock, but by then few could claim it was a total surprise. In fact, as Walvin suggested, it came to seem inevitable because it combined all the rotten elements that had been ringing alarm bells for years: fan violence; dilapidated stadiums; official bungling and neglect; bull-headed policing; and the full range of instant solutions offered by TV pundits (Terry Venables recommended the head-cracking example of the police in Spain, where fans were "really frightened"). The fact that it was broadcast live on television at Europe's showpiece event of the season cemented its symbolism as the apocalyptic climax of all that had gone before.

The most frequently quoted report on Heysel was written by the *Guardian*'s Frank Keating: "One more corpse was carried from the Brussels stadium last night. Soccer itself – draped in the Union Jack. It deserved to be spat upon." In fact, as some protested at the time, the game itself deserved to be rescued and restored to national respectability. But it would take an even greater disaster before that could happen. O

Unjust Deserts

Though cringing slightly herself, Caroline Bailey was keen to defend her team's famous director from media criticism

WSC No 219, May 2005

THERE WAS A TIME WHEN "doing a Delia" meant investing in a non-stick omelette pan. But since that infamous night in February when the Norwich City director, eyes rolling like a colicky mare, tottered on to the Carrow Road turf with a microphone, it has come to mean something slightly different. For Norwich fans already dumbstruck with incredulity at throwing away a perfectly good two-goal lead over Man City, it was all a bit much. As the visiting support treated its hosts to a half-time chorus of "going down with the souffle", Sky Sports busied themselves with yet another action replay of Delia's exhortations.

Needless to say the heady combination of football, celebrity and the scandalous suspicion that Delia had been at the booze proved irresistible. From the playful **Shum people are on the pish** (the *Sun*) to the pompous **How to make a fool of yourself in public** (the *Independent*), the newspapers duly overcooked their pound of flesh and dished it up with a double portion of bad publicity.

The most inexplicably vitriolic attack came from the *Daily Mirror*'s Oliver Holt, whom a panel of strait-jacketed monkeys at the British Press Awards has recently seen fit to name sportswriter of the year. "Delia should be hung out to dry for what she did," he trilled. "If that's not crowd incitement, I don't know what is." The baubled one then compared Delia's incoherent ramble with the gesture that saw Chelsea's manager José Mourinho banished to a broom cupboard during the Carling Cup final: "If the authorities go after him for his trifling shush to Liverpool's supporters, they've got to go after Delia, too. Call her into Soho Square and tell her she's just been garnished with a ten-match ban."

As the week wore on, the scrutiny only seemed to grow. The *Mail* and *Express* pitched in with think-pieces on how Middle England's egg-boiling idol had feet of clay after all; Five Live were still gleefully playing that bloody clip; and the inexorable office jokes were wearing very thin indeed.

I recognised the feeling – it was the same sickly mix of scarlet-faced shame and furious protectiveness I felt when my mum turned up at the school gates with a Norwich scarf tied round her head, bag-lady style, to keep out the cold. Back then the merciless little sods in my class whooped and jeered like something from *Lord of the Flies*; this time the catcalls came courtesy of big egos with picture bylines. Meanwhile, one division down, the Ipswich Town chairman David Sheepshanks, busy with his own stint at the Sky Sports coalface, felt compelled to liken his club's financial collapse of four years ago to the Asian tsunami. His comments made barely a blip on the media's radar.

Some might say Delia has been asking for it – after all, in the Neanderthal world that is professional football, she has committed the twin crimes of being famous and female. Placid old Carrow Road is quite partial to its low profile and even the most devoted fan flinches when, following a rare Norwich goal, the cameras cut yet again to its resident celebrity. When was the last time Sky zoomed up the hairy nostril of Roger Munby, Barry Skipper or Michael Foulger, City's significantly less newsworthy directors?

There is, nevertheless, more to Norwich's majority shareholder than an end-of-the-pier show. When Delia and her publisher husband joined the board in 1996, the club were 15th in the First Division, £8 million in debt and just 24 hours from foreclosure. The couple have since lavished time, energy and the small matter of £7m on their baby – such a large slice of their personal fortune that they have just sold their publishing company in order to secure themselves a pension.

The *Daily Mirror* may find her a soft target, but in bringing Norwich back from the brink Delia has more than fulfilled her side of the bargain – it's just a shame the players have failed to do the same. With a barren forward line and a defence you could drive a bus through, they are fortunate that "doing a Delia" drew a veil not only over their defeat that night but also the end of their Premiership season. ○

Another Kind of Football

Going to a match is the heart of the fan's connection with the sport and the details barely changed for decades, but, as Roger Titford recounted, that familiar routine had been swept away in the past 20 years.

WSC No 219, May 2005 ~ At The Match special

*For a shilling the Bruddersford United AFC offered you Conflict and Art...
it turned you into a partisan, holding your breath when the ball came sailing
into your own goalmouth, ecstatic when your forwards raced away towards the
opposite goal, elated, downcast, bitter, triumphant by turns at the fortunes of
your side... and what is more it turned you into a member of a new community,
all brothers together for an hour and a half... you had escaped with most of
your mates and your neighbours, with half the town, and there you were,
cheering together, thumping one another on the shoulders, swapping judgements like Lords of the Earth, having pushed your way through a turnstile
into another and altogether more splendid kind of life, hurtling with Conflict
and yet passionate and beautiful in its Art*

JB Priestley, *The Good Companions*, 1929

WHEN I STARTED WATCHING FOOTBALL REGULARLY, in about 1970, the
outlines of the matchday experience Priestley describes, in this famous
piece written 40 years earlier, were still just about discernible. Football
didn't cost much more than a shilling, you were all brothers together and
it was "another kind of life", though not one that necessarily attracted
half my town. By 1985, English football's low point, this vision was
laughable. By the year 2005 football has revived immeasurably, but in
ways that have transformed, rather than restored, the old experience of
going to the match.

Any fan over 30 is familiar with the surface changes: the disappearance
of the terraces and half-time scoreboards, the proliferation of seats and
Jumbotron scoreboards. But going to the match has changed in deeper
and more abstract ways, too, over the past 30 or so years. Fans have
gained in many ways – in terms of safety, comfort, better view, efficiency
and choices – and have responded in steadily growing numbers since

1985. While there have been significant and well acknowledged material gains, there are five aspects of the experience of going to the match, less tangible but important none the less, that have been lost: visual purity, physical density, individuality, unpredictability and anonymity.

There was something about the visual purity of the game in about 1970 that you could fall in love with. A small industry has since grown out of selling retro strips from the clean and uncluttered look of that era. Some clubs played in kits without even a badge, let alone a sponsor's name, manufacturers' and competition logos and, on the back, the identity of the player. Likewise some grounds (Highbury, Molineux) carried no perimeter advertising and the idea of "moving" hoardings or scoreboard advertising would have seemed an unthinkable distraction from the spectacle. Against the browny-grey background of the crowd or empty terracing the players stood out like beacons and the match officials, in crisp black with white collars, orange and red flags, were eternally well defined. Now, the most eye-catching men in the stadium are the stewards in yellow and orange plastic bibs, the players might be wearing black, grey or khaki and the referee could be wearing who knows what. Behind them the replica-shirted crowd can play the part of camouflage rather than backdrop.

When Priestley wrote about "another kind of life" and others talked about football as an "escape" you could see what they meant in 1970. But in 2005 all the commercial messages make sure your everyday life follows you every step of the way, even into the stadium toilets with ads asking you about "your WKD side". There are messages even on the back now of your favourite player's shirt, reminding you of that questionable loan with HFS. Even the strip you peel off the back of your car sticker brings news of some service you can happily do without. And when the referee sports the same commercial sponsor (Emirates) as the Premiership leaders you cease to even bother wondering where it will end.

For perfectly understandable safety reasons the physical density of football has changed. By 1985 the missing millions had left spaces around the ground. Twenty years later the millions had returned, but the spaces had got so much bigger. The football experience has expanded in time and space. The ten-minute half-time has become the 15-minute-plus snack break, the desultory five-minute shoot-in at 2.53pm has become the 25-minute choreographed warm-up at 2.10pm. Fans leave earlier for the game, travel, on average, greater distances and get back later. Media reports of the day's football events no longer stop at 6pm.

The modern stadiums are physically vast and consequently more fans are more removed from proximity to the action. Upton Park, once the epitome of a tight English ground, now feels bulky and bitty by comparison with its former self. Its capacity has changed little but its atmosphere is much less charged. The modern stadium not only takes the fans further away from the players but also further away from each other. In seated areas the scope for hearing and joining in banter is much diminished by how few people can hear each other, compared with the old terraces. More space and light have made football less intense, while the time spent in the stadium is used differently.

People no longer wait patiently and communally for the match to start; they are somewhere else in the stadium area busily consuming other goods and services. Where once the match took place in a near information-free bubble, at the leading clubs, it seems, you are never far from a plasma screen bearing the latest Bundesliga table among other useful gems. Legend has it, if I recall correctly, that Manchester City goalkeeper Harry Dowd used to fix appointments to do plumbing jobs during the week with fans behind his goal. You suspect you can no longer get close enough to David James to get him to come round and sort out your PlayStation2 on Monday night.

In 1970, and to large extent in 1985, clubs could be viewed as idiosyncratic entities having their own individuality; institutions without common standards in terms of safety, customer service, marketing and communications. Strong, well entrenched and occasionally disreputable individuals stamped their personal mark all over their club. There was no common way of building a stand or designing a programme. Pocket size or newspaper? Would it be a marching band before the game or the latest Beach Boys hit? Each away game was almost a trip to a different country with different customs and variety was the spice of travel.

Again, a small industry has grown up around chronicling the travel to and architecture of football grounds. But the tales are becoming less interesting as the experiences become more homogenised. The perimeter advertising used to be more local – "Bloggs of the Buttermarket for Finest Rivets" – and everywhere parts of the town peaked into view from inside the ground. While fans in Lincoln can still enjoy a view of the cathedral, in other grounds there is something of a loss of a sense of the locality. The colour of the seats is the best guide to where you are.There are many, many more people involved on the administrative side of football eagerly sharing their experiences of "best practice". There are many, many more regulations involved in ensuring the safety of the crowd (for instance, at some grounds you cannot have a half-time penalty shoot-out in case a stray ball hits someone drinking a cup of tea).

Together with the loss in the individuality of the football-going experience comes the loss of unpredictability. Many people welcome this. Much, but not all, of the unpredictability was caused by hooliganism, the fear of hooliganism and the police response to hooliganism. Unpredictability can be frightening and off-putting. The more football has done to rid itself of unpredictability, to create standardised expectations in the same way you have standardised expectations of McDonald's, the more attendances have grown. Delivering to an expected standard is one of the reasons for the success of such businesses. But it is hard to remember any particular meal in McDonald's in the same way it is hard to remember an escorted coach trip to St Mary's (or was it the Riverside?).

The all-seat era has been synonymous with the explosion in season-ticket holding. Before the 1990s season-ticket holding was very much a minority activity (Manchester United had only 10,000 in 1988-89). Now it is prevalent, certainly in the top two divisions, and dictates a more routine approach to football in terms of how often you go, who you go with and who you sit near. Widespread season-ticket holding has seriously affected the casual fan, either by cutting them out or forcing them into greater commitment. Supporters who used to enjoy watching the game from a different part of the ground have also lost out. The less predictable nature of going to football years ago meant that it was more of a test, more of an adventure, more of a heightened experience; but also more dangerous and very occasionally fatal, lest we forget.

In 1970, with only 600 season-ticket holders and up to 15,000 paying at the gate, my local club, Reading, had no idea who I or most of the rest of us were. We were just a mass of anonymity. Now it can tell not just who each supporter is, where they live and whether they are sitting in their designated seat, but also how many games they have been to this season and whether they would prefer to hear about the latest misfortune by text or email. The relationship between clubs and supporters is changing dramatically and this perhaps is the most significant difference in going to the match; no longer as an anonymous observer but as an acknowledged participant. Clubs, rather than fans, are driving this change and the improved technology of the database and the sound system are the new power tools.

The deafening capability of the modern PA system allows the club or the competition organiser to dictate the pre- and post-match running order and set the tempo for the crowd. Just as the announcer has become more partisan (the music-after-goals business that so helps create a friendly and sporting atmosphere), so has the role of the whole crowd, not just the one stand that used to sing back in 1970. There is a sense of obligation to chant and cheer, quite forcefully directed by some managers, chairmen, even Delia. A large proportion of the crowd now wear the shirt and they really are expected to play a part. If you fall asleep, half-drunk, as one Middlesbrough fan did, you could face prosecution. Ultimately, it would be technically possible for CCTV to focus on a supporter in his designated seat, determine whether he is singing or not and make a note accordingly on his personal account on the database, a kind of speed camera for fans. "Jenkins, for not participating fully in the Two Minutes' Hate v Bournemouth we're taking your season ticket away" the text message tells you on the bus home.

The loyal fan will, at last, benefit from the loss of anonymity when it comes to getting big-match tickets. But he may wonder at the level of crowd manipulation and loss of spontaneity in the modern stadium, if he has memories of football before the Taylor Report. There is less mental comfort for the neutral fan who just wants to watch the game and less scope for the verbal counter-culture of the old terraces.

Today the pitches are better, the players are better, the facilities are better, you waste far less time getting tickets and you worry far less about getting thumped. I park the car in a season-ticket holders' car park, 50 yards from the turnstile and the luxury hotel where I get my pre-match pint (home fans only) for the price of a 1970 season ticket. In 1985 football was at death's door. What we have is so much better than you could have imagined going to the match could be back then. But could a modern-day Priestley have waxed quite so lyrical about our modern matchday experience? ○

Slight Entertainment

Harry Pearson looked at the varied attempts made by clubs to keep spectators' attentions focused on the pitch during the half-time interval

WSC No 219, May 2005 ~ At The Match special

IT IS FAIR TO SAY THAT half-time entertainment at the top end of football is no longer what it was. The reason for this is simple – nobody watches it any more. Nowadays there are far too many things to distract fans in the concourses below the stands. And who would not stand and watch highlights of the first half when the alternative is trying to get your head around the sight of ten teams of small children playing five games of football simultaneously across the width of the pitch?

Perhaps it is not such a great loss, anyway. Since the apparent abolition of police dog display teams and regimental bands, half-time entertainment involves either children, inflatables, celebrities (or would-be celebrities) and tubby, pissed fans whose mates are in the stands nudging one another and going: "Text his missus, Degsy, text his missus." All of these amusements can be subdivided into two distinct categories: the penalty prize and the other crap.

Inflatable entertainment can be dealt with swiftly (and definitely should be, preferably with a hat-pin). Inflatables were abandoned by football fans more than a decade ago, but, ever hip to what the new breed dig, the game's rulers continue to use them at every opportunity. Anything that is large, bouncy and filled with gas is enormous fun, they feel. This will come as news to anyone who has ever watched Eamonn Holmes. Inflatables come in many shapes and sizes, from the bull at Hereford to the giant dice currently being rolled about in Premiership penalty areas as part of some inexplicable ritual presumably connected with sponsorship money.

Perhaps the exemplar was Sky's sumo wrestlers, a pair of giants in nappies who showed an uncanny ability to seek out new and ever more adventurous homo-erotic poses while bumbling around the turf. This may well have been what resulted in the TV station pulling the plug on them. Or indeed out of them. Also loosely connected with inflatables, though only in respect of their egos, are club mascots. The joy the sight of a fluffy tyrannosaurus taking penalties brings to a young fan is impossible to put a figure on – there simply aren't enough noughts in the universe.

Celebrity appearances I've noted at grounds down the years have included a folk-singing family from the synthetic ammonia capital of Billingham, Alastair Griffin (one of the losers from *Fame Academy* – an imprecise description admittedly since it covers everyone involved), and actor and comedian Su Pollard. Pollard made the fatal mistake of yelling "Hi-de-hi!" The massed response was predictably Anglo-Saxon. And it was the same the second time she did it, too.

The tubby-pissed-fans events come in myriad form. Some come on in suits and take penalties against a reserve keeper who looks like John Burridge (possibly because he is), for reasons the PA announcer refuses to divulge. Others, in pairs, take part in a trivia quiz, or, in a troupe, indulge in a humiliating aerobics routine lead by a woman in a leotard and leggings who used to be on breakfast television. One, not necessarily drunk, although he really should have been, walked round the edge of the pitch proudly displaying the longest ever continual line of ring-pull tags which he had bent together and stuck on top of a long pole.

The ultimate example of the tubby-pissed-fan genre was Hartlepool's infamous deckchair challenge. Sponsored by DFDS Seaways, this involved TPFs setting off from the halfway line and dribbling around deckchairs before scoring into an empty net. Three attempts were allowed and the fastest time counted. Incredibly one large man not only failed to find the net at all but also succeeded in falling over several times. Invited back for another go he repeated his abject performance, missing out on a luxury cruise to Norway but becoming a minor local celebrity.

Which brings us to the only half-time entertainment of any merit – the ubiquitous penalty prize. This is quick, elegant and offers the opportunity – rare in this day and age – to sadistically abuse small children without feeling the wrath of the law. Across the country the pattern of the penalty prize is much the same and so is the reaction of the crowd. Kids from schools in rugged working-class neighbourhoods are cheered to the rafters, while those from the affluent suburbs had ridicule heaped upon their bourgeois heads. The reaction of the children to the situation is never without interest. On one occasion at Ayresome Park a boy, possibly from a school in Hartlepool, having experienced a torrid build-up to his penalty from the denizens of the Holgate End, blasted his kick into the top corner of the net and then celebrated by lifting up his school jersey to reveal a Sunderland top beneath. This took some guts and, had life been fair, triumph would have been his reward. Unfortunately life isn't fair. The penalty shoot-out ended all square. It went to sudden death. The boy was forced to confront the Holgate End again. This time he missed. I bet he still wakes up screaming. ○

Take the Highfield Road

Coventry's final match at their old ground was a rare sellout. Neville Hadsley wondered why they had to move to a new venue fit for Kylie and U2

WSC No 220, June 2005

IT HASN'T BEEN A GOOD 12 MONTHS for Coventry City chairman Mike McGinnity and his board. First he sacked a popular manager, Eric Black, then compounded the error with City's worst appointment in living memory – Peter Reid – who, instead of achieving the "instant success" McGinnity declared he wanted, pitched the club into a relegation battle. If that wasn't bad enough, McGinnity then chose to embroil himself in a damaging legal case against some of the club's supporters over some low-level name-calling in private correspondence that was inadvertently made public.

McGinnity scored another yet own goal earlier this year when his plan to replace the club badge with something that looked like it had been designed by a child was overwhelmingly rejected by the club's supporters. The appointment of Micky Adams gave McGinnity some sign that redemption was possible, but if anyone needed a successful send-off for Highfield Road it was him. As it turned out, the last game at Highfield Road after 106 years could not have gone better for McGinnity and the Sky Blues. The sun shone and the ground filled to its 22,700 capacity – no mean achievement in a season when the "Sky Blue Army" was often down to a hard core of 13,000. Perhaps fired by the best atmosphere since the FA Cup-winning season of 1987 – and certainly motivated by the need for a win to seal survival in what they laughingly call the Championship – the Sky Blues gave their best result and performance of the season, a 6-2 drubbing of play-off contenders Derby County.

With the obvious exception of the away end, the whole ground seemed drunk on the emotion of the occasion and emboldened by the unravelling of events on the pitch. Even the obligatory Mexican wave seemed less of an irritant than usual, although starting it at 0-0 when relegation was still a possibility did seem recklessly presumptuous. When the first goal came in it was scored by Coventry kid Gary McSheffrey and, when he made it two from the penalty spot soon after, it was hard not to think of those terrible "soccer" movies in which the sun always shines and the local hero, plucked from the obscurity of park football, wins the cup and is carried, shoulder high, off the pitch at the end.

We were 4-0 up at half-time – even the Hollywood cheese-meisters would have rejected such a plot, but it seemed to be real. The scenes long after the final whistle, with Jimmy Hill, hero-manager in the 1960s but a less successful chairman in the 1980s, leading those who could not bear to leave in a mass rendition of Hill's own Sky Blues Song on the pitch, brought many to the brink of tears, and beyond. But many years ago, I made a rule for myself that I would never cry at a football match and I passed the test again as I walked away from the ground that I had known for almost 40 years.

It's hard, in all honesty, to see any logic behind the move to our 32,000-seat new stadium. Even in the heyday of Premiership football at Highfield Road, there were only one or two sell-outs per season. What's more, poor financial management has ceded control and effective ownership of the new stadium to Coventry City Council, which means that none of the financial benefits of sponsorship will accrue to the club, yet CCFC will have to find a substantial rent, thought to be in excess of £1 million per annum.

In the week before our departure it was announced that the club's new home will be called the Ricoh Arena. Tellingly, and humiliatingly, Ricoh's own website announced that it was sponsoring "the home of entertainment" before going on to talk about the place hosting such artists as Kylie Minogue, David Bowie and U2. At no point did the Japanese company mention that Coventry City would be playing there. Unbelievably, it didn't even mention which city its new arena was in. A humbling start to a new era, then, and it is easy to be sentimental about Highfield Road. For all its faults – the restricted views, the cramped facilities – our now former home was a true community stadium that was accessible to all.

The new place is on the edge of the city and does not have the network of pubs, chip shops and curry houses that are crucial to the matchday experience. What's more, it is only accessible by car and, with limited car-park spaces and a draconian street parking regime imposed, many fear an environmental and logistical nightmare. Die-hard football fans instinctively resist change. Who's to say they are wrong? ○

The Final Insult

Cameron Carter argued that nothing better reflected the drop in interest in the FA Cup final than the absence of Kenny Lynch – Brian Dowling being no substitute

WSC No 221, July 2005

THE *GUARDIAN*'S DONALD MCRAE concluded his preview of last month's FA Cup final with the challenge – "Fireworks and fisticuffs, and a few sublime goals, are the very least we expect." I expect Donald was as disappointed by the absence of all three as anybody, but, for others among us, the most unsatisfactory aspect was the continued shrinking of the pre-match build-up on terrestrial television. I realise the olden days of football on television weren't always better. Yet FA Cup final day, as covered simultaneously by BBC1 and ITV, was an orgiastic celebration of the living world in comparison to the mean little coffee morning we're palmed off with today. Both Cup final specials commenced at around 11 in the morning, the build-up to kick-off gluttonously filled with trivia, foppery and banter.

There was so much banter in those days. Whether it was Saint & Greavsie, Little & Large in Man City gear (remember that banter isn't necessarily funny, it is laugh-fighting between two or more men), or Jimmy Tarbuck and his golfing mates, you could rely on a heart-dilating dose of the stuff every 20 minutes or so for approximately four hours. Banter was in the studio panel, on the team coach, in Tarby's Celebrity Friends Bar of '86 and '87 and in the footage of the players at their relaxing country retreat (disappointingly for rationalists, both sides would stay at lucky hotels). Every year since its mid-Seventies heyday, the banter has been reduced, little by little, until all we were left with in 2005 was Ian Wright on a plastic chair.

BBC1's build-up this year contained nothing that wasn't soberly and directly connected to the match. There was no room for *Supporters' Mastermind* or *Cup Final It's A Knockout* (once an annual standby for the BBC, the team whose fans won always seeming to lose the final); Rod Stewart trying a bit too hard in a celebrity game; Brian Moore having his handwriting read by a psychic, Gerald Sinstadt asking the cast of *Coronation Street* for predictions, Brendan Foster triumphing over a string of famous athletes in a race around the Wembley track – the permutations of celebrity, ex-player and established television format were endless. In the old days it was as if everyone in the country, from Magnus Magnusson to Kenny Lynch, was connected, made brothers, by football for one day.

In 2005, *Cup Final Grandstand* finally started at 1pm and was eight parts tabletalk to two parts recorded interview. Even down to the irritatingly chopped-up editing of the occasional action sequences, this was merely *Football Focus* stretched to breaking point. No round-by-round review of the Road to Wembley, just Adrian Chiles swiftly voicing over his highlights of this year's competition. Instead of Tony Gubba kneeling in to catch the nervous jabber from young players on the coach, we had Gary Lineker struggling to identify a team bus from an aerial shot. The one feature that demonstrated any thought or effort was the review of the 1979 final, with revealing contributions from key participants.

However, this shaft of illumination was offset half an hour later by Around The World in 80 Seconds, in which a chap with a microphone in a Soweto bar stated how popular English football is in these parts, seemingly unaware that only four other people were with him, two of them playing pool. There was apparently time for this kind of nonsense and endless studio speculation concerning the Vieira-Keane confrontation, yet Dennis Bergkamp's career was dealt with in a jerky montage of 40 seconds and there was no time at all for the traditional players' profiles, as presented by their captains. Back in 1979, I learned from this item that Gordon McQueen's nickname in the Man Utd camp was Go-Go, owing to his penchant for discotheques. No such revelations now.

There was precious little Cup fever elsewhere on the BBC. *A Question of Sport* had some themed questions on Cup finals on Friday evening. Radio One dangled a possible link-up with Lineker in the Millennium Stadium throughout Saturday morning, but ultimately I couldn't face waiting through several hours of R&B and Brian Dowling's celebrity gossip to experience this scoop item. As so seldom happens, John Motson hit the nail on the head with the random statistic that, when the clubs last met to contest the trophy, the FA Cup final was one of only three live matches on television in 1979. The specialness has gone, you see. John was trying to tell us this in his oblique, Zen-like way – and the BBC are out to ensure we get the message. ○

Home Fixtures

An MTV series spotlighted the lifestyles of football's super-rich but, to Helen Duff's dismay, they just didn't know how to squander their wealth properly

WSC No 223, September 2005

DREAM TEAM. Gary Lineker's crisp adverts. Ron Atkinson's cultured analysis. Television and sport may have engaged in mutual degradation in the past – but never on the jaw-dropping scale of MTV's *Footballers' Cribs*, a look at the home design choices of professional players. Crass, banal and ill-advised, it is consequently thoroughly wonderful.

Portentously, the series is hosted by Nancy Dell'Olio – a woman whose appeal to balding Scandinavians is beyond dispute, but who couldn't cut less mustard as a presenter if she was required at zero notice to front *Newsnight*. Draped on a *chaise longue* in a posture intended to ooze languid luxury (whereas actually she just looks terrified and rigid, like a dental patient braced for the drill) Nancy rotates her head 180 degrees as she reads the autocue with all the joy, assurance and sympathy for language you or I might employ to recite tongue-twisters in Serbo-Croat.

From here in, things get worse – or, in enjoyment terms, better. Far more compelling than most lifestyle programmes – albeit in much the same way that somebody falling off a cliff would be – *Footballers' Cribs* is an offshoot of an MTV series intended to showcase the extravagant and ludicrous homes of music stars. Which is where its makers haven't really thought things through. Because, whereas the average chart star is a debauched hedonist whose excesses are manifest in their zany decor and possessions, the average footballer is a self-preserving numpty who, if he engages in debauched hedonism at all, certainly doesn't do so on a show his boss might see. Consequently we get a programme about cushions.

Though amusing, this is totally dispiriting. Forgetting, for a moment, the sheer life-affirming wonder of hearing the phrase "Hi, I'm Ashley Ward, and this is my crib" (it's hard to sound like a gangsta when you've got an accent straight outta Congleton) the featured players – or "foooterbollas", as Nancy has it – prove utterly lacking as stylistic role models. Talk about a letdown. We're happy to buy rowdy CDs on the express understanding that their makers will spend the proceeds on voluminous crack habits, compensation to the owners of trashed hotel rooms, and endless paternity suits. It makes sense, then, to pay footballers 80 grand a week only if they're prepared to spunk it away on pretentious tattoos, grotesque furniture, Ferraris in which to irk magistrates and all the other accoutrements the rest of us might contemplate if we had wildly more money and wildly less taste.

Where are the leopardskin carpets? The gold spiral staircases? The lifesize statues of the householder-as-Roman-god? Ian Walker's five-bed newbuild in Surrey, bedecked in irreproachable hues of biscuit and bran, resembles the fruits of a lottery jackpot paid out entirely in Habitat vouchers. Listen pal, I sub your Midas wages so you can live large my suppressed dreams of towering vulgarity. When you painted the walls in "Hint of Fawn", you betrayed not just me and yourself but the whole financial ethos of contemporary football.

Nor do we see much evidence of troubled genius or cosmic cool. Diego Maradona's medicine cabinet or a "morning after" shot of George Best's bathroom might merit a glance. Finding out that Harry Kewell's fridge contains Petits Filous feels less like a scandalous insight. And what, more to the point, is in it for the featured players? *Footballers' Cribs* seems as unlikely to win them presenting work as it is to hasten Dell'Olio on to a *Question Time* panel. Those of us who view Robbie Savage as a gobby little irritant are unlikely to have our views changed by the sight of him deriving self-satisfaction from his worktops – nor will Antoine Sibierski droning "and this is another living room" in the style of an estate agent on the verge of a career change boost Manchester City's fanbase much.

None of these concerns should, however, detract from the joy of watching people engaged on a self-promotion exercise that's busy revealing them to be drab and maladroit. Unintentionally, MTV have added to the debate about the morality of players: not only don't they deserve the money they're on, they don't have a clue how to spend it. Brilliant. If only they'd given the show the title it deserves – Lifestyles of the Rich and Shameless, maybe. ○

Flicker Conspiracy

**Subbuteo – arguably the best-ever football game – had a
legion of dedicated players in its heyday, but few will have
been quite as committed as Simon Price**

WSC No 227, January 2006 ~ Football Memorabilia Special

IF HE'S HONEST ABOUT IT, my dad would probably admit that the Hornby
model railway was more of a gift to himself than to me. From the moment
I unwrapped the huge hardboard-mounted layout, he was biding his
time until I grew up, left home and he could claim it as his own. (It
now resides in his loft, along with the collector's magazines and replica
Stanier Black Five engines.) I may have expressed a passing interest in
a train set and I probably played with it a handful of times, frustrated
with the mail train's postbag collection mechanism, which never quite
worked. Within six months I'd flipped the hardboard over – suddenly a
derelict brownfield site, like Ashburton Grove, ripe for redevelopment
– and used it for a oo-scale passion of my own.

Because, make no mistake, if you were going to get hooked on Subbuteo,
you needed a lot more than they gave you in the box. The picture on the
front, showing two kids happily playing flick-to-kick on a pitch rolled out

on the family carpet, was fraudulent: in real life, it was like playing on sponge. Using the dinner table was a non-starter too: it just slipped off. The only answer was a bucket of wallpaper paste and a big bit of wood. Already, you'd realised that the make-believe world of Subbuteo required a lot of improvisation on the part of the owner. The giant, non-storable pitch presented an instant problem. You couldn't exactly roll it up and put it in the cupboard. The solution I reached was to allow Subbuteo to annexe my entire bedroom, with the pitch permanently laid out on my bed base (while I slept on a mattress on the floor). I'd got it bad.

The attraction of Subbuteo – if you could overlook the players' half-Weeble pedestals – was its realism, a miniature universe in which you could literally play God. I had prior form for this sort of thing. Using a ping-pong ball and a motley selection of Action Men, Star Trek figures and Six Million Dollar Men (the Peter Crouches of the posable doll world), I'd previously created a team called, with the inscrutable surrealism of infancy, Gug City Slaggers. The arrival of Subbuteo inspired me to expand the fantasy to a whole country (Oxanania, a nominally Nordic island in the middle of the Baltic, with a green cross flag) with a whole league of made-up teams competing in a league with proper fixtures.

Using every last penny of my pocket money, I gradually built a whole stadium (although, given its old-fashioned appearance, ground is a more accurate word). Well, three-quarters of one, at least: one flank remained open so I could actually get in. The rubbish peripheral accessories that came with Subbuteo are now the stuff of bad stand-up comedy, notably the completely useless floodlights whose Ever Ready power packs emitted a glow so faint that you needed to rope in an Anglepoise lamp for that "European nights" feel. But change was about to come.

Argentina 78 revolutionised Subbuteo. The dusty old world Waddingtons had previously replicated, redolent of rosettes and wooden rattles, was on the way out, as kids clamoured for the glamour of the World Cup they'd just been watching on telly. Wooden scoreboards were superseded by cool black "digital" ones, and in came sexy goalposts with saggy coloured nets and smaller Adidas Tango balls, although it was still some years until you could buy the modern, custard-covered-forearm-holding-a-grapefruit-shaped trophy instead of the defunct (and meaningless, to a Welsh kid who wasn't even born in '66) Jules Rimet, the size of a water tower relative to the players. And if you wanted *junta* helicopters for dropping dissident trade unionists into the sea, you needed to reach into a more military corner of your toy box.

Other new gimmicks ensued, including, in rapid succession, "Astro-turf" pitches, Letraset numbers for the players' shirts, goalkeepers with springy handles, spring-loaded throw-in men, and corner kickers – the nearest we Subbuteo aficionados came to the tacky thrills of Striker (the ITV to Subbuteo's sober BBC, Striker was the sort of thing you did at other kids' houses, but not at home). Not all innovations were positive. The introduction of players with bolt-upright bodies was a disaster: they fell over like Heskey on ice. Competing with other kids – using our own adapted rules, naturally (the ban on using your thumb for leverage was just stupid) – I deployed my secret weapon: an old Celtic team bought from a church jumble sale, with a crouching posture and heavy lead weights in the base (probably discontinued because they sent you mental if you put them in your mouth).

More grimly, you could now replace the old green picket fence with tall, grey, spike-topped deathtrap caging. Replica supporters were the biggest rip-off of all. With ten to a pack, two quid a pop, you needed to be the richest kid in school to afford enough to fill the stands, and the most patient in order to glue them all in. Again, one had to improvise. I populated my stands with the non-competing players, and gave them makeshift scarves snipped from the red and white piping of a plastic Christmas stocking, for that "Kop" look. Andrew next door, meanwhile, used toy soldiers: Second World War Tommies with flame throwers next to Roman legionaries with shields (giving his terraces the look of a modern-day Italian curva).

The main hazard to this carefully balanced set-up was a careless knock from my mum, disregarding my pleas to stay out of my room (particu-larly if she was wielding a Hoover), or a pitch invasion by my cat, as apoca-lyptic as the Post Office Tower-hugging kitten at the start of *The Goodies*, using the cloth for scratching practice. If a player was broken in such an accident, you needed to be careful which glue you used to fix them: certain brands had the effect of melting their lower legs (Waddingtons missed a trick by failing to market a Princess Diana figurine to visit them in hospital). The last element missing from the realism of the Subbuteo stadium was crowd noise. For this, another makeshift brainwave: in addition to an LP recording of the Kop Choir, I detuned my radio on the VHF waveband and used the crackle to simulate a noisy stadium, whacking up the volume dial when a goal had been scored.

Eventually, inevitably, I grew out of Subbuteo and moved on to other obsessions (music and girls, mainly). But my dismantled stadium is still lurking in a suitcase, reproachfully waiting to be reassembled. And should I ever get around to having kids of my own, they can forget Pro Evolution (or that year's equivalent). I'm buying them Subbuteo. Not for me, you understand... O

Up and Under

Harry Kewell's hair might have been pony, but after 32 years Australia were back at the World Cup and, as Mike Ticher reports, it was not just soccer diehards who were celebrating
WSC No 227, January 2006

SOME THINGS ARE HARD TO FORGIVE. For example: planning a ticker-tape parade to celebrate winning one World Cup qualifier, on penalties; inviting John Travolta on to the pitch and into the dressing rooms; 80,000 people booing the visitors' anthem; banners and chants proclaiming "U R gay"; Harry Kewell's double ponytail; playing Men at Work at full volume after the final whistle. But despite all that, it was impossible not to share in Australia's excitement at finally qualifying for the World Cup again after a wait of 32 years. The shootout win over Uruguay at a feverish Telstra (né Olympic) Stadium in Sydney was like a dam breaking. Over it flowed euphoria, relief, gratitude, bitterness, melancholy and wild expectations, one after the other.

There were good excuses for some of the behaviour – though not Kewell's hair. Diehard soccer fans have been through years of agony and, for all their international sporting belligerence, other Australians are under few illusions about the global status of their most popular pastimes. They know what the World Cup means. Qualification was greeted with a raucous frenzy in the media, on the streets (a respectably disruptive celebration, if not quite up to South American standards) and in dressing rooms from Middlesbrough to Basle, Parma and even Sydney (not least because "Dwight Yorke's Trinidad & Tobago" also made it).

The explosion of delight reflected Australia's yearning to get on stage in a sporting drama that everyone else cares about – bear in mind that the next best thing in 2006 is the Commonwealth Games in Melbourne. The following day several papers carried a variant of Look Out, World!

headlines, when perhaps what they really meant was Look At Us, World! Fans of other sports rushed to proclaim the atmosphere in Sydney as unlike anything they had experienced before. Or, as Mark Schwarzer put it to the *Sydney Morning Herald*: "People have told me that they can't remember feeling like this since Australia won the America's Cup." But if there was a good deal of unrequited sporting nationalism around, it was also a night when everything fell into place for soccer's diehard fans. They invoked the saintly presence of Johnny Warren, who played in the 1974 finals and who, by the time of his death last year at 61, had become father figure, evangelist and tireless promoter of the game as a symbol of multiculturalism and a bridge to Asia.

The crowd's overt aggression may not have been quite in the Warren ideal, but it was what the team needed ("a massive, massive boost" said Mark Viduka of the anthem-booing) and, frankly, what the Uruguayans deserved. They had messed about with the first-leg kick-off time, apparently in an attempt to delay Australia's journey home, and persuaded FIFA to replace the officials for the return, on the laughable grounds that a Belgian referee would favour a team with a Dutch coach. Inter's dim-witted Alvaro Recoba injected a bit more poison by insisting Uruguay had a "divine right" to qualify. And in Sydney they played as though they believed it, putting on a classic display of time-wasting, play-acting and general arsing about, when one away goal would certainly have sent them through. The petulant touchline antics of the gesticulating, Marty Feldman-esque Jorge Fossati barely helped.

Australia, by contrast, at last discovered, in Guus Hiddink, a coach with the detachment and nous they needed. His bold tactical shuffling mostly came off, the team played quick, intelligent football and he coaxed blinding performances from several players who seemed lost causes through age, form or injury. He made Australia believe they could win – even with the creaking limbs of Tony Vidmar and Tony Popovic in defence – and added the previously elusive quality of luck. Hiddink, for reasons best known to himself, wanted to put the 6ft 7in reserve keeper Zeljko Kalac on for the shootout, but Brett Emerton went down with a timely bout of cramp and had to be replaced by the third sub. In the event Schwarzer saved two penalties and, perhaps, Hiddink's bacon.

Qualifying will not instantly transform soccer's fortunes in Australia, but it has lanced a festering boil. However the team performs (and they may only be a central defender or two away from surprise-package status) soccer will occupy an unprecedented space in the public consciousness for the next seven months. No doubt the fans will also add their own special dash of kitsch, self-deprecation and boorishness to the mix, swelled by vast numbers from Britain preparing to turn the tournament into a stop-off on the way to the Pamplona bull-running or the Oktoberfest. If that's a prospect that's suddenly turned you off the World Cup, well – you better run, you better take cover. ○

Trophy Bitter

The FA Cup final was supposedly due back at Wembley in May, but what was once the English game's great showpiece is now almost a sideshow, argued Jon Spurling

WSC No 228, February 2006

ON THE EVE OF LEEDS UNITED'S DEFEAT of Arsenal in the 1972 FA Cup final, captain Billy Bremner said: "I've won a Championship medal, a European medal and countless Scotland caps, but sometimes I think I'd swap the lot for an FA Cup winners' medal." A few hours later, Bremner professed delight "with my new prized possession". How attitudes have changed. In his autobiography, Roy Keane described the showpiece occasion as "little more than an afterthought", and Patrick Vieira admitted that Arsenal's triumph in the 2005 final "can't possibly make up for the disappointment of losing the league crown".

The key to the Cup's popularity was its sheer quirkiness or, in the words of Jimmy Hill, "its quintessential Englishness". The draw on Monday lunchtimes was ridiculously inaccessible in the days before daytime television and the internet, and gave rise to the urban myth that teams from around the country huddled around a battered old transistor in feverish anticipation of hearing whom they'd play. There were (seemingly) regular marathon ties, with endless replays, encapsulating the never-say-die English spirit to which Hill referred.

Then there was the plethora of unlikely heroes that the final brought to the fore. Ipswich Town's Roger Osborne – watched by 34 members of his immediate family in the 1978 final – proceeded to faint with the excitement of scoring the winner. The naff plastic hat worn by victorious Sunderland boss Bob Stokoe in 1973, a raft of even naffer Cup final songs and, on the morning of the final, the BBC's special edition of *Mastermind* all simply added to the distinctive flavour of the event. "Aside from the sheer glory of winning it, there's nothing else really," explained Hill in 1974. "There are no financial rewards to speak of. It's about pomp and glory, and English eccentricity. It works."

Thirty years later, and the competition isn't "working" particularly well. The last truly great final was in 1987, when Coventry beat Tottenham 3-2; the last major upset arrived a year later, when Wimbledon defeated Liverpool 1-0. The competition's quirks have either been completely removed (marathon replays have been swept away due to "player fatigue" and "police advice" and there are no more Cup final songs) or tampered with (the draws were moved to Sunday afternoons to cater for TV, then largely shifted back to Monday lunchtimes in the past two years). Each year seems to bring a new nadir: the 2005 final (a dire spectacle in keeping with the majority of recent finals) was the first to be settled on penalties. At least ten million watched Arsenal edge past Manchester United, bucking the recent trend of waning interest, with just five million watching the Gunners play Southampton in 2003. Contrast that with the 14 million who watched finals up to the mid-Eighties. Tarnished, over sanitised and increasingly devalued, the FA Cup just isn't what it used to be.

The competition – in the eyes of the majority of Premiership and Championship clubs – simply isn't worth the hassle any more. Clubs can expect to make around £3 million if they lift the trophy. Contrast this with the £10m on offer for reaching the Champions League group stages (which can't be reached through lifting the FA Cup), the filthy lucre available for getting into the Premiership in the first place and the horrific financial implications of relegation from the "promised land". Then there are the incremental bonuses for finishing in a higher Premiership position. The FA Cup is regarded as more of an irritation, where key players might sustain potentially serious injuries. Hence the trend towards fielding weakened sides. Little wonder that supporters, still charged the full amount to attend games, are staying away in the earlier rounds.

The full-blooded recent encounter between Burscough and Burton Albion revealed that the sheer kudos of reaching the FA Cup third round (not to mention the guaranteed windfall from an encounter with Manchester United) is undiminished among many clubs lower down the league pyramid. The final remains the most watched domestic football match across the world. Yet the competition's stock continues to fall. In recent weeks, there have been rumours that a seeding system could be introduced, in order to separate bigger clubs in the earlier rounds, and on a recent edition of *Jimmy Hill's Sunday Supplement* on Sky, *Sunday Telegraph* journalist Patrick Barclay advocated inviting Scottish and even South American sides to take part, a suggestion met with universal scepticism by the rest of the panel.

If the FA Cup is at least partially to regain its status, lessons need to be learned from various clubs' approaches to the still more derided League Cup. Sunderland cut ticket prices for their recent game with Arsenal and allowed children in for £1. The result? Their first full house in more than three years, not to mention a much improved atmosphere. Others, the Gunners included, have also reduced ticket prices for League Cup games. A similar approach to the FA Cup, especially if clubs field under-strength teams, would at least ensure that a younger generation of fans are able to take some ownership of the competition, rather than hear their parents rant about the "rip off cup", as it is known in some quarters. Tellingly, Sunderland's commercial manager referred to "all-important profit margins dictating whether this becomes a more universally adopted approach".

Much of the wide-eyed innocence and charm of the Cup disappeared long ago and hard economics make it unlikely that clubs will embrace it with the passion of former times. Yet the FA remain convinced that, with the final poised to return to Wembley, the competition will enjoy a renaissance. The nagging doubt remains: are leading clubs willing to put glory ahead of money and treat the FA Cup – not to mention their supporters – with due respect? O

Gesture Politics

The Curva Nord extremists were backing Paolo Di Canio's right to be a fascist but, as Matthew Barker reported, some Laziali are up in arms. What would the chairman do?

WSC No 228, February 2006

LAZIO MUST HAVE THE WORST PR in world football. The continuing fallout following Paolo Di Canio's Roman salutes is the latest in a long line of far-right associations that have plagued the club over the past 25 years. Di Canio, who saluted the travelling support twice in the volatile atmosphere of a game at Livorno and then repeated the trick a week later during a home match against Juventus, seems determined to take on both the Italian FA and now FIFA, as he prepares to contest charges of inciting racial hatred and violating the governing body of international football's code of ethics. And, for the time being at least, the club seem happy enough to back him.

Interviewed after the Livorno game, he warned: "I expect my president to defend me, just like presidents do at other clubs, otherwise I'm going to be really pissed off." Claudio Lotito, Lazio's president, duly stood by his man, saying he was free to do as he wished. The club issued a statement, stopping short of criticising the player, but insisting they reject "any form of racism and the politicisation of football, both on and off the field".

Meanwhile, team-mate Ousamane Dabo told newspaper *France Soir* that he'd "had it with these fascists". However, Dabo then claimed he had been misquoted and suggested there was an anti-Lazio agenda in the press. Having presented Di Canio with a bouquet of roses, the Curva Nord (home to the most vocal – and notorious – of the club's support) greeted their French midfielder at the start of the Juve game with a banner that read: "Dabo we return your honour, a true man without colour." The FA announced an inquiry into the events in Tuscany and Di Canio was fined €10,000 (£6,900) and handed a one-match ban for his antics against Juventus – the same punishment he received after a similar incident in a Rome derby a year ago. The player's argument, that the gesture dates back to ancient Rome and has no political connotations, now goes to an appeal hearing, where he will be defended by right-wing lawyer Gabriele Bordoni. "I am a fascist, not a racist," Paolo explained.

For Lotito, the player is becoming a serious liability. Now 37, Di Canio remains the club *bandiera* (literally, flag), capable of some wonderful football, despite managing just one goal before the Christmas break and rarely completing a full 90 minutes. Di Canio could well have another season left in him; a year that's going to be crucial for Lotito and the club. The president, keen to be seen as the man who revives Lazio, finds himself criticised for refusing to condemn the striker, while plenty still doubt his motives for taking over the club in July 2004, following the collapse of long-term benefactors the Cirio food group. He inherited a bill for €157 million (£109m) in unpaid taxes.

Plans for a move away from the Olimpico, to a "city of sport", complete with branded restaurants, hotels and shops, are at an advanced stage, with a site already identified. But this proposed relocation out of the city met with strong opposition. Lotito's vision is of Premiership-style consumerism, with supporters of an altogether more passive nature. Fiorentina, at least before recent crowd disturbances, are seen as the model to follow, cleaning up their act after bankruptcy and now pushing for a Champions League spot.

Away from the Celtic crosses and extremist posturing, Lazio are just as much a club of the Roman middle classes, with a support base in the posher suburbs and prim satellite towns. It was this aristocratic air that attracted Mussolini's men to the *biancocelesti*, despite the regime having merged three existing clubs in the capital to form AS Roma. The latter had been set up in direct competition to the dominant Bologna, to create a new footballing power base in the capital. However, upwardly mobile local party members preferred to be seen rubbing shoulders with the moneyed *Laziali*, despite the club's mid-table anonymity.

The idea that Lazio have far-right connections really took hold in the 1970s, with the formation of new *ultrà* groups. In such a highly politicised decade it was a short step from the fireworks, flag-waving and sloganeering of street demonstrations to match-day spectacle. If music and fashion were key elements in defining British terrace culture, politics were very much the dynamic behind its Italian counterpart. With Lazio, right-wing groups filled the void left following the break-up of their apolitical predecessors – and have remained there ever since.

The highly politicised nature of *curva* culture may bemuse most outsiders but, with a general election just months away and prime minister Silvio Berlusconi chipping in with some typically unhelpful comments about the Di Canio affair, both player and club are now at the centre of a very public and potentially very damaging controversy that has already seen share prices stuttering; FIFA president Sepp Blatter has hinted at points deductions, too.

Di Canio's actions have stirred some real anger among the more level-headed of the club's support. Webzine Lazio.net happily appears to speak for many: "[He] may think he's saluting his people, but that does not include us. We are not part of the 'fascist Lazio' equation; it's an historical and cultural farce. We will not accept the oldest club in the capital being associated with the darkest page in our country's history. Don't mess with our Lazio." Whether they can now really stand up to the bully boys of the Curva Nord depends very much on their president. O

Decent Exposure

In the aftermath of Mike Newell's claims about corrupt agents, Neil Rose applauded his integrity and successes with Luton. But not everyone was happy

WSC No 229, March 2006

IT FEELS STRANGE to come over all protective about your team's manager, but that is how I feel about Mike Newell. Here is a decent and honest man who has found himself at the centre of a bewildering furore. Publicly he's bullish and holding up well enough, but I would still like to give him a hug and tell him everything will be all right.

Newell does not necessarily look a passionate man. During the epic FA Cup match against Liverpool in January, Lineker, Hansen and Wright giggled away at replays of the besuited Luton boss in characteristic pose, leaning impassively against the dugout, left eyebrow slightly arched, as his side went 3-1 up. He has been described as looking like 007 waiting for a bus. But passionate Newell most certainly is. He is passionate about referees – for turning football into a "non-contact sport" – he is passionate about agents, but more than anything, he is simply passionate about football and that is why he spoke out.

Few of his comments were news to Luton fans, except his revelation about being offered bungs, and that apparently only came out because he was asked a straight question at the launch of Coca-Cola's "Win a player" competition. Being the man he is, he provided a straight answer, never expecting the headlines. It may also be that a proper question came as something of a shock; his usual dour interviewer on local BBC radio prefers to make a statement – "And then Steve Howard scored" – and expects Newell to come back with more than "Yes, he did". You can tell it drives the poor guy bonkers.

Agents are even more frustrating. He never had one during a career that spanned 14 teams and now, as manager of a club with minimal resources, the complication and cost they bring to the transfer process can be the difference between a signing and one that got away. Just don't get him started on the role of agents in simply renegotiating contracts.

The criticism thrown his way is patently unfair, not least the idea that he has made all this up. Newell has nothing to gain and much to lose, not least if the preposterous suggestion of a disrepute charge comes to fruition (and which of us would put that past the FA?). He must provide documented evidence, demand holier-than-thou agents, safe in the knowledge that it is not exactly common practice to offer illegal payments in writing or carry around a tape recorder on the off-chance.

Newell is an interesting character. A Liverpool nut who was released after spending his schoolboy years at Anfield (and was in Istanbul last May), he models his managerial style closely on that of Bill Shankly and Bob Paisley. And a manager is what he is, leaving the coaching to the coaches on the basis that there's not much point having them otherwise. He only speaks to the squad as a whole on match days to ensure they do not get bored of listening to him, and believes that players switch off if they are being constantly bellowed at from the touchline.

To him, a lifetime in the game is qualification enough for his job. There he was on the prestigious applied football management course at Warwick University when they began studying an imaginary club in administration – at the time, Luton were in real administration. Another thing that annoys him is the "promising young manager" tag. Now 41, he has been in the game for more than 25 years.

What he has achieved in less than three years at Luton must not be underestimated, especially given the desperately unpromising beginnings of the ludicrous "manager idol" poll that got him the job at a time when everyone wanted Joe Kinnear back. He seems to treat his players as adults and that partly explains why a team of no stars has achieved so much more than the sum of its parts – last season's League One title was just the fourth in the club's 120-year history. At their best, which pleasingly the nation got to see against Liverpool, Luton play a high-tempo passing game that overwhelms many teams.

There is an upside to the past few weeks. Newell has been linked with any number of jobs – it does not help that he has so many former clubs, or that his family live in Southport – and Luton fans have every reason to fear that when this ambitious man moves on, the club's fortunes will wane. His uncompromising stance over agents may put off a few potential employers and, if it extends his time at Kenilworth Road, that will do very nicely. ○

The Joy of Text

Barney Ronay and his friends spent many a happy hour following football on Ceefax, but teletext was firmly on the retreat thanks to the digital revolution

WSC No 229, March 2006

THE DISAPPEARANCE OF a defiantly non-interactive, distinctly uncool and often misspelt page of blue-and-white text might not seem such a big deal in the grand scheme of things. But so far the imminent demise of Ceefax seems to have gone pretty much unnoticed. No public protest, no online petitions, no angry letters to national newspapers. Not that it's happened yet, but it will. Ceefax, Teletext and the vaguely knocked-off looking versions that have recently ceased appearing on Channel Four and Five are all about to be sacrificed for good at the altar of digital communication. The government's plans to replace all existing analogue TV signals with digital (the Big Switch Off, in irritating New Labour speak) get into gear later this year. The first transmitters will be junked in 2008, with Scotland's Border region leading the revolution from above.

But what's it got to do with football? On the face of it, more than you might think, in a don't-know-what-you've-got-till-it's-gone kind of way. And by the way, I've asked around. It's not just me. Everybody looks at the football scores on Ceefax. The original internet, there is no better medium to experience that white-knuckle final score moment. Nobody else has brought you news of transfer swoops, groups of death and sudden managerial axings (there is something about Ceefax journalism that warms to these cliches – the lack of space perhaps?). And all without trying to sell you a replica Swiss watch or arrange a gynaecological encounter with an unspecified American teenager. Incidentally, it is just Ceefax I'm worried about. Yes, technically it's all teletext and the ITV service is in fact called Teletext. But for sport, and football in particular, it's always been Ceefax, even if only to avoid the adverts for cheap flights that tend to gatecrash between pages on the commercial channels.

Everyone who watches football on Ceefax will have a favourite text moment, even if it's just the thrill of seeing the screen refresh to reveal, with great dramatic timing, that in fact it's still 0-0 and you're staring intently at a black rectangle with some numbers on it. Occasionally I've watched the last 20 minutes of a cup tie, or sat through a penalty shoot-out. Sad, perhaps, but surprisingly engrossing. It's not just football, either. With my four housemates I watched the last 200 runs of Brian Lara's record-breaking 501 not out for Warwickshire in 1994 on Ceefax. And it was great.

The absence of sound, pictures, or anybody giving you anything but the most basic information is the essence of Ceefax's appeal. Ceefax respects your desire just to know the score. No "analysis" from Chris Waddle. No banks of four or quality in wide areas, no news of a fascinating round-table discussion next Thursday night. Just the score, thanks. The BBC's football website live commentaries strive for an echo of this laconic authority ("attacking throw-in Everton Weir left channel" etc) but end up sounding ludicrously stilted. In fact it's quite tempting to come on all *Newsnight Late Review* about the proto-Beckettian sparseness of the Ceefax semiotic, its stark and pre-modern clarity. But really, it's just about the score.

What comes next? Digital communication abhors a vacuum and there are plenty of 24-hour dedicated rolling football news channels out there, all more than capable of filling the Ceefax-shaped hole. It must be said, at this point, that a form of teletext still exists. It must also be said that it's crap. Press the red button and eventually a sub-standard version of Ceefax will appear, complete with un-navigable Premiership-obsessive football headlines, no lower league fixtures and a big hole in the middle just in case you might be tempted to switch channels without a glimpse of Noel Edmonds's face. The real replacement for football on Ceefax is the kind of round-table you-watch-the-pros-watch-football show available on Sky Sports and the BBC. You know the kind of thing. Gordon McQueen, Paul

Walsh and Tony Cottee stare at a TV screen and tell you that Blackburn have just won a free-kick but it's come to nothing still 0-0 at Ewood Park, Jeff. This is essentially Ceefax, but a crazily over-manned version with a human face. It tells you no more, except perhaps that attempts to turn football scores into light entertainment are doomed. The BBC trailers for their Saturday afternoon talk-it-up feature Les Ferdinand corpsing with laughter at something Gavin Peacock has just said, Garth Crooks and Ray Stubbs high-fiving, Adrian Chiles pulling a moony. Yes, you think. But what's the score? And where's that mute button?

This is more than just a nostalgic harrumph. It's also more than just football. The invention of teletext was an instance of the kind of British technological ingenuity that seems increasingly associated with the past. The BBC announced the existence of Ceefax in October 1972. Engineers at Kingswood in Surrey had found a way of sending information inside the ordinary analogue television signal. The service was formally launched in June 1974 at a press conference attended by the relevant minister, after which the BBC began broadcasting through a small mini-computer known to staff as Esmerelda. By October 1981 the government was announcing the first – and so far only – National Teletext Month, as countries across the world launched their own text services based on the British model. In the mid-1990s an all-time popularity high was followed by a gradual winding down as the future began to look inexorably digital.

According to government figures, 63 per cent of homes in the UK now have digital TV via Sky, Freeview or cable. Can this be right? Certainly in the next few years an unspecified number of old people, occasional viewers and residents in remote areas are going to start wondering why the aerial on the roof doesn't work any more. Just as certainly, another long-standing, generally overlooked, but unpretentiously useful part of the experience of following football will have disappeared. ○

The Bottom Line

The Conference threatened both Stockport and Rushden & Diamonds, but the fans of these supporter-owned clubs would not give up easily. Taylor Parkes went along for a relegation scrap

WSC No 229, March 2006

IT HAS NEVER BEEN FUN being bottom of the heap. The Conference spreads its jaws, so you can smell its breath. It smells of damp, failure and loss, empty stands and uncertainty. When you're low, you think you might never stop falling. The last thing you need is to hear that someone somewhere might consider you "unsustainable". These days, both Stockport County and Rushden & Diamonds are owned by supporters' trusts. This is clearly not a recipe for instant success (certainly no help when trying to attract talent – Rushden were recently rebuffed when trying to sign a striker from Bognor Regis FC). But when you're down on your luck, a sense of self-determination is invaluable, as is the knowledge that you're not going to turn up at your ground to find Texas Homecare there instead.

Rushden & Diamonds were well known (if not well loved) as a new-money team, formed by a merger no one wanted, until they hit harder times: now in the hands of their own fans, they have regained a sense of purpose and some kind of security. It's easier still to be sympathetic to Stockport – only a few years ago they were in the grip of strange wealthy men, trying to move the club to Manchester and rechristen them "Manstock County". Since the fans took over, they've successfully fought off venture capitalists, installed their own man as chair and recruited, in Jim Gannon, a manager who cares about the club and is cared about in return, having been one of the most loyal and best-loved players in their history. There are ways of winning, even when you keep losing.

It was never quite flat caps round here, being Cheshire and all, but, like huge swathes of the north of England, Stockport has now been "modernised" to the point where it looks and feels no different from the south. New ring roads, leisure complexes, redbrick office developments; there's nothing here you wouldn't find in Woking or Maidstone, which would be great if it had ever been anything other than hellish to live in Woking or Maidstone.

Reassuring, then, that Edgeley Park retains some character. A cold cuboid of old wood and girders, built among suburban streets with a view of the moors from the back of the stand, it's a small, ugly ground with charm. There's an electronic scoreboard, seemingly plucked from the 1978 Subbuteo catalogue, which just about manages "COME ON COUNTY" and a two-frame animation of clapping hands; the uncovered stand behind the far goal is completely empty but for a couple of ball boys, hunting under fold-up seats for the debris of hopeful passes. The nearby airport means a constant flow of low-flying jets, gleaming in a weak January light, almost within touching distance. It's jarring – up there looks like the title sequence of a holiday programme, down here we could be watching events from 1935, stored in the ground for spectral replay on dark afternoons.

A League Two relegation scrap is not artistry's ancestral home, but as an extreme six-pointer this game should at least do something to warm the air. But the first half is just leaden, uniformly grim. There's simply no avoiding the fact that neither of these teams are very good, especially not when playing for their lives. It's not brutal – there are only two or three harsh tackles in the whole game – but it's ugly and rushed and desperate, and it's yesterday's mashed potatoes for the neutral.

Of the two sides, Rushden are the more one-dimensional, starting aggressively like starving hod-carriers, greeting every ball with a hoof to the corner flag, making the first half-hour little more than a sequence of ungainly foot races down either touchline (the only player who doesn't do this is Tony Stokes, a young loan signing from West Ham whose ground-in bravado betrays his Premiership roots, along with a look of indignation whenever someone knocks him over, and his resemblance to some mercifully missing member of McFly).

Stockport have a little more natural talent in their side, but it's not helping. Matthew Hamshaw can pull off a decent cross, and the hard, fast running of Harpal Singh would cause serious problems if he only learned to keep going, instead of slowing down around the box and waiting for the tackle that invariably leaves him on his arse, appealing for calls that never come. Most promising are their central midfielders, Danny Boshell, a lively type who hits free-kicks with cruel curl, and Damien Allen, a prospective pin-up plucked from the Manchester United youth ranks and whose speedy brain and eagle-eye passing make him an easy man of the match. Sadly for Stockport, the two of them don't just play like Gerrard and Lampard respectively, they play like Gerrard and Lampard together. For long periods, with Rushden in the lead, they'll both drift deep into the opposition half and, when the visitors break, there's a huge hole in the midfield (invariably filled by Tony Stokes, running from deep on a Beckenbauer tip, until someone runs over and shoulder-charges him into a fuming blond heap).

After half an hour it's getting desperate – County's Robert Clare makes a farcical mess of a simple block tackle and has to sprint 15 yards to make amends, then another Rushden effort is headed off the line. Just before the break, the ball ricochets comically off a couple of Rushden defenders and falls to Jermaine Easter, who lobs the keeper, the goal, and very nearly the stand. I sigh patiently and pop my 50th Tic-Tac.

It's another refugee from a bigger club who breaks the deadlock. Adam Griffin, a tiny, shaven-headed dynamo loaned from Oldham Athletic, comes on for the second half and scores with his first touch, flinging himself on to a good cross from full-back Mark Robinson and heading Stockport in front. A cut above the afternoon, Griffin looks like changing the game – and he becomes invaluable as time wears on – but two minutes later County are flapping like dry fish in the face of a Rushden corner. Phil Gulliver equalises past the comically flailing County keeper, James Spencer (seconds after Spencer's gaffe, three middle aged men behind me start whistling the theme tune from *Some Mothers Do 'Ave 'Em*, in perfect unison, as though they've done it before).

To be fair to Rushden, this refusal to employ any form of attack other than high crosses might be a tactical masterstroke: Spencer is the proverbial good shot-stopper, but faced with any kind of high ball he turns into a liquid. When that high ball is coming from wide, he becomes, technically, a gas. Rushden take the lead just past the hour, as another imprecise cross spreads merry hell in County's defence and bounces off Simeon Jackson into the net. A kind of gloom settles, mixed into the winter twilight like motor oil.

Then nothing for a while but 20-yard head-tennis and nudges. As the cold gets darker, Rushden keeper Daniel Crane, placing and replacing the ball for a restart, spends so long hacking up divots with the heel of his boot that he might be tunnelling to China, or digging a grave. For Stockport, even clearing their lines has become a problem, as a hoofed clearance squirts off sideways into the stands – the remainder are coming down sweetly on the visitors' chests. Rushden's hundred travelling fans, with room to put their feet up, sing songs about glory, or the glory of remaining in League Two.

It's not quite over, though. Last time these teams met, County were 2-1 up until stoppage time, when Rushden grabbed a lucky equaliser – today is a perfect reverse. The fourth official, perhaps trying to put off facing the chilly leather seats of his Hillman Minx, signals a baffling five minutes for stoppages and the home crowd redis-cover a voice. Tin-hatted Rushden practically form a human pyramid in their goalmouth, while County bunch up 25 yards out, set for a round of British Bulldog. After much pinball, and with seconds to go, Griffin manages to grab some space and squares the ball for Stockport's substitute, the lanky Liam Dickinson, whose first and last contribution is a firm drive from the edge of the area that beats Crane to even the score.

Down in the swarm that's chuckling and smoking and heading for the exit, things don't seem all that bad. One point isn't much use, but if your team insist on playing like the dead Keystone Kops, having a hand in your own destiny eases the despair, if not the disappointment. It's in the nature of supporters' trusts that they will flourish first at lowly clubs, in some sort of trouble. But the number of British clubs owned and controlled by their fans is now well into double figures and more than a hundred have supporters on the board or as shareholders. As the bubble keeps bursting in super-slow-motion, it's not too fanciful to see this spreading, as though the game is starting to learn a lesson. Clubs that keep their distance from fans are not just pointless, they're ultimately doomed. When the people in charge are the people who care, even a match like this can't drive them away. ○

Identity Crisis

Chris J Taylor was confused – he's a Manchester United fan, or at least he was. Does he now support FC United as well as or instead of the Glazer-owned Old Trafford team?

WSC No 230, April 2006

IT'S NOT EASY being a Manchester United fan at the moment. Oh, stop laughing at the back. It really isn't. I suppose the playing side of things isn't too bad, you know, relative to everyone else who isn't Chelsea. But off the pitch, where things are suddenly far more important, things are screwed up good and proper. You see, I don't even know if I am a United fan any more. Certainly there's a life-long affiliation, a relationship that's only outlasted by that with my family. But Malcolm sodding Glazer stuck his beak in last year and threw everything right up in the air.

You don't need to know the details of the takeover; everyone has been subjected to them for a year or so now. And this is good, because I am in no position to describe them to you. First, because prodding at that seeping wound is all too painful. And second, because, well, in truth I (still) haven't got a clue about all the minutiae and detail. My E-grade economics A-level didn't stretch to cover preference shares, asset stripping, and what have you. All I know is that Malcolm Glazer and his ilk are bad for football and that might not even matter anyway, because top-level football is unutterably rubbish at the moment.

So here's where FC United of Manchester come in. For the few thousand disillusioned Reds who upped and left Old Trafford in the summer, football has become fun again. Indeed, the game has become of almost a secondary importance. The sense of community that had evaporated at Old Trafford, of going to the match with a group of friends, standing and singing together, and not having to pay through the nose to do so, has returned. And on the pitch things are remarkably rosy, too. Top of North-West Counties League Division Two, attracting crowds bigger than every other non-League team save Exeter, and playing surprisingly decent football. So everyone's happy, right?

Well, no. Not really. It seems that a small section of Old Trafford regulars see FC United fans as traitors and splitters – witness the banner away to Benfica that proclaimed "Fuck FCUM – Salford Reds". Nice. And in turn, there are some at FC United who see those still at Old Trafford as scabs and Glazer stooges. Manchester United? It's a ridiculous situation and the fractious infighting is helping no one.

When the takeover was announced, fans tended to fall into one of three categories. Those who called it a day and vowed never to set foot inside a Glazer-owned Old Trafford. Those who would carry on the fight against Glazer from within. And those who didn't really care. And that's fair enough. No one should have to justify their position, just as no one should criticise someone else's. It was never going to be an easy decision to quit Old Trafford after a lifetime's support and, as has been pointed out many times by many different people, the fans were there before the Glazers and they'll be there long after they've crawled back into whatever hole they came out of.

But what of those still in Old Trafford fighting the good fight? Those subversive, guerrilla tactics meant to bring the empire down from within? Well, nothing much happened. A temporary ice rink was daubed in anti-Glazer slogans. A few people have been removed from the ground for daring to bring in anti-Glazer banners. But that's it. No shows of force like the barricades that kept the brothers Dimm inside Old Trafford for four hours last summer. No peaceful marches, no more flag burning, no nothing. Part of the argument against the formation of FC United was that it would remove those with experience of organising and implementing effective protests from where they are needed most. The more political and militant of fans are now having the time of their life at Gigg Lane. Why should they care about what's going on at Old Trafford any more? They have their own club to support now.

And this, essentially, is the problem. The Glazers have become a part of supporting Manchester United now. No one likes them, no one wants them there, but there they are. A slow acceptance, if not approval, of their presence has emerged. There's nothing we, as fans, can really do to speed up their departure. We just know that with his unrealistic financial planning and unserviceable debts, coupled with Ferguson's hilarious inability to create a team to challenge for Premiership or European honours, the whole sorry mess will soon come crashing down. But by then who knows what might have happened? FC United could be the biggest team in the land and only a few thousand could be rattling round Old Trafford watching Darren Fletcher and the boys. ○

Paperback Writers

WSC first appeared in March 1986 and soon found itself part of a publishing boom. Al Needham cast his mind back to the heyday of football fanzines and what his own favourite, Nottingham Forest's *The Almighty Brian*, meant to him

WSC No 230, April 2006

LIKE MANY WRITERS, I got my start in fanzines. In the mid-Eighties, I had an idea that was so obviously brilliant, I used to lie in bed wondering why no one had thought of it yet. So I bought a typewriter from an old woman on the next estate, emptied the local WH Smith of every bit of Letraset they had, monopolised the Banda machine at college and produced the first ever, erm, American football fanzine. (Five hundred back issues of *Third and Long* are still available in my Dad's loft, if anyone's interested. No? Fair enough.)

Round about the same time, as I was getting every copy of the second issue confiscated outside Wembley Stadium during an NFL friendly that took the concept of "meaningless" to new heights, someone else was doing the same thing with proper football, and you're reading the latest issue of it. Without riding anyone's jock, *When Saturday Comes* was the catalyst for a literary revolution that changed football media (and the fortunes of people who worked at a printers, knew your mate and could do jobs on the sly) for ever. Of course, fanzines had been around since the late Sixties, but – apart from *Foul!*, the ground-breaking mid-Seventies dirt-sheet – they were exclusively put together by people desperate to work on the *NME* asking members of the Newtown Neurotics if they thought pit closures were a good idea or not.

Today, when the colonisation of cyberspace means that we're all only five minutes away from having a really good argument with someone in South Africa over which Seventies Coventry City strip was the worst, it's worth remembering how poorly served the average supporter was 20 years ago, especially if you didn't follow one of the Big Five. If you were lucky, you had the *Football Post*, Pink'Un or Green'Un every weekend. If you weren't, you had a correspondent in the local paper who either trotted out the party line in a *Pravda*-esque manner or carried a barely disguised grudge against your heroes because they never left out enough sandwiches in the press box. And that was your lot. If you wanted to buy something outside the ground that wasn't the programme, it was *Bulldog* (the National Front youth paper) or nothing.

For a town that's not supposed to be a footballing hotbed, Nottingham leapt on the fanzine boom very early. Notts County got in first with *The Pie* (albeit with a sizeable amount of pagination given over to real ale reviews), followed by *Flickin' And Kickin'* (about Notts and Subbuteo). Looking back, it was as if the people who put them together couldn't believe at first that people would actually want to read about their own club, which is incredibly endearing. By the 1990s, Nottingham was awash with fanzines. Forest had four, each with a unique personality. The *Tricky Tree* was the insightful one, which had already clocked that something was rotten in the state of Forest. *Garibaldi* was the *Viz*-like one, with endless slurs about the ovinesexuality of Derby fans. And *Forest Forever* was the work of an incredibly prodigious teenage lad who is now part of the committee that's raising money for a Brian Clough statue.

But the one I fell in love with was *The Almighty Brian*. God, how I loved that 'zine. Like all provincials who end up in London, I expressed my homesickness through devotion to my club and *Brian* was an absolute lifeline. The minute it dropped through the letterbox, posted by a mate at home, I was immediately transported to a pub near the ground on match day, bathing in the bitchings and slaggings and local slang.

Like the best fanzines, *Brian* instinctively realised that you couldn't run a report of an away game without devoting at least two paragraphs on the nearby chip shop that would throw your pie into the deep-fryer before you could stop them; that it was perfectly OK to slag off the club you loved as long as you slagged the club you hated even more (with hindsight, you could see the seeds of Forest's eventual destruction by merely reading between the lines of the mithering of certain *Brian* contributors); that taxi drivers in town provided better source material than a thousand programme notes ever could; and you could never write enough about how much you hated badge-kissing Judases such as Roy Keane. I've never been more proud of being published as I was when my piece on how to jazz up the half-time penalty shoot-out made it into an issue of *Brian* – and it wasn't until I got a letter from the editor that I realised she was female.

Obviously, the very same thing was happening right across the country. We didn't know it at the time, but we were witnessing the last great flourish of collective samizdat, with people in every city in the UK hunched over a typewriter or newly available and very temperamental desktop-publishing program, unable to believe that they were getting away with it. At one point, Nottingham even had its own fanzine shop (the owner of which was the number-one subject of letters in *Brian* during the relegation season of 1992-93, due to his minging jumper and penchant for describing his bowel movements) and a record shop with a sizeable stock of the better ones. Of course, they weren't as good as the local 'zines, seeing as they pursued obsessions of their own that were completely alien to the outsider. That was the whole point, really.

So what happened? Like all street (or terrace) movements, football fanzines were ripped off and subverted by traditional media for their own ends. In the penultimate scene of *Withnail and I*, Danny lamented the fact that they were selling hippy wigs in Woolworths. We watched the first episode of *Fantasy Football* and felt the same way. Before too long, every tabloid had its own "Fanzine" (or FanZone, or whatever) section. Like Jimi Hendrix is blamed for the hundreds of crappy Metal bands that came in his wake, it's a bit harsh to suggest that *Grorty Dick*, *A Kick Up The Rs* and *Brian Moore's Head Looks Uncannily Like London Planetarium* were responsible for the career of David Baddiel. Let's not even think about that. And in any case, as with all publications with a limited consumer base in the mid-1990s, the internet was the real killer.

But we should celebrate the fanzine boom, not mourn it. The heyday of 'zine culture began in an era when football was on the ropes due to Hillsborough, Bradford and Heysel and under threat from ID cards, and ended in a time when an interest in football was practically mandatory. And that's no coincidence. ○